Psychoanalysis
Listening to Understand

Selected Papers of
Arlene Kramer Richards

Edited by Nancy R. Goodman

IPBOOKS.net
International Psychoanalytic Books

A Division of International Psychoanalytic Media Group

Distributed by Jason Aronson, Inc.

Permissions have been granted by their respective publishers for the use of all the articles listed below

Papers in Section I
(All papers by Arlene Kramer Richards)

Chapter 1

(2003). Book Review: The Sexualities in Life and Art. *Journal of the American Psychoanalytic Association* 51:1385–1390.

Chapter 2

(2000). Hilda Doolittle (H.D.) and Bisexuality. *Gender and Psychoanalysis* 5:37–66.

Chapter 3

(1999). Freud and Feminism: A Critical Appraisal. *Journal of the American Psychoanalytic Association* 47:1213–1238.

Chapter 4

(1996). Primary Femininity And Female Genital Anxiety. *Journal of the American Psychoanalytic Association* 44:261–281.

Chapter 5

(1992). The Influence of Sphincter Control and Genital Sensation on Body Image and Gender Identity in Women *Psychoanalytic Quarterly* 61:331–351.

Chapter 6

(1992). Hilda Doolittle and Creativity—Freud's Gift. *Psychoanalytic Study of the Child* 47:391–406. Yale University Press.

Papers in Section II
(All papers by Arlene Kramer Richards)

Chapter 7

(2003). A Fresh Look at Perversion. *Journal of the American Psychoanalytic Association* 51:1199–1217, 2003.

Chapter 8

(1996). Ladies Of Fashion: Pleasure, Perversion Or Paraphilia. *International Journal of Psychoanalysis* 77:337–351.

Chapter 9

(1994). A Review of Freud, Proust, Perversion and Love. By Hendrika C. Halberstadt-Freud. *Psychoanalytic Quarterly* 63:804–810.

Chapter 10

(1993). Perverse Transference and Psychoanalytic Technique: An Introduction to the Work of Horacio Etchegoyen. *Journal of Clinical Psychoanalysis* 2:463–480.

Chapter 11

(1990). Female Fetishes and Female Perversions: Hermine Hug-Hellmuth's "A Case of Female Foot or More Properly Boot Fetishism" Reconsidered. *Psychoanalytic Review* 77:11–23.

Chapter 12

(1989). A Romance with Pain: A Telephone Perversion in a Woman? *International Journal of Psychoanalysis* 70:153–164.

Papers in Section III
(All papers in this section are coauthored by Arlene Kramer Richards
and Lucille Spira)

Chapter 13

Proust's Novel, A Clinical Case, and the Psychological and Social Determinants of Snobbery, Prejudice, and Love [Originally (2012). What We Learned from Proust: Psychological and Social Determinants of Snobbery and Prejudice.

Psychoanalysis
Listening to Understand

========================

Selected Papers of
Arlene Kramer Richards

————————————————

Contents

Contributors to Introductions

Phyllis Beren, PhD is a Training and Supervising Analyst at The Institute for Psychoanalytic Training and Research and the Contemporary Freudian Society and a Fellow of the International Psychoanalytical Association. She is the editor of *Narcissistic Disorders in Children and Adolescents* (Aronson, 1998). She is currently Co-Director of the IPTAR Child and Adolescent Training Program.

Alma H. Bond received her Ph.D. from Columbia University, and became a highly successful psychoanalyst for 37 years in New York City. *Jackie O: On the Couch,* the first of her On the Couch series to be published by Bancroft Press, received a Pinnacle Book Achievement Award, Indie award for Best Historical fiction, and Finalist International Book Awards. *Margaret Mahler, A Biography of the Psychoanalyst* was published by McFarland Press in 2008, and has received two awards. Dr. Bond has had 18 other books published, including *Michelle Obama, A Biography.* She is currently working on a biography of Marilyn Monroe, to be published by Bancroft Press in the fall of 2013. Dr. Bond is the mother of three children and the grandmother of eight.

Nancy R. Goodman, PhD is a Supervising and Training Analyst with the Contemporary Freudian Society, Washington DC and the IPA. Her most recent publications include: *The Power of Witnessing: Reflections, Reverberations, and Traces of the Holocaust—Trauma Psychoanalysis, and the Living Mind* (co-editor/writer with Marilyn B. Meyers, Routledge Press 2012), *Enactment: Opportunity for Symbolising Trauma* (Ellman & Goodman, 2012) in A. Frosch (Ed.) *Absolute Truth and Unbearable Psychic Pain: Psychoanalytic Perspectives on Concrete Experience,* (Karnac 2012), and *Battling the Life and Death Forces of Sadomasochism: Theoretical and Clinical Perspectives* co-editor/writers with Harriet I. B and Paula L. Ellman, Karnac 2013). She maintains a psychoanalytic practice in Bethesda, MD.

Anita Weinreb Katz, PhD is a psychoanalyst on the faculty of NYU Post-doctoral Program in Psychotherapy and Psychoanalysis; the Object Relations Institute, and the Metropolitan Institute of Psychoanalytic Psychotherapy She is a member of IPTAR and fellow of the IPA. She has published on Masochism, Fathers and Daughters, and has written many movie reviews, including: *The Vanishing, A Woman Under the Influence, Proof, American Beauty* and *Utz*. Pending publications include a chapter in the *Psychoanalytic Inquiry* issue on psychosomatic problems. She has written articles on oedipal issues encountered throughout the life cycle, a book chapter on Parents Revisiting Adolescence, and has an upcoming book chapter on "Loneliness" In addition, she states, "I'm passionate about doing ballroom and Argentine Tango dancing and playing classical piano."

Lynne Rubin, PhD is a Training and Supervising Analyst with The Institute for Psychoanalytic Training and Research (IPTAR), a board member of the IPTAR Child and Adolescent training program, and a training analyst at the Contemporary Freudian Society and the International Psychoanalytic Association.

Author's Acknowledgements

I want to thank my family for their forbearance while I was off in my own space thinking and writing. My colleagues have given me very much. Nancy Goodman has been a source of information, inspiration and fun for many years. Phyllis Beren gave me thoughtful and gentle criticism over the years of our friendship and collegiality. I have enjoyed the friendship of Lynne Rubin and the inspiration of her generosity. Alma Bond was a source of support and inspiration when I was worried about balancing work and family. I thank Anita Katz for her capacity for fun, and her ambition that keeps me working on new and interesting projects.

My patients have taught me how to listen, how to hear, and to fulfill the prophesy of my first music teacher who said, "You are not a soprano or an alto. You are a listener."

My husband Arnold Richards to whom I owe it all and who has the grace and generosity to let me understand that he owes it all as well.

Most of all I thank Tamar Schwartz and Lawrence L. Schwartz for their tireless, dependable, tactful, and inspiring work on books, papers and symposia.

—Arlene Kramer Richards, Ed.D.
New York, NY

Editor's Acknowledgements

It has been a pleasure and joy for me to be part of this project—to help organize, write an introduction and read all the chapters as I visited the marvelous ideas that live in the mind of Arlene Kramer Richards and are expressed in her work. I am grateful for being a part of this volume. It contains so much wisdom and demonstrates a way of thinking that allows for growth, expansion of mind, and deep under-standing. Having these articles together in one volume makes each of the ideas more vibrant as it intersects with others. Together they make Arlene's voice soar. Readers will be enriched and delighted to learn and deepen their thinking.

My husband, Louis Goodman, has supported me through these efforts. He has frequently told me that he finds Arlene Kramer Richards to be one of the wisest and most brilliant people he has ever met. This volume is evidence for this. Love is in this work. Tamar Schwartz found all of the articles and more. She is dependable, determined, and persistent. Lawrence L. Schwartz put this book together and showed me where we needed to work harder. He is a guide I wanted to follow. I am grateful for being part of this team, thank you, Tamar and Larry. Matthew Bach offered help with the introductions that made them all better. I thank Amy King of Jason Aronson for bringing the book to print with a special eye for the gestalt of the book and the detail. The intro-ducers wrote from their hearts and souls, each with beautiful individual voices. Thank you for showing what it means to be part of Arlene Kramer Richards' circle. We are such lucky people. Arnold Richards creates all the time and I thank him for IPBooks. Arnie is available day and night to encourage and answer questions, always.

I want to acknowledge how the mind comes alive when psychoana-lytic thought is open and receptive, then ideas can take form and keep expanding in ways that can help people who are in conflict and suffer.

—Nancy R. Goodman, Ph.D.
Bethesda, MD

Travels with
Arlene Kramer Richards

Arlene Kramer Richards represents the essence of psychoanalysis. Any struggle with trying to define what psychoanalysis is could be resolved by traveling with Arlene as she thinks, explores the psyche, practices in her consulting room, teaches, supervises, and writes. The papers in this volume contain her breakthrough ideas and the way she conveys them to us. You find here a world of deep psychoanalytic exploration into areas of female development, creativity and poetry, compromises leading to perverseness of mind and the experience of extreme loneliness. She draws us into the world of film and the layers of the unconscious depicted in the dramas. She brings insight to areas of study with an eye to what others have been afraid to see.

Arlene Kramer Richards always maintains interest in individuals, their well-being and their capacities for growth. She is singularly focused on facing the emotional pain of her patients and the truths of the unconscious. All wishes and fears can be acknowledged, helping shame and guilt turn into pride of accomplishment. She brings students and supervisees to places that were only hints and whispers of understanding in their own minds. She enables those she mentors to decipher mysteries previously unknown, so that they now recognize more fully their own creativity.

One of Arlene's understandings of the mind is in the tradition of Jacob Arlow. As she listens, she is ready to discover and uncover the fantasy, conscious and unconscious, as it appears in metaphor, associations, enactments and the affective fullness of transference and countertransference. In the papers in this volume, the reader finds access to foundational elements of psychic life that build the unconscious fantasy. Arlene's belief that they exist and that finding them liberates individuals from pain and symptoms is present in each of these writings.

You have to be brave and determined to face fears and forbidden thoughts and desires. Arlene Kramer Richards is courageous and helps others be courageous as well. When she discovers something in her work that is puzzling and mysterious she sorts it out with research and writing, giving form to the unknown. Indeed it is Arlene's belief in psychic reality that guides her to open understandings that were closed, often by the way psychoanalytic theory itself was rigidified. For example, she can hear the equivalent of an orgasm in a female patient's felt tension and release when making telephone calls that penetrate the boundaries of others (chapter 12). She recognizes the presence of the female internal genital in referents to body sensation her female patients reveal to her (chapter 5) and gives full acknowledgement to the compromise formations they have come to form as the psyche attempts to thwart fears of retaliation for feminine desire (chapter 4). If a psychoanalyst cannot imagine a woman being afraid of being un-penetrable, or of not giving birth, or of experiencing genital harm, or of being seen as unfeminine because of talent and assertiveness, one cannot hear the complexity of the unconscious life of female analysands. In telling us how the myth of the Gorgon Medusa functions in the film, *Basic Instinct,* (chapters 24 and 26) and in patients' minds, she frees us to know, rather than to live out and enact self-destructively in psychoanalytic treatments. She brings the richness of compromise to understanding loneliness and how it functions as repetition and as defense (chapters 13–16). All of these ideas bring strength to the struggles of understanding the mind. Her work demonstrates how important it is that we keep listening and keep finding.

Arlene Kramer Richards writes poetry (Richards 2010) when confronted with the most difficult aspects of life; for example, about the Holocaust (2012), the tortures conducted in the stadium of Santiago, Chile, and about her mother's death. She helps us reach areas of our humanity we were, perhaps, afraid to fully acknowledge and feel. She examines (chapter 6) the letters of the poet Hilda Doolittle that were written during her analysis with Freud. She finds the way he used interventions concerning the pre-oedipal, the oedipal and the transference to help resolve his brilliant patient's writing block.

With all of this in mind, I began to search for the just right metaphor for my beloved friend and colleague. Feeling a little unsure about what first came to mind, I told her that I was imagining Arlene Kramer Richards, like Paul Revere, riding a steed and galloping along the Freedom Trail bringing news that "the British are coming." She has a lantern held high, lighting the way, helping the cause of revolution and democracy, helping to break away from the monarchy of old constricting ideas. In the best of responses, she laughs and says: "Yes, I loved horse-back riding as a girl and I also loved ballet." So now we have a further articulated fantasy image of Arlene riding her horse dressed in her danc-ing femininity beckoning us to follow on pathways better seen and with more secure footing as she leads the way. The horse and rider is one of Freud's famous iconic images representing life and death forces, and con-cerns about reining in innate instinctual energies. The ego is born on this ride, along with access to desire and affect.

Arlene knows how to keep an exhilarating ride moving forward, gather-ing wisdom as she rides. Freud struggled with understanding "what does a woman want?" I am not sure he ever thought of a woman riding this horse in this way. But we know, Arlene does.

Continuing the metaphor, those who accompany Arlene do not have to line up behind her in any formal processional way. There is something about how she teaches and listens that allows others to take off in their own directions with their own individuality. This is the most special of traits. How does she do this? I think we can begin to find the answer in the "Yes" that Arlene articulated when I expressed the play in my mind with the metaphor of her ride along the Freedom Trail. This is an extremely important "Yes"—a great gift. Anyone who knows Arlene has heard the way she says this. It carries something special, a profound recognition that a psychic discovery is being made by the person to whom she is attending. This "Yes" means she has heard the overcoming of a resistance to express oneself with what is truly known and that a transformation is now taking place. When Arlene delivers this "Yes," her face lights up and emits a believing in the other person that reaches them. I have heard this "Yes" often in consultations when I finally get something I have been struggling with. Perhaps I have been reluctant to acknowledge a countertransference or have been fearing a truth, whether erotic, aggressive, or traumatic that I felt would overwhelm me. She waits as I recognize my narrowing of thought and my dead-ening of mind, in my move away from forbidden knowledge and my own accompanying guilt and shame. Then in the space her mind gives me with my patient, with whom I am so involved, I find the place where this "Yes" takes place. I am sure her patients experience this confirmation in their psychoanalytic sessions when scary deep affect is present with "here and now" and historic significance.

As psychoanalysts, we know that the true "Yes" is intimately con-nected to a large, true "No" and is central to autonomy and a sense of identity that is owned. Arlene's ride through terrains of the mind is fueled by just the right combination of "Yes" and "No."

I first met Arlene in 1992 when she was presenting a scientific paper on female development to our fairly new Institute, The New York Freudian Society, Washington DC Program. She came to nurture us and to make us a part of discussion about new ideas concerning female development. She asserted that the little girl has knowledge of her internal genital through actual sensation in relation to sphincter activity. The little girl discovers pleasure and internality, and develops accompanying fantasies and compromise formations. She was announcing that the inner and outer female genital is alive in the body and the psyche. You could feel the room shake as the idea of penis envy as bedrock came loose. The female genital, rather than being perceived as a "dark continent," is felt and known. There now can be recognition of layers of representations, conflicts, and imagination about the female genital, both in little girl's mind and in psychoanalytic thought.

Arlene Kramer Richards sat in comfort in the front of the room as arguments and tensions grew. One male senior analyst asked how she could speculate such knowledge of the internal sense of the female genital and what proof might she have challenging the claim that penis envy and assorted fantasies about absence of the penis must be primary and sole inhabitants of the feminine mind. Arlene looked out at all of us, saying with clarity that she is female, as are many of her analysands, and she is willing to hear what they have to say in their metaphors and rememberings about what is, not only what is not. She suggested that male analysts, including this questioner, have knowledge of their bodies and need to continue writing what they know from their experiences and that of their patients. You could see her with her lantern lighting up areas of knowledge and fending off skeptics who wanted to hide in the shadows, darkening access to further views of the mind.

Oh, did I tell you? Arlene Kramer Richards is beautiful; and, her writing is glorious. As you listen to her and read her work, there is no doubt that the feminine is spacious, creative and clearly articulated. Here she was on horseback in her ballet best enlightening psychoanalytic thought, and when I ran into a disturbing countertransference with an analysand a few years later, I knew who I wanted to call to help me unravel the story unfolding with my patient.

Understanding femininity is but one of the areas of psychoanalysis Arlene has taken on to find the "No" of orthodoxy and the "Yes" of expanding ideas and practice. When she heard a talk suggesting that Holocaust survivors carry guilt because they all had to commit crimes in order to survive, she was enraged. She recognized the desire to make the victim the aggressor as a disturbing defensive move trying to hide the annihilation and actual extermination of human beings who had bonds and care for each other to the end. She then wrote a paper (2001) about the love and affiliations existing within concentration camps that helped individuals survive and feel human. When new ideas of femininity veered into readiness to derogate Freudian thought in general, she wrote (chapter 3) about the paradox that Freud certainly got some things wrong and also energetically brought women into his intellectual circle at a time when women found they were denied access to institutions of learning and to professional life.

Another monument we find on the Freedom Trail Arlene Kramer Richards has forged is to the breaking apart of the disavowal that the feminine psyche can hold problems of perversion. Having this blind spot, that perversion belongs solely to the male, again narrows psychoanalytic process in understanding the depths of psychic life. When constriction of thought pertains to women, it ends up impacting the analysis of men as well. The idea that bedrock exists in any psyche in any form stops analytic process and uncovering for all of psychoanalysis. Her identification of perversity as belonging in the female psyche (chapters 7–12) as much as the male psyche, helps potentiate the possibility that female patients and male patients can be fully analyzed and understood. Upon reading her paper on "Ladies of Fashion" (chapter 8), it becomes impossible to ever again think of shopping as only shopping. In her determination to reveal the historic finding of the topic of perversion in psychoanalytic literature, she decided to personally translate, from German to English, "A Case of Female Foot or, More Properly, Boot Fetishism" written in 1915 by Hermine Hug-Hellmuth (see chapter 11), and to wonder how the knowledge in it had been lost.

On her ride along the Freedom Trail of psychoanalysis, Arlene is able to identify barriers erected and maintained in the halls of psychoanalytic institutions. She has directed her "No" to the realm of psychoanalytic training that has had lasting impact on who has access to practice and how training is conducted. The shifts she has caused augment respect and wisdom, rather than worship of old pantheons and mandates. Arlene is watching over us to make sure we do not get narrow and destructive in our psychoanalytic communities. Do not identify with the aggressor is a constant in her call for change.

Arlene became a psychoanalyst at a time when clinicians who were not medical were not allowed to train at the American Psychoanalytic Association. To get training, one's own passion and motivation to be able to offer analysis to patients had to be one's guide. I call this the era when individuals self-trained, by being on the couch and under the table with those who supported them and believed in the legitimacy of self-training. There were many analysts willing to supervise and offer courses. With personal motivation in charge, many of those training in this way became strong intellectual voices in the arena of psychoanalytic research, writing, and thinking. Arlene has been an active and indefatigable leader in the many groups which developed psychoanalysis for psychologists and social workers and, now, many medically trained professionals as well. She has helped create and nurture The New York Freudian Society in New York and in Washington, DC; The Institute for Psychoanalytic Training and Research; Section 1 of Division 39 of the American Psychological Association; and the Confederation of Independent Psychoanalytic Societies. She has gone around the world to help psychoanalytic groups study and become legitimate and accepted institutions.

Arlene recognized that in most geographic areas of the United States psychoanalytic training was closed to non-medical clinicians. From 1983 through 1985, she was involved with the decisions of psychologists to organize the lawsuit against the American Psychoanalytic Association, which was not offering training to psychologists, and against the International Psychoanalytic Association, that was not admitting psychologist training institutes as member institutes. This was a revolution indeed. Settlement of what is now known as "the lawsuit" opened the doors of psychoanalytic training throughout the United States, and brought many independent psychoanalytic institutes into the International Psychoanalytic Association.

Arlene not only wanted to train non-medical analysts, she was also determined to teach psychoanalysis to social workers and psychologists. She spent summers in Northhampton, Massachusetts teaching in the Clinical Social Work Program of Smith College, where students earned Masters and Doctoral Degrees. This involved spending 21 days in the beauty of Northhampton, Massachusetts, teaching psychoanalytic technique three times a day, six days a week. Many of these students went on to study at Institutes.

When the New York Freudian Society established training in Washington, DC, Arlene joined the effort with her usual full commitment. She became dedicated to "shuttling" down to DC with Freud volumes in tow, to teach, supervise, mentor, and deliver papers at Scientific Programs. She would teach on Saturdays, spend the night, and offer supervisions on Sundays. Amazingly, she did this with little baggage, having in her large purse all that was needed for an overnight, including Freud volumes. She was always ready to go where psychoanalytic training was needed. She sometimes brought her Arnie (Arnold Richards) with her so he could also become our Arnie. He is definitely a partner at all times, riding with her, continually forging new pathways to expand the world of psychoanalysis. We in Washington, DC became privy to the stories of how they met at the University of Chicago as young intellectuals finding their powerful attraction to each other. Their partnership is a wonderful event for them, for psychoanalysis, and for us.

Oh, there she goes again, heading down the Freedom Trail with beacon in hand, lighting the way to understanding the possibilities of psychoanalytic training and treatment in our very modern world, where we have the technology available to overcome geographic distance. When questions arose about phone supervision for psychoanalytic candidates in satellite locations, distant from the home base of the training institute, Arlene addressed the debate with real work. She tackled the prejudice that telephone supervision was too different from in-person supervision by sending a questionnaire to clinicians to gather information about their actual experiences. She later brought together information about psychoanalytic treatment by telephone with similar scholarship (chapter 18).

Another frontier where "No" and "Yes" have come together is the way training analyst status is granted (chapter 19). She had seen too many people crushed by the process, which too often stopped a talented psychoanalyst from developing further, and was destructive to the integrity and growth of psychoanalysis itself. Arlene was determined to try to change the process and actualized her interest with meetings, more meetings, and effective meetings. The New York Freudian Society developed a process for selecting training analysts emphasizing collegiality of discussion of a case for those members evidencing excellence in clinical experience and supervisory experience. In the American Psychoanalytic Association, she took on directly the controversies around certification that had alienated many talented psychoanalysts. She is fearless and helps us all become less fearful of change and knowledge. Arlene Kramer Richards is likely to jump in to save individuals, patients, students, supervisees, colleagues, and friends from misuses of power and the "gas-lighting" of institutions more interested in maintaining their ways than in the true growth of ideas.

Arlene has traveled far and wide to teach, realizing how important it is to bring psychoanalytic ideas to students. She is enlivened by and enlivens Mental Health Institutions in China, finding ways to provide psychoanalytic treatments, seminars, and supervisions. She is a faculty member of the Tongji Medical College of Huazhong University of Science and Technology in Wuhan, China. I have formed the idea that a particular representation of teacher/student exists in Arlene's mind. She has powerful knowledge to convey and, even more importantly, has a way of finding knowledge that through example and through mentoring she brings to her students. Learning always involves a dialogue between what is known and what is not yet known, allowing each to inform the other. The teacher is often the student; the student, more often the teacher. And it is the patient who is ultimately the one bringing knowledge of psychic function and metaphor to the therapist. Freud learned the 'talking cure' by listening to his patients. Arlene brings her listening to patients and students and supervisees on many continents.

I think Arlene has sought out her own teachers with this very high standard of learning in mind. She has honored three particular "teachers" through editing festchrifts to them, namely: Jacob Arlow (1988), Martin Bergman (1994), and Horacio Etchegoyen (1997). Arlene's thinking is clearly centered on ideas found in Arlow's belief that a core presence of unconscious fantasy is continuously active in patient (and analyst), and lurking in streams of thought and interaction brought to analytic sessions. She was one of the many students to sit in Martin Bergman's splendid office, listening to each other's clinical material and learning from Martin's masterful style of bringing together historic psychoanalytic knowledge and new thinking. By bringing Etchegoyen's ideas about perversion, particularly the perverse transference, to English speaking audiences (chapter 10), she has helped ensure that analysts can reflect on the presence of perverse trends taking place in the consulting room.

Luckily for all of us, Arlene Kramer Richards keeps on traveling, lantern held high, taking us with her. She continues to lead us down new paths where we can learn about the unconscious and how it appears in our patients' minds and in our own. The papers here show us many of the places where she stopped to think, create, and write. We know she will energetically uncover new areas for exploration for us, and that we will gladly follow her as she lights up previously unseen territories of the mind.

REFERENCES

RICHARDS, A.K. (2012). Blood:Reading the Holocaust. In *The Power of Witnessing: Reflections, Reverberations, and Traces of the Holocaust—Trauma, Psychoanalysis, and the Living Mind,* N.R. Goodman & M.B., Meyers, eds. New York: Routledge, pp. 217–234.

——— (2001). Healing the Wounds: A Study of Women Survivors of the Holocaust. Paper delivered Lima, Peru, November 16.

——— (2010). *The Laundryman's Granddaughter: Poems by Arlene Kramer Richards.* New York: IPBooks.

——— & RICHARDS, A.D. eds. (1993). *The Spectrum of Psychoanalysis: Essays in Honor of Martin Bergmann.* Madison, CT: International Universities Press.

——— AHUMADA, J. OLAGARAY, J., & RICHARDS, A.D. eds. (1994). *The Perverse Transference: Essays in Honor of Horatio Etchegoyen.* Northvale: NJ: Jason Aronson.

——— BLUM, H., KRAMER, Y. & RICHARDS, A.D., eds. (1988). *Unconscious Fantasy, Myth, and Reality in Honor of Jacob A. Arlow.* Madison, CT: International Universities Press.

Arlene Kramer Richards:
A Personal History

When I was asked to write a personal history of Arlene as an introduction to her collected papers in this book, I was very touched and readily said yes. I have known Arlene as a friend and colleague for over thirty years. We first met in what was referred to as "The Martin Bergman Study Group." The "The" was emphasized because it was the first private study group that Martin Bergman formed and later was to become one of many. Arlene and I discovered that we lived near each other on the Upper East Side and that we were both joggers. Our friendship blossomed as we began to jog before sunrise every day of the week, rain or snow, accompanied by her husband Arnold Richards. We would run down Fifth Avenue to the Plaza Hotel and with the sun rising we would run back up Madison Avenue, jogging in place in front of one of the store windows when a beautiful piece of clothing caught our eye. It was during this activity that I discovered Arlene's interest in fashion, and that she herself was an accomplished and talented knitter who created her own designs.

As I got to know Arlene better, I discovered that she had many passions, interests, and talents that she patiently and indefatigably pursued, all the while making all that she accomplished look effortless. When I recently looked over her publications, what struck me most was how her papers reflected so many of her diverse interests, both professional and personal. Thinking about her interest in fashion, which I discovered during our jogging, and later in her study of female perversions, it came as no surprise to me that she would write a paper called, "Ladies of Fashion: Pleasure, Perversion or Paraphilia" (chapter 7), and another called "Clothes and the Couch," published in a book entitled *I Shop Therefore I Am* (Benson 2000).

As a clinician, her papers are clearly inspired by her careful listening to her patients in the treatment situation. Yet, at the same time, many of the subjects that she has chosen to write about are also subjects that deeply resonate for her personally. The subjects of her writing reflect interests she had before becoming a psychoanalyst, such as her interest in poets and poetry, which she herself began to write when she was eight years old and has continued to write throughout her life. Her papers on female sexuality reflect her work with patients, but the papers are also influenced by her personal background and experience as a woman determined to meet the challenges faced by countless other women, working hard to balance and integrate their competing roles. Arlene has accomplished this high-wire act both in her personal life as a devoted daughter, wife, mother, colleague and friend, and in her professional life as a psychoanalyst, poet, writer, teacher and mentor.

It is often a joke among colleagues, a joke containing more than a grain of truth, that we become psychoanalysts because we began our training in childhood within our own families. In reviewing Arlene's early background, her childhood and adolescence, it is very evident that she had a bent towards helping and teaching others. She told me that when she was five years old and in kindergarten, her Yiddish-speaking grandmother was her "first great student." She would return home from school and teach her grandmother English and whatever else she had learned that day in school. Arlene's father was a businessman, and "the business was to be for her brother and not her." As Arlene told me this, I had the sense that this was her first brush with identifying herself as a feminist. She also felt identified with her mother's love of work. On the other hand, her mother hated anything having to do with keeping a home, and it was her grandmother that was the loving and nurturing figure. Arlene's life in her family of origin was not an easy one, but she had the good fortune to meet someone who told her about a special program at the University of Chicago that accepted gifted students even before they finished high school. Arlene seized this opportunity and entered the University of Chicago at sixteen. She majored in philosophy and classics and studied German.

She later took education courses to become a teacher—in order to work—while her husband, Arnie, whom she had met at the University of Chicago, went on to medical school in New York. By the time she was eighteen she had already graduated from college, married Arnie, and at nineteen had the first of their three children. She taught fifth grade in New York before moving to Kansas City for Arnie's residency in psychiatry at Menningers. She was hired by the Dean of Washbourn University in Topeka to develop a course in reading and study skills for entering freshmen, many of whom had come from rural areas and one-room schoolhouses. This was a relatively new field in education, and Arlene very much enjoyed teaching these eager students. Her early teaching experience with these students has been repeated countless times throughout her career, as many friends, students and supervisees have personally experienced her as a devoted teacher and an unusually generous mentor. When I one day noted this impression to Arlene, she replied, "It's not like I give something away and I have less; it's like giving and I have more. It is very satisfying. I think it goes back to teaching my grandmother when I was in kindergarten."

Arlene describes a pivotal moment for her, during the time the family moved from Topeka and was living in Petersburg, Virginia, where she was teaching reading and learning skills at a branch of William and Mary College. She was reading a *New Yorker* profile about a clinical psychologist by the name of Anne McKillop who was teaching study skills at Columbia Teachers College. McKillop had been impressed by what she observed of the emotional issues that seemed connected to learning disabilities. She and others at the time were also working on dyslexia and the neurological basis of learning disorders. From Arlene's telling, she became very excited about this work and called McKillop immediately to ask her if she would be her mentor. This is quintessential Arlene, as is the story that follows. She arranged that Arnie would stay with the children and she would take a night bus to New York City and return the next day. They drove to a rural town where she was to take the bus, but the bus never came. Arnie insisted that she keep the interview, so they piled all three sleeping children into the car and drove to New York. The children were astonished to wake up in the city the next morning. Arlene went into a coffee shop and changed in the bathroom into her interview clothes. When she appeared for the interview she told McKillop about how she had gotten to the interview. McKillop accepted her on the spot, noting that anyone with such motivation had to be in. This was the year 1964 when she began her Masters studies at Columbia Teachers College.

I love this story, because it represents so well Arlene's personality and her capacity not to let the extraneous details of everyday life stand in the way of her objectives. Most of us facing the same situation would have felt crushed, returned home, and gathered our nerve to rearrange the interview. Of course, her partner in this complementary marriage played a part, but it is who Arlene is that makes these things happen.

I recall a visit to Arlene's former vacation home in Stonington, Maine. At breakfast, she mentioned that she was having a party that evening and had invited, at that point, about twenty people. At about four-thirty in the afternoon I began to get nervous, because she had as yet not made any preparations for the party. She was busily working in her beautiful Japanese garden, which she had designed. I interrupted her and trying to be diplomatic asked if there was something I could do for the party. Arlene, stopped her work and said, "Oh, we can go down to the deli and get the food." And so we did. She bought all kind of delicacies, provided a sumptuous spread for her guests, and never at any moment seemed harassed or concerned about it all going well. Arlene approaches life with an unending sense of optimism, perseverance, humor and boundless energy that she brings both to her work and play. She is seemingly never daunted by the challenges she undertakes.

After receiving her Masters, she became increasingly more interested in psychology, feeling she had done all she wanted in the learning and reading field, and she decided to go on for a doctorate. In thinking about her dissertation subject, she decided to investigate the development of language structure in young children, and so it was not a coincidence that her youngest child, then six years old, was enlisted into a pilot project to test out her hypothesis. In attempting to write her proposal she developed a serious writing block. This writing block coincided with her son turning thirteen, being Bar Mitsvahed, and going off to high school. She found herself very sad about all that was occurring, and she could not understand her sadness or the writing block. These events led her to enter psychoanalysis.

Jacob Arlow had just published a paper on the significance of Bar Mitzvah. She sought him out for a consultation and then entered an analysis with him. Arlene also understood that some of her issues had to do with being a woman and a mother, her fears of separation and loss, and her guilt over her personal ambitions.

True to her character, after a year of analysis her writing block disappeared. So it is of little surprise that one of her early papers was about the poet H. D. who had writer's block and sought analysis with Freud. She had read Hilda Doolittle's poetry since childhood and had loved it. She views some of Doolittle's poetry as she views her own writing, as an adaptive response to a loss or a tragedy and a sense of despair, and ultimately as way to deal with thoughts and feelings that seem unacceptable.

Her interest in the subject of female development, and specifically female sexuality, was kindled by a female patient who spoke to her mother on the telephone countless times a day. While this looked like severe dependency and separation problems, Arlene discovered that these telephone talks also pervaded the patient's sexual life and this led her to write, "A Romance with Pain: A Telephone Perversion in a Woman" (chapter 11). There was little in the literature about female perversions, and very little about female genital anxieties. The area of female sexuality became of interest to her. A number of papers on the subject of female perversions and female genital anxiety followed, including her papers: "Primary Femininity and Female Genital Anxiety" (chapter 4), and "The Influence of Sphincter Control and Genital Sensation on Body Image and Gender Identity in Women" (chapter 5). Her interest in the study of loneliness also derived from a number of her patient's concerns, and she and Lucille Spiro have written on this subject and have an ongoing workshop dealing with the subject of loneliness at the annual Winter Meetings of the American Psychoanalytic Association.

Arlene's creativity, curiosity and willingness to risk writing about subjects that push the envelope of conventional psychoanalytic thinking has deepened our understanding of psychoanalytic technique and expanded the possibilities of discussion. This is seen in her paper, "Talking Cure in the 21st Century: Telephone Psychoanalysis" (chapter 17). It is not that analysts have never before had telephone sessions, but few had ever written about it and, of course, today, in our global world, it would be impossible not to consider using the telephone for sessions. As Arlene said to me, "If you're not supposed to think it, it fascinates me." As this book will attest, Arlene has made some very original contributions to our psychoanalytic literature, contributions from which we have all richly benefited. The word "original" best describes Arlene, not only in her writing but in how she has navigated her different roles, and lived her very rich life to the fullest.

REFERENCE

RICHARDS, A.K. (2000). Clothes and the Couch. In *I Shop, Therefore I Am: Compulsive Buying the Search for Self* (A.L. Benson, ed.), New York: Jason Aronson, pp. 311–337.

Arlene Kramer Richards,
One of a Kind

At Arlene's 65th birthday party, her young grandson Joshua, told a story about Arlene that nobody who was there will ever forget. Grandmother and grandson trudged up to the top of a steep roller coaster at an amusement park. When they went to get in the car, the child got frightened and refused to go on. Arlene pushed him into the car. "My grandmother is not like other grandmothers," Joshua said. Guests are still laughing at the remark.

Joshua summed up Arlene perfectly. Not only is she different from other grandmothers, she is not like other people, either. She is that unique kind of person we call an original. She is herself, and nobody else. For example, I experienced a terrible tragedy in my life, and went to spend some time with Arlene. Did we discuss my grievous loss? Not at all. We went to the movies. It was just what I needed.

Then she wrote me this poem:

For Alma
Even stars shiver
in the alone night cold silver,
cold black, crying in.

Another time, Arlene was held up by a mugger, who stole her purse. Anyone else would have been glad to escape with her life. Not Arlene! She charged into the mugger and proceeded to beat him up. The mugger knew when he was licked and handed the purse back to Arlene. I asked her, "Weren't you frightened that he would kill you?" "I didn't think about that," she answered. "A rage came over me. I couldn't help myself."

Arlene, another analyst, and I wrote a book together. Our coauthor was a fine professional woman, but her writing left something to be desired. She had been raised in Europe and educated to write in a ponderous German style. The title she came up with for the book was a long, academic chain of words that one would have to read at least twice to understand. Arlene renamed it *Dream Portrait,* a lovely simple title that conveyed to the two of us, if not to our disgruntled colleague, the essence of the book.

The Richardses have a darling dog called Winnie, named after Churchill, of course. Arlene adores Winnie, and rarely goes anywhere without him. Sadly, they were informed by their co-op board that they would have to get rid of the dog, if they wanted to remain in the co-op. Arlene announced that they would not get rid of the dog, but would move elsewhere instead. Fortunately, they found a clever way of keeping both Winnie and their home.

A few years ago, the Richards and I went on a cruise together to Mexico. Near the end of the trip, Arlene said, "I want to do something in the water. Anybody want to come with me?" Arnie and I, who were exhausted from days of sightseeing, groaned. Did that deter Arlene from proceeding with her wish? Of course not. She went off scuba diving by herself. Par for the course, Arlene's fiftieth birthday party was held at a swimming pool. Her mother, who shared some of Arlene's uniqueness, and I were talking about the achievements of her daughter. I asked, "Aren't you proud of her?" She answered, "I'm so proud of her I could bust!" So are her friends.

A friend of mine told me a story that fits right into my thinking about Arlene. My friend and the Richards had joined a tour to visit Alaska. She had been brought up by a helicopter to a plateau of a glacier, and was gazing up at some distant hikers who were attached together by a rope. They had climbed high up on the glacier and were continuing upward, hacking their way with the aid of pick axes. She looked carefully at the tiny figures of the climbers, one of whom, despite the distance between them, looked vaguely familiar. "Oh my God, that's Arlene Richards!," she exclaimed.

As Joshua so astutely pointed out, Arlene's responses are often one step to the side of anyone else's. She loves their summer home in Garrison, New York. I asked Arlene what she would have done if they hadn't found the house, thinking she might have responded with a remark such as "We'd travel more." "I would have looked for another one just like it," she said.

Recently, Arlene asked me to review a paper she had written. I spent a good deal of time reading it and making suggestions. I emailed them to her, and waited for a response. It never came. After several weeks, I asked her, "Didn't you like my suggestions?" She answered, "Of course I did, and am using most of them." "Why didn't you let me know?"

I asked. "Didn't I?" she responded. "I guess I thought you would know I liked them."

Arlene is a strange combination of character traits. Who else do we know who is an exquisite poet, a fine psychoanalyst, teacher and writer, a superb wife and mother, and spends her spare time playing Solitaire on the computer? In addition, she swims like a dolphin through the dark cold waters of the lake near their summer home. Arlene wears the same size now that she did at their wedding. Her husband thinks she looks like Marilyn Monroe. I think he is a lucky man.

Even Before:
Teaching, Reaching, Writing

Arlene Kramer Richards is easy to describe—more difficult to imagine. She is a full-time adult analyst and has worked with and spoken for young people as a teacher, author, researcher and social activist. She is completely in the realities of this century; she is completely faithful to lessons from the past. One hundred percent of the time she is a poet, analyst, teacher, supervisor, parent, friend and wife. These exist not as competing commitments, but as inner worlds fueled by multiple talents, each fully lived, each nourishing one another.

After teaching a multilingual class in the elementary division of Williamsburg Vocational High School in Brooklyn, she went on to teach at a land grant college in Topeka, Kansas. There she worked with students from one-room schools in rural parts of Kansas who needed to learn reading and study skills in order to do college-level work. All of this left her with an understanding of how to speak to young people with little or no academic achievement.

Is it a coincidence that Dr. Richards's poetry, books, and analytic papers—which all hinge on the effectiveness of *language*—were written by someone whose family communications were early-on deeply influenced by the fact that even loved-ones had different "first" languages, and were not easily understood by one another?

In four books written for and about young people, she partnered with Irene Willis, a deeply respected colleague, and a former High School principal, and now online poetry editor of the website www.InternationalPsychoanalysis.net. Dr. Richards describes Dr. Willis's enormous ability to depict the "normal" kid's voice. Dr. Richards contributed how the child with specific troubles might feel and act. They met, no surprise, in a poetry seminar, each already taking pleasure from using words to absorb and stretch reader, writer, and listener. Their first collaboration, in 1976, was *How to Get It Together When Your Parents Are Coming Apart.*

These books spoke to teens: their parents and caregivers, their teachers, the administrators of their schools, and to them. The language respectfully but directly answered life questions that crossed generations. Years before her analytic training, Dr. Richards almost casually captured transference and the repetition compulsion in the (biographical) story of a young man who can neither get along nor leave home:

> It was the same old story everywhere, as far as Tim was concerned. As soon as you let (any)one of them get away with it, they'd walk all over you. To Tim, it seemed that his old man was just like that too. Let him get away with pushing you around even once and he'd follow up the advantage. Tim couldn't trust anybody to treat him fairly . . . Tim wasn't ready to move on to a new stage of life because he was still stuck in an old one, that of the little kid trying to win some freedom from his parents (p. 120, *Leaving Home*, 1980).

Throughout the books, the message for parents and their kids alike, is that who we are and what we become arises from a blend of powerful but silent expectations, often accumulating over generations. The books encourage communications that will soften and even extinguish the explicit but unknown expectations of the parents' own lives now, as they become expectations of their children.

With Irene Willis, Dr. Richards "translated" developmental theory into language as real as the teen's day just lived: the helplessness of the infant these teens once were; the earliest ways they learned to connect, to stay attached and be cared for; the rebellion and energy of their toddlerhood; the out-there school kid they needed to be; their confused efforts to simultaneously stay in the familiar and escape its confines. Mahler, Pine and Bergmann, Anna Freud, Joe Sandler, John McDevitt; Bowlby and Ainsworth, Fonagy and Target, and countless other explicators of development, are taught in these books mostly through the first-hand experience of the young people who are hurting.

The teens' stories infuse every chapter of the books. They are believable because they come directly from interviews with thousands of young people. True to the mission of the task, not one parent was interviewed. These were written for the benefit of teens whose power to change adults is usually limited. Through these interviews, the objectivity of a fine researcher and educator, and eventually an analyst, highlights the subtle foundations of disharmony, and worse. Here is the eventual supervisor pointing out the nuanced choreography of family collapse. In the realistic anecdotes lie operatic but real renderings of parent-child,

teacher-child, friend-to-friend, sibling-to-sibling, parent-to-parent relationships. The young and older reader, alike, watch as the fallout from
misunderstanding acquires incendiary force. Through the vignettes—the
stories of connection, broken hearts, anger, and love—the reader learns
about transference, ambivalence, separation-individuation, defense, the
repetition compulsion: the stuff of the treatment they may one day turn to.

The emphasis in all of the books is on understanding one's own
and another's actions. Subtly readers are encouraged to express emotions, rather than behaving as reflex might otherwise prompt. Throughout
the books is the sense that anger, rebellion, and even self-destruction
need not be pathologized to validate the seriousness of a young person's
predicament. The message comes through to offspring and caregiver
that the first response to adolescent outrage and despair would best be
reasoned-communication, not a hardening of lines between the parties.
Evidence emerges on every page that the emotional core of the young
is every bit as valid and vulnerable as that of its caregivers. The concept
that pervades the books is that helping a young person feel understood
may lessen inevitable disappointments, anger, and hurts enough to allow
him and her to work optimistically toward a wished-for future.

In *How to Get It Together When Your Parents Are Coming Apart*,
the authors

> . . . help adolescents deal with the effects of their parents' marital
> troubles on their own lives . . . Parents want to help their children
> through the pain and fear of dissolving marriage, but many do not know
> how to begin . . . [p. xii]

Here both audiences, one stated, one tacitly invited, confront their effect
on one another. For the young, it may be the first view of their parents as
neither all-powerful nor without pain of their own. For the older reader,
it may be the first unguarded opportunity to realize how their own unfinished family business is replayed in the failure of their own marriage,
and how the current failure can injure their own children as much as themselves. Always playing in the background of the vignettes of upset, splitting families is how easy it is to be and act angry and to hurt one another,
how much more difficult it is to feel pain and not retaliate in kind.

Elsewhere in the book, Dr. Richards warns that "No book can replace
therapy," but these books are the stuff of good therapy: they *ask questions*. They help sort real intent from the imagined. The books alter
premises. They question the wisdom of denial, explain the use of defense,

and by teaching this psychological substrate, the books ultimately empower:

> When parents are only pretending to be happy together, kids are kept from recognizing and adjusting to the real situation . . . (p. 7)

> She was ashamed of her parents. They didn't live up to her picture of a happy, warm family . . . they lacked self-control . . . her shame spilled over from them to herself . . . (p. 14).

> No matter how lonely or isolated you feel, *someone* in the world will want to listen to you and will be able to understand and help you through difficult times . . . We hope you will discover ways of finding those people who can share and help, and also learn how to find help, strength and action within yourself (p. xvii).

> The best way to get rid of that feeling is to tell your parents about it . . . in a quiet controlled way . . . to prove to yourself that you are different. You can see that you are not the screamer, not the person out of control; you are a separate, controlled person. You are separate, yet not uncaring (p. 14).

Dr. Richards looks at the imperfections of some adult behavior realistically and validates the adolescents' fears and feelings:

> If your parents fight physically instead of with words, you may have to deal with that. You are right to be afraid . . . (p. 17).

And even more starkly, different dangers after a separation or divorce:

> The scariest part of having a person living with your parent while you are still at home is the fear that you may be seduced. Some kids are teased or forced into having sex with other people . . . (p. 132).

But empowerment even as a member of a "falling apart" family is the goal:

> may be asked to talk to the judge. This is your chance . . . talking to the judge does guarantee the chance to express your wishes directly . . . (and) see how to get a lawyer who can advise you . . . (p. 67).

> If you are having problems you need to tell other people. Talking with other people about the problems helps keep you from being overwhelmed and ashamed. Other people can help you judge whether you're coping with those problems reasonably well or not. If you can't talk to your friends about your problems, you need to think

through for yourself whether you should look for someone with special training in helping others with their problems (p. 161).

In 1979 came *Boy Friends, Girl Friends, Just Friends*. Having conveyed that parents may be the beginning but they aren't all that matters in one's life, they write: "It is possible to grow up successfully without a parent, perhaps, but not without a friend . . . " (p. 12).

They talk to the power of peers and call friends "the mirrors in which to see yourself apart from the identity created for you by your parents" (p. 23).

They venture into the power of the group, often a test of confidence and identity for many young people. They talk about the magnified power of certain rejections. They talk about the strength of the wish to be acceptable and what that acceptance is worth. They talk about teasing and being teased; what behavior is it necessary to accept from a "friend"; and one's obligations to others who trust us. They talk about preparing for work, love, individuality, and teamwork. They talk about the obligations of being a leader and how to evaluate would-be leaders. They talk about resolving conflicts with people one values, and what can be expected and requested from others. This is ostensibly about friendship, but it is about getting ready to emerge from the family.

Under 18 and Pregnant was written in 1983, ten years after Roe v. Wade and six years after the FDA proclaimed that the first early (home) pregnancy test was ready for the public.

In narrative and diagrams the relevant factual details of teenage sex and sexuality are told in teen language. Here also are the potential consequences of wishing away—denying—the possibility of pregnancy.

This was a bold book. A small sampling of the full page of acknowledgements tells how deep and fair the research was: the head of a Maternity Services and Family Planning agency; a representative of the Salvation Army; directors of Women's and Youth services; the director of Student Health Services; Family Court judges; OB/GYNs; Principals; Planned Parenthood; a Center for Alternative Planning—on and on. But perhaps the thanks to ". . . All the pregnant teenagers at the Edna Gladney Home, Inwood House and elsewhere, who shared their experiences with us . . ." adds any necessary credential to this book's already stark believability.

Under 18 and Pregnant is a book about consequences, about impulses, about delay, about planning, about displaced feelings. It avers that ignorance and denial can be a temporary salve; it warns about

25

external pressures that ultimately affect only the pregnant teen and the father of the not-yet born; about responsibility for another person—for the rest of their lives. It talks about wanting to be assured of love through sex, about every step of an abortion, feelings afterward, resisting pressures to have one, or to not have one. It describes the process of giving a baby up for adoption; of how to continue school if it's kept; about conducting one's self at job interviews as a new parent. It helps the adolescent figure out whether to marry as a consequence of the pregnancy and, again, how to resist pressure. Nowhere is an author's opinion offered. Only encouragement to think it through, talk to whomever you can, and a 43-page appendix telling where to read about and get direct help with every possibility. It's a book about reality and responsibility.

It is in *Leaving Home* that the simultaneously freeing and excruciating process of being physically apart from the known characters of family and friends coalesces. This book is about how emotional understanding of what one is feeling—and what the caregivers are experiencing—affects one's planning. *Leaving Home* is about transforming the powerlessness of youth into a life with appropriate and growth-promoting options.

It is the reasoned assessment of some emotional issues in *Leaving Home,* not the stern voice of a cautious parent, that gets the caring message through the generational barrier. The book has its warnings, but they are presented as developmental realities: "One way a girl separates from her mother is by having sex . . . (p. 18)."

About choosing new role models:

> . . . People who are satisfied with themselves and what they have done with their lives make kids want to be like them . . . an older person who is unusually self-satisfied can be too attractive. A kid has to think seriously about whether the person is really worth imitating. (p. 52).

Understanding aggression as a part of developmental energy:

> Coming back home is (also) a way of settling old scores . . . showing their families and friends they were wrong about them . . . (p. 114).

The development of the capacity for self-reflection:

> When you are grown up you are your own boss; your sense of self-worth comes from inside you and not from what other people say . . . (p. 162).

And, the sense of agency and independence that are requisites of real adulthood:

> You have to be able to stand being away from your parents without feeling that you have been lost or abandoned and to stand being close to them without feeling that you are being swallowed up (p. 162).

Needing, loving, loss, and leaving are the stuff these books are made of, but the last—the experience of leaving and being left—seems to test all that came before. When Dr. Richards wrote the poetry that became another language, she wrote about the loss of her own mother:

> *. . . Stars and simple icebergs froze us*
> *when your arm slipped out of mine*
> *Goodbye I came to say Woe I Say Woe is us.*

And *After She Dies:*

> *Without you*
> *I hang out*
> > *On the line*
> > *Like wash*
> > *Left until it tatters.*

Her writing recognizes that only with maturity can one safely acknowledge dependency: Who will notice me, motivate me, partner me, mirror me, when the grown-ups are gone? The mutual need is accepted and mourned. She describes life as a system where youth outlasts the old, and armed with knowledge of one's self, can be ready for the legacy and obligations ahead. She describes how the unevenness of power adjusts over time. She pictures the adjustment of an internalized duet becoming a solo.

Mother's Night:

> *Less days*
> *less height*
> *Less.*
> *As she dies, my Mother grows less*
> *Even her skin grows tight.*
> *Less.*
> *Her lids droop.*
> *Her gaze is less*
> *Her hands grasp air*

Her smile loses curvature.
A moon no longer cup, now saucer.
STOP TIME.
Go no further.
Because I, the one to bring home blue stars,
Need you to bring them home to . . .

The educated plea of Dr. Richards, the eventual analyst, was that adults listen to young people and—having listened—listen, learn and possibly change themselves. The same plea is spoken by the twelve-year-old Paloma, who is looking forward to suicide as a release from her affectively deaf family in *The Elegance of the Hedgehog* (2006). Paola feels useless to all but equally underrated adults in her life. She emotionally connects with the manifestly ignored neighbor and concierge, Madame Michel:

> You know I wonder if I haven't missed something. A bit like someone who's been hanging out with a bad crowd and then discovers another path through meeting a good person . . . I understood that I was suffering because I couldn't make anyone else around me feel better . . . I can see their symptoms clearly but I'm not skilled to treat . . . Briefly, I thought I had found my calling . . . I could heal others . . . So what does this mean—I'm supposed to become a doctor? Or a writer? It's a bit the same thing, no? (p. 290).

Yes, and Dr. Richards is both.

REFERENCES

BARBERY, M. (2006.) *The Elegance of the Hedgehog.* New York: Europe Editions.

RICHARDS, A.K. & WILLIS, I. (1976). *How to Get it Together When Your Parents Are Coming Apart.* New York: David McKay.

——— (1979). *Boy Friends, Girl Friends, Just Friends.* New York: Atheneum.

——— (1980). *Leaving Home.* New York: Atheneum.

——— (1983). *What to do if You or Someone You Know is Under 18 and Pregnant.* New York: Lothrop, Lee & Shepard Books.

Back when I began writing about female development I was reacting to the work of Charles Brenner. He had just written a book in which he claimed to explain the empirical finding that depression was more common in women and anxiety was more characteristic of men. His explanation was that men are anxious because they fear loss of the penis n the future while women are depressed because they believe that they have already lost the penis. I thought that women were anxious about genital damage. I also thought that men could be depressed because of their lack of the more responsive and more richly innervated female genital. I thought that the social treatment of women accounted for much of the depression. When I told this to Dr. Brenner, his response was: "GET THE DATA. WRITE IT UP." I was honored and grateful for the challenge. I set my course for writing about my experience with women patients and my research into the analytic literature about women written by women.

Looking at the work on femininity now I think of it as quite autobiographical. For me the essence of being female has been the female body. The family lore had it that I bounced to music before I could sit up. My earliest memory is of rage that my younger cousin had a ride in my walker when I was 15 months old and I walked alone for the first time toddling after him hollering "Give back, give back." As a young child I loved to ride my trike, loved to climb the monkey bars in the park, to run and feel my body move. Later I loved to ice skate, roller skate, dance ballet and tap dance. Swimming was my great pleasure. But best of all I loved riding horses. All of these pleasures contributed to my feelings about my female body.

All this time I had little interest in dolls. I had no younger siblings until age ten. So my interest in babies was limited as was my experience with them. My maternal feelings came later and were much less compelling than the bodily experience of being a girl. In addition I was the only girl grandchild and was brought up by my grandparents until age six. I was valued by the family as a girl and as the first person born in the United States. Much later I learned that being so valued had to do with their legal status at the time. Because I was born in the United States, I could never be deported. And the laws of that time stipulated that my parents could not be deported either. And because they could not be deported, neither could my grandparents and uncles. All of them were rooted in this country through me. Of course none of that mattered to me as an infant and toddler, but the way they all cherished me did matter a lot.

All of this meant that when I read the analytic literature about female development, it made little sense to me. The idea that the little girl experienced herself as a boy made no sense. It did not seem to me that I did not have anything. It did not seem that I had lost anything. I had always experienced my body as a source of pleasure and my "bottom" as a special source of good feeling. The idea that this good feeling was not important to me was an alien idea, not consonant with my experience at all. I felt it to be delicate, did not want to think of hurting there, did not want it touched by anyone I did not trust. The idea that a girl becomes aware of being a girl only when she sees that a boy has a penis seemed alien to me. Later amendments to analytic theory, that posit that the little girl understands herself to be a girl when she is told by her social environment that she is a girl, made sense to me. The idea that the genital is disappointing to a little girl because a boy has "more" or that the little girl must necessarily envy the little boy's genital and think that she has none was not consonant with my own experience.

In addition the idea that the girl accepts what she believes to be the inferior genital because it comes with a promise that she can have a baby when she grows up was not believable on three counts: (1) my genital provided pleasure; (2) I felt valued as a girl; and (3) being grown-up was very far away.

Surely there are many little girls who experience themselves as potential little mothers, and play dolls and house and mommy and daddy. They look forward to being able to have babies of their own. But there are other little girls who are pressed into service taking care of their younger siblings. Some of them look forward to not having to take care of more babies. For them the idea of having the capacity to have babies of their own may seem more like a punishment than like a prize. Having seen women with such diverse infantile experiences and such varied fantasy lives derived from those bodily and social experiences, I am now impressed by the diversity of development more than by its regularity. Altogether I now find the individual differences even more fascinating than the similarities among people. Does this make the analytic attitude more of an art than a science? Maybe the technique of listening and responding to patients has changed the way we think about female development as it has so many other aspects of our understanding of people.

PAPERS IN SECTION I
(All papers by Arlene Kramer Richards)

Chapter 1
(2003). Book Review: The Sexualities in Life and Art. *Journal of the American Psychoanalytic Association* 51:1385–1390.

Chapter 2
(2000). Hilda Doolittle (H.D.) and Bisexuality. *Gender and Psychoanalysis* 5:37–66.

Chapter 3
(1999). Freud and Feminism: A Critical Appraisal. *Journal of the American Psychoanalytic Association* 47:1213–1238.

Chapter 4
(1996). Primary Femininity And Female Genital Anxiety. *Journal of the American Psychoanalytic Association* 44:261–281.

Chapter 5
(1992). The Influence of Sphincter Control and Genital Sensation on Body Image and Gender Identity in Women *Psychoanalytic Quarterly* 61:331–351.

Chapter 6
(1992). Hilda Doolittle and Creativity—Freud's Gift. *Psychoanalytic Study of the Child* 47:391–406.

A Book Review

CHAPTER 1

THE EMERGENCE OF SEXUALITY: HISTORICAL EPISTEMOLOGY AND THE FORMATION OF CONCEPTS. By Arnold Davidson. Cambridge: Harvard University Press, 2001, xvi + 254 pp., $42.00.

In this scholarly and closely reasoned book, Arnold Davidson considers the origin of a conceptual schema that created three institutions: psychiatry as a medical discipline, psychoanalysis as a theory of the mind and a treatment modality for mental illness, and sexuality as a science of desire. He elegantly shows how this schema—the medical diagnosis and treatment of actions, thoughts, and feelings—developed in the nineteenth century, replacing the idea that madness was a theological problem. Following Foucault on this path, he extends historical epistemology to assert that concepts (in the philosophical sense) are not fixed and given Platonic ideals, but rather pieces of a world view that changes with historical circumstance and, he implies, with the evolution of thought. His book is timely now that the paths of psychiatry and psychoanalysis seem to be diverging—the former toward medicalization, while the latter develops into a talking cure administered by psychologists, social workers, and others. In our time, the concept of mental illness is developing along a bifurcation between (on the one side) dispensers of medications for anxiety, depression, hyperactivity, schizophrenia, and other specific symptom constellations, and (on the other) patient and painstakingly slow exploration of a person's thoughts and feelings with the goal of achieving the most adaptive and least painful compromises among one's wishes, fears, moral ideals, and relationships with others. To see where we are going, it may help to see where we have been. From this point of view, Davidson's history of our concepts and their relations is valuable for analysts.

Davidson credits Foucault with the discovery that medicalization of the behaviors previously categorized by Augustine as religious heresy or as punishments from God marked a shift in power from the Catholic Church to hospital and from priests to doctors. Where the Church had categorized types of sins, psychiatry now classified types of people (that is, personalities) and types of disorders. In the world of the Church there had been plenty of flagellation, but only when Sacher-Masoch, by naming and describing it, made a concept of masochism did *masochism* enter the realm of discourse. Now it became possible to speak of masochism—his books had provided the context, the examples, that made the concept possible. Mental aberration and "perversion" were now considered malfunctions of the sexual instinct, rather than the result of a degenerate brain. But the function of the sexual instinct was taken to be propagation of the species, and all sexual behavior that did not serve reproduction had to be thought of as perversion. Thus stood psychiatry's functional system until Freud replaced it in his "Three Essays"; for Foucault, psychoanalysis was historically the next step in the medical treatment of thoughts and feelings. By taking patients out of the hospital and into consulting rooms, and inquiring into their thoughts and feelings, Freud replaced the perversion-heredity-degeneracy system of understanding mental illness with a new set of concepts to go with his new method of treatment. Most notably, according to Davidson, Freud replaced the concept of sexual instinct that had itself been part of the then prevalent psychiatric perversion-heredity-degeneracy system. In philosophy, sociology, and history, madness replaced badness and ideas about pleasure and pain replaced the notions of good and evil.

Davidson asserts that the first of these essays is Freud's point of departure from the previously accepted view of perversion as any nonreproductive sexual activity. The crucial change is Freud's definition of the sexual drive as distinguishing an aim and an object that are independent of each other and only "soldered together" during the course of development. In Freud's conception, a drive differs from an instinct in that a drive is independent of its object. From this he concludes that inversion or homosexuality is not a perversion, since it involves a different object only, not a different instinct. Further, Freud shows that the genital nature of the sexual drive is not absolute, but that the genital zone is one in a succession of zones that provide impetus for sexual behavior.

If kissing is making love with the lips, Freud reasons, why is oral-genital contact any different? Davidson wants to follow this argument to the conclusion that there is no such thing as a perversion. He reads Freud as saying that nongenital sexuality is not perversion, and that what Davidson calls *fixity* cannot be perversion, since fixity on a genital relation to an object other than a child or animal is not perversion. Davidson concludes from this that there is therefore no perversion. But

Freud himself takes his argument to a different conclusion. Although he believes that homosexuality is not perversion, he concludes that perversion does exist. But he defines perversion as the intersection of two domains: the nongenital aim of the sexual drive and its fixity.

To illustrate this point, a Venn diagram is useful. Imagine two circles overlapping. Circle A (nongenitality) is not perversion. Circle B (fixity) is not perversion. Now imagine that one circle is yellow, the other blue. You can show that neither circle is green. But the intersection of the two will be green. Davidson has followed Freud's assertion that the first circle is not green and the second circle is not green. Therefore, Davidson says, there is no perversion. But Freud says that the intersection where they overlap *is* perversion. The area where there is both fixity and nongenitality is the area of perversion.

As a philosopher, Davidson is no doubt familiar with this kind of reasoning, but he does not seem to understand it in this context. He is writing as a twenty-first-century philosopher and successor to Foucault in a time when the concept of perversion is seen as sexist and coercive; Foucault, in whose honor he writes, saw it that way as well. Freud, on the other hand, was writing as a twentieth-century psychoanalyst. The concept of perversion was useful to Freud because it described a certain kind of symptom and could explain a certain associated difficulty in the course of treatment.

Davidson cites the definition of perversion in Laplanche and Pontalis's (1973) dictionary of psychoanalytic terms as the best summary definition of the way the term is used in Freud. Laplanche and Pontalis contrast the use of the term in other contexts with the purely sexual meaning it has in psychoanalysis. They emphasize Freud's refusal to separate homosexuals from other people as a special group—his rejection of the psychiatric model—since, he says, all human beings have made a homosexual object choice at some time in their development. This same consideration, they maintain, applies to the fixation argument; that is, all human beings have experienced early states of organization in which pleasure derived from other bodily zones is preferred to genital pleasure with another person. They conclude that Freud's later work develops the idea that perversions exist (as in the psychiatric model) as fixed and compulsive behaviors, but that they possess complex layers of historical precursors and determinants, and implications for the structure of an individual's defenses and way of experiencing the world.

Freud's relationship to the problem of perversion was thus not simple. He began with a refutation of the psychiatric way of looking at it, and then went on to formulate genetic and developmental theories of perversion. Laplanche and Pontalis, however, do not include Freud's final step in the evolution of his thinking on this subject. That was to pose aggression as a counterweight to sexuality, thus suggesting a dialectic between the drives rather than a single drive theory. This step was decisive for later analysts because it allowed the earlier view of perversion as aggression toward law to come back into the theory, making room as it did for the superego, for conscience, for guilt, for self-hatred, and for self-punishment. By stopping short of this last step in the development of Freud's thinking, Davidson keeps his own argument pure, but also simplifies it unneccesarily. He would make his point— that perversion is not a fixed concept—better, I believe, by including the evolution of the concept of perversion beyond the early days of Freud's theory and into the changes that led to more current thinking.

Davidson also devotes an essay to the presentation of knowledge. Here he asks why we assert knowledge, and he discusses how the use of evidence can serve as a communication only when the context is clearly delineated—not only by choice of word, but also by grammatical indicators of mood, tense and degree of certainty. He shows how narrative is never free of argument. While he does not directly concern himself with the instance of the case study as a form of history, the analyst will inevitably see the connection with Davidson's account of the divergence of the judicial and historical styles of thinking about evidence. For the judge, focusing on events that can be ascribed to particular persons, times, and places is useful. For the historian, such evidence is limiting in that it excludes such phenomena as social life, ways of thinking, and the other elusive but powerful forces that affect historical argument.

The ends of the judge differ from those of the historian, and so their methods of evidence collection and evidentiary reasoning must differ as well. As an analyst, I think that the method of data collection used for psychiatric diagnosis is akin to that of the judge, in that specific bits of evidence are required to categorize a disease, or a person as an exemplar of that disease: for instance, schizophrenia or a schizophrenic. Yet more global and less discrete evidence is not only valid but crucial if historical accounts are to have context and meaning. Context is useful in that it allows the listener the use of repetitions, gaps, metaphors, and other narrative clues to evaluate the truths sometimes hidden in the facts. Rather than insist that a narrative stick to the facts when speculation and context are required in order to make meaning, the responsible narrator tries to present both speculation and facts while carefully distinguishing between them. Thus Davidson urges that we be more profoundly aware of the interventions of the historian, rather than attempting to eliminate them—a strategy similar to that of the current moment in psychoanalysis and in literature.

All of this comes around to Davidson's major point: that perversion does not exist except in the particular time and place that gave rise to the theory of sexuality that has perversion as its centerpiece. He says: "The concept of perversion, for example, must not be identified with some mental state that can be found by introspection to, so to speak, bear the label 'perversion.' Nor is the concept of perversion or sexuality to be identified by the uses that are made of them, by the connections that govern their employment and that allow them to enter what Foucault called 'games of truth' *(jeux de vérité)*" (p. 181). Davidson warns analytic philosophers who want to treat the concept of perversion as though it were an eternal truth that they have to understand it in the context of the medical way of thinking that creates perversion as a category of sexuality. He chooses the idea (from Foucault) of "the field of utilization" as the context that stabilizes the meaning of such concepts as perversion and sexuality. This means, as I understand it, that even if a clinician uses the idea of perversion as a psychoanalytic concept to help a person who is in trouble with the police for fondling a minor (rather than using it to denigrate that person), he remains within Foucault's paradigm in which the medical establishment uses the power of medical concepts to punish. To name something, Foucault considered, is to punish it, however sympathetically (as opposed to sadistically) the naming is offered.

Power, however, like other concepts, gains meaning through its context, and the context of the clinician does differ from that of church or of state. Furthermore, the concept of power in the context of psychoanalysis differs from the same concept in the context of psychiatry. Power for the psychoanalyst is not the power to punish as exercised by church and state, or the power to classify and medicate as exercised by psychiatry; it is the power to liberate through empathy and understanding from the pain of even the most socially unappealing and disgusting symptoms of the human psyche—even perversion.

REFERENCE

LAPLANCHE, J., & PONTALIS, J.-B. (1973). *The Language of Psychoanalysis.* New York: Norton.

****
****

Original publication of this chapter:

RICHARDS, A.K. (2003). Book Review: The Sexualities in Life and Art. *Journal of the American Psychoanalytic Association* 51:1385–1390.

Hilda Doolittle (H.D.)
and Bisexuality

Bisexuality is investigated in the pair of poems H.D. wrote in the summer following her analysis with Freud. The idea that this analysis enabled her to integrate, value, and fashion a work of art out of her conflictual bisexuality is explored in detail in this paper. These poems explore the male in female and female in male that together delineate creativity.

Bisexuality is a concept which has not received the kind of attention from analysts that Freud's ideas on childhood sexuality have received. But bisexuality is a concept without which it is very difficult to understand the ubiquity of conflict. Children raised in what appear to be difficult families seem to turn out well while others reared in what appear to be favorable environments do poorly, suffer with neurotic manifestations, and fail to live up to their potential. The almost universal experience of not getting what one wants, not knowing what one wants, and being desperately miserable turns out, on analytic investigation, to have to do with wanting it all. Both boys and girls want what the other sex has. Both boys and girls want to be able to do what the other sex does, to have what the other sex has, and, eventually, to become both. This idea appears in Freud's thinking early in his letters to Fliess (Masson, 1985) and in his clinical (Freud, 1905a) and theoretical (1905b, 1908) work. More recently MacDougall (1991) and Stimmel (1996) have focused on women's bisexual fantasies and their relation to creativity. The impossibility of having everything accounts for so much misery that the notion of universal bisexual wishes is almost inescapable (Fast, 1984). But we have relatively little analytic data on bisexuality as behavior and lifestyle. One of the few bisexuals who was analyzed was the American poet H.D. She left an account of her analysis (1975) and a pair of poems dealing with feelings inspired by her newly gained self-understanding directly after it.

In a talk on the influence of psychoanalysis on modern American poetry Helen Vendler (1991) remarked that not only the content but the structure of poetry has been influenced by poets' experience of psycho-analytic psychotherapy. She was building on the way Holland (1989) uses psychoanalytic ideas to analyze the mind from the poetry and the poetry from the knowledge of the poet as a person. Vendler remarked that both Robert Lowell and John Berryman had written epics in the form of short pieces strung together into longer wholes as the analytic hour is strung together with other hours to form the analytic experience. Epic poetry has always taken the form of episodes strung together to form a larger story. But both Lowell's *Life Studies* (1972) and Berryman's *Dream Songs* (1959) have a different form from that of the epic. In both *Dream Songs* and *Life Studies,* the episodes have a recursive relation to each other that contrasts with the string of adventures in epic poetry. It seemed to me that Vendler had opened a new path to understanding modern poetry. Her idea led me to think about the work of another modern poet who expe-rienced psychoanalytic psychotherapy, H.D. I wondered whether the form of H.D.'s poetry had been affected by her analysis, and if so, in what way. She had written epic poetry after her analysis, something she had been unable to do before it. In another place, I hope to explore her epics with regard to Vendler's hypothesis. It seems to me that the first place to look for an influence of analysis on poetic form is in the first work produced after the analysis. H.D. went to Switzerland and worked there immediately after leaving Freud, psychoanalysis, and Vienna. That sum-mer she produced three poems. She published one poem, *The Master* (H.D., 1983), separately. The other two she published as a pair: *The Poet* and *The Dancer.* It seemed a clue to the meaning of the poems that they were published as a pair. A pair can be a dialectic. That is why I am focus-ing on this work here.

H.D.'s analysis with Freud was undertaken to deal with her writer's block (Duplessis, 1986); that she wrote for several hours every day after her analysis and produced work of such quality that she was the first woman elected to the American Academy of Arts and Letters seems to me to show that the analytic treatment was successful in relieving her of her symptom. What she had learned about herself in the brief analysis with Freud had changed her so significantly that her writer's block disappeared for life. To pose the question of how she changed is to ask what she learned. She believed that Freud gave her two major insights. The first was that she, like all women, suffered from a form of penis envy which entailed depreciating her own genital endowment. The second was that she was "perfectly bisexual." In an earlier paper (Richards, 1992), I focused on the usefulness of the interpretation of penis envy for her creativity. Here I would like to examine the influence of the interpretation of her bisexuality on the *form* of her work.

The poet in question was D. H. Lawrence, an early love of H.D.'s, dead by the time this poem was written, the dancer a woman she saw for the first time shortly before the poem was written.

The Poet

> There were sea horses and mer-men
> and a flat tide-shelf,
> there was a sand-dune,
> turned moon-ward, and a trail of wet weed
> beyond it,
> another of weed'
> burnt another colour,
> and scattered seed-pods
> from the sea-weed.
> there was a singing snail,
> (does a snail sing?)
> a sort of tenuous wail
> that was not the wind
> nor that one gull,
> perched on the half buried
> keel,
> nor was it part of any translatable sound,
> it might have been, of course,
> another sort of reed-bird,
> further inland;
> inland there was a pond,
> filled with water lilies;
> they opened in fresh water,
> but the sea was so near,
> one was afraid some inland tide,
> some sudden squall,
> would sweep up,
> sweep in,

over the fresh-water pond,
down the lilies;
that is why I am afraid,
I look at you,
I think of your song,
I see the long trail of your coming,
(your nerves are almost gone)
your song is the wail
of something intangible
that I almost but not-quite feel.

2
But you are my brother,
it is an odd thing that we meet here;
there is this year,
and that year,
my lover,
your lover,
there is death,
and the dead past:
but you were not living at all,
and I was half living,
so where the years blight these others,
we, who were not of the years,
have escaped,
we got nowhere;
they were all going somewhere;
I know you now at this moment, when you turn,
and thank me ironically,
(everything you say is ironical)
for the flagon I offer,
(you will have no more white wine;)
you are over-temperate in all things;
(is inspiration to be tempered?)
almost, as you pause,
in reply to some extravagance,
on my part,
I believe that I have failed,
because I got out of the husk that was my husk,

and was butterfly;
Oh snail,
I know that you are singing;
your husk is a skull,
your song is an echo,
your song is infinite as the sea,
your song is nothing,
your song is the high-tide that washed away
the old boat-keel,
the wet weed,
the dry weed,
the seed-pods scattered,
but not you;
you are true
to yourself, being true
to the irony
of your shell.

3
Yes,
it is dangerous to get out,
and you shall not fail;
but it is also
dangerous to stay in,
unless one is a snail:
a butterfly has antennae,
is moral
and ironical too.

4
And your shell is a temple,
I see it at nightfall;
your small coptic temple
is left inland,
in spite of wind,
not yet buried
in sand-storm;
your shell is a temple,
its windows are amber;

you smile
and a candle is set somewhere
on an altar;
everyone has heard of the small coptic temple,
but who knows you,
who dwelt there?

5
No, I don't pretend, in a way, to understand,
not know you,
nor even see you;
I say,
"I don't grasp his philosophy
and I don't understand."
but I put out a hand, touch a cold door,
(we have both come from so far;)
I touch something imperishable;
I think,
why should he stay there?
why should he guard a shrine so alone,
so apart,
on a path that leads no where?
he is keeping a candle burning in a shrine
where nobody comes,
there must be some mystery
in the air
about him,
he couldn't live alone in the desert
without vision to comfort him,
there must be voices somewhere.

6
I am almost afraid to sit on this stone,
a little apart,
(hoping you won't know I am here)
I am almost afraid to look up at the windows,
to watch for that still flame;
I am almost afraid to speak,
certainly won't cry out "hail,"

or "farewell" or the things that people do shout;
I am almost afraid to think to myself,
why,
he is there.

The Dancer

I came far,
you came far,
both from strange cities,
I from the west,
you from the east;
but distance cannot mar
nor deter
meeting, when fire meets
ice or ice
fire;
which is which?
either is either,
you are a witch,
you rise out of nowhere,
the boards you tread on,
are transferred
to Asia Minor;
you come from some walled town,
you bring its sorcery with you;
I am a priestess,
I am a priest;
you are a priestess;
I am a devotee of Hecate,
couched by a deep jar
that contains herb,
pulse and white-bean,
red-bean and unknown small leek-stalk and grass blade;
I worship nature,
you are nature.
I worship art;

2
I am now from the city
of thinkers, of wisdom-makers,
and I watch as one come from afar
in a silver robe;
I carry no wine-jar;
I watch intent,
as one outside with whom is the answer;
intelligence alert,
I am here to report,
to say this is
or is not
God;
I am perfectly aware,
perfectly cold;
a girl clutches at her lover's wrist,
I do not care,
(I am perfectly aware of what you are doing,
of what seeds you are sowing)
I know what this youth thinks,
what nerve throbs in that old man,
how that wan soldier
back from the last war,
feels healing, electric, in a clear bar,
where an arm should be;
nothing is hidden
from me;
If you make one false move,
I will slay you;
I hate and have no fear,
you cannot betray me,
you cannot betray us,
not the Sun,
who is your Lord;
for you are abstract,
making no mistake,
slurring no word
in the rhythm you make,
the poem,
writ in the air.

3
Fair,
fair,
fair,
do we deserve beauty?
pure,
pure
fire,
do we dare
follow desire
where you show
perfection?
loveliest,
O strong,
ember
burns in ice,
snow folds over ember;
fire flashes through clear ice,
pattern frozen is red-rose,
rhododendrons bend under full snow,
yet each flower retains colour;
the rhododendrons are in flower
and snow covers
the flame heat
of purple,
of crimson,
of dark-blue,
of pale-blue,
of white
crystal
calyx;
miracle,
miracle of beauty returned to us,
the sun
born in a woman.

4
We are more than human,
following your flame,

O woman;
we are more than fire,
following your controlled
vibrance;
we are more than ice,
listening to the slow
beat of our hearts,
like undercurrent of sap in a flowering tree,
covered with late snow;
we are more than we know.

5
Give us the strength to follow,
the power to hallow
beauty;
you are wind in a stark tree,
you are the stark tree unbent,
you are a strong bow,
you are an arrow,
another arrow;
your feet fling their arrows,
your twin arrows,
you then pulse into one flame;
O luminous,
your feet melt into folded wing,
to the mer-maid's tail;
O love in the circle
of opening,
of closing,
of opening;
you are every colour of butterfly,
now in a frail robe, you are a white butterfly;
burning with white fervour,
you are a moon-flower,
seen in water.

6
You are every flower,
I cannot stop to name;

nor do I claim
precedence among the harp-players;
my song-note falters;
I claim no precedence among the flute-players,
for I could not maintain
presence enough to stand,
there at your feet
with the rest,
making that music;
I can not name
the Doric nor the Ionic
measure,
nor claim greatness;
I have gained
no laurel
at Delphi;
but he,
your Father,
burning son-lover
has yet had his jest,
has said, among all these
there is one voice,
one councillor;
listen,
Rhodocleia,
he says;
"dance for the world is dead,
dance for you are my mistress,
you are my stylus,
you write in the air with this foot,
with that foot,
with this arrow;
your flung hand
is that pointed arrow,
your taut frame
is one arrow,
my message;
you are my arrow,
my flame;

I have sent you into the world;
beside you,
men may name
no other;
you will never die;
nor this one,
whom you see not,
sitting, sullen and silent,
this poet."

7
O let us never meet, my love,
let us never clasp hands
as man and woman,
as woman and man,
as woman and woman,
as man and man;
O let us never speak, my love,
let us never utter
words less than my heartbeat,
words less than your throbbing feet;
white cygnet,
black missel-thrush,
let us never crush
breast to breast,
let us never rush
purple to purple fire,
wide flowers,
crushed under the glory
of god in the whirl-wind,
of god in the torrent;
O chaste Aphrodite,
let us be wild and free,
let us retain integrity,
intensity,
taut as the bow,
the Pythian strings
to slay sorrow.

8
There is much to know
and little time,
O bright arrow;
there are many to heal
and few to feel
the majesty
of our King;
there is little to know
and all eternity,
O my sister;
there is no hurry,
no haste,
not waste,
only leisure;
infinite leisure
to proclaim
harmony,
our Master.

9
So haste not,
bright meteor;
waste not strength,
O fair planet,
singing-sister;
move delicate strength,
pause,
never-weary palour;
gather blue corn-flowers,
bind poppies in your hair,
O Priestess;
teach men
that the sun-disk
is bearable,
and his ardour;
dare further,
stare with me
into the face of Death,

and say,
Love is stronger.

10
Rhodoceia,
rhododendron,
sway, pause, turn again;
rhododendron,
O wide rose,
open, quiver, pause
and close;
rhododendron,
O strong tree,
sway and bend
and speak to me;
utter words
that I may
take
wax
and cut upon my tablets
words to make men pause
and kneel,
broken
by this pulse we feel;
rhododendron,
laurel-tree,
sway, pause,
answer me;
you who fled your Lord and Sire,
till he pulsed to such desire
that no woman ever
could
after,
bear his sacred brood;

11
only singing fools and delf
trees
might speak

his prophecies.
Rhododendron,
O wild-wood,
let no serpent
with drawn hood,
enter,
know the world we know;
rhododendron,
O white snow,
let no mortal ever know
mysteries
within the fold
of purple
and of rose
and gold
cluster
of this sacred tree;
rhododendron,
swear to me,
by his mountain,
by his stream,
none shall mar
the Pythian dream.

12
We will build an altar here,
swear by wood, by hill, by star,
swear by wind, by curve of bay,
where his leaping dolphins lay,
singing to the priests, on high
build the altar
let life die,
but his song shall never die.

13
Leap as sea-fish
from the water,
toss your arms as fins,
dive under;

where the flute-note
sings of men,
leaving home
and following dream,
bid men follow
as we follow;
as the harp-note tells of steel,
strung to bear immortal peril,
(pleasure such as gods may feel)
bid men feel
as we feel.

In looking for evidence of the effect of H.D.'s analysis on her writing, I propose to look at content and form (form will include imagery). The form of the work is at first glance a diptych. The poems are bound together. Looking more closely, the first poem is six stanzas long, the second thirteen. But the thirteen stanzas are themselves divided into a first section of six stanzas and a second section of seven. Now we have a triptych. The form lends itself to the dialectic mode of thought: thesis, antithesis, synthesis. This is a mode of thought found in the analytic hour. Patient talks, analyst talks, patient and analyst create a new understanding.

In this work the dialectic is on the theme of love. The first poem is heterosexual, the second is lesbian in its first six stanzas and in the final seven achieves a reconciliation and integration of her bisexuality. In this sense, form adds emphasis, adds affect to content.

A theme common to all of this work is the seashore. The first stanza of *The Poet* sets the scene:

There were sea horses and mer-men
and a flat tide-shelf,
there was a sand-dune,
turned moon-ward, and a trail of wet weed
beyond it,
another of weed'
burnt another colour,
and scattered seed-pods
from the sea-weed.

The lines alternate wet and dry, sand and water, the tide shelf is sometimes underwater, sometimes not. The poem explores ambiguity and doubleness. It shows a region that is sometimes sea, sometimes land, a place where both are there at different times. This serves as a setting for a poem in which deep feelings of internal bisexuality are explored. The setting is metaphor, the poems, if they did not have the internal ambiguity and conflict in the foreground, could be seen as flawed by the pathetic fallacy. It is H.D.'s genius and the fruit of her analysis that the structure of the poems carries through the metaphor without devaluing bisexuality.

In the poem to Lawrence, Doolittle recalls his hypermasculine cult of the male orgasm. The poem starts with the bisexual seahorse, a species in which the male carries the egg pouch and nurtures the young. The mermen are less familiar to the Western eye than mermaids and evoke the latter even as they shock the reader. This shock prepares the reader to think about the ambiguity of the sex and sexrole in this poem. The flat tide shelf and dune turned moonward provide a landscape with feminine connotations. The sea and its moontides evoke female periodicity echoed by the repeated trails of seaweed left by the tide. Images of cries and singing introduce Lawrence himself, the singing snail. Remembering him in the poem, Doolittle recalls a scene in which "I see the long trail of your coming,/(your nerves are almost gone)." The ejaculation is accompanied by a "wail of something intangible/that I almost but not-quite feel." There is a suggestion of a love scene on the beach, but of an ambiguous kind. Agony is suggested in the cries, disbelief is expressed in the question "Does a snail sing?" This is a love song infused with pity for the beloved, and with fear of his impotence, in short, a tragic love song. The poet Byron, who had a club foot and was a very strong swimmer, had called himself a merman. Byron, like Lawrence, presented a hypermasculine idea of himself and exalted romantic love; and Byron drowned. Doolittle evokes the tragic early death of Byron to foreshadow and thus intensify the tragic effect of the early death of Lawrence.

In the second stanza, Doolittle reproaches Lawrence for being "over temperate in all things." She clearly wanted intimacy, "But you are my brother," and after the first taste, he declined, "you will have no more white wine." She believes that he regretted his moment of freedom with her when "in reply to some extravagance,/on my part," he says "I believe that I have failed,/because I got out of the husk that was my husk,/and was butterfly." She reminds him that the butterfly which goes out of its pupal shell "is moral and ironical too." Besides, staying in the snail shell is dangerous, unless one is a snail. The danger quickly overtakes the poet-muse, Lawrence. He had actually died in New Mexico by the time this poem was written. In the poem, as in reality, his shell has become a temple in the desert. No one there knows him. The only sign of life in his temple is a drop of amber, a souvenir of ancient life. The temple in the desert has a sort of placid, brooding female quality; it is a womb. Paradoxically, Doolittle, the female poet, has moved and done, flown like the butterfly, while Lawrence, the male poet, has retained his sexually ambiguous snail shell to the end of his life and has died and been enshrined in a female image, a kind of dried-out shell, a dessicated vagina. The poem ends in a fearful hush as Doolittle, sitting on a stone, barely dares to let herself think of him.

The images of fire and ice which recur in the second poem come from Petrarch, a great poet of heterosexual love. He owed that image to Sappho who had used fever and chill to describe lesbian love. Like the sexual imagery in *The Poet,* that in *The Dancer* is reversed. The dancer is a woman, but her attributes are among those traditionally regarded as masculine. The poem opens with travel; both women have completed a journey, "I came far,/you came far." Yet in the very next lines otherness rather than similarity is stressed: "I from the west,/you from the east." The difference is emphasized even though both Doolittle and her beloved are women. Shifting between similarity and difference, the form of the poem is ambiguous just as the depiction of the female is ambiguous. Similar to the male, yet more adventurous than he is, the female lover is paradoxically more masculine. And the meeting with the female lover creates fire and ice, as in heterosexual Petrarch, rather than chills and fever as in lesbian Sappho. The theme of difference and sameness continues in images of priest/priestess, nature worship/nature, and art worshiper/art. Doolittle portrays herself as the rational observer and contrasts herself with the dancer who needs no logic and no words, who writes poems in the air.

The dancer is ember in ice, red rose in snow, fire in ice. Even more fantastic, the flame is purple, crimson, dark blue, pale blue, and white crystal. The dancer's beauty is masculine: "wind in a stark tree," the "stark tree unbent," "a strung bow," "an arrow." All of these are taut, spare, masculine images. But she is also the mermaid, an echo of Lawrence as the merman. She is the butterfly Lawrence never dared to be, she pulses in the circle, opening, closing, and opening. Here is the ideal image of the vaginal sphincter, the woman's power and the promise of immortality. Here is the hymn to immortality to parallel the mourning stanza for

Lawrence's death. Here end the six stanzas which parallel the six to Lawrence.

Having posed the problem of love for man or love for woman, H.D. resolves her sexual doubleness in another paradox. She opens the seventh stanza "O let us never meet, my love." She wants never to clasp her lover's hand, or even talk to her, but rather to join with her in honoring the one who is Master to them both; "stare with me/into the face of Death,/and say,/Love is stronger." She invokes the classical Greek image of Rhododendron. The maiden Daphne who fled Apollo, ran from him so hard and fast that he lost his potency by pursuing her. According to Ovid, she prayed to be released from the beautiful body that caused the god to pursue her, her prayer was answered and she was changed into a laurel tree. The leaves of this tree were then used to crown poets with immortality. Later they were also used for the victors in the Roman wars. The maiden was pleased to exchange her fate of sexually subject woman for that of the tree of poets' honor. At the site of Apollo's mythic castration, H.D. and the dancer will build an altar together, an altar like Lawrence's, but by the life-affirming mother sea, not in the arid desert. H.D. alludes to the first images of the poem here, the seahorse and the mermen, for mer means sea and mere means mother and the seahorses are male mothers with egg pouches. And there at the edge of the sea the women will teach men to feel the pleasures of gods, to leap and dive, to leave home, and follow one's dreams, to feel as artists feel.

It is clear that H.D. accepted and welcomed her charge from Freud. She wanted to become a poet rather than a beautiful woman pursued by lovers. Practically, this made sense for a woman who was then 48. It also made sense for a woman who was raising her child with a female lover who had been the family provider and taken the role of father from the child's birth. But it also had a deeper and more universal sense. To negotiate her way in her art, H.D. needed all the time and energy she could muster for writing. Yet it took a great deal of courage and conviction for Freud to suggest this resolution to H.D., just as it had taken a great deal of courage for him to recognize the bisexual wishes in his own nature that led him to become the kind of artist he made of himself.

Conclusions and a Speculation

The existence of these poems shows that the writer's block was removed by the analysis. But analysts believe that psychoanalysis is more than symptom removal. Questions about the possible mechanisms of removing symptoms vex the analytic mind. Where does a symptom go after it is removed? How does loss of the symptom affect the rest of the psychic organization? These questions seem to me related, in this instance, to the question of the influence of analysis on the forms the poet uses.

To return to the question of whether Doolittle's poetic form had been affected by her analysis in the same way as had Lowell's and Berryman's, I believe that in this pair of poems the effect of the analysis on the poetry is different from that of the effect on *Dream Songs* or *Life Studies*. Doolittle's *The Poet* and *The Dancer* seem to me to reflect the structure of the dialogue within a single analytic hour. They contain a dialectic and resolution similar to the pattern experienced when the patient's voice alternates with that of the analyst. They also reflect the more hypothetical alternation of wish and prohibition with the synthesis of a compromise formation within the patient.

Most profoundly, they reflect the competing impulses toward love for a man and love for a woman. The conflict has not been removed. The symptom of inability to write has been replaced by the work of art. As the impulses are aroused again or continue to be important to the woman, they require the production of more poetry and the writer's block is replaced by a need to write. The intensity of the need and its continuous imperative are structured by the patterns of thought, the ego functions, developed in the analysis. Thus, the analysis influences both the poet's productivity and the form of the product.

Anna Freud (1936) described psychic change in terms of changes in defenses: on a naive level, this was considered to be elimination of defenses, on a more sophisticated one, it was thought of as exchanging rigid all-purpose defensive structures for more flexible situation specific ones. Brenner (1982) has proposed that we consider change in compromise formations with gratification, defensive maneuvers, and superego prohibitions altered in a way that allows more self-acceptance and better functioning. Arlow (1987) believes that analysis increases one's awareness of fantasies as well as allowing one to accept them as welcome organizers of psychic functioning. Bach's (1985) work implies that ease of transition from one way of seeing the world to another perspective is a measure of analytic success. What these points of view seem to me to have in common is the idea of satisfaction. I believe that all of these authors would agree that H.D.'s analysis with Freud would have to be considered successful if it resulted in her feeling satisfied—and it did.

What H.D. and Freud accomplished in her analysis was to enable her to deal with oedipal issues and issues of sexual identity and sexual object choice. That she learned to accept her bisexuality and to believe in her creativity as part of her femininity was crucial. Freedom to love both men and women and to sublimate that love in her work was what H.D. believed she had accomplished in her analysis. These poems support the idea that H.D. succeeded in this life goal in a way that reflects unmistakably the attainment of the analytic goal of self-knowledge (Ticho, 1972).

What is bisexuality? H.D. wrote a letter to her lover Bryher, in which Freud is referred to as "papa." H.D. says:

Also, usually, a child decided for or against one or the other parent, or identifies himself with one. But to me it was simply the loss of both parents and a sort of perfect bi-sexual attitude arises, loss and independence. I have tried to be man or woman, but I have to be both. But it will work out, papa says and I said now, in writing [cited in Richards, 1992, p. 400].

Friedman (1981) believes that Freud empowered H.D. by allowing her to disagree with him and to argue with his points of view. She believes that this represents a conventionally masculine role and would therefore allow H.D. to be creative, a conventionally masculine activity. Women believe that they can create, but do not believe that men will value their creations. Therefore, Freud was able to help H.D. to write because he valued her as a woman and as a writer. Benedek (1968) says:

In our language, the term bisexuality refers to a specific predisposition to certain psychological reactions to environmental influences which exert control over the development of the personality. Infants of both sexes introject memory traces of responses to both parents. . . . This implies the basic assumption that children of both sexes have a biological predisposition to develop empathic responses to individuals not only of their own, but of the opposite sex: without this communication between the sexes would not be possible [p. 427].

For Freud (Sulloway, 1970) the psychological concept of bisexuality was a transformation of a biological idea. It was rooted in Freud's first research: a study of the gonads of the eel. Since the eel lives part of its lifetime as a biological male and the other part as a biological female, research on its sexual organs is the perfect prototype for psychological inquiry into the psychological bisexual dispositions of human beings. It also reflected the content of Freud's second research project: a study of the spinal nerves of the bisexual organism petromyzon. Sulloway concludes: "Thus, when Wilhelm Fliess brought the theory of bisexuality to Freud's attention in the mid-1890s, he found in the latter a biologically prepared listener who not only had trained with a leader in this field but had also conducted firsthand research himself on a bisexual progenitor of man" (p. 160). Freud's scientific relationship with Fliess is widely known to have been the source for Freud's ideas about bisexuality, but Sulloway explains why Fliess's idea had such an impact on Freud. The biological underpinnings of the idea are reflected in Benedek's definition. That argument based on anatomy and its development had already been superseded by Horney (1924) in a paper in which she showed how identification with the father contributed to the little girl's idea that she would like to have a penis. Benedek, however, emphasizes the identificatory and object relations aspects of bisexuality, thus encompassing the psychological transformation Freud wrought in the theory of psychoanalysis when he accepted Horney's idea on the identificatory origin of bisexuality.

Early ideas about bisexuality in females included Wittels's (1934) suggestion that women used their beauty as a phallus. He believed that the narcissistic self-enhancement of cosmetics and beauty routines was neurotic, homosexual, and masculine. Penis envy, he thought, was the cause of neurotic attachment to beauty. Bryan (1930) considered manifestations of bisexuality in sexual stimulation and gratification of the heterosexual man and woman.

A more directly biological basis for female psychological bisexuality was adumbrated by Sherfey (1968). She described the embryological development of the sexual organs in humans as going from a morphologically female to a male configuration in the presence of male hormones. Biologically, she argues, the female cannot be seen as a defective male, but the male must be seen as a variant of the female. It is not clear to what extent this biology is mirrored in psychology, but the idea that the girl's first identification is with her mother supports the analogy.

Identification is most powerful when the love and hate are at their most intense. Schuster (1969) described a patient who: "attributed the penis to his mother and thus explained her dangerous tendencies." Schuster believed that this fantasy evolved from primal scene experiences: "His identifications tended to oscillate between father and mother in their sexual encounter; at times he was the attacker, at other times he was the attacked" (p. 78). Earlier, Schuster (1966) had described a woman whose image of herself included a masculine lower part of her body with a hidden penis. A dream in which she was beating her stepdaughter led to associations of leading to the conclusion that: "Mother and child in the dream represent father and mother having intercourse, the patient identifying with both. She identifies with the sadistic, attacking father and becomes violent herself in order to defend against identification with the helpless, violated mother. The dream goes beyond the feminine incestuous wish and the wish to be punished: it also represents a triumph through identification with the aggressor" (pp. 362–363).

Friedman (1976) described a little girl who became fascinated with her father's umbilicus. She wanted to poke her finger in it, laughed when she saw it, and spent time watching her father change his shirt in hopes of seeing it. An adult woman patient of Friedman's reported in analysis that she always experienced an urge to poke her finger in her husband's umbilicus after intercourse. This substitute area in which men and women are the same is also an area in which one is vulnerable to being poked. The umbilicus is bisexual image personified.

Wisdom (1983) has shown that male and female trends in both sexes could be understood as the result of a process he called early personality exchange. This process is similar to identification, but also involves reciprocity. Traits are first internalized by identification, then subjected to transformation as the other reidentifies with the child. This process implies that all children brought up by male and female parents or surrogates would acquire traits from both sexes and would therefore have bisexual personalities. The process of attaining self-understanding which we call psychoanalysis would then necessarily result in the patient learning to appreciate the qualities of both sexes in oneself and to value them. The analysis of H.D. seems to have achieved that.

Bisexuality is the subject of both fear and condemnation among heterosexuals as well as homosexuals. Proust (1913–1972) in Sodom and Gemmorah regarded it with horror. He wrote: "Vice begins for the invert when he takes his pleasure with women." His idea was that being loyal to one's first choice is essential to being a whole person. For Proust it was not a matter of being faithful to one person, but of being consistent with one's own character, which he regarded as being decisively shaped by one's object choice. For H.D., the problem was one of integration of the object choices with her choice of profession.

H.D.'s integration of the conflict into a truly adaptive compromise formation took place, I believe, in this complex work. Images like the snail shell, mermen and tide pools for the man and arrows and the stylus for the woman contribute to the integration of male and female into the creatively human. By finding the feminine in the masculine and the masculine in the feminine, H.D. was able to integrate a self that would later work in a masculine way, producing epic poetry, and yet make feminine work, showing the epic nature of the female experience. The poems considered here show a stage in her development toward this achievement and to illustrate the profound effect Freud's interpretation of her bisexuality made on her.

In this context, I would like to venture a speculation about how the specific form of bisexuality found in women who have a dual object choice develops. From what we know from the psychological literature about infant development, mothers treat their male and female infants very similarly, concentrating on nurturance and protection. Fathers, however, treat male infants more roughly and treat female infants more flirtatiously (Maccoby, 1998). My own idea, which comes from fantasy and observation, is that both female and male infants develop an expectation of nurturance and a close attachment to the mothering person. But rivalry with others for mother's love appears later when, as toddlers, they have the capacity to understand that another person is an independent source of initiative. Tomasello (1999) puts this at the end of the first year, Mahler, Pine and Bergman (1975) at between 18 months and 3 years. Only then can the fantasy that a rival for mother's love put one at risk of losing her to that rival. I think that for both little girls and little boys this is a terrible blow, one of the catastrophes of childhood and one that haunts the developing mind. I do not think that it matters whether the rival for mother's love is a man or a woman. Lesbian couples and gay couples report that their children are as rivalrous as those brought up in heterosexual families. What I think matters is the basic constellation of loved one, rival, and self. The particular circumstances of each person's development determine the endlessly fascinating variations in the story. This makes what we are accustomed to calling the negative oedipal constellation the basic and most definitive structure in a girl's development. Thus, a female object choice is the first in development and the bisexuality of a girl is based on the inherent conflict between her negative oedipal longings and the wish to become a mother and have a baby. It is the flirtatious father or other flirtatious adult, who tries to woo the little girl away from her mother, who offers a compromise that many, if not most little girls are tempted to take, though rarely without resenting mother for not having chosen the little girl as her one and only best beloved.

REFERENCES

ARLOW, J. (1987). The Dynamics of Interpretation. *Psychoanalytic Quarterly* 56:68–87.

BACH, S. (1985). *Narcissistic States and the Therapeutic Process.* New York: Jason Aronson.

BENEDEK, T. (1968). Discussion of Sherfey's Paper on Female Sexuality. *Journal of the American Psychoanalytic Association* 16:424–448.

BERGMAN, J. (1954). *The Dream Songs.* New York: Farrar Straus.

BRENNER, C. (1982). *The Mind in Conflict.* New York: International Universities Press.

BRYAN, D. (1930). Bisexuality. *International Journal of Psycho-Analysis* 9:150–166.

DUPLESSIS, R. (1986). *H.D. The Career of That Struggle.* Bloomington: Indiana University Press.

FAST, I. (1984). *Gender Identity.* Hillsdale, NJ: Analytic Press.

FREUD, A. (1936). *The Ego and the Mechanisms of Defense.* New York: International Universities Press, 1966.

FREUD, S. (1905a). Fragment of an Analysis of a Case of Hysteria. *Standard Edition* 7:1–122. London: Hogarth Press, 1953.

——— (1905b). Three Essays on the Theory of Sexuality. *Standard Edition,* 7:123–243. London: Hogarth Press, 1953.

——— (1908). Hysterical Phantasies and Their Relation to Bisexuality. *Standard Edition,* 9:155–166. London: Hogarth Press, 1959.

FRIEDMAN, S. (1976). On the Umbilicus as Bisexual Genital. *Psychoanalytic Quarterly* 45:296–298.

FRIEDMAN, S.S. (1981). A Most Luscious Vers Libre Relationship. *Annual of Psychoanalysis* 14:319–343. New York: International Universities Press.

GUEST, B. (1984). *Herself Defined.* New York: Doubleday.

H.D. (1975). *Tribute to Freud.* New York: McGraw-Hill.

H.D. (1975). *The Poet and the Dancer.* San Francisco: Five Trees Press.

H.D. (1983). *Collected Poems.* New York: New Directions.

HOLLAND, N. (1989). *Poems in Persons.* New York: Columbia University Press.

HORNEY, K. (1924). *On the Genesis of the Castration Complex in Women. International Journal of Psycho-Analysis* 5:50–65.

Lowell, R. (1972). *Life Studies.* New York: Noonday.

Maccoby, E.(1998). *The Two Sexes.* Cambridge, MA: Belknap Press/Harvard University Press.

MacDougall, J. (1991). Sexual Identity, Trauma and Creativity. *Psychoanalytic Inquiry* 11:559–581.

Mahler, M., Pine, F., & Bergman, A. (1975). *The Psychological Birth of the Human Infant.* New York: Basic Books.

Masson, J., ed. (1985). *The Complete Letters of Sigmund Freud to William Fliess (1887–1904).* Cambridge, MA: Harvard University Press.

Proust, M. (1913–1972). *Remembrance of Things Past.* New York: Random House.

Richards, A. (1992). Hilda Doolittle and Creativity. *Psychoanalytic Study of the Child* 47:391–406. New Haven, CT: Yale University Press.

Schuster, D. (1966). Notes on "A Child is Being Beaten." *Psychoanalytic Quarterly* 35:357–367.

——— (1969). Bisexuality and Body as Phallus. *Psychoanalytic Quarterly* 38:72–80.

Sherfey, M. (1968). The Evolution and Nature of Female Sexuality in Relation to Psychoanalytic Theory. *Journal of the American Psycho-analytic Association* 14:28–128.

Stimmel, B. (1996). From "Nothing" to "Something" to "Everything." *Journal of the American Psychoanalytic Association (Suppl.)* 44:191–214.

Sulloway, F. (1970). *Freud, Biologist of the Mind.* New York: Basic Books.

Ticho, E.A. (1972). Termination of Psychoanalysis. *Psychoanalytic Quarterly* 41:315–333.

Tomasello, M. (1999). *The Origins of Human Cognition.* Cambridge, MA: Harvard University Press.

Vendler, H. (1991). Freud and Postwar American Poetry. Paper presented at IPTAR Symposium on Applied Analysis, New York.

Wisdom, J. (1983). Male and Female. *International Journal of Psycho-Analysis* 64:169–186.

Wittels, F. (1934). Mona Lisa and Feminine Beauty: A Study in Bisexuality. *International Journal of Psycho-Analysis* 15:25–40.

****
****

Original publication of preceding chapter:

Richards, A.K. (2000). Hilda Doolittle (H.D.) and Bisexuality. *Gender and Psychoanalysis* 5:37–66.

Freud and Feminism:
A Critical Appraisal

This paper traces the contributions made by women to Freud's ideas about women. Freud paid back the gifts he received from women with encouragement and support for their careers and with a theory that was instrumental in freeing women from both domestic bondage and fantasies of inferiority, but which was used by later "Freudians" as justification for returning women to an exclusively domestic life. Paying particular attention to Sabina Spielrein, Lou Andreas-Salomé, and H. D., the paper illustrates some of the contributions of women to early psychoanalysis, and speculates on ways in which Freud's thinking was guided by his belief that women are, and should be considered, equal to men.

Sigmund Freud invented psychoanalysis as the art and science of listening. He was a listener who tried to hear and who worked hard at making sense of what he heard, and he listened to voices that in his day received very little attention—the voices of women. Unlike many of his professors, he listened to his patients, and he broke ranks even further with the men of his time by listening especially to women

I owe much of my thinking and all of my interest in this topic to what happened in my own analysis, where the most essential thing I learned was that my status as a woman did not have to limit my ambitions or my achievements. Years later, reading Hilda Doolittle's *Tribute to Freud* (1975), I found an echo of my own experience. H. D. had found in her analysis encouragement, a sense of purpose, and belief in her own creative powers. What had given that to her? I wrote this paper to answer that question. When I finished a draft, I gave it to some feminist colleagues to read. Much to my dismay, some of them objected that I was ignoring the other aspect of Freud: the misogyny of which his feminist critics accuse him. I could see that Freud's theories of female sexual development were insulting to women, but I was puzzled by the clash between the feminist outcomes of some psychoanalyses and those aspects of his theory of female sexual development that led later feminist psychoanalysts to condemn him for his ideas about women. After thinking this through, I came to the conclusion that it would be better to examine the evidence on Freud's attitudes towards women and then consider the very important ways in which his theorizing led feminist critics to believe that he, and by implication psychoanalysis, denigrated women.

I will argue that Freud was an equality feminist. The challenge of his time was to show that women were worth educating, could participate in the modern scientific world that was emerging, and could earn money and deserve social value for their participation. Part of his achievement was to show that women were the equals of men with regard to work and intellectual capacity. I hope to show that his accounts, now discredited, of identical development in boys and girls until the fateful discovery of the penis were not attempts to show that women were less than men because they had no penis, but rather that women had the same equipment as men in all other respects. But if Freud was a feminist in the equal-opportunity tradition, how could he have created a theory that offends so many women and so many feminists?

In this context, it is useful to recall that feminism is and was a movement with a tripartite agenda. Feminists have worked for: (1) equality in voting, education, and opportunities; (2) respect for sexual differences; and (3) support for motherhood, including childcare and education for young children. These three parts of the feminist agenda are not always compatible, and sometimes conflict. Susan B. Anthony wrote to Elizabeth Cady Stanton in 1857,[1] "My soul was on fire. This [idea that women are emotional while men are rational] is but a revamp of the world's idea from the beginning, the very same doctrine that consigned women from the beginning to the sphere of the affections and that subjugated her to man's wisdom." Stanton was an equality feminist. She argued that women could and should be self-supporting, and she believed that sexual attraction lay "in the *knowledge* of the *difference of sex*." She believed that this knowledge was social, not biological, and that it could be changed by dress and grooming, the socially conventional signals of sexuality. Underneath, she believed, men and women are the same. In modern terms, she was a social constructivist. Her point of view was the feminist point of view that Freud knew and followed. In our own time, Carol Gilligan (1982) is an example of a difference feminist. She argues for respecting women's value systems in connectedness, rather

---

[1] New York Times feature, July 18, 1998.

than assuming defective superegos because women, unlike men, are inclined to place persons above principles. Feminists who want government support for mothers who choose to stay home, or who argue that women need to be devoted to home and family, and so must allow their husbands to take care of them, are in the third feminist tradition. All are feminists, but there are clashes between the values and policies espoused by the different groups.

Freud was an equality feminist, squarely opposed to the idea that women should be content to exchange servility for support and protection. Freud's equality feminism, like Stanton's and Anthony's, was formed in the climate of opinion that resulted from the American Civil War. So many men were killed that many middle-class young women were left with no hope for marriage or protection from a man. They had to learn to fend for themselves. One response to this situation was the foundation of women's colleges to prepare women for professional and academic work. This particular history, and this special consequence of that history, left feminism with a flavor of failure and envy that combined ironically with a strong sense of option and privilege. Equality feminism spread from the United States to Europe, where it influenced Freud. These contradictory currents influenced both Freud and feminism in ways that have yet to be recognized.

Freud missed the boat on the feminism that privileges motherhood. He refused to enter fully into the idea of difference feminism, and he admitted that he did not know what the equality agenda might entail in the way of sacrifice of "femininity." He famously asked women to figure all of this out. For these reasons, he become the target of feminist repudiation and hatred.

Second-wave feminists of the 1970s began criticizing Freud in reaction to the popularizing of his theories of feminine development in magazines and newspapers. I believe that the agenda of the advertising industry, and the businesses that hired it in the United States in the 1950s, was to avoid postwar depression and unemployment by directing half the work force to leave its employment and go home to full-time consumering, depending on the other half of the work force for support. If women were home doing the childrearing and household maintenance, the jobs they had held in wartime would be open for men. The men would support the women, and all would be well. To this end, women were told that Freud believed that they had to choose between the natural fulfillment they would find as wives and mothers, and the substitute satisfactions enjoyed by spinsters with jobs or professions. Simone de Beauvoir (1952) argued that this postwar propaganda showed the profound disrespect for women's intellect and women's work then pervasive in Western culture. Betty Friedan's *The Feminine Mystique* (1963) argued against the view that one pattern fits all women—that the happy homemaker ideal is ideal for all. Ironically, Freud would have argued against this view as well. Shulamith Firestone in *The Dialectic of Sex* (1970) insisted that Freud's argument that anatomy is destiny enslaved women by chaining them to their roles as childbearers. She called for new technology to replace pregnancy and lactation. Kate Millet (1970) argued that not only motherhood but also sexual intercourse serve patriarchy, and that men dominate women by making them sexual slaves. For her, Freud's idea that women desire sex was another way of enslaving them. Phyllis Chesler (1970) argued that marriage and psychotherapy both promote dependence on men. Naomi Weisstein (1971) argued that Bettelheim was foreclosing on women's choices by insisting that they must all be nurturers, and pointed out the impact of social thought on concepts of femininity. Rather than target the followers who had distorted Freud's ideas, these feminists attributed the sexism of their era to Freud himself.

How to make sense of the contradiction between Freud's respect for the intellect and talents of the women he learned from and taught, and the denigrating descriptions of female sexual and emotional development that were attributed to him and that, in some cases, he did indeed espouse? I reread Freud. In 1886, at the beginning of the *Standard Edition,* Freud is thirty years old and already a physician, with the best training in neurological diagnosis and treatment of the nervous disorders to be had in his day. After his studies with Charcot in Paris and his translation of Charcot's work, Freud begins his own writings on psychoanalysis (he had written research papers in biology and physiology previously) with an investigation of the connection between the "genital system" and neurosis. By the end of the *Standard Edition* in 1941, his posthumously published last paragraphs tell of his final thoughts: that identification with the clitoris is the girl's source of inferiority feelings, not penis envy. He begins and he ends with the riddle of female sexuality. His answer to this riddle failed to satisfy the Sphinx; he certainly failed to convince many women that he understood them, and his answer has earned him criticism from feminists. But this is getting too far ahead of the story. He was working very hard at the riddle, not for abstract or patronizing reasons, but in the service of the women he was attempting to understand—not just as sexual beings, but as people who needed relief from psychic pain. Beyond his interest in female sexuality, Freud was interested in, and influenced by, women. And that is the story.

Freud learned from his patients. These women suffered from the psychological disturbance most common on the Viennese scene in the second half of the nineteenth century: hysteria. First there was Bertha Pappenheim, the Anna O. of Freud and Breuer's book *Studies on Hysteria,* which they wrote between 1892 and 1893. Freud's account of her includes a respectful comment on her fluent command of several languages and her cultural sophistication. Bertha eventually became a radical spinster. She founded a home for unwed mothers and their infants, translated Mary Wollstonecraft's *Vindication of the Rights of Woman* (1792) into German, discovered and was first to publish a diary written by a woman in Europe, the memoirs of Glückel von Hameln,[2] and lived a life devoted to feminism in every way. Then came Anna Van Lieben, whom Freud treated from 1887 to 1888, and whom he called his "teacher." Just as he and Breuer had learned from Bertha Pappenheim that following the thoughts and feelings related to a particular symptom could play an important part in relieving it, so did Freud learn from Anna that the thoughts and feelings that fueled symptom formation could also fuel the creative process. In a letter to Fliess, Freud called Anna "a highly intelligent woman to whom I am indebted for much help in gaining an understanding of hysterical symptoms."

From his patient Fanny Moser, Freud learned that talking with his patients was better than hypnotizing them, and that listening was better still. With Fanny, whom he called "Emmy von N" in *Studies on Hysteria,* listening allowed Freud to learn the family secrets that caused the shame and guilt fueling her insomnia, depression, tics, and neuralgias.

From the girl he called "Katharina" he learned that premature incestuous seduction was a trauma capable of causing neurotic symptoms. If Freud was a student of hysteria, his teachers were the women he treated. Being a good student, he learned a great deal from them. His working relationships with them were not those of an authoritarian man

---

[2] In his introduction to the 1977 Schocken edition of *The Memoirs of Glückel of Hameln,* Robert S. Rosen states that "The first of two translations into German was made by a descendent of Glückel, Bertha Pappenheim, and printed privately, in Vienna, in 1910" (p. xii).

with a submissive woman. Rather the reverse; these hysterical women had much to teach, and Freud was eager to learn. This is the kind of relationship that has become the model of what good psychoanalytic treatment can be. It may at times have been misunderstood, and subsequent practitioners have sometimes had very different attitudes toward their patients, but the model stands as the ideal toward which psychoanalytic therapy strives.

Learning from Patients

Freud learned from the women he saw in consultation. Did he treat them simply as patients? A colleague of mine has objected that "being solicitous or sympathetic to women patients does not necessarily make them equal in the doctor's eyes." She thought that Freud's attitude was just "good bedside manner," not real respect. But the evidence is to the contrary. Appignanesi and Forrester (1992) described Freud's attitude this way:

> *This credulity and gullibility in the face of the female patient—in Jones's eyes so characteristic of Freud, and so much a necessary precondition for the development of psychoanalysis—was the inevitable accompaniment of the sympathetic attention Freud always found for those most inaccessible of patients, the female paranoiacs. With them, his curiosity in the kernel of truth to be found in all delusions and illusions was unencumbered by the expectation of therapeutic benefit, while at the same time, his sympathy for any woman deprived, by whatever means, of sexual fulfillment could find adequate expression. The slightly cold disinterestedness that some of his patients noticed in him could then be exercised in the most profitable way, through maximizing his own gain in understanding* [p. 182].

I think this shows that Freud was not just a physician with a bedside manner, but that his sympathy and concern for his women patients extended from them to other women. His biographer Ernest Jones thought that he was less motivated by zeal to heal any particular woman than by interest in what he could learn from the particular women who showed up in his consulting room that would benefit all women (Jones 1955, p. 421).

This same attitude of wishing to learn, and this same solicitousness for female patients deprived of sexual pleasure, is evident not only in the early treatments, but later in his case studies (Freud 1915, 1920). In "Fragment of an Analysis of a Case of Hysteria" (1905), also known as the "Dora" case, Freud diligently attempts to understand what women want. Dora was a teenage girl who experienced disgust when a friend of her father's embraced her. The fact that the man was married Freud saw as no obstacle; he could get a divorce. Critics have attacked Freud's technique in this case, averring that he was too abrupt, too demanding of Dora, too eager that she conform to her family's wishes, too intent on getting her married, too dismissive of her moral scruples (Shainess 1970; Glenn 1980; Scharfman 1980; Langs 1980; Kanzer 1980; Bernstein 1980; Bernheimer and Kahane 1985). Marcus, remarking on Freud's suggestion to Dora that she could marry her father's mistress's husband and resolve the family's problems, says: "No one—at least in recent years—has accused Freud of being a swinger, but this is without question a swinging solution that is being offered" (1985, p. 87).

But this is a misreading of Freud's intentions. He suggested to Dora that she was less afraid of her suitor's intentions than of her own desire. He did not see her as a mere respondent to male desire, but as the subject of her own wishes and the owner of her own sexual desire. Critics of Freud's views in this case, especially those writing in Bernheimer & Kahane's *In Dora's Case* (1985), have pointed out that she was only a young virgin, as if virgins were immune to desire. But Freud believed, contrary to the views of the Victorians of his day and the wishes of some modern psychoanalysts, that even female adolescents could enjoy a first experience of their desire if they were not neurotic. In this way, he was both very modern, and very empowering of women.

Freud has also been faulted for empowering only the heterosexual desires of women and for not attending to the revolt against patriarchy that is implied by Dora's refusal of heterosexual desire (Ramas 1980). "Dora," the pseudonym Freud chose to cover the identity of his patient, was also the name of a servant, who had been forced adopt it in place of her own name (Rosa) when she became nanny to Freud's sister Rosa (Moi 1981). Ramas points out that all unmarried women were potential servants, relegated to the care of children and to household labor of every kind, and that the devaluation of servant women had become so extreme in Victorian society as to allow men like Dora's suitor Herr K. to seduce and abandon them with impunity. Dora explained to Freud that she could not accept her suitor because he had seduced and abandoned his children's governess. He was degrading her by courting her as he had the governess, and he might have spurned Dora also, once she gave in to his wishes. This view does deal with why Dora would not accept her suitor. But I think it fails to explain Freud's question: why did she get sick instead?

Freud tells us that Dora was fascinated by a portrait of the Madonna, a woman who earned endless veneration by the preservation of her virginity, which endured even after she gave birth to a child. Being a Madonna herself would insure that Dora could have heterosexual fulfillment without being debased as the servant girls had been. She would triumph both as a biological woman and as an exemplar of the ideal and the spiritual. But Freud noted this only as a by-the-way. He was more interested in why this solution had not worked for her—why she had not chosen a marriage in which she would be the idealized Madonna-wife, but had become hysterical instead.

There he relied on her own statement that she saw her father's mistress as having "an adorable white body." He hypothesized that her wish for the love of her father's mistress interfered with her wish to have a man. His daring conclusion was that this woman wanted sex with a man and sex with a woman, but that each wish interfered with her ability to satisfy the other.

I think that the Dora case shows Freud trying to follow his patient's narrative. He did not always succeed, but he did strongly suggest to her, as well as to others, that being sexual was better than being hysterical. In his introduction to "On the History of the Psychoanalytic Movement," Freud (1914) tells three stories. All have to do with older and more experienced colleagues remarking in an offhand manner that the real cause of hysteria is always sexual deprivation. This amazing talk about women being sexually deprived is very far from the Victorian notion that women's sexuality consisted only of enduring their husbands' sexual demands.

Up until 1914, although Freud was asked about female sexuality, he published no theoretical papers on the subject. Instead, according to Buhle (1998), he hung back while the bestseller on the subject of female psychology (Weininger 1908) differentiated women from men in many dimensions, always invidiously. The most plausible explanation for Freud's silence is that he was looking for a more rigorous understanding of women that the facile view of his day that they were simply inferior beings. Deeper analyses of women, and a more thorough study of early female development, would be required to provide the kind of substantive data and coherent theory that he could find persuasive.

Women Colleagues

Meanwhile, he argued for equality for women in his own circle. According to the minutes of April 6, 1910, of the Vienna Psychoanalytic Society (Nunberg and Federn 1967), Freud specifically stood up for women:

> SADGER declares himself to be opposed in principle to the admission of women.
> ADLER would be in favor of admitting women physicians as well as women who are seriously interested in the subject and want to collaborate with us.
> PROF. FREUD would take it as a gross inconsistency were we to exclude women on principle.
> In the test balloting conducted after Freud's remark, it turns out that three out of eleven votes are opposed on principle to the admission of women; this will oblige the president to proceed with extreme caution on this point [p. 477].

Freud thus stood in staunch opposition to the patriarchal position, even to the point of risking dissension within the ranks of his fragile little band of eleven followers. His statement that he is opposed to the exclusion, "on principle," of women, because it would be inconsistent, is very important. As a colleague has pointed out, this statement can imply that excluding women would contradict the fundamental principles on which psychoanalysis rests. If so, this means that Freud thought that women should be viewed as equal from the point of view of psychoanalytic theory, as well as within the psychoanalytic movement.

The woman proposed for membership on that occasion, Margarethe Hilferding, had been listed as one of the twenty-three members of the Society in October 1909. Her nomination was referred to the executive committee, brought up again at the meeting on April 20, delayed, and then finally voted upon on April 27, when she was admitted by a margin of twelve to two. She attended her first meeting as a full member on May 4. These details tell the story of a Freud willing to put his power and prestige on the line for women. He was even willing to risk division, something so small a society could hardly afford. He was clear on where he stood on equality for women.

But Freud wrote his first paper on what women want only after he read Lou Andreas-Salomé's monograph *Die Erotik* (1910), in which she described what she considered to be normal female development in the sexual sphere. Lear (1998) points out that Freud left Eros out of psychoanalytic thinking until the 1914 paper "On Narcissism," which he wrote after reading Andreas-Salomé's essay. After reading her account of the importance of Eros, Freud used that concept as a less biological and more psychological way of thinking about positive feelings than "libido." Once again, Freud had listened to a woman—this time not as a patient, but as a colleague. One could wish that he had cited her in that paper, but he only thanked her in private letters.

From their letters to each other it appears that Freud had the highest respect for Andreas-Salomé's thinking. His respect for her work later extended so far that he sent his own daughter Anna to her for analysis after his attempt to analyze Anna himself.

What did Andreas-Salomé have to say about women that Freud could respond to? Freud was an equality feminist, certain that women could do what men could do. Andreas-Salomé was a pioneer of the branch of feminism that has emphasized the differences between men and women. She described heterosexual love as the bond that could unite two very different sexes. If Freud had previously been on the side of the feminists who emphasized equality between the sexes and demanded equal education, equal opportunities, and equal treatment in the political arena, his reading of Andreas-Salomé made him aware that the argument for differences need not be an argument for inferiority, as it had been in Weininger's work.

Freud was no longer satisfied with his previous belief that conclusions about male development could be assumed to apply to females. Now attention to differences did not necessarily imply invidious comparisons. He was no longer in danger of siding with the dismissive Weininger if he spoke of sexual difference. Difference had become a female claim, and attending to it was a mark of respect.

Many feminists of the time were influenced by Ellen Key, a Swedish writer (*The Woman Movement,* 1912) and lecturer who believed that woman's role was motherhood and that this primary responsibility should be given great support and respect by society. Andreas-Salomé did not go along with this idea, which was later championed by Karen Horney. For Key and Horney, motherhood was a little girl's ambition and a grown woman's achievement. But Andreas-Salomé, childless herself, saw that there were other possibilities for satisfaction as a woman. Freud learned at least two things from Andreas-Salomé: the first was that recognizing female psychology as different from male psychology was not necessarily a disparagement of the female; the second was that women could be self-assured in a way that men were not. His paper "On Narcissism" can be read as a study of Andreas-Salomé's character as the female ideal.

Andreas-Salomé fascinated Freud, as she had other men, in her capacity for pleasure and satisfaction. She was complete in herself. Freud remarked on this as the essence of the female character in "On Narcissism," and he contrasted it with the character of the normal male. For the male, Freud contended, winning the beautiful woman was essential. Man wants to love. Woman wants to be loved. The male gives up part of his self-esteem to idealize the female. The female keeps her self-esteem, which is bolstered by the love of the male. This formulation depicts the relationship between Freud and the women he loved, especially Andreas-Salomé.

For example, he wrote to her (Pfeiffer 1966) after she had not attended one of the series of Wednesday evening lectures: "I am very sorry that I have to answer your letter in writing, i.e., that you were not at my lecture on Saturday. I was thus deprived of my point of fixation. . . . You spoil people like me who are continually tempted to complain about mankind, by a degree of understanding which extends beyond what has been said" (p. 13). Freud valued her opinion on both political and scientific issues. For example, Andreas-Salomé says in a letter to Freud, "I owed you an answer last evening when you passed me the note asking me how I had found Sunday's lecture" (p. 12). His letters to her reveal a similar interest in her opinions of political matters: "But all the same one cannot help feeling a covert desire to know how the whole thing might appear to another person, to a judge male or female, and I confess that it is to you that I would most gladly have entrusted such an office" (p. 17). At the same time, he was interested in her scientific productions as well. He wrote in reply to her mention of a paper she was writing: "And if you have recited 'Anal and sexual' to yourself, the brothers will also want to hear it" (p. 19).

She wrote to him about that paper on October 19, 1919:

It always seems to me: since our body must play for us a double role, since it is just as much 'we ourselves' as also at the same time the most immediate piece of external reality, to which we are in the most various ways forced to adjust ourselves in exactly the same fashion as to all the rest of the external world—for this reason it can only accompany us a little way along the road of our narcissistic behavior. If it is charged with libido beyond this point ('overeroticized') then it reacts with unpleasure tension and rids itself of the excess of this libido, i.e., behaves as something no longer quite identical with us, and enters into a bad relationship with us [pp. 25–26].

He wrote in response to her detailed critique of his paper "On Narcissism": "I do not interpret your remarks on narcissism as objections, but rather as a stimulus to attempt a further conceptual and factual clarification of the subject. I am in agreement with what you say without being able to solve the problems you have raised" (p. 26). His need for her opinion was especially intense when he introduced new concepts: "The essay on the unconscious will contain a new definition of the term which is really tantamount to a restatement. I shall ask your opinion on this" (p. 28). He not only wanted her opinion, he also craved confirmation:

You know how to cheer and encourage. I would not have believed, least of all in my present isolation, that psychoanalysis could mean so much to someone else or that anyone would be able to read so much in my words. And at the same time you have a subtle way of indicating where gaps become visible and where further argument is needed [p. 35].

He regarded her as his most acute reader: "I have never received a letter containing your reaction to my paper on the Unconscious. Actually there is a point in that paper about which I am very curious to know who will be the first to have seen its significance. I am sure it will again be you" (p. 39).

Most important, he relied on her understanding to figure out how to take the next step in his thinking:

I cannot believe there is any danger of your misunderstanding any of our arguments; if so, it must be our, in this case, my, fault. After all, you are an 'understander' par excellence; and in addition your commentary is an amplification and improvement on the original. . . . Then you come along and add what is missing, build upon it, putting what has been isolated back into its proper context. I cannot always follow you, for my eyes, adapted as they are to the dark, probably can't stand strong light or an extensive range of vision. But I haven't become so much of a mole as to be incapable of enjoying the idea of a brighter light and more spacious horizon, or even to deny their existence" [p. 45].

But he was not only interested in her opinion of his work; he also valued her original contributions:

Your manuscript has arrived and is now in the hands of the editors, who send you their thanks. In my opinion it is the best thing you have given me to date. Both your incredible subtlety of understanding and your impressive gift of making a synthesis out of the material you have sifted in your investigation find admirable expression in this work [p. 36].

Most telling was Freud's fascination with and respect for her 1916 paper "Anal and Sexual." He referred to it twice, more than any other single work by any author. He used it in the long footnote he added to the 1920 revision of Three Essays on Sexuality (1905b, p. 187). This work was one of the most important of all his writings: on a par with the dream book and The Ego and the Id in importance and in the frequency of its use in teaching and in references. Therefore, Freud's basing such a long addendum on Andreas-Salomé's work conveys his belief that not only he, but all analysts, could learn from her.

Was this friendship based on the pattern of submissive woman student and authoritarian man teacher? Some feminists have asserted as much. But here is Andreas-Salomé in 1921, writing a paper on narcissism that she intended as a reply to and correction of Freud's 1914 work on this subject. Andreas-Salomé says: "Let me not be expected to take too seriously Freud's account of feminine libido, a view which emphasizes clitoridal sexuality to the passivity of the vagina" (pp. 9–10). Not only did she not agree that a child was a substitute for a penis, she understood the experience of motherhood quite differently: "This very activity fulfills her almost to the point of bisexuality, but, on the other hand, holds her grounded in primary narcissism: for nowhere else in the world can it be seen but in the image of the mother, who procreates herself, and holds herself at her breast" (pp. 11–12). This self-fulfilling, self-nurturing mother is the very antithesis of Freud's ideal of the selfless mother. Whether Freud got it right or not, the point is that Andreas-Salomé was ready and able to present her own ideas, and not apologetic at all about disagreeing with Freud. Nor did this assertiveness in any way at all disrupt their provocative and mutually stimulating intellectual relationship. And after this paper he continued to send her patients, and to write to her about his work and his life. It was also after this paper, in 1930, that he wrote to her that "I have today instructed my son Ernst to transfer to you 1000 marks out of the money from the Goethe prize which is deposited with him. In this way I can reduce by a little the injustice that was committed when they awarded the prize to me"

(p. 190). Thus he expressed his respect and gratitude in deed as well as in word.

Freud's respect for her work, her thinking, and her creativity lasted until the end of their correspondence in 1936, when both were old and infirm, but still caring for and concerned about one another. Meanwhile, Freud cultivated the friendship and the scholarship of other women. One of these was Hermine Hug-Hellmuth, also an early member of his scientific circle. She had earned a Ph.D. in physics from the University of Vienna in 1909, as one of its first women students (MacLean and Rappen 1991), and had been analyzed by Isidor Sadger between 1907 and 1910. When her analytic interests superseded her involvement in physics, Freud championed her admission to his Wednesday evenings, urged her to make observations of child development, and encouraged her in establishing the field of child analysis. By 1912 she was publishing papers sponsored by Freud. She wrote about children's dreams, letters, and memories, about psychic structures and war neuroses, and, most important, about the technique of child analysis. Through the teens and twenties she also wrote on female sexuality, female perversions, and war neuroses in women. The modernity and clinical acuteness of her thinking on women is amazing (Richards 1992). She was the first to publish a paper about female perversion, clearly showing that sexual perversions in women did not only have to do with compliance to male perverts as later writers thought, but was based rather on fantasies relating to early development and its effect on female desire.

Soon after the first women entered the Wednesday evening circle, another woman presented Freud with what would turn out to be a very serious dilemma. On March 7, 1909, he received a letter from Jung, who was then his protégé. Jung wrote that he had a woman patient who "has kicked up a vile scandal solely because I denied myself the pleasure of giving her a child" (McGuire 1974). Freud replied that this was one of the hazards of the profession and that Jung should not take it too seriously. But the difficulty did not go away. In June Sabina Spielrein contacted Freud and asked for an interview. Freud put her off; in a letter of June 4, 1911, he wrote: "Dr. Jung is my friend and colleague: I think I know him in other respects as well, and have reason to believe he is incapable of frivolous or ignoble behavior" (Carotenuto 1982, p. 114). But Freud then asked for Jung's side of the story. Jung prevaricated. Spielrein acceded to Freud's advice that she settle it herself with Jung, and made Jung promise to tell her parents and Freud that he had taken advantage of her. Freud apologized to her for his previous skepticism. He wrote to her on June 24:

> *I have learned today something from Dr. Jung himself about the sub-*
> *ject of your proposed visit to me, and now see that I had divined*
> *some matters correctly, but I had construed others wrongly and to*
> *your disadvantage. I must ask your forgiveness on this latter count.*
> *However, the fact that I was wrong and the lapse has to be blamed*
> *on the man and not on the woman, as my young friend himself*
> *admits, satisfies my need to hold women in high regard. Please*
> *accept this expression of my entire sympathy for the dignified way*
> *in which you have resolved this conflict* [Carotenuto, pp. 114–115].

Freud not only apologized to her. He also showed his respect for her by becoming her mentor. He allowed her to attend the Wednesday seminars, and she was elected a full member of the Vienna Psycho-analytic Society on October 11, 1911. Her thesis on that occasion began with a consideration of the "Death Instinct," a concept that she origi-nated, and that was later to have a profound influence on both Freud and Jung. She explicated the concept of transformation of instincts, an idea that is still under discussion today, and also elaborated on her 1908 idea that sexuality is destructive to the individual even while it is cre-ative for the species.

Jung acknowledged her contribution only in 1952. Freud had given her credit for it in *Beyond the Pleasure Principle* of 1920, where he made his first theoretical statement on destructiveness—a problem he would return to periodically for the rest of his career. He said then: "A consid-erable portion of these speculations have been anticipated by Sabina Spielrein (1912) in an interesting and instructive paper which, however, is unfortunately not entirely clear to me. She there describes the sadistic components of the sexual instincts as 'destructive'" (p. 55). It did take him the better part of a decade to think through the contribution Spielrein had made, but he continued thinking about it from the time he heard her thesis until the time he wrote about it, and also after that. His willingness to credit her with the contribution makes it clear that he valued her as well as her idea, and that he thought of her as a colleague, not just as a source of intellectual supplies.

By 1912, Freud was referring patients to her. He had remarked to her that: "You could have the child, you know, but what a waste of your tal-ents." She subsequently followed Freud's (only apparently) contradicto-ry advice to marry and have children if that was what she wanted. But she did not give up her career. With Freud's help she managed to have it all. By 1920 she was pursuing a new line of thinking. She gave a paper on "The Origin and Development of Spoken Speech." Freud encouraged her move to Geneva, where she started a new analytic institute.

Her concern with language had a great influence on three of her analysands: Piaget, Vygotsky, and Charles Odier. Piaget and Vygotsky published papers taking sides in the debate on whether language influenced thought or thought preceded language in child development. Their work in turn influenced the fields of child development, education, linguistics, and philosophy. Freud's recognition of Spielrein's genius, and his encouragement of her work, allowed psychoanalytic thought to influence Western culture in momentous ways.

Freud realized early how important the translation and publication of his work would be for the future of psychoanalysis. That this was not just the sort of secretarial work that women get stuck doing is indicated by the fact that Ernest Jones wanted the job.

However, Freud insisted on Joan Riviere for both *The International Journal of Psycho-Analysis* and for the English edition of his *Collected Papers*. He thus entrusted her with the presentation of his own work to the English-speaking world, and that of all the other German-language contributors to psychoanalysis as well—a position of great trust indeed. Freud also praised a 1927 paper of Riviere's in which she disagreed with his daughter Anna on matters of psychoanalytic theory and technique. About that paper he said: "Incidentally, Mrs. R.'s logic and perspicacity are revealed even in her error; she has quite rightly discovered the theory which alone fits Mrs. Klein's technique. Is it not time to end this not altogether agreeable episode? I should be sorry if Mrs. R. continued to be discouraged and estranged" (Appignanesi and Forrester 1992, p. 361).

Then there was Freud's intensely proud and intensely touching relationship with his youngest daughter, Anna. Anna was allowed to attend the Wednesday evening seminars from the time she was fourteen. Freud trained her from the earliest possible age to think psychologically, to take part in learned discussions, and to consider herself part of his scientific circle. Did he allow her to develop her talents on her own? Well, he did not send her to a university. On the other hand, there is no evidence that she wanted a university education. Since education at that level was rare in those days even for men, this is a circumstance that looked very different then than it does from today's perspective.

Anna did develop her talents in a teacher-training course, and having finished this she was allowed to translate Hug-Hellmuth's work on play therapy with children into English. This enabled Anna to start on an analytic career of her own that would parallel Freud's, without being entirely in his shadow. Freud encouraged Anna in her work, but discouraged her in her love life. He objected to her male suitors, but he finally approved of her love for Dorothy Burlingham, a woman who had come to Vienna with her two children, and without her husband, in order to be analyzed by Freud. Dorothy and Anna became lifelong partners and best friends. They shared a home, shared the upbringing of Burlingham's children, and had, in short, what biographers have called a "Boston marriage."

It seems to me important to point out, in considering Freud's relationship with Anna, that although one's politics may sometimes succumb to the dynamics of one's closest relationships, that does not mean that the politics do not exist. Freud was controlling and possessive of Anna, but in a way that was consistent with his idea that women could find fulfillment and pleasure in the same sorts of careers that men enjoy. He paradoxically pushed her into a brilliant career, and into a position of importance in the world that none of his sons or other daughters achieved. His satisfaction with this outcome was expressed in a letter to Andreas-Salomé dated June 1, 1935:

> *My one source of satisfaction is Anna. It is remarkable how much influence and authority she has gained among the general run of analysts—many of whom, alas, have derived little from analysis as far as their personal character is concerned. It is surprising, too, how sharp, clear and unflinching she is in her mastery of the subject. Moreover, she is truly independent of me; at the most I serve her as a catalyst* [Pfeiffer 1966, p. 204].

Freud's worries about losing Anna to a man were resolved when she settled in with Dorothy Burlingham, but her reputation as an analyst was still in question. Her 1927 book, *Introduction to the Technique of Child Analysis,* was important in establishing her reputation as an independent thinker. Freud wanted to make clear that he respected her views, but that she had formed them on her own. According to Appignanesi and Forrester (1992) he wrote to Andreas-Salomé: "You will not believe how little I contributed to her book, nothing but curtailing her polemic against Melanie Klein. Apart from that, it is a completely independent work" (p. 288). That exception, the curtailing of the polemic against Melanie Klein, is a tremendous statement. All through his life Freud was partial to his daughter. But his partiality had bounds. He would not support her against another woman when he believed that the other woman was right. This even-handedness can be seen also in the above-mentioned comment about Riviere.

Freud cited two women in his 1931 paper "On Female Sexuality." From Jeanne Lampl-de Groot he had received the idea that the girl's development is parallel to that of the boy in the preoedipal phase. From Helene Deutsch he took the idea that female masochism results when the girl gives up her intense phallic attachment to her mother in order to turn to her father passively. Both of these ideas are among those seen by contemporary feminists as derogatory. Yet Freud had accepted them from women, and his use of the women's ideas is evidence of his respect for them as psychoanalysts.

The idea that women are primarily interested in reproduction, while men are most interested in sexual pleasure, is another idea that contemporary feminists see as demeaning women. This idea, basic to difference feminism, is one that Freud took from Karen Horney (1924). While Freud argued that women wanted what men had, Horney countered that women wanted the thing that only women could have: a baby. As soon as Freud accepted this idea as elaborated by Deutsch (1925), however, it became for some feminists (Dimen 1998) proof that he was patriarchal.

Freud learned about preoedipal development from Ruth Mack Brunswick, another early female analyst. His ideas about the importance of the little girl's early love for her mother were influenced by Mack Brunswick's observations, which she eventually published in an influential paper of 1940.

To my own mind, the most interesting evidence for Freud's extraordinary ability to learn from women comes from his analysis of Hilda Doolittle, the American poet known as H. D. (Richards 1992). Doolittle had a writing block. She was forty-seven years old when she went to Freud in 1933. Freud was an old man, held in awe by the Viennese. Doolittle wrote home on her first day in Vienna: "The manager is terribly impressed, we of Vienna did not know that Doctor Freud took any but the most learned professors, does he now take—ah, er, patients?" Yet Freud was impressed with Doolittle. She reports that he ushered her into his consulting room with the words: "Enter, fair madame." She had the highest hopes of her treatment with him: "And note all papa's remarks which may be ammunition against the world, for all time" (H. D. 1933; emphasis H. D.'s). (Papa was Doolittle's pet name for Freud.)

Freud trusted H. D.'s judgment on something that was very important to him. On May 3, 1933, she wrote to her long-time companion Bryher:

> *Papa has a completely new theory but he says he does not dare write it, because he does not want to make enemies of women. Apparently we have all stirred him up frightfully. His idea is that all women are deeply rooted in penis envy, not only the bi-sexual or homosexual woman. The advanced or intellectual woman is more frank about it. That is all.[3] But that whole cult and development of normal womanhood is based on the same fact; the envy of woman for the penis. Now this strikes me as being a clue to everything. The reason women are FAITHFUL when men are not, the reason a Dorothy R. or a Cole will stick like grim death to some freak like Alan or Gerald, the reason Mama or my mother went insane at the oddest things, the reason for this, the reason for that. I was awake all last night and up this morning just after 7.... as this seemed to convince me more than anything. What got me was his saying the homosexual woman is simply frank and truthful, but that the whole of domestic womanhood, is exactly the same, but has built up its cult on deception. Well, he did not say deception. He just flung out the idea. I screamed at him. 'But the supreme compliment to women would be to trust women with this great secret.' I said Br., the princess and myself would appreciate it and keep it going. Or something like that. ... This is a thing, for instance that Chaddie fought against, and tried to make out that the monthly is interesting and that men envy women. Well men do. . . . Now you see all this in the ucn may also be assisted by our liking the little-dog, as I think we certainly do"* [H. D. 1933].

Here Doolittle is convinced that Freud's great contribution to the psychology of women is the idea of penis envy. She links the idea to women's pleasure in the clitoris, which she calls "little-dog." Because she was enthusiastic about the idea, she may have inadvertently misled Freud into thinking that other women would be, as well. It could be an answer, she thought, to the question of why so many women seemed to be willing to collude in their own oppression. Perhaps it was to be attributed to the little girl's belief in the power of the penis. If the girl saw her mother and her sisters treated as lesser beings than men, if she saw them tolerating oppression, Freud thought, it must be her idea that this was

---

[3]Underlined italics indicate H.D.'s use of red ink in the letter.

because they were not whole as men were whole, but deficient, defective, and therefore deserving of this societal oppression. As it turned out, other women have found that idea offensive and wrong. By Doolittle's description, her previous analyst Elizabeth Chadwick appears to have been nearer to the current feminist position with her idea that men are envious of women. In this Chadwick was apparently influenced by Melanie Klein's (1921) assertion that the first envy is envy of the breast. Chodorow's (1978) belief that the mother is the infant's first object of awe broadens this concept and has had great influence among feminists. Later Lacanian feminists have been interested in the penis as metaphor, as "phallus"—as the symbol of power and respect. They have not taken physical sensation and the value of pleasure as seriously as did Freud in his idea of penis envy as the fantasy that the penis had the power of the clitoris only multiplied by its greater relative size.

Doolittle had to wrestle with Freud's notion of penis as metaphor. On May 15 she wrote to Bryher: "But the cure will be, I fear me, writing. . . . It is important as book means penis evidently and as a 'writer' only am I equal in ucn in the right way with men." Thus, Doolittle's understanding of penis envy was much more physical, concrete, and unsymbolic than Freud's. Yet this understanding allowed her to write and publish not only in quantity, but with such quality that in 1960 she was the first woman ever to receive the medal of the American Academy of Arts and Sciences. Freud's valedictory message to her in 1933 had been: "I am deeply satisfied to hear that you are writing, creating, that is why we delved into the depths of your unconscious mind I remember" (H. D. 1933).

The Controversy

Freud wanted to foster H. D.'s creativity as he had that of all of the women discussed above, and many others. Feminists assert that Freud's views on women in his scientific writings denigrate women and, after all, that it is not the private person who matters in this instance. It is the public figure, the scientist and scholar, who affected the views of the psychoanalytic world, and all the other sciences and arts that have been influenced by his work and that of his followers. Feminists in our time have especially resented the idea that penis envy was the bedrock of female psychology (Horney 1924; Fliegel 1973, 1982). Worse yet was Freud's (1925) statement that: "Their [women's] superego is never so inexorable, so impersonal, so independent of its emotional origins as we require it to be in men" (p. 257). Among the many who have objected to this particular statement are Bernstein (1983) and Tyson and Tyson (1990).

As Hoffman (1999) has argued, Freud missed the importance and ubiquity of aggression in women, particularly towards their infants. He also missed (Richards 1996) the importance of female genital sensation in forming the little girl's appreciation of her own genital, the genital anxieties that accompany the possession of a sensitive and thus potentially vulnerable area of the body, and primary femininity and its importance in shaping the little girl's sense of self. I think that his misunderstandings of women in these crucial ways led women to feel misunderstood and undervalued. As long as he failed to understand the intensity and particularity of genital sensation in the development of the female child, women felt that he failed to understand them.

In reply to the critiques of Freud's views on female sexuality, female aggression, and the female superego, Freudian feminists began to update the psychoanalytic understanding of women. Chasseguet-Smirgel's (1970) *Female Sexuality* showed how women could study together to learn about their own minds. Mitchell (1974) argued that psychoanalysis was not about prescriptions for social arrangements, but was really about the unconscious and about sexuality. She stated that the attacks on Freud had to do with his abandonment of the trauma theory and exposure of childhood sexuality, and with his theories of female narcissism, female masochism, and passivity as a female trait. Mitchell showed that these theoretical ideas were not directed at subjugating women, but at freeing neurotic people from the domination of crippling unconscious sexual fantasies.

Strouse (1974) brought together a group of essays showing how analysis can empower women as individuals. Miller (1976) not only stressed the importance of the conjunction of feminism and psychoanalysis, but showed how they could work together. Blum (1978) edited a *JAPA* supplement that illustrated these updates of female psychology: the effort was to understand women's thinking, rather than to prescribe what an ideal woman should think. Since Blum is very closely identified with Freud and his work, his interest signified a willingness on the part of the Freudian keepers of the flame to rework the understanding of women in the Freudian tradition.

Especially influential has been Nancy Chodorow (1978, 1989), who reconciles two feminist insistences—on the special knowledge of female psychology that is available to women, and on the special knowledge of feelings that is available to mothers—and concludes that women are especially able to implement the analytic focus on feelings. Susie Orbach (1999) makes the complementary point: that by encouraging women to speak their feelings, psychoanalysis empowers them. Prozan (1992) has shown that some of the feminist agenda has been accomplished by women who have themselves had psychoanalysis or psychoanalytic psychotherapy. Because Freud listened to women, he empowered them. Because he took women's ideas seriously, they acquired a new platform from which to present them. Many of these authors have acknowledged that they were empowered by the Freudian movement. The changes in Freudian theory since the 1970s led to another landmark in the understanding of women: the second *JAPA* supplement on female psychology, which appeared in 1996. Here papers on feminism, on the psychoanalytic treatment of women using the new understanding of the female genital and primary femininity, and on the implications of female gender for the work of the female analyst, were all thoughtfully considered. Thus Freud's legacy has not only provided employment for women on a professional level, but has also provided opportunities for women's ideas and innovations to be taken seriously.

Other contemporary feminist psychoanalysts (Young-Bruehl 1990; Dimen 1998) are coming around to this view as they read Freud in the *Standard Edition* and in the various compilations of his letters that have become available. Young-Bruehl argues that feminists have mistaken Freud to mean that femininity is failed masculinity, when he actually argued that femininity is really a limitation of an original bisexuality, just as masculinity is. Neither patriarchal theorist nor misogynist, Freud is coming to be seen for what he attempted to be: an equal-opportunity feminist.

REFERENCES

ANDREAS-SALOMÉ, L. (1910). *Die Erotik.* Frankfurt am Main: Literarische Anstalt Rutter und Loening.
——— (1921). The Dual Orientation of Narcissism, Transl. S. Leavy. *Psychoanalytic Quarterly* 31:1–30, 1962.
APPIGNANESI, L., & FORRESTER, J. (1992). *Freud's Women.* New York: Basic Books.
BERNHEIMER, C., & KAHANE, C., Eds . (1985). *In Dora's Case.* New York: Columbia University Press.
BERNSTEIN, D. (1983). *The Female Superego: a Different Perspective.* International Journal of Psycho-analysis 64:187–202.

BERNSTEIN, I. (1980). *Integrative Summary: On the Reviewings of the Dora Case. In Freud and His Patients,* ed. M. Kanzer & J. Glenn. New York: Aronson, pp. 83–91.

BERNSTEIN, P. (1999). Personal Communication.

BLUM, H., Ed. (1977). *Female Psychology.* New York: International Universities Press.

BREUER, J., & FREUD, S. (1893–1895). Studies on Hysteria. *Standard Edition* 2.

BRUNSWICK, R.M. (1940). The Pre-oedipal Phase of the Libido Development. *Psychoanalytic Quarterly* 9:293–319.

BUHLE, M. (1998). *Feminism and Its Discontents.* Cambridge: Harvard University Press.

CAROTENUTO, A. (1982). A Secret Symmetry. New York: Pantheon.

CHASSEGUET-SMIRGEL, J., ed. (1970). *Female Sexuality.* Ann Arbor: University of Michigan Press.

CHESLER, P. (1972). *Women and Madness.* New York: Doubleday.

CHODOROW, N. (1978). *The Reproduction of Mothering.* Berkeley: University of California Press.

——— (1989). *Feminism and Psychoanalytic Theory.* New Haven: Yale University Press.

DE BEAUVOIR, S. (1952). *The Second Sex.* New York: Vintage Books.

DEUTSCH, H. (1925). The Psychology of Women in Relation to the Functions of Reproduction. *International Journal of Psycho-Analysis* 6:405–418.

DIMEN, M. (1998). Strange Hearts: on the Paradoxical Liaison Between Psychoanalysis and Feminism. In *Freud: Conflict and Culture,* ed. S. Roth. New York: Knopf, pp. 207–221.

DOOLITTLE, H. (1933). H.D. Archive, Beinecke Library, Yale University.

——— (1975). *Tribute to Freud.* New York: Mcgraw-Hill, 1956.

FIRESTONE, S. (1970). *The Dialectic of Sex.* New York: Morrow.

FLIEGEL, Z. (1973). *Feminine Psychosexual Development in Freudian Theory. Psychoanalytic Quarterly* 42:385–409.

——— (1982). Half a Century Later: Current Status of Freud's Controversial Views on Women. *Psychoanalytic Review* 69:7–28.

FREUD, A. (1927). *Introduction to the Technique of Child Analysis.* New York: International Universities Press.

FREUD, S. (1905a). Fragment of an Analysis of a Case of Hysteria. *Standard Edition* 7:7–122.

——— (1905b). Three Essays on the Theory of Sexuality. *Standard Edition* 7:125–247.

——— (1914). On the History of the Psychoanalytic Movement. *Standard Edition* 14:7–65.

——— (1915). A Case of Paranoia Running Counter to the Psycho-Analytic Theory of the Disease. *Standard Edition* 14:261–272.

——— (1920a). Beyond the Pleasure Principle. *Standard Edition* 18:3–71.

———— (1920b). The Psychogenesis of a Case of Homosexuality in a Woman. *Standard Edition* 18:145–172.

———— (1925). Some Psychical Consequences of the Anatomical Distinction Between the Sexes. *Standard Edition* 19:248–258.

———— (1931). On Female Sexuality. *Standard Edition* 21:223–246.

FRIEDAN, B. (1963). *The Feminine Mystique.* New York: Norton.

GILLIGAN, C. (1982). *In a Different Voice.* Cambridge: Harvard University Press.

GLENN, J. (1980). Freud's Adolescent Patients. In *Freud and His Patients,* ed. M. Kanzer & J. Glenn. New York: Aronson, pp. 23–47.

GLÜCKEL (1977). *The Memoirs of Glückel of Hameln,* Transl. M. Lowenthal. New York: Shocken.

HOFFMAN, L. (1999). Passions in Girls and Women: Toward a Bridge Between Critical Relational Theory of Gender and Modern Conflict Theory. *Journal of the American Psychoanalytic Association* 47:1213–1237.

HORNEY, K. (1924). On the Genesis of the Castration Complex in Women. *International Journal of Psycho-Analysis* 5:50–65.

JONES, E. (1955). The Life and Work of Sigmund Freud, Vol. 2. New York: Basic Books.

KANZER, M. (1980). Dora's Imagery. In *Freud and His Patients,* ed. M. Kanzer & J. Glenn. New York: Aronson, pp. 72–82.

KEY, E. (1912). *The Woman Movement.* New York: Putnam.

KLEIN, M. (1921). The Development of a Child. In *Love, Guilt and Reparation and Other Works.* [New York]: Delacorte Press, 1975, pp. 1–53.

LANGS, R. (1980). Misalliance Dimension in The Dora Case. In *Freud and His Patients,* ed. M. Kanzer & J. Glenn. New York: Aronson, pp. 58–71.

LEAR, J. (1998). Open Minded. Cambridge: Harvard University Press.

MACLEAN, G., & RAPPEN, U. (1991). *Hermine Hug-Hellmuth.* New York: Routledge.

MARCUS, S. (1990). Freud and Dora. In *In Dora's Case,* ed. C. Bernheimer & C. Kahane. New York: Columbia University Press, pp. 56–91.

MCGUIRE, W., ed. (1974). *The Freud-Jung Letters: The Correspondence Between Sigmund Freud and C.G. Jung.* Princeton: Princeton University Press.

MILLER, J.B. (1973). *Psychoanalysis and Women.* Baltimore: Penguin Books.

———— (1976). *Toward a New Psychology of Women.* Boston: Beacon, 1977.

MILLET, K. (1970). Sexual Politics. Garden City, NY: Doubleday.

MITCHELL, J. (1974). *Psychoanalysis and Feminism: Freud, Reich, Laing and Women.* New York: Pantheon Books.

MOI, T. (1981). Representation of Patriarchy. Feminist Review 9:60–73.

NUNBERG, H., & FEDERN, E. (1967). *Minutes of the Vienna Psychoanalytic Society.* New York: International Universities Press.

ORBACH, S., & EICHENBAUM, L., (1999). Relational Psychoanalysis and

Feminism: a Crossing of Historical Paths. In *At the Threshold of the Millennium,* ed. M. Lemlij & M. fort Brescia. Lima: Sidea pp. 175–181.

PFEIFFER, E., ed. (1966). *Sigmund Freud and Lou Andreas-Salomé: Letters.* New York: Harcourt Brace Jovanovich.

PROZAN, C. (1992). Feminist Psychoanalytic Psychotherapy. New York: Aronson.

RAMAS, M. (1980). Freud's Dora, Dora's Hysteria. *Feminist Studies* 6:472–510.

REISNER, S. (1999). Freud and Psychoanalysis: into the Twenty-first Century. *Journal of the American Psychoanalytic Association* 47:1037–1060.

RICHARDS, A.K. (1990). Female Fetishes and Female Perversions: "A Case of Female Foot or More Properly Boot Fetishism" by Hermine Hug-Hellmuth Reconsidered. Psychoanalytic Review 77:11–23.

——— (1992). Hilda Doolittle and Creativity: Freud's Gift. *Psychoanalytic Study of the Child* 47:391– 406.

——— (1996). Primary Femininity and Female Genital Anxiety. *Journal of the American Psychoanalytic Association* 44(suppl.):261–283.

SCHARFMAN, M. (1960). Further Reflections on Dora. In *Freud and His Patients,* ed. M. Kanzer & J. Glenn. New York: Aronson, pp. 48–57.

SHAINESS, N. (1970). A Psychiatrist's View. In *Sisterhood Is Powerful,* ed. R. Morgan. New York: Vintage Books, pp. 257–274.

STROUSE, J. (1974). *Women and Analysis.* New York: Dell, 1975.

TYSON, P., & TYSON, R. (1990). Gender Differences in Superego Development. In P. Tyson & R. Tyson, *Psychoanalytic Theories of Development: An Integration.* New Haven: Yale University Press, pp. 228–245.

WEININGER, O. (1908). *Sex and Character.* New York: Ams Press, 1975.

WEISSTEIN, N. (1971). Psychology Constructs the Female. In *Woman in Sexist Society,* ed. V. Gornick and B. Moran. New York: Basic Books, pp. 133–146.

WOLLSTONECRAFT, M. (1792). *A Vindication of the Rights of Woman.* New York: Norton, 1967.

YOUNG-BRUEHL, E. (1990). *Freud on Women.* New York: Norton.

****
****

Original publication of preceding chapter:

RICHARDS, A.K. (1999). Freud and Feminism: A Critical Appraisal. *Journal of the American Psychoanalytic Association* 47:1213–1238.

Primary Femininity And
Female Genital Anxiety

Primary femininity implies that female development proceeds along lines that generate anxiety about damage and loss similar to the fears of castration that trouble males. The female fears are classified as fear of painful penetration, fear of loss of pleasure, and fear of loss of procreative function. The first two fears are illustrated with clinical material showing the ways in which they manifest themselves in adult women.

After Reading *Mickey and the Night Kitchen*
for the Third Time Before Bed

My daughter spreads her legs
to find her vagina:
hairless, this mistaken
bit of nomenclature
is what a stranger cannot touch
without her yelling. She demands
to see mine and momentarily
we're a lopsided star
among the spilled toys,
my prodigious scallops
exposed to her neat cameo.

—RITA DOVE (1989)

The poet describes an intimate moment between mother and little daughter, which might have been unmentionable a decade earlier. The little girl wants to see her mother's genital and the mother shows it to her. They compare. The education in sexual openness, in the

I thank Dr. Leon Hoffman, the members of the RAPS Study Group on Female Psychology of the Society for Medical Psychoanalysis, Dr. Arnold D. Richards, Dr. Jules Glenn, and all the other readers of this paper who asked incisive questions and did not let me get away with easy answers.

permission to be curious and in the child's right to be in control of her own sexuality, is clearly delineated in a few lines. Are we up to this?

We psychoanalysts have learned much about female psychology since Blum's (1976) major effort to update our views. Of particular interest to me is the new understanding of female sexuality as it relates to body image, self-esteem, and sense of productive possibility. Part of the new understanding is a sense that women have a genital which they value and which they can worry about losing. This idea is not a new one, but one which has been controversial. I want to support with clinical data the idea that female anxiety about genitals could be anxiety about loss of specifically female anatomical features, functions and sensations.

The other side of this debate in the early analytic literature (Freud 1905, 1908; Deutsch 1930; Rado 1933; Jacobson 1936) developed the idea of penis envy as the bedrock motivator of female behavior. Associated with that idea was the belief that females suffered from castration anxiety in the form of fear of loss of a fantasied penis (Freud 1924) or in the form of an idea that they have already been castrated (Freud 1933, Brenner 1982).

My special interest is to examine the received wisdom of the concept of castration anxiety as it is applied to normal female development and as it is used to conceptualize female experience when development goes awry and leads people to our offices for help with dealing with their symptoms. The idea that forms the basis of this paper is that girls, like boys, value pleasure and fear unpleasure. From this it follows that girls would value the pleasurable sensations arising from genital stimulation. It also follows that girls would not need to experience anything more complicated than genital pleasure to value that pleasure. Nor would they need to experience anything other than genital pain to fear that pain. The fear of unpleasure would have to be understood as fear of pain and fear of loss of positively pleasurable sensation. Once this stance is adopted, ideas of pain and of loss of pleasure would be evident in the analytic work with almost any female patient. If loss of pleasure is understood to include aphanisis and frigidity, it becomes a concept often reported in the analytic literature, and especially as a presenting complaint in neurotic women patients. Since fear of genital pain is almost always associated with fear of painful penetration in adult women, I have postulated the idea of painful penetration. Quinodoz (1989) puts the more inclusive idea this way:

This anxiety about losing the female function and organs is present in girls just as its counterpart is in boys (Klein 1932), but has never been given a specific term. Freud reserves the term castration loss for loss of the penis and not even the testicles (p. 58).

Stoller (1968) delineates the idea of primary femininity that entails a belief that one is a female and values femininity and one's female genital. This idea of primary femininity rests on clinical evidence that women and girls have fears of genital damage. Since the term "castration anxiety" means fear of loss of the penis, these female fears are best labeled "genital anxiety" (Goldberger, unpublished; Lax 1994).

This paper is both a critique and an elaboration of D. Bernstein's (1990) and other authors' idea that females have fears of genital damage. It presents new clinical material in support of this idea. Bernstein proposes that female genital anxieties can best be conceptualized as fears about access, penetration, and diffusivity. While I agree that fear of penetration is ubiquitous in female patients, I also believe that it overlaps with what Bernstein calls access. Thus, I have condensed access into the category of penetration. I differ from Bernstein in that I have not found diffusivity to be a felicitous concept in regard to female genital anxieties. Interpretations to my patients about such fears have led to surprise and interest, but not to psychic change. Unlike Bernstein, I have inferred loss of function as a primary fear in many women. This loss sometimes appears to me to be loss of the pleasure-giving function of the genital, and sometimes as fear of loss of the reproductive function. For these reasons, I shall modify her categories. The purpose of the clinical material in this paper is to illustrate these concepts. My hope is that this formulation will enable the reader to listen to patients differently from the way they listened before.

Female genital anxiety consists of many manifest fears: first, fear of painful penetration (Horney 1926; D. Bernstein 1990); second, fear of loss of pleasurable sensation (Jones 1927); third, fear of loss of reproductive function of the genital apparatus (Mayer 1985; Bergmann 1985). I shall not address the third category here. Little girls can have fears of any or all these calamities. In my clinical experience adult women clearly have one or more such fears. They also fear loss of love, loss of the object, and experiencing guilt and shame. In the material that follows, separation issues (Olesker 1990) and other fears can be seen, and clinicians might choose to focus on one of these other issues. The question I address is whether female genital fears are worth interpreting or whether seeing the issues as related to penis envy, as had been done in the past, is sufficient.

PAINFUL PENETRATION

How are fears of painful penetration manifested? Some women fear being alone in their homes and hearing noises in the night; some fear dark streets and parking lots. They have realistic concerns about such dangers. Besides their realistic concerns, some women have fantasies about rapists under the bed or in lonely or deserted spots. These women may also wish for forceful or involuntary penetration, but their fears are more than mere repudiations of desire.

An example of such a fantasy comes from a woman who had put up with an abusive husband for several years rather than face her fears of being alone. She had always been compliant in the analysis, reporting dreams, telling of her current life, and recalling the events and feelings of her childhood. This behavior paralleled her behavior in her current life and what she reported of herself in her past. She often remained silent when she had been hurt, slighted, or snubbed, or when she believed she had been mistreated by her analyst. When confronted with her compliant and self-effacing manner and given interpretations about the covert aggression expressed by her creating a situation in which the other person was the bad guy and she was the good girl, she was able to explore the fantasy of the object's potentially explosive aggression and to modify her behavior. She was gradually able to talk more about her feelings that the analyst was hurting her, then about interactions in which her husband physically abused her. Gradually, she recognized that she enjoyed seeing herself as the analyst's passive victim rather than the person who had initiated the exploration of her pain and suffering. She began to recognize that she had needed her husband's abuse for displacement of her own aggressive wishes. Accepting how violent her interior life actually was, allowed her to ask her abusive husband to leave. Shortly after his departure, he forcefully reentered their home, ostensibly to collect his possessions. He shattered a mirror in the hallway in his rage over the end of the marriage. Her first dream after this violent intrusion was:

Someone is flying a plane. It's a war mission. It's a secret mission. People are on the ground waiting for him. The gas leaked; the pressure

was down. I felt like I could have stopped it. I closed my eyes. The back
of his head began to explode. Blood started coming out and went all over
his face. Then it switched to the ground. People were looking for him.
They found things on the ground. A flare. A parachute case. Spreadout.
It was a field, but overgrown. Then they found him. He was alive. I
didn't really want to see him. I was afraid. I didn't know if he was alive
at first. I didn't know if I wanted to see it. There was blood on his face.
It was O.K. I wasn't in the dream. They went into the water. I was swim-
ming around. This joined with the part of the dream I was in. I can't
remember any of it. I'm trying to remember.

The patient's affect was muted. She said the dream had to do with
her fear that her husband would crash and burn without her. She said
she felt "sympathetic, painful, and curious." Her associations were to
thoughts of a penis with blood coming out of it, circumcisions, and other
dreams she had recently about drowning, floating, and swimming. What
led me to ask whether she was the pilot was a series of remarks: her
denial that she was in the dream, her remark that she felt she could have
stopped it, her assertions that she closed her eyes and did not want to see,
and her confusion about what she remembered. She hated that idea, but
it seemed to me that she confirmed it when she responded thoughtfully
that flying was like swimming underwater.

The dream took place in a war. We both knew that her father had
been in a war. The idea of harming men's penises and of not knowing
where the blood came from led to thoughts of seeing her father naked. He
liked to swim naked and would not wear a bathing suit even when he was
teaching her to swim when she was a little girl. This led to thoughts of
having intercourse while menstruating, thus allowing herself to bloody
her lover's penis in a way that did not hurt him. The idea that her father
would let her fall in the water was linked with the pilot's crash in the
dream. The most hidden idea, the unconscious fantasy, was that she had
been the one to bleed. Eventually she came to state that her genital was
the damaged and painful one.

The fear underlying her apparently aggressive and destructive attitude toward men, and the male genital in particular, was only recovered
when we got to the understanding that she was both the author and the
protagonist of her dream. Because she was the author, the war was her
war. The aggression was her aggression. Her fear of her own aggression
was displaced onto the wartime enemies in the dream. Her fear that her

husband would "crash and burn" if she left him was also a displacement of what would happen to her if she left him. She would be damaged. She had refused to talk to her father about paying my fee, which she would have to ask him to do if she were to continue her treatment when she no longer had a husband to share her expenses. She was sure that her father would "explode at her" if she asked him to help her. We reconstructed a childhood fantasy that her father damaged her in an explosive version of intercourse. The fear that she would be damaged did not simply serve as a defense against the wish to be penetrated by her father. That fear was defended against by her displacement onto the husband. She was afraid to be alone with her aggression toward the husband and men in general. Even though her analyst was actually a woman, the ideas she had about me were similar to those she had about men. I was the father in the transference, always to be fended off, guarded against, and placated. I often felt hesitant about making interpretations, as if I would hurt her by saying what I was thinking. The fear that she would be damaged had been elicited by the conviction that her father's penis had damaged her genital. Thus, her fantasy followed the pattern outlined by Devereux (1957), but with the important difference that she did not experience herself as having a fantasy penis. Instead, she fantasied that she had a female genital that had been damaged by penetration and could be damaged again in the same way. The difference may be attributable to the fact that she, unlike Devereux's patient, had not actually been raped.

Many other female patients imagine imminent danger whenever they are alone at night. Their manifest fantasies of being killed, robbed, mugged, and raped derive from infantile fears of genital damage like those of this patient. Even women who enjoy intercourse with their chosen partners imagine pain and suffering as consequences of their masturbation fantasies when they are alone. This pain is partly punishment for the wish to have sexual gratification from the stranger who represents the father. The infantile origin of the wish accounts for another part of the fear. The father's penis seems to the little girl too large to fit into her genital without damaging it. Therefore she believes that penetration must be painful.

What the concept of fear of painful penetration added to my understanding of this specific female patient was the specifically sexual component of her fear of recognizing her own aggression. Examples of her fantasy that she had no aggressive wishes were frequently found in the transference. She always paid for her sessions promptly, even when she had to deprive herself to do so. She used silence to efface her aggressive wishes toward me. Because she imagined that I would feel guilty about hurting her if she cried, she stopped herself from crying in sessions. The analysis of the sexual component of her fear of aggression—her fear that she would damage the penis and its associated fantasy of damage to her own genital—provided another link to her fear of leaving her husband.

Aggression, penis envy, castration wishes, fears of separation and loss as well as other themes could have been interpreted here. But thinking of the dream in terms of fear of painful penetration allowed the patient to see the part of her struggle that had to do with her own body and her own mind. This issue went beyond the present interaction with her husband and her present struggle with me. It went back to an earlier time when her father exposed himself to her in a swimming pool by teaching her to swim while holding her face down in the water, supporting her on his forearms while he wore no bathing suit. I believe that the unique value of the concept was that it allowed her to think about what she had fantasied about that experience, how she had organized it in her memory, and how she had used it in shaping her view of the world as a dangerous place and her own body as too small and too vulnerable to contain or express her aggression. I believe that our exploration of this fear contributed to her later being able to choose a lover who was gentle.

LOSS OF PLEASURE

How do fears of loss of pleasure manifest themselves? Women fear they will not find a sexual partner. Some believe they must marry early to avoid such a fate. Others make themselves available to men they do not desire to ensure that they will not be without a partner. Other women fear they will become frigid because of rape, masturbation, or failure to find the man they can love. The fantasy that there is only one "Mr. Right" clearly reflects their belief that pleasure can only be had with the man who was unique: the father. Their idea that this man only exists in the future reflects their understanding that the father they are looking for only exists in the past. In the childhood fantasy the father was the giver of sexual pleasure. As adults they still believe that they will never have sexual pleasure without him.

A fantasy of losing genital pleasure was inferred late in the analysis of a woman who had an unusually ascetic way of life. By the end of the analysis we came to the conclusion that her asceticism was a defensive maneuver, a way to allow herself the sexual pleasure she feared losing as a deserved punishment for having experienced sexual pleasure with a grandmother. Several years of analytic work had allowed her to take her first vacation since finishing college and beginning work. In the week following her vacation, she began a session by saying she had a curious dream about something that happened "in real life":

L. It was last night or this morning. There were lots of people there. It was in the subway. All my friends were going to dance somewhere. Dana and Ellen were trying to decide what to do with their purses. I was going to put mine in a locker in the subway. I decided not to wear long pants because I would get really hot. Everybody else was wearing long pants. They were progressing. Men showed up. Robert was there. They were collecting money for something. They were, I don't know what . . . I am annoyed at myself for being so complicated. For making it complicated. Yet it happened in real life, too. It always happens. I always take long to get ready to go. I am amazed when my roommate gets ready so fast when we decide to go out.

It was in a restaurant in the dream. I saw Harry, but in reality Harry is in Israel ... with Pam. I was staying in her apartment in the dream. Last night I actually went back home to Connecticut. Sally is back but she wasn't there, she must have stayed at Bill's last night. He got an apartment in the Village so that will change Sally's plans. I drove my clothes to Sam's street. There was nowhere to park, so I went back to the garage, then walked back.

A. It sounds like you complicate your life with many people and many plans and activities.

L. In Phoenix there was no way to get to the Grand Canyon. The bus didn't work out, so I had to figure out a way to get to Phoenix before the plane left. I had to take a 10:00 a.m. bus to Flagstaff. I went to the Bright Angel Lodge. They are all owned by the same person. Joe had said I could use his phone. I had run into Jim. I was trying to make the phone calls. The phone ate my change. I said to Jim I was going to use Joe's phone. So in two seconds Jim had made a reservation on the plane. I feel I do things the worst way possible when I try to do them my own way. I complicate things. I see things as being really big problems when they really are not.

I didn't really talk with Sally about dividing our furniture. I can live with a few extra pieces of furniture until she has time to deal with it. She said all I have to do is call Goodwill and they'll come and take it. I see problematic solutions. It made me think of my father and the phone calls he doesn't make. The only time he called me in the past couple of years was to get my brother's phone number. But he sends me a card and money twice a year—on my birthday and Christmas.

A. I had not called so much either. I had said very little.

L. I agree.

A. I wonder why you had to do so much. You were putting all your change into the phone in our session also and not allowing me to respond to you. I admired your skill in showing me what you are telling me about.

L. I always felt other people could go straight to the point. Only I have to be complicated.

A. You had that problem in the dream when you were getting ready to go to a dance. You stood in the way of your own chance to have pleasure.

L. I understood that as a reprimand. You are saying that I didn't deserve to have fun because I always screwed things up.

This was typical of her way of understanding everything as proof that she should not allow herself pleasure. She believed that everyone around her wanted to deprive her of pleasure also. What she did not understand before her analysis was that her renunciation of other pleasures was in the service of protecting herself from the loss of sexual pleasure.

She said the image of putting her purse in a locker in the subway before going to a dance represented what she wanted to do with her genital. She did not want to wear long pants because she did not want to be "hot." She understood her dream as a representation of her defenses against sexual excitement and pleasure. As she saw it, she wanted to be safe and she sacrificed pleasure for safety. I suggested that she imagined external danger to ensure that she got no pleasure. The dangers she was protecting herself from were internal. One danger was of condemning herself for wanting sexual pleasures from her father. Another was losing her father's love by demanding more of him than he was willing to give. Although she understood the demand as wanting more frequent telephone calls and visits, she also came to understand that this represented her childhood wishes to sleep with him and have sexual pleasure from him.

She expressed the same idea when she told of her difficulty in arranging a part of her vacation trip. What made it so problematic for her was that it was a pleasure trip. She could not allow herself pleasure even in the sublimated sphere of travel. She had to spend her time and her change trying to arrange to go by bus when it was so easy to go by plane. In her view, her male friend had no trouble arranging things because he was a man. Women, she believed, are more fussy, more focused on details, more in need of being sure of what they are doing. Men are more willing to take a chance. Besides, the plane would cost more than the bus. In her view men are willing to spend more money than women are because men will pay for their pleasures when women will not.

Another theme of the session which I interpreted to her was her insistence on crowding her account with many names and her life with many friends. In this she was using a compromise typical of latency children. She had a gang so that she would not get too close to any one person. That fended off sexual intimacy. She had orgastic but casual sex, always at the price of having little or no pleasure in the rest of her life. Her college years had been spent with a group of other young women. She felt deserted as most of them settled into long-term relationships. Her last roommate, Sally, was now leaving the house they had all shared in the early years of their careers.

She had to dispose of the extra beds and all the old furniture they had left. It was as if they had left her behind with all of their discards. They had gone on to live with sexual partners. Only she stuck with the shell of their life together. They had many parties. Each of them, including the patient, had dates with men, some of whom they had sex with. Yet as long as they lived together, she maintained the fantasy that their primary loyalty was to the group (Kernberg, 1980) and their current sexuality was unimportant.

As she mourned them, she also mourned the loss of her family when her parents divorced. She had never felt comfortable letting people go or letting old relationships end. That was part of why she had so many people in her life. She had several early caretakers and had formed special relationships with each of them. Her multiple early love objects seemed to have resulted in multiple love objects in her later life. She had experienced as forbidden her wishes for sexual pleasure with each of those early objects. Now she clung to many images of people with whom she was forbidden to have sexual pleasure.

One important precursor of her fantasy of a dirty and dangerous female genital was the circumstance of her birth. Her parents had been divorced before she was born and she had been told repeatedly, as part of the family lore, that it was because her father did not find her mother attractive when she was pregnant. Her own fantasy was that her mother hated having a female genital and found it dirty and disgusting, and that she should also. Her compromise was to enjoy her genital but deprive herself of other pleasures.

Shortly after the session presented here she recalled that she had been very sad when her father's mother died. She had masturbated while in bed with her grandmother when she was a little girl. Her guilt over this transgression haunted her. The "Bright Angel" in her story of making her reservations was important. Her grandmother had called her "Angel" as a term of endearment and was now with the angels herself. She believed that angels were like people, only better in that they were nonsexual. Angels had no sexual urges. Thus, her apparent asceticism had to do with defending herself from losing genital pleasure as a punishment for her early incestuous pleasure.

Transference fantasies were difficult for her to acknowledge. She rejected my idea that she involved so many friends in her life and names in our sessions as defensive shields against losing me. She did not like my inference that she was holding on to me by telling me stories in order to prolong the treatment. Her understanding of the analytic work was that I wanted her to get "hot" while I would keep "cool," thus humiliating her. Worse yet, she believed that I had many patients, all of whom loved me, and that she would be seduced into loving only me and thus be hurt by what she believed would be my inevitable rejection of her. We came to see that she believed I would divorce her as her father had divorced her mother. At the point in the treatment when she experienced me as dangerously leading her into temptation, I became the grandmother in the transference.

After months of continuing to work on this problem, I came to this formulation: she was describing the interference with pleasure that resulted from her fantasies about sexual greediness. Masturbation and its accompanying incestuous fantasies are universal. They lead to severe inhibitions only when accompanied by special circumstances. For this patient the experiences with her grandmother were crucial. For other women memories of early experiments with siblings, being forced to have sex with adults, and seductions can be such circumstances. What the focus on the concept of fear of loss of pleasure added to her treatment was the notion that she was depriving herself of pleasure of loving and being loved in the present because she believed she should be punished for experiencing sexual pleasure in the past. By punishing herself, she was preventing punishment from the outside. Her punishment was especially effective because it was a talion. As she experienced pleasure, so she must renounce pleasure. As she had many objects, so she should have none. Her understanding that she was doing all this to herself to pay for infantile sexual "crimes" made the punishment seem ludicrous to her, and she could give it up.

The experience of pleasure can be forbidden to such a degree that the taboo threatens or destroys the capacity to function sexually. This is true both for the process of menstruation and the capacity to bear children. Some patients have to suppress their menstrual function by starving themselves down to below the percentage of body fat needed to maintain it. Some manage this effect by dieting, purging, fasting, exercising, or combinations of these methods. Such suppression can only be fully understood when the component of punishment is considered. This category of fear adds another dimension to female genital fears, one that I hope to address at another time.

DISCUSSION

It is time to come back to the questions about the relationship of theory and clinical observation. It is for the reader to decide whether the concepts of primary femininity and female genital anxiety illuminate the clinical material in the cases sketched here. Painful penetration seems to me to fit the fears of the patient with the war dream. Fear of loss of pleasure seems to fit the patient with the prolonged reliance on a cast of friends and an inhibition about moving on to a more adult status. These descriptive concepts seem a closer match to what the patients were thinking and feeling than would ideas of penis envy, even if penis envy is understood as a metaphor for the social valuation of masculinity (Grossman and Stewart, 1976).

The clinical utility of this version of the concept of genital fears can be evaluated in each case. For the first patient the idea that what she is afraid of is damage to her own genital from painful penetration allows her to see the problem as her own. Interpreting her fear as fear of loss of a fantasied penis might easily have led to more concern about loss of the husband, and been understood as an injunction to stay with him and tolerate his abusive behavior because as long as he was around, she had a penis in the house. For the second patient, the interpretation of fear of loss of pleasure and conviction that she deserved to have no pleasure seemed to have worked because it encompassed her history of depriving herself of pleasure and addressed her symptom of holding on to outgrown patterns of life. An interpretation focusing on penis envy would not have had the same immediacy. Therefore, I believe it would have been less likely to change her behavior. For both patients and, I think, for women in general, the idea that penis envy is the motivator of their behavior only serves to support the idea that the penis is the only genital worth having, a notion contradicted by every experience of pleasure and functioning girls and women have.

Because the clinical material shows how the theory of primary genital anxiety changes the interpretations given to the patient, I think it may actually be validated by the clinical material. The theory gains validity as it explains the observations better than previous theory. It seems to me to have been more effective than the theory that regarded penis envy as primary in allowing these patients to understand themselves and change their behavior.

Functions of the female genital have been understood as important motivators of behavior ever since Horney (1926) postulated the wish for a baby as the little girl's premordial desire. Motherhood has been central to the image of woman in recent thinking. While Person (1986) advocates understanding motherhood as a limited part of a woman's role rather than as her entire identity and Welldon (1991) warns against the idealization of motherhood as a full-time career, their views show that the idea of motherhood is a currently powerful metaphor for womanhood. Freud (1917) believed that the wish for a baby was a secondary compromise formation. Deutsch (1944) and Erikson (1968) believed this longing for a baby led the developing girl to value the inner portion of her genital. Mayer (1991) has shown that little girls today still prefer structures containing enclosed spaces, while little boys prefer towers. While Mayer cautions against concluding that this preference reflects awareness of an inner genital, Bassin (1982) reasons that early experiences of inner space contribute to a schema that structures later cognition so that the girl constructs a world partly on the model of her inner experience. Ironically, Freud, in his insistence on the importance of the clitoris, had the kernel of the idea that the little girl was aware of her external genital all along. The possibility of viewing the little girl as valuing the vulva and the surrounding area had taken another 50 years (Richards, 1992). Now a new literature of neuropsychology (Damasio, 1994) points to the inextricable part bodily sensation and the resultant body image play in all of mental functioning. While bodily sensations of a steady state can only form a background for continuous mental functioning, it seems plausible that body sensations, which wax and wane dramatically as do genital sensations, must reach foreground early, and the pleasure and pain associated with such genital functioning would have to play an important part in the formation of body image as well as in the formation of fears of genital damage.

Mayer's suggestion that the girl values the vulva and fears loss of openness seems to correspond with the fears of loss of pleasure and loss of function. If the opening to the female genital is lost, the possibility of the pleasure of intercourse is lost also. Similarly, loss of the opening implies loss of the capacity to menstruate as well as the capacity to bear children.

Why had psychoanalysts so long believed that little girls look at boys' genitals and see something enviable while believing that they themselves have "nothing"? Is it true that little girls think they have "nothing"? No. Why would analysts think so? It is my hypothesis that the idea that girls have "nothing" is a defense against the male fear of the female genital.

Representations of the female genital have struck fear in both men and women since ancient times. The Medusa image has been horrifying people (Hamilton, 1940) since the Greeks moved from an agricultural matriarchal society to an urban manufacturing patriarchy (Gimbutas, 1989; duBois, 1988). According to duBois the Greek representations of woman evolved as the social structure changed. Early representations of woman as all-giving mother-field gave way successively to various metaphors of: furrow, ploughed into fertility by man; stone enclosing a secret space from which life comes and into which mortality sinks; oven in which male seed is baked into food sustaining life, and tablet on which man inscribes his will on his property. All of these images coexisted in ancient times. Of them Medusa is the image most frightening because the sight of her turns men into stone. Her image was, according to Gimbutas (1989), the image of the earth goddess, an image, in turn, preserved in stone.

In contrast to Lacan and the Lacanian feminists, duBois thinks such a mother is not a phallic mother, but a mother empowered by her own fertility, a power that precedes and stands apart from that of the phallus. Her view coincides with Bergmann's (1985) description of the importance of motherhood in the empowerment of modern woman. It also intersects with Lax's (1994) view of primary femininity as emanating from the female experience. My own emphasis on the power of the sensations emanating from the entire genital and perigenital area (1992) and Bass's (1994) on the sensations of the urinary sphincter also support this position. Gilmore (unpublished) adds an object-relations perspective to Burton's (1994) work on the anatomical roots of conflation of anal and genital sensations in the girl. Gilmore sees this conflation as a regressive fantasy "compensating for feelings of castration as well as fears of helplessness, penetration, and injury arising from oedipal fantasies of the paternal phallus, sexual intercourse, and childbirth." These feelings of castration correspond to what I am calling fear of loss of pleasure and fear of loss of function. The fantasies of the paternal phallus, intercourse, and childbirth correspond to what I am calling penetration fears. Fears of damage to the body from penetration are frequent in little girls, and fears of bodily damage from babies are seen both in adult women and little girls (Bonaparte 1935; Luquet-Parat 1970; I. Bernstein 1976; Blum 1976; Parens et al. 1976; Friedman 1985).

In discussing a previous version of this paper, J. Glenn (unpublished) cited two cases of congenital absence of the vagina. One was a woman analyzed by Greenacre (1958), the other a girl who had been treated in psychotherapy by a colleague of Glenn. Both patients wanted to be more womanly, asked for plastic surgery to create a vagina, got it, and were very pleased with the result. He described a woman in treatment with him who had fantasies of damaging men's penises and fears of being damaged by her analyst. He analyzed these fantasies as revenge for molestation by a gang of boys when she was still in late latency, rather than primary envy. He believes that this evidence bolsters the case for the secondary and special place of penis envy in women. Like Rees (1987), he believes that masculine identifications and the vicissitudes of development complicate the fantasies of girls and make it impossible to attribute penis envy or castration fantasies to simple "castration shock" at seeing the penis.

IMPLICATIONS FOR FUTURE RESEARCH

Why had genital anxiety in women been studied so little between 1930 and 1970? Hoffman (1996) suggests that Freud and his followers could not understand feminine sexuality because they could not conceive of feminine subjectivity. He believes that the consequence of this was that Freud defined any active wish on a woman's part as masculine. Could primary femininity be frightening to men because the active woman is powerful? Why should a powerful woman frighten men? Chodorow (1978) believes that she evokes the image of the powerful mother of infancy, reducing the other to his or her passive helplessness of that stage of life.

Castration anxiety seems self-evident. No one asks what men are afraid of when they are afraid of being castrated. Abelin (1994) attributes extreme submissiveness and lack of aggressivity in women to their fear of eliciting castration anxiety in men. Fears of pain, of loss of pleasure, and of loss of function seem to be prominent components of castration fear. Reserving the term "castration anxiety" to fear of loss of the penis and/or scrotum and using the term "female genital anxiety" for fear of damage to the vulva and inner genital structures may help to clarify the differences between the experiences of the little boy and the little girl on the way from the anal to the oedipal stage. Goldberger (unpublished) proposes replacing the term "phallic" stage with "infantile genital" stage to make it clear that girls have their own fears and developmental line. Alternatively, such a stage could be called the "narcissistic-genital" stage. This would imply that boys and girls understand their own genitals as normative, experience fear of losing what they have and envy what they perceive or imagine the other sex to have. Infant observation like that of Galenson and Roiphe (1976) and Olesker (1990) as well as theory-building about infantile development (Tyson and Tyson 1990) could add to our understanding of the genesis of the fears of this stage.

The research that could make a difference in this regard is not another look at observations made when penis envy was the only reaction thought to be noteworthy. In order to investigate whether little girls show evidence of enjoying, valuing, and fearing the loss of their own genitals, researchers would have to be looking specifically for such reactions at the time of gathering their data. Observations made in day care centers and infant nurseries would be relevant. So would anecdotal evidence from parents and other caretakers.

Evidence from adult analyses would have to be gathered by analysts who were open to the idea that girls, like boys, value pleasure and fear unpleasure. Reich (1964) has described the enormous effect of female genital pleasure in bolstering self-esteem. The fear of unpleasure would have to be understood as fear of pain and fear of loss of positively pleasurable sensation. The experience of genital pleasure can be renounced to such a degree that the taboo threatens or destroys the capacity to function sexually. This symptom can be seen as a compromise formation in which the fear of loss of feeling or the conviction that feeling has already been lost plays a crucial role. Although the wish may be for sexual pleasure with a beloved caretaker, the fear is of unpleasure, either through pain or through aphanisis.

But it is still the case, unfortunately, that students and seasoned analysts read papers that assert as facts such ideas as: (1) female genitals are internal and invisible; (2) female genitals are incapable of focused sensation or direct erotic discharge; (3) the girl becomes sexually awakened by a man; (4) women do not masturbate; (5) women prefer hugging and fondling to intercourse. There are many such ideas accepted as truth by otherwise rational analysts. In the course of our scientific work, I believe we have the responsibility to challenge the received wisdom, especially when it contradicts sensory experience and common sense.

Is the fear of genital pain or loss of pleasure always object-related? I believe so, and I believe that it is important for an analyst to take account of the object in understanding fantasy as well as conflict. But that is not the whole story. The idea of primary femininity is part of a view that shows female sexuality to have a complex development with strands woven from body image, object images, fantasy development, and interactions with the caretakers (Breen 1993). Having a good mother does not protect from all of life's vicissitudes. Having an inadequate one does not necessarily presage disaster. One of the factors other than the adequacy of the object is experience with one's own body.

The body as a source of pleasure is rivaled by the body as a source of knowledge. As Piaget, Dewey, Montessori and many others have amply demonstrated, learning takes place on a sensorimotor level long before the language system is fully developed. As Vygotsky and others have shown, language-mediated learning is increasingly important with age. As many educators have known, motoric learning is more stable, less conscious, and more permanent than linguistically mediated learning. Once you know how to ride a bicycle, you are likely to know it forever. But you can easily forget the theorems of geometry if you have never learned them by pacing out the earth to make fields.

All of this is to say that the sensory experience a little girl has of her genital may not be one she can put into words, but it is deep, going back to her earliest life. It is permanent as the result of flexing and relaxing the sphincters and surrounding musculature, and it is valued as it gives a great deal of pleasure. By comparison, seeing a boy's genitals is a relatively transitory, usually purely visual and not necessarily formative experience. To base a whole theory of female development on that one experience while discounting the ongoing deep musculature sensation and the surface experience of clitoral and labial stimulation is, to my mind, not reasonable. I believe that the experience of female genital sensation and its importance in the developing girl's sense of her own body is a kind of experience Heinz Hartmann referred to as the body ego. It is basic to the experience of being female. Paying attention to it in analyzing female patients can only enhance the analytic experience for them.

REFERENCES

ABELIN, G. (1994). The Headless Woman. In *The Spectrum of Psychoanalysis.* A.D. Richards & A.K. Richards, eds. Madison, CT: International Universities Press, pp. 161–184.

BASS, A. (1994). Urinary Sphincter. *Psychoanalytic Quarterly* 63:491–517.

BASSIN, D. (1982). Woman's Images of Inner Space. *International Journal of Psychoanalysis* 9:191–205.

BERGMANN, M.V. (1985). The Effect of Role Reversal on Delayed Marriage and Maternity. *Psychoanalytic Study of the Child* 40:197–220.

BERNSTEIN, I. (1976). Masochistic Reactions in a Latency-age Girl. *Journal of the American Psychoanalytic Association* 24(suppl.):589–607.

BLUM, H.P. (1976). Masochism, the Ego Ideal, and the Psychology of Women. *Journal of the American Psychoanalytic Association* 24(suppl.):157–192.

BONAPARTE, M. (1935). Passivity, Masochism and Femininity. *International Journal of Psychoanalysis* 16:325–333.

BREEN, D. (1993). *The Gender Conundrum.* New York: Routledge.

BRENNER, C. (1982). *The Mind in Conflict.* New York: International Universities Press.

BURTON, A. (1994). The Meaning of Perineal Activity to Women: An Inner Sphinx. *Journal of the American Psychoanalytic Association* 44(suppl.):241–259.

CHODOROW, N. (1978). *The Reproduction of Mothering.* Berkeley, CA: University of California Press.

CLOWER, V. (1970). (Panel Report) The Development of the Child's Sense of His Own Identity. *Journal of the American Psychoanalytic Association* 18:165–176.

DAMASIO, A. (1994). *Descartes' Error.* New York: Putnam.

DEUTSCH, H. (1930). The Significance of Masochism in the Mental Life of Women. *International Journal of Psychoanalysis* 11:48–60.

———— (1944). *The Psychology of Women,* Vol. 1. New York: Grune & Stratton.

DEVEREUX, G. (1957). The Awarding of a Penis as Compensation for a Rape. *International Journal of Psychoanalysis* 38:398–401.

DOVE, R. (1989). *Grace Notes.* New York: Norton.

DUBOIS, P. (1988). *Sowing the Body.* Chicago, IL: University of Chicago Press.

ERIKSON, E.H. (1968). *Womanhood and the Inner Space. In Identity: Youth and Crisis.* New York: Norton, pp. 261–294.

FLIEGEL, Z.O. (1973). Feminine Psychosexual Development in Freudian Theory. *Psychoanalytic Quarterly* 42:385–409.

FREUD, S. (1905). Three Essays on the Theory of Sexuality. *Standard Edition* 7.

———(1908). On the Sexual Theories of Children. *Standard Edition* 9.

———(1917). On Transformation of Instinct as Exemplified in Anal Erotism. *Standard Edition* 17.

———(1924). The Dissolution of the Oedipus Complex. *Standard Edition* 19.

———(1933). Femininity. *Standard Edition* 22.

FRIEDMAN, L. (1985). Beating Fantasies in a Latency-age Girl. *Psychoanalytic Quarterly* 54:569–596.

GALENSON, E. & ROIPHE, H. (1976). Some Suggested Revisions Concerning Early Female Development. *Journal of the American Psychoanalytic Association* 24(suppl.):29–58.

GIMBUTAS, M. (1989). *The Language of the Goddess.* New York: Harper & Row.

GREENACRE, P. (1958). *Early Physical Determinants in the Development of the Sense of Identity. In: Emotional Growth,* Vol. 1. New York: International Universities Press 1971, pp. 113–127.

GROSSMAN, W. & STEWART, W. (1976). Penis Envy. *Journal of the American Psychoanalytic Association* 24(suppl.):193–213.

HAMILTON, E. (1940). *Mythology.* Boston: Little Brown.

HOFFMAN, L. (1996). Freud and Feminine Subjectivity. *Journal of the American Psychoanalytic Association* 44(suppl.):23–44.

HORNEY, K. (1926). The Flight from Womanhood. *International Review of Psychoanalysis* 12:360–374.

JACOBSON, E. (1936). On the Development of the Girl's Wish for a Child. *Psychoanalytic Quarterly* 37:523–538.

JONES, E. (1927). The Early Development of Female Sexuality. *International Journal of Psychooanalysis* 8:459–472.

KERNBERG, O.F. (1980). Love, the Couple, and the Group. *Psychoanalytic Quarterly* 49:78–108.

KLEIN, M. (1932). The Effects of Early Anxiety Situations on the Genital Anxiety of the Girl. In *The Psychoanalysis of Children.* New York: Norton, pp. 194–239.

LANGER, M. (1992). *Motherhood and Sexuality.* New York: Guilford.

LAX, R. (1994). Aspects of Primary and Secondary Genital Feelings and Anxieties in Girls During the Preoedipal and Early Oedipal Phases. *Psychoanalytic Quarterly* 58:271–296.

LUQUET-PARAT, C. (1970). *The Change of Object.* In *Female Sexuality,* J. Chasseguet-Smirgel, ed. Ann Arbor, MI: University of Michigan Press, pp. 84–93.

MAYER, E. (1985). Everybody must Be Just like Me. *International Journal of Psychoanalysis* 66:331–348.

————(1991). Towers and Enclosed Spaces. *Psychoanalytic Inquiry* 11:480–510.

OLESKER, W. (1990). Sex Differences During the Early Separation-individuation Phase. *Journal of the American Psychoanalytic Association* 38:325–346.

PARENS, H., POLLOCK, L., STERN, J., & KRAMER, S. (1976). On the Girl's Entry into the Oedipus Complex. *Journal of the American Psychoanalytic Association* 24(suppl.):79–108.

PERSON, E.S. (1986). Working Mothers. In *The Psychology of Today's Woman,* T. Bernay & D. Cantor, eds. Hillsdale, NJ: Analytic Press, pp. 121–138.

QUINODOZ, J. (1989). Female Homosexual Patients in Analysis. *International Journal of Psychoanalysis*70:55–63.

RADO, S. (1933). Fear of Castration in Women. *Psychoanalytic Quarterly* 2:425–475.

REES, K. (1987). I Want to Be a Daddy. *Psychoanalytic Quarterly* 56:497–522.

REICH, A. (1964). Masturbation and Self-esteem. In *Annie Reich: Psychoanalytic Contributions.* New York: International Universities Press 1973, pp. 312–333.

RICHARDS, A.K. (1992). The Influence of Sphincter Control and Genital Sensation on Body Image and Gender Identity in Women. *Psychoanalytic Quarterly* 61:331–349.

STOLLER, R.J. (1968). The Sense of Femaleness. *Psychoanalytic Quarterly* 37:42–55.

TYSON, P. & TYSON, R.I. (1990). *Psychoanalytic Theories of Development: An Integration.* New Haven, CT: Yale University Press.

WELLDON, E. (1991). *Mother, Madonna, Whore.* New York: Guilford.

****
****

Original publication of preceding chapter:

RICHARDS, A.K. (1995). Primary Femininity and Female Genital Anxiety. *Journal of the American Psychoanalytic Association* 44:261–281.1.

The Influence of Sphincter Control and Genital Sensation on Body Image and Gender Identity in Women

The development of one aspect of feeling female is hypothesized to account for certain phenomena in the treatment of young women patients. Fear of loss of genital pleasure experienced as contractions of the anal and genital-urinary sphincters is seen as the central issue in conflicts manifested in genital, oral, and anal modalities. It is suggested that the female's awareness of her genital arises from the generalization of sphincter sensation in the little girl, which is then represented in the body image. The body image is postulated as a link between genital pleasure and the valuing of femininity.

> *Everyone in me is a bird.*
> *I am beating all my wings.*
> *They wanted to cut you out*
> *but they will not.*
> *They said you were immeasurably empty*
> *but you are not.*
> *They said you were sick unto dying*
> *but they were wrong.*
> *You are singing like a school girl.*
> *You are not torn.*

> From "In Celebration of My Uterus"
> —ANNE SEXTON (1981)

We know what we mean when we say that men are afraid of castration. And many psychoanalysts believe they know that when women are afraid of castration, they are afraid of losing a fantasied penis or they are afraid of their masochistic wishes in reaction to their wish to castrate a man. True or not, this seems to me not to be the whole story, or even the primary part of it. In this paper I am going to present some evidence for the idea that women believe they have an internal (and an external) sexual organ which is a source of pleasure and which they fear losing. Anne Sexton's poem says so. Some women I have analyzed think so. Mayer (1985) and Renik (1990) think so, too. For Sexton, the fear is fear of the loss of her uterus, a uterus experienced as "singing like a school girl," an internal source of pleasure.

When a woman says that she is afraid she will lose her femininity, she could be talking about secondary sexual characteristics, the external genitalia, or, like Sexton, she could be referring to her inner genital. The experience of the interior genital and its relation to an aspect of body image, as well as to an aspect of the gender identity of women, is what I would like to explore here. I think that contractions of the perineal musculature in toilet training result in sexual excitement which is felt as genital by the oedipal girl and which she fears losing as a punishment for oedipal wishes. The question to be addressed is: To what extent is the female's fear of castration a fear of loss of genital sensation? The following case examples are intended to show how this fear appeared in the analyses of some women who differed from one another with respect to kind and level of pathology.

CASE EXAMPLES

A young executive who had quickly reached the highest levels in her career, entered a four-times-a-week analytic treatment because she wanted help in deciding whether to end her relationship with her lover; if the relationship continued, she needed help in improving it. Her success had left her feeling cut off from her roots. When she realized that her lover was from a wealthy family, she had begun to lose her spontaneity with him. She believed that his mother disapproved of their relationship, and she complained whenever he took her to family events. Yet she clung to him desperately, tolerating neglect and abuse from him. As treatment progressed and he became less abusive (because she provoked him less about his close relationship with his family), she lost interest in him.

During the waning of this relationship, in the fourth year of her analysis, she got into a taxi one day on her way home from work. The driver told her that if she would come home with him, he would "eat" her. She went and enjoyed the encounter, with no sense of fear or shame. As she explained in her session the next day, when she did this, she did not have that image of her father standing at the foot of the bed, watching her and disapproving, which she had regularly experienced when having sex with her lover. We came to understand that she felt too powerful and too phallic with her lover, but felt feminine when degraded by the cab driver. I interpreted that this was related to her belief that her father had wanted her to be a boy. She thought he had wanted a son, but she also believed that he detested masculine women. What she both valued and depreciated in herself was her femininity.

She was afraid that if she stayed with her lover, the sexual roles would be reversed. Her need to be treated as inferior, dirty, an outsider, and immoral derived from her disdain for sexual activity of any kind. It also derived from her guilt over her wish to be penetrated by her father and, most terrifying of all, from her fear that she would lose her femininity and the possibility of ever having children if she succeeded in her career and in her relationship with her lover, who was too deferential to women.

Her dilemma had plagued her as long as she could remember. For example, she was the only girl her father and uncles took along when they went to their hunting cabin each fall. She was also the only girl in her class who did better in math than she did in other subjects. At puberty she had continued to do well in math and science, but believed, as a result, that there was something wrong with her as a girl. She had acquired a boyfriend as soon as she could and had remained with him, believing that she could not be less of a woman than the others if she had a man. Any lapse of what she considered masculinity on the part of her man threw her into a panic. She had left her boyfriend when he decided to go into an artistic field in which he would never earn as much money as she would earn in business. The femininity she was afraid to lose was her orgastic potential. What she said she valued was the "fluttering" sensation in her vagina, which I understand to represent the sphincter clenching of orgasm. That fluttering sensation corresponds to Sexton's image: "Everyone in me is a bird." This case illustrates something that I have observed with other women patients: some women who fear losing their femininity are afraid of losing the inner experience of the female genitalia.

Like this patient, other women who succeed in traditionally masculine occupations seem to me to be especially prone to allowing themselves to be exploited by men because they need to prove themselves desirable and feminine rather than masculine. Any perceived softness or openness in a man is frightening because it threatens role reversal and consequent loss of genital sensation. The hypermasculine man is valued by such women because they can feel more feminine in contrast to him. They are likely to be the victims of impostors (Gediman 1985) because they feel themselves to be impostors as women when they succeed in masculine roles. This was even more pointedly illustrated by a patient whose ordinarily regular menses suddenly appeared two weeks early, just at the moment she was giving a lecture in which she would be seen as a serious and successful scholar by a very large audience. Her pride in her accomplishment was countered by her embarrassment at not being able to sit down again on stage after she finished at the podium. The achievement, which felt masculine to her, was countered by her bodily reminder to herself that she was only a woman, but this was also a comfort, a reassurance that her achievement had not cost her her femininity. The social role of successful career person may be understood by such women as a threat of loss of feminine genital function.

Another patient, a writer in a three-times-a-week treatment, had an eating disorder. She drank quarts of artificially sweetened coffee every day. Much distressed when her doctor told her that her recurrent bladder infection was probably related to her caffeine and saccharine intake, she determined to try to stop drinking so much coffee. Yet she had to eat lemon cookies while she wrote, and only coffee went well with the cookies. She had learned to write from her father, who used to keep these cookies on his desk. I interpreted her identification with him. But, she protested, her father did not drink coffee. We came to understand the coffee as a poison she used to punish herself for indulging in fantasies of being her father's darling, as well as fantasies of being just like him and doing everything he could do. The symptom of endless desire for coffee had become exacerbated when she became more successful than he. It abated when we understood it as a bid for his love and for the attention and concern of her physician and of her mother. Using the coffee to become sick would put an end to her striving, which she saw as too masculine and therefore castrating to her as a woman. I interpreted the self-filling as a masturbatory equivalent of being penetrated. I told her that she was penetrating herself with food, but in fantasy she was being penetrated by her father. Therefore, she had to punish herself by taking in the poisonously sweetened coffee.

The oral displacement upward of the genital wish to be filled represented control over sphincters, conflating glottal closure with vaginal sphincter control. She used eating as an area in which she could maintain control, reassuring herself that her vocational activity, which, to her, represented masculine activity, did not destroy her femininity. She became able to give up the coffee when sphincter control was brought into the analytic discourse as the issue which linked her sexual concerns with eating.

Clenching and unclenching the perineal sphincters becomes important when the need for mastery is evoked by trauma resulting from physical or sexual abuse. The ordinary experience of mastery obtained in the course of toilet training can become a nodal point for regression when the girl feels threatened with intrusion or penetration. This sphincter mastery can also serve to ward off other threats, as in the following instance.

A young woman analysand with an intense devotion to ballroom dancing was able to gather the courage to tolerate a break with her abusive lover when she began to understand her complex need for an abusive and antisocial sexual partner. She had been unable to even contemplate leaving him as long as she remained terrified of confronting him. An interpretation of her use of ballroom dancing to allow him to lead, yet to keep him behaving within an acceptable social pattern, made sense to her. She then uncovered a memory of being terrified by her parents' quarrels when she sat alone in the back of the family car. She recalled having hummed to herself while crouched in the space between the front and back seats of the car, clenching and relaxing her perineal musculature to the rhythm of her music.

Recalling the soothing effect of this intense preoccupation with her own inner sensations, she was able to accept my interpretation that her sense of her own power to tolerate the disruptive parental quarreling derived from her awareness of the power of her sphincters. This made her feel powerful enough to end her affair with her abusive lover. She said that she no longer needed him "to be the bad guy." I understood this to mean that she no longer needed the opportunity to project her aggression onto him and seduce him into acting it out for her.

In attempting to understand the origin of her early solution to the shattering effect of her parents' quarrels, she recalled that her artist mother would spend hours painting what looked to her like abstractions, but required that her father pose nude while her mother painted what were supposed to be pictures of him. As a little girl she had felt intense envy of her father's body and especially of his penis. She had believed that her mother allowed him to do anything, to break any rules, because she wanted to be allowed to look at his body. The early fantasy that the man's body is so beautiful to look at that he can have anything in exchange for the favor of exhibiting it contrasted with her attitude toward her own body.

She described her own body as being "strong, like a peasant or a machine. Not fine, well defined, or elegant." Her fantasy of the primal scene involved a gangster-type man, elegantly groomed and dressed, but doing bad things and getting away with them. She envisioned the woman as a love slave, enthralled by the man's "suave" penis. The parental quarrels had been so frightening to her partly because they evoked the primal scene fantasy too vividly. I interpreted that she must have wished they were making love instead of fighting and that she must have felt so powerless to stop them that she had used masturbatory clenching and unclenching in order to feel powerful and loved. Her position in the car had guaranteed that she was alone, protecting her from feeling like she was intruding. Thus, I now think, she was protected from superego condemnation for intrusion on the primal scene. She remarked that one good thing about her lover's antisocial activities was that by contrast with him, she always could feel like a good person. In my opinion, she projected her guilt onto her lover in order to allow herself what she perceived as the guilty pleasure of making love actively.

For this patient, anything was all right as long as she could blame the other person. Adult masturbatory clenching and unclenching was bad because she was doing it on her own initiative. Ballroom dancing was not bad, even though she had the same kinesthetic experience, because she could rationalize that she was just responding to the music and to the partner who led her. She could enjoy it while appeasing her superego by seeing herself as only a passive tool.

For all of these women, the complaints about their social role, their interactions with men and women in their environment, and their self-understanding seemed to me to be colored by their experience and valuing of genital sphincter sensation. Issues raised by these observations are: (1) How does the girl's awareness of her inner genitals develop? (2) How does awareness of inner genital sensation relate to castration fears in women? (3) What does the female's awareness of her anatomy contribute to the development of object relations? (4) What is the relation between this awareness of inner genital sensation and perversion?

INTERIOR AND EXTERIOR

The psychoanalytic treatment of adult women has given rise to a complex view of the development of female gender identity. Bernstein (1990), Mayer (1985), Kestenberg (1956), (1968), Horney (1924), and others see female psychosexual development as being an elaboration on early, specifically female gender identity. It seems to me that several different strands of development converge to produce the adult woman's sexual orientation and view of her own sexuality. While penis envy may be part of it, and feelings about early objects certainly enter into it, the strand of female sexual development highlighted here is a line based on the kinesthetic experience of the interior genital.

Freud (1932) saw sexuality as the most complex and difficult to trace of motivators. He encouraged women analysts to expand understanding of female development. From the start, they emphasized primary femininity. This is in contrast to Freud's view (1931) that female psychological development starts out male, veers with the girl's discovery that she does not have a penis, and is ever after determined by that fateful turn. Early attempts by women to understand vaginal awareness addressed the problem. Bonaparte (1953) pointed out that vaginal mucosae have almost no sensitivity, even to heat or pain. She believed that arousal depends on sensitivity of the vulva, meatus, or perineum and kinesthetic sensitivity of the erectile tissue lining the vagina. Beating fantasies symbolize stimulation of the vagina by blows of the penis. I infer that beating fantasies would have developed from the sensation of flexing the sphincters and would then provide the mental representation linking the early sphincter experience with later coital sensation.

Laqueur (1990) asserted that Freud's "vaginal orgasm" was known to be anatomically impossible by the time Freud wrote about it, because it had long been well known that the supply of nerves in the vagina is quite sparse, while the supply of nerves in the vulva is luxuriant. Of the "vaginal orgasm" Laqueur said: "It involves feeling what is not there. Becoming a sexually mature woman is therefore living an oxymoron, becoming a lifelong 'normal hysteric,' for whom a conversion neurosis is termed 'acceptive'" (p. 243). This absurdity could not have escaped Freud. Thus, his humble conclusion that he did not understand female sexuality was justified.

The idea of vaginal orgasm seemed finally to be laid to rest by Sherfey's (1966) careful and exhaustive review of the anatomical and developmental data and behavioral evidence derived from the data of Masters and Johnson. Sherfey concluded that there is no vaginal orgasm, and that clitoris, labia minora, and the lower third of the vagina function as a unit during intravaginal coitus. More specifically: ". . . there is no such thing as psychopathological clitoral fixation; there are only varying degrees of vaginal insensitivity and coital frigidity" (p. 101). My understanding of this is that instead of a transfer of sensitivity, there is an integration of clitoral sensitivity into the larger functioning of the complex assembly of part organs.

This leaves the question of how this interior space is reached. The idea of a body opening with no sphincters, and therefore no control of access, appeared in Barnett (1966), and was elaborated by Bernstein (1990). It seems to me that while this idea may be relevant to the sensation of no control over menstrual flow, it fails to account for the toddler girl's awareness of the presence of a competent set of muscles in the female perineum. The girl cannot be unaware of this musculature since voluntary control of it is necessary to toilet training (Kestenberg 1956). Even though the voluntary control of the sphincters is not in awareness at all times, it becomes the center of a girl's attention several times each day.

Erikson (1950) found that girls built enclosures and played in them, while boys built towers, roadways, and houses and played outside them. He concluded that girls were motivated by their interior genitals as boys were by their exterior ones. Piaget and Inhelder (1966) described early learning as sensorimotor. By this they meant that early learning occurs through gross motor activity. It is while the girl is in this early sensorimotor stage of development that gender identity is formed (Fast 1984). At the same stage, toilet training takes place. In addition, the crucial events of separation-individuation occur (Mahler, et al. 1975). The meaning of gender is therefore influenced by the girl's discovery of it in the context of toilet training.

The most significant event of toilet training for the development of the girl, I believe, is the discovery of voluntary control of the anal and urethral sphincters. The girl gains control of these sphincters as early as eighteen months. Mothers universally report that little girls are toilet trained earlier than boys. One mother of twins described her experience: "Jane was trained by eighteen months. It seemed like she wanted to be. It took forever with John. He was three and a half" (Bond 1990). I believe that the sense of mastery that the girl achieves in controlling her sphincters is magnified by the sexual pleasure she achieves by this control. Cloacal fantasies bother women throughout life (Goldberger 1991); (Spitz 1955). Making the distinction between the highly valued genital product and the devalued anal one is so important to women that any threat to this distinction can invoke danger (Stein 1988). The woman writer with the eating disorder suffered from this confusion, never knowing whether her product was "great" or "shit."

The little girl's pleasure in her control of her sphincters may be the origin of her tendency to enjoy cleanliness, neatness, and orderliness. Montgrain (1983) posited oral and anal roots of vaginal erotism as foci for regressive psychic representation of the vagina. According to Barnett (1966): "The complete sequence of normal female development may be based totally on orifice and cavity cathexis" (p. 130). From oral to anal to vaginal cavity, the girl may always experience sexual pleasure from internal mucosae. This may be the prototype of how pleasure from interior or exterior stimulation is experienced as vaginal (Glenn and Kaplan 1968).

The writer with an eating disorder was greatly concerned with elimination. This paralleled her conflict over intake. Her generalized sphincter concerns, I believe, defended against the superego prohibitions over experiencing genital sensations while engaged in activities which she associated with her father.

Bernstein (1990) said: "'Wetness' necessarily invokes a regressive potential to all the anxieties and conflicts surrounding early bladder and sphincter control . . . " (p. 154). The bladder in particular is the source of genital stimulation in girls from the earliest years of life. Urinary retention, with tightening and relaxation of the sphincters to release urine, are the prototype of vaginal excitement and orgasm in women. Galenson and Roiphe (1976) asserted that the little girl is awed by the discovery of the male urinary stream as much as by the penis. I believe that this follows from her pleasure in regulating her own urination. The vulva as a whole is squeezable and distendable from the earliest years. Little girls can and do squeeze and release their sphincters rhythmically to gain pleasure from their sexual organs (Clower 1976). Latency age girls have been reported to masturbate by running, horseback riding, gymnastics, bicycle riding, rubbing their legs together, and similar activities. Their passionate attachment to these activities may attest to the high value they place on the pleasure they get from them. It seems to me that fear of the loss of this capacity, experienced as fear of forcible penetration or rape, is the basic female sexual fear.

In normal development, the sensory experience of the girl is not of an isolated clitoris or vagina, but of a global area around the inner upper thighs, the vulva, and the lower abdomen (Sherfey 1966), including the anal area; there powerful sphincters of the anal, urethral, and vaginal openings are brought under conscious control and experienced as the site of stimulation from the bowel movement, the urinary stream, and the shifting positions of the abdomen. Because little girls are taught that it is not socially appropriate to communicate these sensations (Lerner 1977), I believe that they learn to enjoy the feelings without registering them in conscious thought. Hägglund and Piha (1980) described this process as one in which access to the inside is by means of sensations induced by manipulations outside. Girls experience the inner and outer portions of the genitalia as connected through the sensation of pleasure. Mastery attained in this way can defend against the unpleasure associated with aggressive impulses which are unacceptable to the girl. The patient who rocked in the back of her parents' car used her sphincter sensations as a defense against awareness of her rage at her parents for failing to protect her and her fear that they would kill each other.

The executive described above recalled being convinced throughout latency that she was not like other girls. It was not a matter of being better or worse, only different. For her, the mind was inside and her pride in her mental functioning bolstered her sense of being female until the situation became more complex as she began to understand her intellect as masculine. Once that happened, she needed to bolster her sense of femininity by having a lover as an external sign of her feminine identity.

CASTRATION FEARS

A woman patient expressed the fear that her vagina would dry up like a raisin and fall out. This form of castration fear in a woman contrasts with the view that women only fear loss of a fantasied penis. Girls, like boys, value genitals for the pleasure to be derived from them. Fear of loss of the pleasure genitals provide is common to both sexes. But the exquisite innervation of the genitals which produces pleasure also entails vulnerability to pain. It seems to me that these fears of loss of pleasure and the experience of pain are necessary and sufficient to account for castration anxiety even in children who have never been threatened with castration. Ideas of specific ways in which the loss of pleasure and the experience of pain can occur elaborate pleasure and pain into fantasy. Bonaparte (1953) regarded "castration fear," or loss of an imaginary penis, as secondary in women, with what she called "fear of perforation" as the more general problem. Bernstein (1990) understood rape fears as fear of penetration rather than castration. This accords well with Bonaparte's "fear of perforation" and Barnett's (1966) idea that the girl suffers from fear of lack of muscular control over the vagina. Bernstein showed how female castration anxiety is manifested as fears about "access," "penetration," and "diffusivity."

Girls' genitals, which are highly pleasurable from infancy onward, are located so close to the organs of excretion that excretory functions are confused with genital ones. Thus, disgust with excretions and the excretory function endangers genital pleasure. McDougall (1988) described the girl's castration anxiety as fear that "her mother will attack her whole inside" (p. 67). This view of female sexuality emphasizes the internal and makes vivid the equation of rape or forced penetration with death and the fantasy of death as turning the body into feces (Bach and Schwartz 1972).

Mayer (1985) showed that female castration anxiety is best understood as fear of loss of the female genital. She based her view of female development on the girl's awareness of her vulva. For Mayer, the girl's development parallels that of the boy, in that the small girl experiences her own body as the prototype of what a body should be and experiences the difference between the sexes as a defect or deformity in the male, just as the little boy experiences that difference as a defect or deformity in the female. I agree that the visual sense of the vulva and surrounding area are crucial to the value the woman attaches to her genital openness. But I want to emphasize the role of the invisible but kinesthetically perceived sphincter muscles as generating the body image.

Renik (1990) described a female patient's fears related to her active phallic strivings as he uncovered her wish to penetrate and impregnate her male analyst. He attributed these strivings to denial that she could actively seduce through her feminine sexuality. To wish for the sexual equipment of the opposite sex implies castration for women as for men. To have a penis is something women wish for but also dread, because having it would entail loss of the treasured source of pleasure. The ballroom dancer was dependent on a man to dance with because she needed to deny her female power to seduce as well as because she envied and feared male power. Fear of loss of internal genitalia is explicit in Sexton's poem to her uterus, written in response to a recommendation of hysterectomy. It was hidden in the symptoms my patients presented, but the symptomatic relief produced by this interpretation confirmed that the fear of loss of genital sensation had played a role in forming the symptoms.

The executive who worried about being too controlling and powerful with her lover believed that the external power she wielded would destroy her internal control. In treatment she set up a choice between having frequent sessions or using her money for surgery to have her "too high arches" restructured. I interpreted to her that she could change inside or outside, but not both. Changing the outside seemed less frightening, and it protected from her the greater danger of changing inside. Since she believed that I wanted her to continue to advance in her career, she needed the surgeon to take her money so that she would not have so much treatment that she would become too masculine. Treatment would also deprive her of the fantasy of being wounded and inadequate and therefore the sort of woman her father would choose. In this sense, her dilemma could be seen as a choice of whether she was to be castrated outside, on her feet, or inside, in her mind.

ANATOMY OR OBJECT RELATIONS

Wisdom (1983) emphasized the extent to which society defines what constitutes femaleness. While Person (1980) viewed sexuality as determined by object relations rather than by a biological "drive," she agreed that gender "plays an organizing role in psychic structure similar to other modalities of cognition, such as space, time, causation and self-object differentiation" (p. 49). Chodorow (1989) contrasted the concept of primary genital awareness with that of parent labeling as explanations for female gender development. She cited Galenson and Roiphe and Kestenberg in the first camp and Stoller, Kleeman, Lerner, and others in the second. Money and Ehrhardt (1972) might well be added to the latter group. The idea that sphincter awareness contributes to body image and thus to gender identity supports the importance of primary genital sensation in the formation of sexual identity. I believe that new evidence from the history of science supports this view.

A history of theories of female sexual anatomy was offered by Laqueur (1990). Laqueur showed that the idea that female sexual anatomy is inverted male anatomy pervaded medical and scientific thought in the Western world until relatively recent times. In this view, a female is an imperfect male. Laqueur dated to the eighteenth century the idea that the uterus is different and that this difference determines the physical and mental life of the person who has one. Here the female is the opposite of the male. This belief, restated by Freud in his famous dictum, "anatomy is destiny," places an emphasis on the biological difference which Laqueur believed the facts do not support. Thus, female anatomy produces sensations specific to a muscular sphincter covered by a mucosa which is partially hidden from view but rich in sensation, a specifically female organ which should not be defined in terms of difference from the male or in terms of lack of the male organ.

In contrast, Laufer (1991) agreed with Freud's (1933) idea that the girl accepts femininity only with the oedipal realization that she cannot take father's place with mother because she lacks a penis. Laufer viewed self-mutilation, anorexia, bulimia, and suicidal behavior as responses to a harshly punitive mother image which appears to the girl when she attempts manual masturbation at or after puberty. The adolescent girl sees her body as a punitive object attacking herself. For Laufer, therefore, the object relation with the mother determines the girl's body image. Here Laufer is similar to Chasseguet-Smirgel (1988) who said that "the first category is mother/father" (p. 126). For Chasseguet-Smirgel, the awareness of difference between male and female is not based on one's own anatomy, but on the differences between the primary objects. Parens (1991), in contrast to Laufer, stated that the girl starts out non-specific and develops a feminine identity in the late preoedipal period.

According to Fisher (1989), early relationships with parents predict later sexual behavior, which speaks for the primacy of object relations over anatomy in the development of body image. He did not take into account the possibility that recall of early interactions with parents may be affected by subsequent sexual and cognitive development. Such linear thinking may hamper understanding of female development. According to Ritvo (in Panel 1989),

> ... gender identity formation is not a simple dichotomous variable or a fixed normative endpoint in a linear developmental sequence. It should be viewed instead as a complex construction which includes the possibility of retroactive transformations of previous meanings in the light of libidinal and aggressive aims (p. 801).

Thus, thinking about anatomical development is needed to supplement what is known about development from the object relations point of view. I believe that we can now specify one more aspect of this early female development: the experience of the sphincters.

To illustrate the complex interaction between object relations and bodily sensation in the formation of adult gender identity, I would like to return briefly to the cases with which I began this paper. The executive had developed a fantasy of her father wanting her to be a boy to explain to herself her own wish to be a boy, its disavowal because of the threat to her femininity if it were fulfilled, and her need for her father's love. This fantasy had developed into the idea that as long as she had a lover she was not too masculine. This, in turn, had led her to become subservient to her lover and unreasonably demanding of proof of his masculinity. Any man who could be macho enough to make her feel feminine, however, was so unsuitable and so unable to accept her achievements, that she could not accept him. I view all of this as based on her female genital pleasure, a pleasure she was unwilling to give up.

The writer also had fond memories of being special to her father. She experienced severe conflict because she both identified with him and wanted his love. When she believed herself to be like him, she experienced herself as too masculine to be loved by him. Again, this object relations view of her conflict was a simplification, in that it needed to be supplemented by understanding of the sphincter control issues which, I believe, contributed so much to her psychopathology.

The ballroom dancer identified primarily with her artist mother. Her need for a man to lead her placated her superego. Instead of feeling guilty for seeing her father naked and for being present at her parents' quarrels, she admired the antisocial activities of her lover. But this also had a physical component. She enjoyed the ballroom dancing as a kind of stimulation that would not force her to punish herself for masturbating.

FEMALE SEXUALITY AND PERVERSION

The early recognition of sexual perversion in women (Richards 1990) was followed by a relatively long period in which most analysts thought that women did not have sexual perversions at all (Richards 1989). Denial of sexual perversions in women reflected the view of female sexuality as passive, responsive to the male, or simply absent. For Chasseguet-Smirgel (1978), perversion is a negation of the oedipal prohibition, a denial of both the generational taboo and the differentiation between the sexes. Stoller (1985) held that a hostile desire to humiliate the other is central to perversions. These definitions allow for female as well as male perversions. Recognizing the existence of perversions in women entails recognition of spontaneous female sexual desire. As we have seen in considering anatomy and object relations, the sphincter sensation may be one basis for female sexual desire.

Stoller reported varieties of female sexual experience, including erotic vomiting, which illustrate the interplay of internal and external genital imagery. In bulimia (Sours 1974), a girl enacts a wish to gain and to repudiate the huge belly and breasts which the little girl fantasies are emblems of the mother's capacity for pregnancy. The wish to be pregnant may, in turn, relate to the wish to fill and empty an inner space. This fantasy was seen in the patient who had to eat the lemon cookies and drink coffee, and is an extension of early sphincter pleasures.

Such fantasies make gender a complex achievement, from the toddler's labeling the self as a boy or girl to the mature adult's negotiating gender identity, gender role, object choice, and object relationships. Dahl (1988) put it this way:

> *"Gender identity" is not a fixed normative end point in a linear developmental sequence but a complex construction involving the interrelationships between body and mind and between inner and outer reality . . . The mind must find a balance between the needs and demands of outer reality and the needs and demands of the body ... it does so through the creation of the configuration of fantasies we subsume under the term "gender identity"* (p. 363).

SUMMARY

The experience of female sexuality seems to have to do with experiences of both the exterior and the interior portions of the female genitalia. Mental representation of this experience seems to interact with early perceptions of the parents and their roles, and with socially normative maleness and femaleness, in producing the fantasies which govern the possibilities for female sexual development and functioning. A vital and, I believe, insufficiently emphasized aspect of female genital representation is the flexing of perineal musculature, originally in the voluntary control of the anal and urethral sphincters, and later in the involuntary contractions of the orgasm. The degree to which this is the preferred method of masturbation may have important consequences for the girl's development. The concept of a body image based on a model of body activity rather than on visual image alone is an important and neglected factor in formulating a theory of the development of self-representation and body ego. I believe that paying attention to this aspect of female sexual development in the clinical situation can enrich our understanding of our female patients.

REFERENCES

BACH, S. & SCHWARTZ, L. (1972) A Dream of the Marquis De Sade: Psychoanalytic Reflections on Narcissistic Trauma, Decompensation, and the Reconstitution of a Delusional Self. *Journal of the American Psychoanalytic Association* 20:451–475.

BARNETT, M.C. (1966). Vaginal Awareness in the Infancy and Childhood of Girls. *Journal of the American Psychoanalytic Association* 14:129–141.

BERNSTEIN, D. (1990). Female Genital Anxieties, Conflicts and Typical Mastery Modes. *International Journal of Psychoanalysis* 71:151–165.

BONAPARTE, M. (1953). *Female Sexuality.* New York: Interntional Universities Press.

BOND, A. (1990). Personal Communication.

CHASSEGUET-SMIRGEL, J. (1978). Reflexions on the Connexions Between Perversion and Sadism *International Journal of Psychoanalysis* 59:27–35.

——— (1988). Interview in *Women Analyze Women.* E.H. Baruch & L.J. Serrano, eds. New York/London: New York University Press, pp. 109–126.

CHODOROW, N.J. (1989). *Feminism and Psychoanalytic Theory.* New Haven/London: Yale University Press.

CLOWER, V.L. (1976). Theoretical Implications in Current Views of Masturbation in Latency Girls. *Bulletin of the American Psychoanalytic Association* 24:109–125.

DAHL, E.K. (1988). Fantasies of Gender *Psychoanalytic Study of the Child* 43:351–365.

ERIKSON, E.H. (1950). *Childhood and Society.* New York: Norton.

FAST, I. (1984). *Gender Identity: Advances in Psychoanalysis, Theory, Research, Practice Vol. 2* Hillsdale, NJ: Erlbaum.

FISHER, S. (1989). *Sexual Images of the Self.* Hillsdale, NJ: Erlbaum.

FREUD, S. (1931). Female Sexuality. *Standard Edition* 21.

——— (1932). the Acquisition and Control of Fire *Standard Edition* 22.

——— (1933). New Introductory Lectures on Psycho-analysis. Lecture xxxiii. Femininity *Standard Edition* 22.

GALENSON, E. & ROIPHE, H. (1976). Some Suggested Revisions Concerning Early Female Development. *Bulletin of the American Psychoanalytic Association* 24:29–57.

GEDIMAN, H.K. (1985). Imposture, Inauthenticity, and Feeling Fraudulent. *Journal of the American Psychoanalytic Association* 33:911–935.

GLENN, J. & KAPLAN, E. (1968). Types of Orgasm in Women: A Critical Review and Redefinition. *Journal of the American Psychoanalytic Association* 16:549–564.

GOLDBERGER, M. (1991) Pregnancy During Analysis—Help or Hindrance? *Psychoanalytic Quarterly* 60:207–226.

HÄGGLUND, T.-B. & PIHA, H. (1980). The Inner Space of the Body Image. *Psychoanalytic Quarterly* 49:256–283.

HORNEY, K. (1924). On the Genesis of the Castration Complex in Women. *International Journal of Psychoanalysis* 5:50–65.

KESTENBERG, J.S. (1956). Vicissitudes of Female Sexuality. *Journal of the American Psychoanalytic Association* 4:453–476.

—— (1968). Outside and Inside, Male and Female. *Journal of the American Psychoanalytic Association* 16:457–520.

LAQUEUR, T. (1990). *Making Sex: Body and Gender from the Greeks to Freud.* Cambridge, MA: Harvard University Press.

LAUFER, M.E. (1991). The Female Oedipus Complex and the Fear of Passivity. Presented to the Meeting of the New York Freudian Society.

LERNER, H.E. (1977) Parental Mislabeling of Female Genitals as a Determinant of Penis Envy and Learning Inhibitions in Women. *Bulletin of the American Psychoanalytic Association* 24:269–283.

MAHLER, M.S., PINE, F. & BERGMAN, A. (1975). *The Psychological Birth of the Human Infant: Symbiosis and Individuation.* New York: Basic Books.

MAYER, E.L. (1985). 'Everybody must Be Just like Me': Observations on Female Castration Anxiety. *International Journal of Psychoanalysis* 66:331–347.

MCDOUGALL, J. (1988). Interview in *Women Analyze Women.* E.H. Baruch & L.J. Serrano, eds. New York/London: New York University Press, pp. 63–86

MONEY, J. & EHRHARDT, A.A. (1972). *Man & Woman, Boy & Girl: The Differentiation and Dimorphism of Gender Identity from Conception to Maturity.* Baltimore: Johns Hopkins University Press.

MONTGRAIN, N. (1983). On the Vicissitudes of Female Sexuality: The Difficult Path from "Anatomical Destiny" to Psychic Representation. *International Journal of Psychoanalysis* 64:169–186.

PARENS, H. (1991). The Female Oedipus Complex. Presented to the Meeting of the New York Freudian Society.

PERSON, E.S. (1980). *Sexuality as the Mainstay of Identity: Psychoanalytic Perspectives in Women, Sex and Sexuality.* C. Stimpson & E.S. Person, eds. Chicago: University of Chicago Press, pp. 36–61.

PIAGET, J. & INHELDER, B. (1966). *The Psychology of the Child.* New York: Basic Books, 1969

RENIK, O. (1990). Analysis of a Woman's Homosexual Strivings by a Male Analyst. *Psychoanalytic Quarterly* 59:41–53.

RICHARDS, A.K. (1989). A Romance with Pain: A Telephone Perversion in a Woman. *International Journal of Psychoanalysis* 70:153–164.

—— (1990). Female Fetishes and Female Perversions: Hermine Hug-Hellmuth's "A Case of Female Foot or More Properly Boot Fetishism" Reconsidered. *Psychoanalytic Review.* 77:11–23.

Sexton, A. (1981). *Complete Poems.* New York: Houghton Mifflin.

Sherfey, M.J. (1966). The Evolution and Nature of Female Sexuality in Relation to Psychoanalytic Theory. *Journal of the American Psychoanalytic Association* 14:28–128.

Sours, J.A. (1974). The Anorexia Nervosa Syndrome *International Journal of Psychoanalysis* 55:567–576.

Spitz, R.A. (1955). The Primal Cavity: A Contribution to the Genesis of Perception and its Role for Psychoanalytic Theory. *Psychoanalytic Study of the Child* 10:215–240.

Stein, Y. (1988). Some Reflections on the Inner Space and its Contents. *Psychoanalytic Study of the Child* 43:291–304.

Stoller, R.J. (1985). *Observing the Erotic Imagination.* New Haven/ London: Yale University Press.

Vogel, S.A. (panel report) (1989). Current Concepts of the Development of Sexuality. *Journal of the American Psychoanalytic Association* 37:787–802.

Wisdom, J.O. (1983). Male and Female. *International Journal of Psychoanalysis* 64:159–168.

****
****

Original publication of preceding chapter:

Richards, A.K. (1992). The Influence of Sphincter Control and Genital Sensation on Body Image and Gender Identity in Women. *Psychoanalytic Quarterly* 61:331–351.

Hilda Doolittle and Creativity—
Freud's Gift

The problem of work inhibition in a woman is addressed in terms of a specific case. The paper investigates the patient's view of how such an inhibition was cured in a brief analytic treatment of the American poet Hilda Doolittle conducted by Freud in 1933–1934.

F REUD MAY WELL HAVE WONDERED WHAT IT IS THAT WOMEN WANT, but in the case of one woman who went into analysis with him and went on to tell the tale, it was clear that he gave a woman what she wanted. That woman was Hilda Doolittle (1886–1961), an American poet with a purported writing block, a work inhibition. Applegarth (1977) observed work inhibitions among women in our times. If Freud managed to help Doolittle with it, there may be inferences to be drawn for current versions of this problem in women.

Doolittle had written some wonderfully terse imagist poems, a minor play, and letters to her friends before her analysis with Freud. She was 27 when her first poem was published in *Poetry* magazine. Four years later a slim volume of her poetry was published. The quality of her early work excited other poets so much that Pound considered her to be the founder of a whole new poetic aesthetic, a school which became known as Imagism. The only way to convey what that early work was like is with a sample. This is the first poem in *Sea Garden,* her first book of poetry, published in 1916:

> *SEA ROSE*
> *Rose, harsh rose,*
> *marred and with stint of petals,*

Thanks are due to the Beinecke Rare Book and Manuscript Library, Yale University for their hospitality and cooperation in the research for this paper. Mr. Louis H. Silverstein was particularly helpful. The letters quoted are all from their collection. Unusual spellings, grammatical peculiarities, pet names, and code words may make reading them difficult. I chose not to alter them in order to preserve immediacy even at the expense of correctness.

> *meager flower, thin,*
> *sparse of leaf,*
> *more precious than a wet rose*
> *single on a stem—*
> *you are caught in the drift.*
> *Stunted, with a small leaf,*
> *you are flung on the sand,*
> *you are lifted*
> *in the crisp sand*
> *that drives in the wind.*
> *Can the spice-rose*
> *drip such acrid fragrance*
> *hardened in a leaf?*

This poem is on the small scale typical of women's poetry, but brings this scale down to the exquisitely tiny, making the moment in time and the few square inches of space occupied by the rose itself fill the entire poem. The rose is unsentimental, absolutely opposite to the lush, sweet, round, full-scented flower of prior poets. It is not given by a lover to his lady, it conveys no sentiment. What is important is the image, the thing itself. And the image is a tough one. Consider the words used to describe the rose: "harsh," "marred," "meager," "thin," "sparse," "stunted," "flung," "acrid," and "hardened." The action of the poem is what happens to the passive rose. She is "caught," "flung," "lifted." Doolittle's inventive use of language is as new as today; the sand is "crisp." Surely this is the contradiction of everything the rose had been in Western culture. Yet the image of this rose is sweeter, the poet asserts, than the overblown fullness we have been accustomed to admiring. And the image convinces.

Although there was no break in Doolittle's productivity, the quality and originality of her work had diminished by the time she sought analysis (Duplessis 1986). She wrote three unpublished and undistinguished novels in the 1920s. A play of no great interest had been completed when she entered treatment with Freud in 1933 at age 47. Freud had requested copies of her work prior to her analysis, in order to become acquainted with her personality through her work. Once he took her on as a patient, he was clear in his intent to enable her to create and equally clear in his recall of this goal afterwards. He wrote to Hilda Doolittle on October 27, 1933: "I am deeply satisfied to hear that you are writing, creating, that is why we delved into the depths of your unconscious mind I remember."

After her analysis she wrote and published epic poetry of a scope rarely attempted in our century and even more rarely in any age attempted by a woman. Her epics are remarkable for their quality and coherence. In 1960 she was the first woman to receive the American Academy of Arts and Sciences medal. She also published several distinguished works of prose in the 25 years of her life after her brief analysis. What, one may wonder, was it that Freud gave Hilda Doolittle?

Fortunately, she left much evidence in her published works about what she thought he gave her. Moreover, inferences may be drawn from the letters she wrote to her friends and those she received from Freud and others. From March 1 to June 12, 1933, she visited Freud six days a week for her treatment. She resumed treatment for five weeks from the end of October through December 2, 1934. By modern standards, this would be far too short a period of treatment to qualify as a complete psychoanalysis, but by any standards, the therapeutic effect would have to be considered spectacular. Whatever it was that Freud gave her, it was clear that she lived on it for the rest of her life. She described it most directly in *Tribute to Freud* (1956), her memoir of that analysis. Her most important novels, *Bid Me to Live* and *The Gift,* bear the imprint of her experience with Freud. In addition, her major poems, "Trilogy," Helen in Egypt, and "The Master" all deal with her analytic experience, reworked through several metaphors: as a war, as an island idyll, as a rebirth, and a journey. It provided not only material to be worked over for the next quarter of a century, but also the freedom and inner wholeness to do the work even without immediate access to publication.

Doolittle's life was a sexually ambiguous one. Her position in the world of letters was established early by a man, her then former fiancé Ezra Pound. Her career, her daughter, her analysis, and her life were supported by her wealthy female lover Bryher (born Winifred Ellerman). Doolittle had married once and had become pregnant twice before her liaison with Bryher. She also had several male lovers even during the time she was living with Ellerman. Thus her sexuality was complex, with male and female partners both important to her. Furthermore, there is general agreement (Duplessis 1986); (Friedman 1981); (Robinson 1982) that Doolittle retained intimate friendships with former lovers for decades after their passions had cooled.

Yet her work prior to analysis was not androgynous, but entirely in the female tradition. She wrote lyric poems, short and full of intense private emotion, like that of other major women poets. But after her analysis she wrote epic poems, in which adventure themes like those explored in *The Oddessy* and *The Iliad* were dominant. Thus, not only the fact of her work but the form of it was what had previously been thought of as exclusively masculine. In addition, she was able to use the epic form to express content no poet had ever used before to express it. She developed a way to explore the classical themes of war and its aftermath which combined travel, exploration, and adventure with specifically female concerns of maternity and nurturance.

The puzzle is how she was able to achieve this creativity. Her letters to Bryher, written daily, and even several times some days, attest to her sense of the importance of what she was doing, her awe of Freud, and her determination to make the analysis work for her. Her letter to Bryher of February 28, 1933 relates the awestruck attitude she encountered in the manager of her hotel before the actual beginning of her treatment: "The manager is terribly impressed, we of Vienna did not know that Doctor Freud took any but the most learned professors, does he now take—ah, er, patients? I said I was working with him through a friend also a lieber Gott Herr Professor of London or words to that effect."

The fact of the letters and their frequency support the idea that she was eager to keep in touch with her family through the analysis, and to reassure them that she was not forgetting them. The family at that time was a complicated one, including Bryher, Doolittle's daughter, and Kenneth MacPherson. MacPherson had been Doolittle's lover. Bryher had married him, supposedly to stabilize the relationship. Although he subsequently became homosexual, the three adults lived together as a family and raised Doolittle's child. If every family has trepidations about what the change in the family members in analytic treatment will mean for the others, this particular, highly irregular family would have had even more to worry about than most. Would Doolittle become heterosexual? Would she lose interest in Bryher? Would Freud try to "cure" her of homosexuality? The reassurance she attempted to provide in her letters surely colors her presentation of Freud himself and the process of her work with him. But it is worth sifting through her correspondence for evidence of what the effective therapeutic action of her analysis consisted of in her own opinion as well as for clues to what may have affected her without her awareness.

On March 1, 1933 she writes: "I stuck to the coat, was ushered into the waiting room and before I could adjust before joyless street mirror, a little white ghost appeared at my elbow and I nearly fainted, it said 'Enter fair madame' and I did." Doolittle presents Freud as both little and a ghost. She refers to this ghost as "it," a presence rather than a person. She may be minimizing the power of this ghost by calling it "little," or she may be emphasizing his spiritual power by contrast with his lack of physical strength. She goes on in this first account of her first visit with Freud: "We talked of race and the war, he said I was English from America and that was not difficult. 'What am I' [asked Freud] I said 'Well, a Jew.' He seemed to want me to make the statement—then went on to say that that too was a religious bond as the Jew was the only member of antiquity that still lived in the world." Here Doolittle describes the opening phase of the treatment in which Freud encouraged transferential statements, especially of a negative kind, since to be a Jew in that time and place was to be hated and persecuted. Freud would have had to know of Doolittle's preoccupation with the ancient world from her poetry which used images of the classical Greek world as its universe of discourse. Therefore, by describing himself as a member of an antique people, Freud fostered her identification with him. To describe himself as a member of an antique race was also to say that he was allied to the source of her poetry.

By March 2, she described him in quite different terms: "He got off his desk, an Ivory Vishnu that the Calcutta psychs sent him, and dug out a Pallas, about six inches high that he said was his favorite. O lovely, lovely little old papa." On March 10 she already saw what the outcome of her treatment was to be: "And note all papas remarks, which may be ammunition against the world, for all time." This intense positive transference was the vehicle for her exploration of her past. On March 23 she described their work together as follows:

F. says mine is the absolutely FIRST layer. I got stuck at the earliest pre-OE stage and 'back to the womb' seems to be my only solution.
My triangle is mother-brother-self. That is, early phallic-mother, baby brother or smaller brother and self. I have worked in and around that, I have HAD the baby with my mother and been the phallic baby, hence Moses in the bulrushes. I have HAD the baby with the brother hence Cruikshank, Cecil Grey, Kenneth, etc. I have HAD the 'illumination' or back to the womb WITH the brother hence you and me in Corfu (island = mother) with Rodeck always as phallic mother . . .[1]
well, well, well I could go on and on and on but once you get the first

[1] Doolittle's ellipsis.

idea, all the later diverse looking manifestations fit in somehow. Savvy? Its all too queer and at first I felt life had been wasted in all this repetition etc., but somehow F. seems to find it amusing, sometimes and apparently I am of a good 'life' vibration as I went on and on repeating, wanting to give life and save life, never in that sense to destroy life (except self-rat to get back to the womb phase, all most natural).

This view of her life and the repetitions of situations of her earliest days seem to have been an acceptable story to tell her lover and patron, to reassure her that the analytic work was not a danger to the relationship and that she was getting her money's worth.

But all was not so simple. No letters from Doolittle survive to tell of the negative transference, but two letters to her from Kenneth MacPherson, undated, but probably from 1933, imply that it not only existed, but was communicated to Bryher as well. Bryher is referred to by her pet name "Fido." "Chaddie" is Doolittle's first analyst, an Englishwoman who seems to have also treated MacPherson. Kenwin is the name of the country house they shared in England. The first letter says:

I understand from Fido that your hour with Papa is now becoming the hour of the dog-fights. That must be too Kenwin to be pleasing! Certainly it wouldn't induce a smooth flow of inner consciousness.

The second letter enlarges on this theme:

You! You and your old man of the mountains. It must be a peculiar state of affairs. I wonder if you like it as much as you thought you would? More? Less? Certainly its an unique experience, if that's any consolation. That playwright female who committed suicide got tangled up with p.sa. I expect she went to some sort of Chaddie. No, someone worse, for it must be said for Chaddie, awful as she is, she DOES put one on one's mettle, till one feels to hell with the old baggage, who is SHE anyway! . . .[2] Anyhow I expect you to yowl gloriously on Papa's couch. Power to you.

MacPherson encouraged her not to be too much in awe of Freud's power or prestige, to keep her sense of humor and her sense of self intact, thus implying that he believed her to be frightened or discouraged by her anger toward Freud. Her fears that psychoanalysis might

---

[2]MacPherson' ellipsis.

precipitate suicide were addressed, but MacPherson tried to reassure rather than alarm her.

By May 3, Doolittle had a completely new understanding of her difficulties which she communicated to Bryher this way:

> *Papa has a complete new theory but he says he does not dare write it, because he does not want to make enemies of women. Apparently we have all stirred him up frightfully. His idea is that allwomen are deeply rooted in penis-envy, not only the bi-sexual or homosexual women. The advanced or intellectual woman is more frank about it. That is all. But that the whole cult and development of normal womanhood is based on the same fact; the envy of woman for the penis. Now this strikes me as being a clue to everything. The reason women are FAITHFUL when men are not, the reason a Dorothy R. or a Cole will stick like grim death to some freak like Alan or Gerald, the reason mama or my mother went insane at the oddest things, the reason for this, the reason for that. I was awake all last night and up this morning just after 7 . . .[3] as this seemed to convince me more than anything. What got me was his saying the homosexual woman is simply frank and truthful, but that the whole of domestic womanhood,is exactly the same, but has built up its cult on deception. Well he did not say deception. He just flung out the idea. I screamed at him 'but the supreme compliment to women would be to trust women with this great secret.' I said Br.,[4] the princess and myself would appreciate it and keep it going. Or something like that. Any how, do you see what I mean??? We have evidently done some fish tail stirring, and if Papa bursts out like the Phoenix with his greatest contribution NOW, I feel you and I will be in some way responsible. This is a thing, for instance that Chaddie fought against, and tried to make out that the monthly is interesting and that men envy women. Well men do. But the whole thing must be 'built on a rock' anyhow, and I feel S.F. is that rock and that perhaps you and I (as I did say half in joke) ARE to be instrumental in some way in feeding the light. Now you see all this in the ucn may also be assisted by our liking the little-dog, as I think we certainly do, . . .[5]*

This letter is partly written in red ink, indicated here by the bold lettering. It contains much underlining and some words in all capital letters. It is the only place in all the correspondence with anything like such

---

[3] Doolittle's ellipsis.
[4] Bryher.
[5] Doolittle's ellipsis.

emphasis. Doolittle was clearly excited as she wrote it, excited by the idea, and perhaps excited by the notion that Freud himself was afraid to say it aloud lest women become too angry with him. More than 50 years later, feminists still find penis envy the most provocative of Freud's ideas. It is considered insulting to women, destructive to the development of young girls, and to be understood, if at all, only as a metaphor. For Doolittle the idea was not a metaphor. Her reference to the "little-dog," a coy pet name for the clitoris, shows that she is thinking of the actual penis, not an equivalent or metaphor. Doolittle's excitement suggests that she considered it the crux of her analysis. It was an idea Freud had been elaborating since he first proposed it in his "Three Essays" (1905). What may have seemed new was the notion that all women, homosexual and heterosexual, shared this dynamic.

The idea of the actual thing, rather than the metaphor, became a theme in the analysis.

On May 15, H.D. wrote to Bryher:

> But the cure will be, I fear me, writing that damn vol straight, as history, no frills as in Narthex, Palimp and so on. I keep dreaming of literary men, Shaw, Cunningham, Grahame, now Noel Coward and Lawrence himself, over and over. It is important as book means penis evidently and as a 'writer' only am I equal in ucn in the right way with men. Most odd. However we will work it all out, only I am sick of myself at this moment. I do, do, do wish you were here.

Doolittle seems to have had a need to feel equal to these literary men in her circle. She could achieve the equality she longed for only by writing, not by the relationship with Bryher. By May 18, Doolittle was regretting having communicated this idea that she could be cured only by writing of her experiences from the time of her marriage in 1913, through pregnancies and the establishment of her relationship with Ellerman in 1919. Their habitual use of initials, nicknames, and pseudonyms, the searching for metaphors in ancient cultures, all the ways that reality had been falsified and evaded must be given up, at least temporarily. Doolittle knew that this would not be easy for Bryher to accept. She wrote:

> This is a bone to you, I realize, but Papa seems to believe explicitly that it would be best for me to make this vol. of mine about 1913–1920 explicit. I am merely collecting data, from the outside, not working with the dream or "stream of consciousness" at all. Papa says that my dreams show that a bridge in the uc-n has been

made somehow and that the whole ps-a is more or less 'over' in the primitive sense, but it will need a lot of guts (my word) my end, to get the thing done in a stern manner and not leap goat-like on the top of things in a dope-y stream of consciousness like Narthex.

This part of her analysis was complete. Doolittle went alone to Switzerland to write of her analysis and what she had learned. The manuscript she produced that summer remained in Switzerland during World War II. In London in 1944 she wrote *Tribute to Freud* (1956). On her return to Switzerland after the war, she wrote a gloss on *Tribute,* using her personal notebooks. It was published as "Advent," the coda to *Tribute.* Many of the details in the letters are reproduced in "Advent": the Vishnu, the Athene, the discussion of Freud's Jewishness, the triangles, the literary friends, and the concern about what is real, what is dream, and what is fantasy. "Advent" skips over the events of April and May, but in June Athene is mentioned again and connected with earlier goddesses. The final note reads: "Some of us, a group of six or eight, now seated on a mountain slope, ask, are we dead?" (p. 187).

The theme of death was to be prophetic. When Doolittle returned to Freud in the autumn of 1934 for more analysis, it was to deal with questions relating to the fear of death. Her manifest impetus was the death of another of Freud's patients, the young man who had had the hour before hers during her first treatment. He had died in an airplane accident. Doolittle feared Freud's death, both because he was an old man and because of her understanding of the Nazi intentions toward all Jews. This had revived her fears of her father's death when he had a severe head injury with much bleeding when she was a child. On November 14, 1934, she wrote to Bryher: "The whole now of the psa is about death, not so very cheerful, but I suppose the boil in the uc-n has bust." This theme was no doubt very important to Doolittle. She had grown up in a family in which death was all too present. Her father's first wife and their daughter had died; her two older brothers had survived their mother's death. Her own mother's eldest child, a girl, had also died. The family often visited their graves when Doolittle was a little girl. Her earliest experiences thus included the idea that females were especially vulnerable to death. When she was a young woman, she experienced the death of her first child as well as the deaths of her parents, grandparents, and siblings. Shortly following Doolittle's first treatment with Freud, Bryher's father had died. He was so significant a figure to Doolittle that she had written to Bryher on September 22, "THE FATHER is the great mind, the sweep of sea and sky, my own father, yours and our dear old 'papa' . . . Those three men are the three wise men to me." Of them, only Freud was now left alive.

But death was not the only theme of the second phase of Doolittle's treatment. The issue of sexuality reappears as the decisive issue in her letter to Bryher of November 24, 1934.

> *It appears that I am that all-but extinct phenomina [sic], the perfect bi-.*
> *I can keep up being a 'woman', even a 'nice woman' for about two hours, then I get a terror of claustrophobia, this is no joke—and have to get to an intellectual retreat, book or pages—to prove I am a man. Then I prove back again. The only thing I want is the cloak of invisibility. That is why it is so hard to be at Audley for more than a few hours. I can act perfectly, the part, for a few hours, then I feel I shall go mad. This makes me, as a 'genius', if I may use the word, but breaks me, as a person. I know you will make allowances and try to understand. It has meant everything to have this connection with Freud.*

The understanding achieved was that creative work, not social or sexual gratification, was Doolittle's satisfaction in life. The bisexuality was a resolution that allowed Doolittle to bow gracefully out of the lesbian activity without rejecting Bryher, and thus without biting the hand which had so generously fed her. The resolution was strengthened by a consideration of the role of identification in forming the perfectly bisexual personality.

On November 27, Doolittle wrote to Bryher:

> *Also, usually a child decides for or against one or other parent, or identifies himself with one. But to me it was simply the loss of both parents and a sort of perfect bi-sexual attitude arises, loss and independence. I have tried to be man or woman, but I have to be both. But it will work out papa says and I said now, in writing. Masturbation with me only breaks down the perfection, I have to be perfect (in bo bo mica?) I may get that in writing and will become more abstract toward the writing in life, now that I know WHAT I am. O, I am so grateful and happy, Fido*

At this juncture Doolittle had found a way out of her dilemma. By seeing herself as perfectly bisexual, by finding childhood roots for her choice, and receiving the permission from Freud to consider herself perfect, she was able to give up trying to make what was for her an impossible choice; now she was free to pursue writing as her main source of pleasure and satisfaction. As it turned out, she wrote for several hours a day, seven days a week for the next two decades and produced poetry and prose of great quality. Some of these works were produced during the time she lived with Bryher in very tight quarters in London during the blitz.

It was especially amazing that World War II with its hardships and terror did not interfere with her ability to write. She had terrible experiences in World War I; the cold, starvation, loss of her baby, the deaths of her younger brother and her father, and the break-up of her marriage had all happened in that war and its aftermath. World War II evoked memories of all of that. She had always required peace, solitude, and freshly sharpened pencils on her desk in order to work. In the blitz nothing was orderly, solitude was impossible, and quiet did not exist. Her newfound capacity to write what she thought undisguised allowed her to write even under these trying conditions.

Among the things she produced in London during the blitz was an account of what she recalled of her experience with Freud. And the central interpretation as described in this book consisted of a moment when Freud handed her a small bronze statue of Pallas Athene, " 'She is perfect,' he said, 'only she has lost her spear' " (p. 69). Such an interpretation would hardly seem likely to empower a woman writer. But for this particular woman writer, the remark had resonances other than the universal one of penis as organ of power and woman as castrated person without power. Freud had asked for and read her published works. In 1927 she had written a play called *Hippolytus Temporizes* which contains the line: " 'let tall Athene have the broken spear' " (p. 31). The tall Doolittle may well have seen Athene as one aspect of herself. The spear is, in fact, not part of Athene, it is only her weapon. If she loses it, she has lost her tool, not her capacity. Similarly for Doolittle, if she does not have a penis, she is perfect anyway. She still has her capacity to create. All she needs is the pencil, the paper, and the will.

"The Master," a poem written in homage to Freud, expresses the same idea:

> *I was angry with the old man*
> *with his talk of the man-strength.*
> *I was angry with his mystery, his mysteries,*
> *I argued until day-break;*
> *O, it was late,*

and God will forgive me my anger,
but I could not accept it.
I could not accept from wisdom
what love taught,
woman is perfect [1983, p. 455].

The alternative to accepting the idea that a woman could be perfect without a penis was, for Doolittle, to hallucinate. The play deals with this possibility. In the play Hippolytus tries to attain love and passion by entering the woods of Artemis, the huntress, and rejecting the rational world of his father Theseus, king of Athens. By choosing the woods over the city, and Artemis in place of Athene, Hippolytus winds up in the bed of his stepmother Phaedra, loses his moral judgment, his sanity, and ultimately his life.

Freud's understanding of the play as well as his recall of the line must have been condensed into the interpretation. His meaning is not that the woman is castrated, but that she is subject to the laws of reason, and that reason is preferable to madness, restraint to lawlessness, and human interaction to the life of the outlaw. Athena is the lawgiver, the goddess who delivered the Greeks from the horrors of talion law, and the passing down of feuds and sins from generation to generation in the House of Atreus. To accept the perfection of Athena is to accept reason, balance, the possible rather than the perfect. It is better to live with the world one is given than to run away into madness.

For Doolittle, madness had been preferable to the acceptance of her woman's body. She had actually courted the hallucinations she experienced years earlier on a trip to the Greek Islands with Bryher. Freud seems to have convinced her that her hallucinations were symptoms, not illuminations, and had helped to reconcile her to her femininity and her bisexuality. After the analysis, Doolittle understood her bisexuality to entail elaboration of the fantasy through her work. She came to understand as well the need for activities that shored up her feminine identity to alternate with the more masculine activity of writing. The fantasy (or theory) of bisexuality replaced her earlier fantasy of damaged femininity. The hallucinations had been a maladaptive compromise. The poetry was a supremely adaptive one (Breener 1982). Freud had not only helped her to become more creative, but had also helped her to accept herself as a person. He bade her not only to write, but to live.

DISCUSSION

Would a modern analyst have attempted to analyze this woman? The hallucinations are diagnostic of psychosis, or, as Freud called it, narcissistic neurosis. The unorthodox household arrangements, Doolittle's age at the time of seeking treatment with him, her failure to benefit from previous analytic treatments, all were factors suggesting that analysis could not help this woman. Modern analysts inclined to diagnostic categories different from the ones Freud used would certainly consider her to have a "borderline personality." Based on these diagnostic possibilities, an inference of early narcissistic trauma would be made. Early narcissistic trauma would be expected to make analysis long, difficult, miserably painful, and likely to precipitate a psychotic episode or end in a stalemate. The particular interpretation of penis envy would not be used even if she was treated with an analytic therapy. Such an interpretation would be thought to be likely to be misunderstood because such a patient would be unable to hear it as a metaphor (Grossman and Stewart 1977).

These ideas make it very difficult to accept what happened in this particular treatment. One way of understanding it is to say that the treatment was not, after all, an analysis. Freud was old by then, worn down by his continual bout with cancer, his endless pain, and his precarious situation as a Jew in the increasingly anti-Semitic political climate of Germany and Austria as well as the rest of Europe. One could say that he was merely assuaging her pain as he faced his own, that he taught her to bear her troubles as he bore his.

Theories about what Freud gave Hilda Doolittle have been put forth by Holland (1969), Riddel (1969), Friedman (1981), (1986), and Jeffrey (1992). While Riddel focuses on the interpretation of her penis envy, Holland considers all psychosexual stages. Jeffrey emphasizes object relations, i.e., Doolittle's idealization of Freud and her identification with him. Friedman (1986) concludes that Doolittle attributed to her treatment with Freud the "explosion of her creativity in the last twenty-five years of her life" (p. 329). In Friedman's view, Hilda Doolittle came to Freud with a readiness to oppose him and gained from him the permission to do that. Friedman specifically discounts any possibility of a therapeutic benefit from interpretation based on Freud's theories of female sexuality. She understands that theory thus: "He argued that in reaction to the traumatic revelation of their 'castration,' girls either became 'normal' feminine women, passive in their relation to men; or masculine women who sublimate their desire for a penis into their competition with men; or neurotic women, blocked in love and work." It is Friedman's conclusion that this theory cannot serve as "a source of empowerment for women's creativity" (p. 329).

Friedman therefore attributes the therapeutic effect of their work together to the complexity of Freud's character. She believes that Freud's maternal aspects and his delight in independence encouraged Doolittle to oppose what Friedman considers his destructive ideas. She argues that Freud succeeded with Doolittle by breaking his own rules, by using intuition (a code word for feminine style intellectual functioning), and by reciprocity rather than hierarchy. Friedman concludes that Freud and Doolittle had a sort of symbolic intercourse which enabled her to continue producing their mutual gifts to posterity for the rest of her life.

Friedman's ideas seem to me to have some serious contradictions. If what enabled Freud to help Doolittle was his feminine way of receiving opposition passively and thinking intuitively, how can he have helped her by fertilizing her? The image of impregnation is surely the quintessential image of male functioning, the one thing anyone must understand to be the good masculine act. To attribute this impregnation to Freud's feminine side results in a muddle of feminine and masculine traits rather than a blend or interaction of them. There must be more to it than this. While I am not satisfied with her conclusions, I believe that Friedman is on exactly the right track to finding the answer to the puzzle of what happened in the brief treatment that allowed Doolittle to leave with such a brilliant result. The issue of sexual ambiguity is the crucial one.

Brenner (1982) would see the therapeutic action of the interpretation to have been a revision of the compromise formation. While Doolittle had been androgynous in her sexuality and feminine in her poetry before the analytic work, she became essentially feminine in her love life and capable of encompassing both feminine and masculine themes in her poetry after the analysis. This view describes the situation elegantly, but I believe that it can be supplemented by a consideration of the narcissistic features of sexual ambiguity.

One could hypothesize that Freud considered Doolittle to be a possible disciple, taught her some principles of psychic functioning and some ideas about development, and thereby gave her narcissistic gratification which helped heal the early narcissistic wound. This point of view would rest on ideas about the etiology of narcissism advanced by several theorists (Kohut 1971); (Kernberg 1975). These ideas are, to my mind, best adumbrated by Bach (1985):

Similarly narcissistic "phantoms" such as transitional objects, imaginary companions, doubles, vampires, ghosts, muses and the creative product itself may be regarded as readaptation phenomena to correct distortions in the sense of mental and physical well being, particularly when these distortions have occurred before the establishment of a firm sense of self [p. 15].

The idea that the "phantoms" are in principle interchangeable suggests that the principle of treatment for these narcissistic phenomena is interchange. For Bach, the therapeutic action of psychoanalysis derives from the capacity of the patient to see multiple perspectives. If she can only tolerate a world in which everyone is concerned with her, she is hurt every time other people fail to respond to her needs. If she fails to see herself as the center of her world, she experiences a catastrophic loss of self-esteem. Either experience can precipitate psychic disaster. If the patient can see that she is simultaneously the center of her own world and a peripheral person in someone else's world, she is not vulnerable to narcissistic wounding. Psychoanalysis allows the person to see both sides of the truth at the same time. If this idea is applied to Doolittle's analysis, by seeing herself as not having a penis but being perfect, and by seeing this as a wonderful secret of which she and a few trusted others are the keepers, Doolittle changes from a patient to an acolyte. By seeing herself as perfect and bisexual, she changes from a sexual outlaw or freak into the perfect artist, the genius. As she remakes her view of herself, she turns symptom into adaptation.

I believe that the capacity to understand fantasy as unreal while at the same time treating it and experiencing it as real is crucial. The idea of alternating between being a man in fantasy and feeling like a woman, which Doolittle so poignantly describes as her bisexuality, is so important because it provides the prototype of the fantasy experience of being and not being, having and not having, doing and not doing. It also seems to me that this view takes account of the adaptive value of fantasy formations as well as the potentially maladaptive consequences (Arlow 1969a), (1969b). In this view, psychic change may consist of the development of multiple points of view, multiple fantasies, and relatively easy transition from one fantasy to another, rather than replacing fantasy with reality or accepting the inevitable.

SUMMARY

Hilda Doolittle's successful analytic treatment for work inhibition, a writing block, was conducted by Freud in a way which impressed the patient as especially helpful because he made two important interpretations. The first was a reconstruction of her early wish to be a phallic partner in a relationship with her mother and little brother. This was encoded in her book about her analysis in the statement that Pallas Athene was perfect, only "she has lost her spear." "She is perfect" was the idea which enabled Doolittle to accept her capacity to create while acknowledging her femininity. Second, the idea of bisexuality as "perfect" was implied in the later interpretation of her identification with both parents at once as having resulted from her infantile belief that she was suffering loss of both parents at the same time. The resolution she achieved was to tolerate alternating views of herself as masculine in her work and feminine in other aspects of her life, especially her love life and social relations.

REFERENCES

APPLEGARTH, A. (1977). *Some Observations on Work Inhibitions in Women in Female Psychology* H.P. Blum, ed. New York: International Universities Press, pp. 251–268

ARLOW, J.A. (1969a). Unconscious Fantasy and Disturbances of Conscious Experience. *Psychoanalytic Quarterly* 38:1–17.

———— (1969b). Fantasy, Memory and Reality Testing. *Psychoanalytic Quarterly* 38:28–51.

BACH, S. (1985). *Narcissistic States and the Therapeutic Process.* New York: Aronson.

BRENNER, C. (1982). *The Mind in Conflict.* New York: International Universities Press.

DOOLITTLE, H. (1916). *Sea Garden.* Boston: Houghton Mifflin.

———— (1927). *Hippolytus Temporizes Redding Ridge.* CT: Black Swan, 1985.

———— (1956). *Tribute to Freud.* New York: Mcgraw-Hill, 1975

———— (1960). *Bid Me to Live.* New York: Grove.

———— (1961). *Helen in Egypt.* New York: New Directions.

———— (1969). *The Gift.* New York: New Directions.

———— (1983). H.D. *Collected Poems.* New York: New Directions.

DUPLESSIS, R. (1986). *H.D.: The Career of That Struggle.* Bloomington: Indiana University Press.

FRIEDMAN, S. (1981). *Psyche Reborn.* Bloomington: Indiana University Press.

———— (1986). A Most Luscious Vers Libre Relationship. *Annual of Psychoanalysis* 14:319–343.

FREUD, S. 1905 Three Essays on the Theory of Sexuality *Standard Edition* 7 3–122.

———— (1937). Analysis Terminable and Interminable *Standard Edition* 23 209–254.

GROSSMAN, W. & Stewart, W. (1977) *Penis Envy in Female Psychology* H.P. Blum, ed. New York: International Universities Press, pp. 193–212.

HOLLAND, N. (1969). H.D. and the "Blameless Physician." *Contemporary Literature* 10:474–506

JEFFREY, W. (1992). Lazarus Stand Forth. *International Journal of Psychoanalysis.*

KERNBERG, O.F. (1975). *Borderline Conditions and Pathological Narcissism* New York: Aronson.

KOHUT, H. (1971). *The Analysis of the Self.* New York: International Universities Press.

RIDDEL, J. (1969). H.D. and the Poetics of "Spiritual Realism." *Contemporary Literature* 10:447–473

ROBINSON, J. (1982). *H.D.: The Life and Work of an American Poet.* Boston: Houghton Mifflin.

****
****

Original publication of preceding chapter:

RICHARDS, A.K. (1992). Hilda Doolittle and Creativity—Freud's Gift. *Psychoanalytic Study of the Child* 47:391–406, 1992.

My understanding of perversion emerged from my own experience of it. I recognized this with a shock when I read Freud's *Three Essays on The Theory of Sexuality*. Of course he was right that oral and anal, and then genital, pleasures mattered most as babies develop into toddlers, and toddlers into children. I could recall having experienced all of these and relishing them as I was growing up. It made sense that the earlier pleasures continued even as later development made them subordinate. And Freud was right when he thought that the genital pleasure subsumed the others in adulthood for many people. And he was right that the pleasures of looking and hearing and smelling went along with these other pleasures and that they all got orchestrated together in a fully functioning adult. But some people did not find genital pleasures supreme. For some people the sensations of feeling pain, giving pain, giving and accepting humiliation, guilt, and shame loom larger than the act of intercourse. For some adults anal pleasure is as important or more important than genital touch. For some, oral pleasure is paramount even in adulthood. The thrust of his argument was that even in the face of the most socially unacceptable perversions, one was looking at a person like oneself except for his or her not having given up the primacy of the infantile pleasures.

I recalled reading some quasi-anthropological but pornographic book about the sexual practices of people in Africa and Oceania when I was about twelve years old. Interest in these exotic peoples had been kindled and sanctioned by study units in elementary school that brought together the geography and history of various countries around the world. That rather sophisticated curriculum included study of the culture of the people of each country. Included in the topics we studied were: climate, food, shelter, clothing, manufacture, commerce, music, art, political arrangements, and dance. Sexual practices were never mentioned. So, at the time, I was just continuing the learning I had been taught to value. But reading about these practices turned out to be sexually arousing. I felt that I had had a secret and forbidden thrill. The idea that it was forbidden increased the thrill. Later when I read Sacher Masoch's *Venus in Furs*, I thought the intensity of a childhood experience like being beaten or being exposed to naked bodies or the primal scene or horrific events accompanied by sexual stimulation could fix the pleasure so that it remained paramount even in adulthood. The thrill would have to be accompanied by the thought: "This is the best. Nothing could possibly be better than this." And that thought would have to remain fixed regardless of the push toward maturation that would ordinarily lead to changes in the forms of desire. But even then, it required meeting the patient in whom I would later recognize a perversion to alert me to the idea that psychoanalysts at the time had fixed beliefs, one of which was that only males could have perversions because all perversions were caused by fear of castration and only males could be castrated. I had to think along a lonely path to find out that castration really meant removal or destruction of the reproductive organs: the testes in males or the ovaries in females. That path occurred to me, in part, because of my having been so interested in horses. I knew that penile ablation was the right way to name what psychoanalysts had been calling castration, and that females prized their gonads just as much as males did theirs.

But even as recently as this year, Loeb and Loeb (2012) published a book about perversions in clinical practice that insists that perversion is the result of male castration anxiety. They support this claim with very good clinical evidence in every one of their beautifully detailed and convincingly therapeutic analytic cases noting that a major aspect of each history was a mother who initiated the boy into perverse activities. Is not such an initiation a female perversion? Their cases all would substantiate Estela Welldon's (1992) idea that the common female perversion is child abuse perpetrated by the mother on a child she sees as a hated extension of her own hated self. Returning to the early studies of female sexuality I found support of this idea:

> [T]he chief effect that the sight of the child produces consists in the revival of the mother's own infantile sexuality. On the one hand, sexual envy is awakened; on the other hand, the sexual repression that often enough has been carried through and maintained only with great effort takes place again. And thus it could be that the hostile impulses that express themselves in the maltreatment of children are also connected with the reawakening of the mother's childhood sexuality. (Nunberg & Federn 1962–1975)

A concise restatement of the work of Laplanche (2004) calls perversion the sexual crime. In this view child abuse is the model for all crime, whether the crime is obviously sexual or more disguised as in the cases of theft, robbery and white-collar crime. Crime always involves a dominance-submission dynamic and thus always has a sadomasochistic form. Whether the person views their perversion as using another person as if they are an inanimate object or consciously enjoys the suffering of the other person, the dominance of the person with the perversion is the point of the behavior. And the end of the perversion is not the creation of new life, but the destruction of the life of the other. It seems to me that the concept of the death drive could only have been posited by someone who understood perversion. Freud attributes this concept to Sabina Spielrein. She was a woman who had herself reached orgasm by being beaten and who understood masochism from the inside.

A new thought: Is masturbation a perversion? Laqueur (2003) describes the history of how modern medicine redefined what had been a common practice as a sin and a danger to mental and physical health, a misuse of the sexual potential and a danger to society. He credits Freud with challenging this view by showing that masturbation belongs to a normal developmental stage which Freud called "phallic." The soothing and calming effect of masturbation can allow it to be seen as parallel to perversion, but then Freud's theory challenges the moral and religious contention that sex is only legitimate if it leads to conception and that delegitimizes pleasure as the goal of most sexual activity. This has a profound connection to Freud's revelation of infantile sexuality as the basis for all adult sexuality and sexual intercourse between adults of opposite sexes with the intent of conception as a relatively infrequent variant of a much larger and more diverse variety of pleasures.

REFERENCES

FREUD, S. (1905). Three Essays on Sexuality. *Standard Edition* 7.

LAPLANCHE, J. (2004). The So-Called 'Death Drive': A Sexual Drive, *The British Journal of Psychotherapy* 20(4):455–471.

LAQUEUR, T. (2003) *Solitary Sex.* New York: Zone Books.

LOEB, L.R., & LOEB, F.F., Jr. (2012). *Helping Men: A Psychoanalytic Approach.* New York: IPBooks.

NUNBERG, H., & FEDERN, E. (eds.) (1962–1975). *Minutes of the Vienna Psychoanalytic Society* (vol. 3), transl. Margaret Nunberg with the assistance of H. Collins New York: International Universities Press, pp. 119–120.

WELLDON, E. (1992). *Mother, Madonna, Whore.* London: Karnac.

PAPERS IN SECTION II
(All papers by Arlene Kramer Richards)

Chapter 7

(2003). A Fresh Look at Perversion. *Journal of the American Psychoanalytic Association* 51:1199–1217, 2003.

Chapter 8

(1996). Ladies Of Fashion: Pleasure, Perversion Or Paraphilia. *International Journal of Psychoanalysis* 77:337–351.

Chapter 9

(1994). A Review of *Freud, Proust, Perversion and Love.* By Hendrika C. Halberstadt-Freud. *Psychoanalytic Quarterly* 63:804–810.

Chapter 10

(1993). Perverse Transference and Psychoanalytic Technique: An Introduction to the Work of Horacio Etchegoyen. *Journal of Clinical Psychoanalysis* 2:463–480.

Chapter 11

(1990). Female Fetishes and Female Perversions: Hermine Hug-Hellmuth's "A Case of Female Foot or More Properly Boot Fetishism" Reconsidered. *Psychoanalytic Review* 77:11–23.

Chapter 12

(1989). A Romance with Pain: A Telephone Perversion in a Woman? *International Journal of Psychoanalysis* 70:153–164.

A Fresh Look at Perversion

The history of ideas about perversion is considered, along with an examination of whether the concept is clinically useful. Three cases of varying degrees of severity are presented, illustrating the clinical value of the concept in the analytic situation. All three cases are women, and the particular usefulness of the concept of perversion for women is noted. The place of aggression and the pleasure resulting from its expression are highlighted.

I want to consider a subject with a long history in the field of psychopathology: perversion. I especially want to focus on the rather murky but fascinating idea of female perversion. First, what is *perversion?* Historically, the term developed in a theological context, and meant doing something contrary to "the laws of God"—especially the use of sexuality for anything other than procreation. In the Enlightenment, perversion came to mean any act contrary to "the laws of nature." As Nature replaced God, physicians replaced priests. With the medicalization of "deviant" behavior, perversion came to be understood as a class of symptoms delineated by psychopathologists. This was the situation just before Freud came on the scene.

In his *Three Essays* (1905), Freud enumerated the perversions: intercourse with a minor or an animal, oral sex, anal sex, fetishism, masochism, and sadism. He then attempted to go beyond classification to define the set of behaviors by its characteristics, and came up with the following definition: *perversion* is a fixed and exclusive sexual aim other than genital intercourse. His definition contrasted perversion with *inversion,* which name he used for homosexuality. He saw perversions etiologically as prolongations in the adult pervert of normal infantile stages in which erotogenic zones other than the genitals were primary. He followed Sacher-Masoch (1870), Sade (1966), and others who posited that perversion is characterized by the need to experience or inflict pain as a necessary and sufficient condition of sexual discharge.

This point of view responded to the need to define oral-genital and anal-genital sex as normal when not used to inflict pain on the other. Having established that the *wishes* enacted in perversions exist in all normal people, Freud accounted for the lack of perverse *behavior* in normal people by positing the repression of such wishes as the necessary sacrifice required by civilization. But the price of this repression, he concluded, was neurosis. "Thus, symptoms are formed in part at the cost of abnormal sexuality; *neuroses are, so to say, the negative of perversions*" (p. 165; Freud's emphasis).

The second essay's developmental emphasis, and its suggestion that perversions are the forerunners of neurotic symptoms, foreshadowed the third, in which Freud asserted that the transformations of puberty led to the subordination of oral, anal, and phallic pleasures to genital pleasure, and that the union of tenderness and lust provided the capacity for permanent union in marriage. This view led him to the conclusion that the endpoint of normal development is "normal" heterosexual union in which sexual excitement and tender concern for the other are permanently attached to one person: the beloved. Others (Foucault 1978; Laplanche and Pontalis 1973) have critiqued this position, as did Freud (1927) himself in his later work on fetishism. While Freud concluded the essays with the idea that normality is the endpoint of development, this view does not convince modern analysts; the perversions are just as highly developed—that is, just as complex and multi-layered— as "normal" sexuality. And the difficulty with "normality" itself, as Foucault pointed out, is that what is accepted as normal is not what is "natural," but is socially determined and changes with social values. How then are we to understand perversion in modern analytic theory?

In this discussion, I will look at perversion as a range of behaviors, and associated thoughts, feelings, and fantasies, that are felt as compulsions. I understand perversion as a source of pleasures that induce a person to devalue the pleasures of making love. Perversion has an antisocial connotation, in that it is sexual pleasure that coincides with inducing pain in oneself or another person. As Chasseguet-Smirgel (1984) put it, perversion is using the other person coercively, rather than in the service of the other person's pleasure. It involves self-esteem in that the pervert asserts pride in being special and better than those who experience ordinary sex (Sacher-Masoch 1989; Khan 1979, Goldberg 1995). Some sadomasochism may be found in any relationship (Kernberg 1991), but the *predominance* of hatred and sadomasochism characterizes perversion. The defining attributes of perversion are, then: (1) valuing a particular scenario, animal, inanimate object, or part of a person more than another person's happiness or approval; (2) compulsion, (3) sexual pleasure and pleasure in the discharge of aggression; (4) shame and attendant grandiosity; and (5) coercion masquerading as love. Any of these attributes can be traced to particular wishes and prohibitions just as neurotic symptoms can be traced to their antecedents in childhood wishes and prohibitions. All of them, combined in a single behavior that is then valued above sex with a loved person, constitute a perversion. This view is new in that it takes into account the complexity of perversion—not only from the point of view of etiology, but also, and more importantly, from the point of view of clinical treatment. My view is also different from that of the mostly male theorists cited so far in that I do not see male perversion as the template for understanding behavior or motivation in women. I think here of female development as seen by Horney (1924), Blum (1976), Tyson (1982) and others as the norm for female behavior; I will not treat it as a variant of male development as Freud (Orgel 1996) seemed to do even when his clinical material came from women.

The comment that neurosis is the negative of perversion seems to mean that if the repression of the wish for the pleasure of a perverse act is the cause of neurosis, the realization of such a pleasure is its opposite. Implied in this definition is the idea that undoing repression will result in mental health. The history of psychoanalytic technique is the story of attempts to refine theory in order to treat more effectively patients with symptoms that do not yield to release from repression. I want to argue that treatment of some of these people can be enhanced by understanding perversion in a new way that includes all five of the attributes of perversion listed above, and highlights the idea of pleasure in the discharge of aggression. I will use three cases to illustrate a range of difficulties common in the treatment of perversion.

After describing these cases, I will look at what has been written about female perversion in the past, and then bring the discussion up to date to examine what more modern ideas about perversion can add to our understanding of the cases discussed here. Throughout, I will keep in mind the question: What does calling a particular behavior a "perversion" add to our ability to treat the person in the consulting room?

CASE EXAMPLES

The first patient is a young woman who presented with what seemed to be chronic severe separation anxiety, manifested as a need to telephone her mother many times each day (Richards 1990). The second is a young woman who could not write the required papers for her college courses, and who, when this symptom cleared up, complained of a compulsion to shop for fashionable clothing. The third patient is a woman in her thirties who came to me complaining that she could not find a husband. She turned out to have a severe anxiety disorder with sadomasochistic features, and as her treatment progressed it became evident that she could be diagnosed a borderline personality. None of these women came complaining of a perversion. In general, people do not come to treatment specifically for the treatment of perversions, because perversions are behaviors that give them pleasure. Perversions are diagnosed and understood over the course of working on the presenting complaints and symptoms. I will argue that these three patients delineate a spectrum of perversions from the relatively treatable to the much less so. I also want to say that perversions are worth treating even though the results may not be the attainment of "complete" mental health.

My own interest in perversions began with the first of these cases. The young woman who kept telephoning her mother had been in analysis with me four times a week for over a year, attempting to deal with what appeared to be her separation anxiety, when she reported one Monday morning that she had called a friend at college in a different city. She called late on Saturday night, and was told that her friend was at a guy's house. She managed to persuade the friend's roommate that this was an emergency, got the man's number, and called. Her friend was irate. "Why do you call me when I am in bed with a guy? What are you, some kind of a pervert?" This chance remark gave me the idea that she might indeed be deriving sexual pleasure from these telephone calls that kept her mother at home awaiting them whenever the patient was away at school or at camp. Her rage at me for saying this led to the idea that keeping her mother chained to her was an enactment of the rageful neediness she felt toward her. Several years followed in which aspects of her development were analyzed: these included torture by her older brothers, being forced to witness their "pissing contests," and being taken to evening parties by her mother when her father was away on business. The torture resulted in an identification with the aggressors that led to her sadism. The way her mother protected her against the torture, by taking her along to parties rather than leaving her alone with her brothers, fostered her fantasy that she was her mother's escort and true love.

Her relationship with her distant and sadistic father was intensified by the belief that he saw in her the brightest of his children; she was the only one he was willing to send to expensive private schools. His distance, combined with preferential treatment, constituted for her a kind of teasing that fed into her sadomasochistic fantasies. I think that this is a clear-cut case of perversion as a symptom that caused pain to others, but was experienced by the patient herself as a triumph as well as a shameful blemish. The patient responded to the interpretation that she had constructed a fantasy of herself as a tough cookie to ward off her fear of being tortured by her brothers and abandoned by both father and mother, and that she imprisoned her mother by seeming to cling to her. She seemed better able to work, began dating, and saw herself as more competent. Several years of analysis later, she called me with her usual complaints of pain, and said that she had been withholding urine until she got all shivery. We both recognized the orgasm that had accompanied the telephone calls to her mother and later to me as the hallmark of her perversion. Interestingly, using the telephone as a medium for sexual discharge against the other person's will is easily identified as a perversion when the caller is male, but at least one colleague has found it difficult to see it as a perversion in this case because the caller was female.

The second patient was a college student who was also afraid to leave her mother. She had returned home from her school in a nearby city after her therapist there told her that her dependence on calling her mother several times a day was evidence that she had separation-individuation issues and should try to separate from her mother by calling her less often. She now lived at home with her parents. Each week they would spend a day together shopping for fashionable clothing. As she described it, her parents would look at luxury items. Her mother would choose something and her father would admire her in it. After several such choices, her mother would actually buy something. Then it was her turn. Her parents would insist on her trying on clothes that were like her mother's, and then tell her that those were too expensive. Pleading for the clothes she wanted was part of the experience, as were dressing and undressing and having her body admired.

Finally her father would give in and allow her to buy something she wanted, but her mother always insisted that it be less expensive than what she herself had bought.

I first interpreted this as an oedipal reenactment in which the mother was asserting her triumph over her daughter, and I asked the patient whether this was her father's teasing way of loving her. She responded with a story about one of her father's friends who was rumored to have impregnated his daughter. Her own father, she said, would never do anything like that. Her response led me to conclude that in her mind, the teasing was a subtle form of incest. The shopping trips were the most important and exciting events of her life; she found her boyfriends much less interesting. When she was finally able to establish a relationship with a man, it was with a professor at her college. Even he was discarded on the pretext that her mother thought him not good enough for her (because he had an ethnic last name). Her continual fascination with a movie in which a scene of anal rape was the central feature led to my interpretations that she experienced her shopping trips with her parents as a forced and painful way of giving and getting pleasure with them; it was so important to her that no man and no other way of making love could compete. Her belief that she was being a good daughter by devoting herself to her parents added to the intensity and immovable quality of this pattern. It was the ego-syntonic nature of this enactment, and its anal and exhibitionistic features combined with the way it replaced sexual intercourse, that caused me to understand it as a sexual perversion. The previous therapist's focus on separation-individuation issues failed to take into account the possibility that clinging behaviors may defend against the emergence of oedipal wishes—especially the oedipal wish to destroy one's mother in order to have exclusive rights to one's father's love (see Hoffman's article in this issue; see also Brenner 1982; Kulish and Holtzman 1998).

The third patient was a woman who had been diagnosed as borderline. She met all the criteria. But she was also a mother and a professional who functioned very well at times—so well that she was successful in her career despite erratic behavior. Once again, the idea of female perversion was so uncomfortable that it was not on my mind as I began to treat her. She began treatment with a propensity to cling, to act babyish, and to demand attention. She reported that she had seen a male analyst for five years starting at age nineteen. During that period she married, had a child, divorced, and completed college. Settled into a profession and busy caring for her baby son as a single mother, she had terminated analysis with a sense that she had gotten a great deal out of the treatment. Her first analyst began to write about boundary issues shortly after she completed her treatment with him. She believed that this had something to do with her treatment, but would not elaborate. When she did not connect with another man, she began to feel quite desperate about her chances for marriage and more children. She then saw another male analyst for several years. That treatment ended badly when she accused the analyst of boundary violations and threatened to bring charges against him for those violations. The case was settled when he "voluntarily" agreed to retire and not to renew his license to practice.

By the time she came to me she was thirty-four. Her son was a late latency child by then. He had begun to have trouble in school, and was questioning her treatment of him. Because she was a single mother, she had enrolled him in an all-boys religious school where she thought he would have male role models and mentors. She still hoped to be able to remarry and have at least one more child, the little girl she had always wanted. Her goal was to find out what was making this so difficult for her. In the course of our treatment she related tales of what had happened between her and her second analyst. He had pushed her out of the office when she refused to leave at the end of her sessions. He had pushed her to the floor when she attempted to sit on his lap. He had spoken to her on the telephone late at night when she was calling him from her bed. She would sometimes masturbate during these calls. She claimed that this was the only way she could fall asleep. She understood that all of these actions were boundary violations. I understood that she had provoked the man constantly and mercilessly. While I initially felt only horror and repulsion at these tales, I gradually came to pity the analyst. As she provoked me, I also came to feel sorry for myself for having this tiger by the tail. As Hoffman has suggested to me in a personal communication, this behavior could be seen as a separation issue masking a sadomasochistic oedipal enactment.

She found many ways to make me angry with her. She called incessantly, managed to figure out my telephone answering machine code (so that she could listen to my messages from other patients), picked up items in my office and threatened to throw them at me or at the window, and annoyed other patients in the waiting room who came before or after her by asking them personal questions. The deprivation involved in our work became too much for her when she refused to leave at the end of one of our sessions, and I would not push her out of the office After having to ask the patient who had the hour after hers to come back another time, I put it to her that if she would not leave at the end of each session, I could not continue to treat her. She still refused to leave. After calling the police to evict her, I accompanied her to the emergency room. After a brief stay in a general hospital, she began looking for further treatment. I referred her to a colleague. They worked together for some months. She believed that she was not getting any better with his treatment, so she called me for another referral. That treatment lasted for another few years. Eventually she felt that it was not helping her enough either.

At that point she began a frantic series of consultations with experts in all different forms of psychotherapy. She "recovered" memories of sexual abuse in an intensive treatment program for survivors of sexual abuse. She tried interpersonal therapists, cognitive therapists, intersubjectivists, a self psychologist. Each consultation ended with the same disappointment. She called and asked to come back into treatment with me. I agreed to treating her in analysis, on the couch, four times per week, with the intent of putting her feelings and thoughts into words. I also told her that I could provide no more than that. If she needed more, she was to go to someone else.

She agreed to this, but immediately began provoking me by sitting up, turning around, reaching her hand out to touch me, bringing me presents, asking to take home bits of things from my office: a pencil, a ballpoint pen, some Kleenex, a plastic cup from the bathroom. I told her each time that she could put her wishes into words and that I would think about their meanings with her, but that I could not provide anything more than words. She wept, said that I hated her, that she was valueless, that she had no right to live, that I despised her, that she was hopeless, that all I felt for her was hate and that I wanted her to go away and leave me alone. I began to think that the last accusation had some truth to it.

Meanwhile, she told tales of her intervening treatments. The first person she had seen after me was a follower of Winnicott. He told her that she wanted infantile comfort, which (he assured her) was nonsexual. He therefore allowed her to sit on the floor next to him with her head in his lap during her sessions. He told her that he was not allowed to touch her, but that she could touch him. She said that she had enjoyed their sessions, but grew tired of them when it became clear that he would not help her attain her goal of getting a husband. She also believed that her work life was deteriorating as a result of her increasingly infantile behavior. He had acknowledged that they seemed to have reached a stalemate and referred her to his mentor.

This man had more experience with severely regressed patients, and had developed a technique that he too claimed to be derived from Winnicott and the British object relations school. He talked to her, but also accepted gifts of food and other things. He introduced her to his wife and children. He held her hand when she was frightened. After a few years she believed that she had been integrated into that therapist's family as an extra child. Eventually she decided that he was exploiting her, and left him. Like all of her therapists, he had told her that she was extraordinarily gifted intellectually. In addition, he encouraged her to believe that all of her symptoms were the result of her very deprived and abused early childhood. I told her that I could not understand why she would want treatment from me when I was so much more withholding and discouraging. She insisted that I had helped her in the first treatment.

She continued to provoke me by putting her hand in my face, by begging me to touch her, by calling and saying that she was going to take just enough medication to put herself into a coma and then lock her door so that I would be forced to send the police to take her to the hospital. In every way she could, she invited rejection by asking for more closeness than I could offer.

During much of the treatment I thought about the feelings evoked in her by my having broken off treatment the first time. I constantly brought our conversation back to the last day of the treatment, to how she had felt and what she had thought. Sometimes I wondered whether I was just being masochistic in doing that, but it did make some space in the room so that we could talk to each other about what was happening between us as well as how that connected with her other treatment experiences. She was the one to bring in experiences of her early life, and we both tried to connect those to that fateful day. Whenever things got too hot for her she would reach back over the pillow and I would see her hand coming toward me; I told her that her only chance to mature seemed to me to be to put her wish to touch me into words rather than into action. She would cry and throw the pillows from the couch, but she always managed to settle down on it the next time.

Of particular interest to me were the feelings she had had when she was allowed to touch the other therapists. Just as she complained about everything and everyone, she also complained about the therapists who allowed her to do that. They, according to her, were not as smart as she was. They did not know that she was manipulating them. I recognized that this was just a variation of her theme of seducing the therapist into feeling superior to the other therapists and to her parents, a fairly common countertransference seduction. I could see how the therapists who wanted to be better parents than her parents got pulled into this kind of thing, and that I was getting pulled into it also. I told her that all of her carrying on was in the service of not talking about what she was worrying about. She insisted that she could not talk about it. I insisted that if she could not talk, I had nothing to offer her. Having read the literature on perversions and on boundary violations, I believed that the greatest danger to the treatment was her insistence on provoking rescue fantasies in me. I thought that as long as I saw her as an extraordinarily bright and talented person, I was playing into her grandiosity and allowing my own grandiose fantasies to overrule my judgment. I decided that I had to think of her as one of many patients, probably someone who could be helped, but neither appreciably smarter nor appreciably worse off than the others.

This attitude on my part enraged her. She insisted that I was not believing what she told me. All of her previous therapists had thought she was extraordinarily smart. Even I had thought so in the past. She mischievously said as she was leaving a session: "I almost got you to hold my hand that time. I am the smartest patient you have." I was shocked to hear myself say, "What makes you think you are the smartest among my patients?" When I interpreted the resulting fury as disappointment at my refusal to take part in her game, she became even more enraged. "Oh, you think I am dumb. You think I am not as educated or as professionally advanced as your other patients. But that's because I am an animal to you. I am subhuman in your eyes. I don't deserve to live." The alternation between grandiosity and catastrophic loss of self-esteem was amazingly rapid and extreme.

Again and again she attempted to get me to prove that I did not want her dead, or to touch her to show that I did not feel disgusted by her. Again and again I pointed out how she left no middle ground for either herself or me. Once she told me that she had sent herself flowers the previous weekend, signing the card as if it had come from me. She grew more insistent that we should be lovers as I interpreted to her that she both wanted and did not want such a thing to happen. I felt her behavior as a constant challenge, requiring me to steer between the regression-inducing gratification of her wishes and the communication of a fear or loathing that I believed would inflict iatrogenic wounds. The counter-transference was what Racker (1953) has defined as *concordant*. Just as I felt helpless to deal with her, so she felt helpless against her desires. I felt at the same time my rage at her and her rage at me. I also felt the disgust she talked of, and understood it to be a reaction to her wish for sadomasochistic sex with me. It aroused the complementary countertransference in me as well. Hers was a prime example of what Etchegoyen called *transference perversion*.

OUTCOMES

The woman with the telephone perversion, the first of these cases, was the most treatable. She completed an analysis, and established a successful career and a satisfying marriage. She was never able to enjoy sex without some enactment of a sadomasochistic fantasy, but the enactment was playful and not objectionable to her husband. The fantasy of power over her mother—enacted by keeping her at home answering the telephone—remained the predominant feature of her affective life, but she was able to understand it and to protect those she loved from it.

The woman with the shopping perversion was less treatable. I think that this was due to her father's death and her mother's insistence that she become her (the mother's) companion not only on the shopping trips, but also in the rest of her life. The transference turned into a tug of war between mother and analyst for the allegiance of the daughter. The mother won. No matter how much I interpreted the triangle, the patient experienced the shopping as more exciting that anything an analyst or a boyfriend had to offer. Yet this woman did finish college and establish a career. She made a "conscious" choice to remain her mother's companion. Unlike the woman with the telephone perversion, she fell prey to the loss of her father and the sudden possibility of turn-ing the tables by becoming as indispensable to her mother as she had felt her mother to be to her. Here again the fantasy of having power over her mother (by forcing her to buy the clothes that the daughter chose) remained powerful, and the predominant mode was phallic. Yet the awareness of what she was doing enabled this woman to find satisfaction in academic life and in her social life with her friends and the rest of her family.

In the last case, the transference was refractory to interpretation perhaps because the patient had had too much success in seducing her therapists and could not forgo this pleasure for any other. Yet she was able to remain in treatment long enough to allow her son to grow up, leave home, and establish himself in both a loving relationship and a career. The mother exercised her power in the transference over and over again, an enactment that made her therapists miserable but may have served to spare her child the brunt of her enraged exercise of retaliatory power. All the patients benefited greatly from their treatments, even though the outcomes were not optimal in the last two cases. Perhaps results like these are what led to the conventional wisdom that perversions are not treatable. I believe that if we accept less than total restructuring, they are treatable to varying degrees, and that the effort to treat them is both worthwhile and interesting.

LITERATURE

Female perversion entered the analytic literature early in the twentieth century when Hermine Hug-Hellmuth (Richards 1990) described a case of a boot fetish in a woman. Hug-Hellmuth asserted that the young woman's love for a man who wore particularly well-polished high riding boots was based entirely on those boots and not on any qualities of his own. Furthermore, this young woman could trace her love of such boots back to her childhood experience of standing beside her father when he was reviewing his troops in his elegant boots. She could not think of loving a man who did not wear such boots. A very long gap in the literature on female perversion ensued. The Hug-Hellmuth paper was ignored until Greenacre (1953) cited it in her work on fetishism.

Meanwhile, Bak (1953) claimed that perversion is always the outcome of castration fear, and assumed that castration means penile ablation. Therefore, he concluded, only men suffer from perversions. That view was shown to be both narrow and inaccurate (Richards 1989) because castration actually means removal of the testes or ovaries. What had been labeled castration fear in the prior literature was therefore actually men's fear of losing potency, of experiencing pain and/or of loss of pleasure. This was shown to correspond, in women, to fear of

loss of genital pleasure, fear of genital pain, and fear of loss of reproductive function. This more accurate definition of castration implies
a whole person with complex feelings rather than focusing on part of
the genital of one sex, and makes it clear how "castration fear" and
perversion apply to both sexes.

Masochism was thought to be a necessary part of female character
(Freud 1924, Deutsch 1930) as it allowed women to tolerate the pain of
childbirth and the ensuing self-denial and renunciation of pleasures
that the raising of children demands. This assertion was interpreted
to mean that masochistic females were not perverted, even when the
behaviors they indulged in were the same as those that would be
considered perversions in men. Zavitsianos (1971) discussed a woman
who masturbated while driving a car on a highway, displaying herself
so that truck drivers could see into her car. His labeling this exhibitionism a perversion caused some people to rethink the idea that perversions did not exist in females. The crucial aspect of his case was the
aggressive nature of his patient's enactment. She was masochistic, but
her behavior was endangering the truck drivers' lives as well as her
own. It was so clearly parallel to the behavior of a male flasher that
it could not be dismissed as normal female masochism.

If women *can* have a perversion, how do we know when a patient
does have a perversion? The perverse activity my third patient repeated
over and over is what Etchegoyen (1978) has labeled *perverse transference*. In the terminology of scientific reasoning, I believe, the
observation is the perverse transference, and the *inference* is the
perverse ego. In my experience, the first observation is the countertransference to the perverse transference. The analyst experiences rage
at the patient. From the rage, the analyst infers an intent to provoke in
the patient. If, on inquiry, the patient is seen to be unaware of any intent
to provoke, or does not see what is wrong with provoking, the analyst
infers that the patient has a perverse ego. The perverse ego is similar
to what Arlow (1971) has called the character perversion: namely, it
appears in an analysis as a flaunting of the rules of the analysis and
in everyday life as a flaunting of the accepted rules of behavior.

Etchegoyen discusses the work of Betty Joseph (1971), who
believes that perversion can be resolved only by being experienced in
the transference. Erotization of the transference, silence, flooding with
words, and passivity all may reflect the wish to attack the analyst—not
merely defensively, but in order to destroy. These perverse aspects of

the personality can appear in neurotic or borderline patients, according to Etchegoyen (1991). The pervert seduces the analyst into scoptophilia, or subverts the analysis so that interpretations are surface pseudo-interpretations that can destroy the analyzing instrument. Etchegoyen takes from Lacan (1966) the idea that the fetish is the incarnation of the female penis. I take this to be the female genital in all its frightening power, as depicted in the Medusa myth. In synthesizing Etchegoyen's clinical observation and Lacan's theory with the idea that the female genital has psychological reality, my view of perversion allows for an understanding of disruptions and distortions in the analytic process as sexual-aggressive perversions in the analytic hour itself.

The great question introduced by the concept of perverse transference is whether the perverse transference provokes the perverse countertransference or the perverse countertransference is a dynamic provoking perverse transference. Those who advocate soothing the patient by hand-holding and other forms of touch argue that the patients who need this are those with preoedipal pathologies or "archaic" needs. They compare their treatment approach to the touch provided by the mother to the young infant. But the mother's touch is not necessarily benign. Can abusive touching be a perversion? Etchegoyen's view is that touch in the analytic situation is always a perversion, because perversion is pleasure in breaking a rule. Understanding touch as sexualized (Goldberg 1995) implies the misuse by the patient of what the analyst may intend as nonsexual touching.

Goldberg (1995) has argued that a physician who had his female patients perform fellatio on him had a perversion. According to Goldberg, "The behavior qualifies as perversion because it was episodic, associated with anxiety, and followed by what John described as guilt, but was often clearly shame" (p. 86). For Goldberg, the sexualized abuse of the other person in the service of shoring up the perpetrator's self-image is a perversion. This definition brings him close to Estella Welldon's (1991) definition of perversion: perverse mothering. In *Mother, Madonna, Whore*, Welldon shows how women use their power as mothers to inflict sexual and aggressive harm on their children through perverse mothering. In her view, the mother is caught in a world where she is powerless except for her power over her child. Isolated, neglected, and disempowered by being denied the opportunity to earn money, she has no other object than the baby for either her lust or her aggression. This leads her to use her child to meet her sexual needs and satisfy her aggressive impulses. Welldon defines this as perversion. According to her, perversion is a syndrome in which the sufferer feels compelled to substitute some aggressive action for genital satisfaction. Here Welldon harks back to Foucault's formulation of powerlessness as the bedrock of perversion. This powerlessness is similar to what Ogden (1996), following Khan (1979) and McDougall (1978), described as a sense of deadness. Ogden's view is that the sense of deadness derives from a belief in the deadness of the parental couple's relationship to each other. I think that the several cases described above show that it can derive from diverse fantasies like that one; what all of them have in common is the sense of powerlessness derived from the infant's inability to evoke caring from a mother, from the toddler's inability to control anal and urethral productions, from the young child's inability to master what is outside the zone of proximal development (Vygotsky 1962, Wilson and Weinstein 1990), and from the oedipal child's inability to seduce each of the parents away from an adult partner—and from the pain of experiencing parental aggression and hatred in each of these stages of development.

In this sense, the frustrated mother beating her child is the epitome of perversion. Welldon (1991) enables us to understand that the mother who sees her child as part of herself also maltreats her child as an expression of her own self-hatred. When she beats her child, it is as much a masochistic self-injury as it is a sadistic attack. There is a paucity of analytic data on child abuse from the abuser's side, but Welldon's case vignettes show the way violent child abuse may lead to perversion.

The essential aspect of perversion is the aggressive dehumanization of the object. The other person is made to serve the pervert as a piece of equipment, valued equivalently with (or even less important than) the whips, chains, dildos, and other props of the obligatory scenario. This is so much the case that when the other person does not appear to be pained or humiliated, the whole thing becomes unsatisfying and the perverse scenario is over. Welldon gives this example: "Suddenly she stopped these beatings altogether when she realized that her baby had a triumphant look and, according to her, "was even enjoying" her ill-treatment of him (p. 74).

Welldon describes a similar outcome in Shengold's (1978) case of mother-son incest. The mother stopped the abuse when the son ejaculated for the first time. Shengold and Welldon both attribute this to the mother's fear of becoming pregnant by her son. But it seems to me possible that the mother stopped for the same reason Welldon's patient stopped beating her two-year-old. When the "victim" enjoys the experience, the perversion no longer serves as aggressive discharge. This fits nicely with Goldberg's definition of perversion as use of the other in a sexualized way in the service of one's self-image or self-esteem. It also fits the alternative explanation offered by Etchegoyen and by Joseph: that the aggression felt toward the other causes the abuse that is the essence of perversion. All perversion is then aggression in the name of love. All perversion is objected to by the pervert's "love objects" precisely because the pervert uses them as objects, not subjects, and thereby dehumanizes and debases them.

Is this dehumanizing another way of looking at what used to be called castration? I think so, because it renders the other powerless. But castration seen in this way is no different for women and girls than it is for men and boys. Being powerless, worthless, disregarded is equally enraging for both sexes. Being used sexually for the pleasure of another rather than for one's own desire is equally enraging for both sexes. Being the one who has to endure pain for the pleasure or convenience of another is equally enraging for both sexes. And all of this is to some degree an inevitable consequence of infancy. Klein (1932, 1953), Etchegoyen (1991) and the Kleinian tradition in general emphasize the inevitability of aggression in human development. Goldberg (1995), Kohut (1971), and others in the self psychology tradition emphasize the damage to self-esteem that is an unfortunate consequence of lack of empathic parenting. Both traditions add to the Freudian view of the decisive role of oedipal fantasies in shaping the later sex life of the person. By emphasizing the self-esteem and self-cohesion issues, the self psychologists strengthen our understanding of oedipal as well as preoedipal influences in the formation of perversions. By bringing the aggressive and envious feeling of the infant to the fore, the Kleinians add another important dimension. By integrating these dimensions, we can rid ourselves of the false dichotomy between perversions in men and identical symptoms in women that cannot be thought of as perversions as long as we use the narrow definition of perversion as a response to fear of castration by penile ablation. The Lacanian idea is that desire fueled by a perceived lack situates perversion close to creativity and to sexuality in general (Jacobson 2003). Both Chasseguet-Smirgel (1984) and Whitebook (1995) argue that creativity is the adaptive alternative face of perversion. More recently, Hoffman (2003) and Pender (2003) have shown that mothers experience aggressive urges toward their infants and children in ways that have not been acknowledged in much of our literature. Pender's cases suffered losses of support or major catastrophes that they understood to require them to "protect" their children in abusive and even fatal ways. By understanding such maternal perversions as attempts to restore a sense of mastery, we can see how women's perversions are precipitated by fears of loss of power stemming from difficulties of every stage of development.

Now we can come back to the original question: What does calling a behavior a perversion add to our ability to treat the person in the consulting room? I think that my emphasis on the pleasure derived from the behavior and the sense of power and control gained from it are more evident when we call the behavior a perversion. By contrast, a symptom is a dysfunction, something we believe the person wants to be rid of; a complaint is clearly something a person wants to be rid of. To classify them all as compromise formations does take the stigma away from perverse behavior and allows the therapist to feel compassion for what might otherwise be disgusting or repulsive. It also allows for investigation of the negative affects of anxiety or depressive affect—the wishes, the fears, the moral injunctions, and the defenses that go into that compromise formation. These are helpful to patient and therapist both. But identifying the behavior as a perversion makes it possible to focus as well on the positive affects. The pleasures of the behavior and the values are vital parts of what needs to be understood if the patient is to have even a hope of giving up the behavior, or of choosing to continue it in the belief that it is worth the loss of the social approval that would go with giving it up. Choice is the important freedom that analytic work can give a person. I believe that this is a worthwhile goal and an achievable one for at least some of those who come to us with perversions.

From a theoretical point of view, the model I am tentatively proposing here suggests that the central fantasy in female perversion has to do with maternal aggression as perceived by the infant and child at each stage of development. The individual fantasies are all different, but they cohere around a core of pain and failure to master what the child or infant perceives as the key to pleasure. This unpleasure is perpetuated by real or imagined experiences of pain, provoked by the conviction, that grows as the child does, that pleasure must be wrested from a cruel adversary or a deadeningly indifferent one.

REFERENCES

ARLOW, J.A. (1971). Character Perversion. In *Psychoanalysis: Clinical Theory and Practice*. Madison, CT: International Universities Press, 1991, pp. 318–336.

BAK, R. (1953). Fetishism. *Journal of the American Psychoanalytic Association* 1:285–298.

BLUM, H.P. (1976). Masochism, Masochism, the Ego Ideal, and the Psychology of Women. *Journal of the American Psychoanalytic Association* 24(Suppl.):157–191.

BRENNER, C. (1982). The Concept of the Superego: A Reformulation. *Psychoanalytic Quarterly* 51:501–525.

CHASSEGUET-SMIRGEL, J. (1984). *Creativity and Perversion.* New York: Norton.

DEUTSCH, H. (1930). The Significance of Masochism in the Mental Life of Women. *International Journal of Psychoanalysis* 11:48–60.

ETCHEGOYEN, R.H. (1978). Some Thoughts on Transference Perversion. *International Journal of Psychoanalysis* 59:45–53.

——— (1991). *The Fundamentals of Psychoanalytic Technique.* London: Karnac.

FOUCAULT, M. (1978). *The History of Sexuality.* New York: Pantheon.

FREUD, S. (1905). Three Essays on Sexuality. *Standard Edition* 7:145–246.

——— (1924). The Economic Problem of Masochism. *Standard Edition* 19:157–172.

——— (1927). Fetishism. *Standard Edition* 21:147–157.

GOLDBERG, A. (1995). *The Problem of Perversion.* New Haven: Yale University Press.

GREENACRE, P. (1953). Certain Relationships Between Fetishism and Faulty Development of the Body Image. *Psychoanalytic Study of the Child* 8:79–98.

HOFFMAN, L. (2003). Mothers' Ambivalence with their Babies and Toddlers: Manifestations of Conflicts with Aggression. *Journal of the American Psychoanalytic Association* 51:1219-1240.

HORNEY, K. (1924). On the Genesis of the Castration Complex in Women. *International Journal of Psychoanalysis* 5:50–65.

JACOBSON, L. (2003). On the Use of "Sexual Addiction": the Case for "Perversion." *Contemporary Psychoanalysis* 39:107–113.

JOSEPH, B. (1971). A Clinical Contribution to the Analysis of a Perversion. *International Journal of Psychoanalysis* 52:441–449.

KERNBERG, O. (1991). Sadomasochism, Sexual Excitement, and Perversion. *Journal of the American Psychoanalytic Association* 39:333–362.

KHAN, M.M.R. (1979). *Alienation in the Perversions.* New York: International Universities Press.

KLEIN, M. (1932). The Effects of Early Anxiety Situations on the Sexual Development of the Girl. In *The Psychoanalysis of Children.* London:

Hogarth Press, 1980, pp. 192–240.

———(1953). *Envy and Gratitude and Other Works.* London: Hogarth Press.

KOHUT, H. (1971). *The Analysis of the Self.* New York: International Universities Press.

KULISH, N., & HOLTZMAN, D. (1998). Persephone, the Loss of Virginity, and the Female Oedipal Complex. *International Journal of Psychoanalysis* 79:57–71.

LACAN, J. (1966). *Ecrits.* Paris: Editions du Seuil.

LAPLANCHE, J., & PONTALIS, J.-B. (1973). *The Language of Psychoanalysis.* New York: Norton.

MCDOUGALL, J. (1978). The Primal Scene and the Perverse Scenario. In *Plea for a Measure of Abnormality.* New York: International Universities Press, 1980, pp. 53–86.

———(1986). Identifications, Neoneeds, and Neosexualities. *International Journal of Psychoanalysis* 67:19–31.

OGDEN, T. (1996). The Perverse Subject of Analysis. *Journal of the American Psychoanalytic Association* 44:1121–1146.

ORGEL, S. (1996). Freud and the Repudiation of the Feminine. *Journal of the American Psychoanalytic Association* 44:45–67.

PENDER, V. (2003). Female Aggression. Paper presented at the Winter Meeting of the American Psychoanalytic Association, New York, January 2003.

RACKER, H. (1953). The Meanings and Uses of Countertransference. In *Transference and Countertransference.* London: Hogarth, 1968, pp. 127–173.

RICHARDS, A.K. (1989). A Romance with Pain: A Telephone Perversion in a Woman? *International Journal of Psychoanalysis* 70:153–164.

———(1990). Female fetishes and female perversions: Female Fetishes and Female Perversions: "A Case of Female Foot or More Properly Boot Fetishism" by Hermine Hug-hellmuth Reconsidered. *Psychoanalytic Review* 77:11–23.

SACHER-MASOCH, L. (1870). *Venus in Furs.* In *Masochism,* ed. and transl. Gilles Deleuze. New York: Zone Books, 1989, pp. 142–272.

SADE, D.A.F. DE (1966). *The Marquis de Sade: The 120 Days of Sodom and Other Writings.* Comp. & transl. A. Wainhouse & R. Seaver. New York: Grove Press, 1966.

SHENGOLD, L. (1978). Assault on a Child's Individuality: A Kind of Soul Murder. *Psychoanalytic Quarterly* 47:419–424.

TYSON, P. (1982). A A Developmental Line of Gender Identity, Gender Role, and Choice of Love Object. *Journal of the American Psychoanalytic Association* 30:61–86.

VYGOTSKY, L.V. (1962). *Language and thought.* Cambridge: MIT Press.

WELLDON, E. (1991). *Mother, Madonna, Whore.* New York: Guilford Press.

WHITEBOOK, J. (1995). *Perversion and Utopia.* Cambridge: MIT Press.

WILSON, A., & WEINSTEIN, L. (1990). Language, Thought, and Interiorization: A Vygotskian and Psychoanalytic Perspective. *Contemporary Psychoanalysis* 26:24–39.

ZAVITZIANOS, G. (1971). Fetishism and Exhibitionism in the Female and Their Relationship to Psychopathy and Kleptomania. *International Journal of Psychoanalysis* 52:297–305.

Original publication of preceding chapter:

****
****

RICHARDS, A.K. (2003). A Fresh Look at Perversion. *Journal of the American Psychoanalytic Association* 51:1199–1217, 2003.

Ladies of Fashion: Pleasure, Perversion or Paraphilia

The author considers the reasons why interest in fashion is important in female development. Freud's comment that "all women are clothes fetishists," and his explanation that a woman uses clothes to show that "one can find in her everything that one can expect from women" are amplified and challenged by other authors and psychoanalytic evidence. Caper's (1994) focus on the erotic meaning of his patient's clothing is contrasted with the use ego-psychologists have made of 'appropriate' clothing and grooming as markers of mental health and intact functioning. A case of a woman who had a shopping symptom is considered. The roots of the symptom in her fantasy life, its replacement of genital satisfaction, its precursors in interactions with her parents and its use in enacting sado-masochistic fantasies is elaborated in the case material. A second case briefly illustrates the role ascetic refusal of clothing may play in some women's psychic lives. Use of clothing as a way of displaying the body, as an indicator of economic power, as an incitement to envy, and as a sexual enticement is discussed. Examples of understanding of the psychological aspects of interest in clothing are drawn from art, anthropology, sociology, political science and philosophy. The paper concludes with the idea that clothing, and shopping for clothing, can range from normal pleasure to paraphilia, and leaves open the question whether it can be a perversion. Focusing on clinical material about shopping for fashionable clothing, the author shows how shopping can become central in some women's lives as it is important in many. It considers the boundaries between source of pleasure, paraphilia and sexual fetish as they are exemplified in women's attitudes towards clothing and their use of it.

> *Full nakedness! All joys are due to thee;*
> *As souls unbodied, bodies unclothed must be*
> *To taste whole joys. Gems which you women use*

Are like Atalanta's ball cast in men's views;
That when a fool's eye lighteth on a gem,
His earthly soul might court that, not them.
Like pictures, or like books gay coverings made
For laymen, are all women thus arrayed.
Themselves are only mystic books which we
—Whom their imputed grace will dignify—
Must see revealed. Then, since that I may know,
As liberally as to thy midwife show
Thyself, cast all this white linen hence;
There is no penance due to innocence.
To teach thee, I am naked first; why then,
What needst thou have more covering than a man?

From "To His Mistress Going to Bed"
—JOHN DONNE (1994, p. 246)

Why are dress, fashion and shopping for clothing so important to women? Freud (Rose 1988) stated that:

All women . . . are clothes fetishists . . . It is a question, again, of the repression of the same drive, this time, however, in the passive form of allowing oneself to be seen, which is repressed by clothes, and on account of which, clothes are raised to a fetish. Only now can we understand why even the most intelligent women behave defenselessly against the demands of fashion. For them, clothes take the place of parts of the body, and to wear the same clothes means only to be able to show what the others can show, means only that one can find in her everything that one can expect from women (p. 156).

At that time Freud thought that the clothes were overvalued because they covered ("repressed") the naked body that women wished to display in what he then thought of as a passive kind of perverse pleasure. But he went on to say that clothes are prostheses for parts of the body. Did he mean that they were substitutes for the penis? He said that he meant that clothes give the message that the wearer possesses all that can be expected of a woman. This is a display of all of the erotic parts of the feminine body. This view, unlike some of his later ideas, seems to refer to a woman's wish to possess an erotic body that is the essence of female allure and function.

For a woman the act of dressing and display are not passive pursuits. They are activities with many steps and many pleasures. The female body is displayed as part of courtship, can be flaunted aggressively to frighten and humiliate men and can be the centre of a woman's consolidated sense of self. In this regard, Freud's comment that not even the most intelligent woman is free of the dictates of fashion suggests that the motivation for that interest is not frivolous, but has psychological import.

Clothing has been of interest to psychoanalysts as an expression of feelings and thoughts of which the patient is not necessarily aware. Clinical case reports often mention that the patient began treatment dressed sloppily or inappropriately and came to look better groomed and more appropriately dressed as treatment progressed. Schwaber (1977), for example, has used grooming as a measure of her patient's self-regard and therefore as a measure of his mental health. Similarly, Bergmann (1985) used femininity of dress and adornment as an indicator of her patient's ease with her gender identity and therefore of her mental health. Bergler (1953), writing in the heyday of conformity, cited many cases of what he believed to be improper or unfashionable dress as evidence of the presence of neurosis.

Bergler also took issue with Flugel's (1930) idea that female clothing was used for modesty. While Flugel believed that there is an essential tension between decoration and modesty in dress, Bergler thought that feminine clothing was always used to draw attention to female sexuality. Even when apparently modest, it enhances attractiveness by allaying men's fears of the unclothed female genital. Flugel pointed out that clothing was used to enhance the body by enlarging salient features of it. The skirt, he noted, would make the female body appear wider and therefore more powerful, especially when it was extended by crinolines, hoops or bustles. Flugel also showed that by enlarging a body part some, but not too much, a maximally enhancing effect was achieved.

Protective functions of clothes are noted by Flugel in that a mother will always suggest to her child that he or she should wear more, but rarely less, clothing. According to Flugel strict differentiation between male and female dress has been essential for propping up the male heterosexual orientation. He hoped that in the future clothing would be eliminated altogether.

Hollander (1994) builds on Flugel's ideas. She believes that the trouser suit as worn by western men since the eighteenth century contrasts with the skirt by emphasising the possibility of activity rather than the capacity for reproduction epitomised by the skirt. In my view, this line of reasoning can lead to the conclusion that by wearing trousers, women signal an intent to be active participants in the work of their society. They then repudiate the exclusively reproductive role signalled by the wide skirt. The clothing presents not only the contours of the body, but also functions for which the wearer intends it to be used.

Clothing has been of importance to women not only in the wearing, but also as the object of a quest in shopping. Winestine (1985) described a woman with a shopping fetish that she traced to a childhood seduction. For Winestine's patient the seduction had resulted in a feeling of helplessness that she attempted to overcome by experiencing power when she shopped in fancy stores and imagined herself the wife of a powerful rich man. Because the patient could not afford the clothes, she enjoyed using credit cards that she then would not pay for, thus cheating the bankers while blaming them because they kept extending credit to her.

Many reasons on many levels of discourse have been adduced to account for the apparently gender specific female interest in clothes. There is the economic view which cites consumerism and the need for someone to consume the products which will keep business going. Advertising to make women believe that they need clothes certainly is part of it, but this does not explain why women are targeted to be the consumers in the first place. Veblen (1899) pointed out that men use women to display their economic success by wearing expensive jewellery and clothing. But this socio-economic explanation does not address the issue of why women are willing and eager to comply, nor why in other times and places, men have worn the fruits of their economic success themselves, as many do today.

Anthropologists and social critics (Simmel 1904; Bell 1976; Lurie 1981; Dalby 1993) have studied the cultural meanings of dress and come up with important conclusions about what rules and status particular kinds of clothing communicate. Dalby has shown that in Japan kimono styles and patterns not only distinguish men from women, but also women of reproductive age from those no longer capable of reproduction. She has also shown that clothing can be exquisitely attuned to seasons, expressing a convention of season which may not correspond to weather. In such uses of clothing the wearer conveys information about her aesthetic sensibility and awareness of social convention without uttering a word.

Why do women need new and differently styled clothes? What purpose does women's clothing serve that makes the garment industry the largest in the world, larger even than the "defence" establishment worldwide? Bell states: "Nor is it easy to know what effect fine clothes have upon a woman when they are worn by a man, or whether women's clothes have an erotic effect upon those who wear them or upon other women" (1967, p. 48). Do women use clothing as a fetish (Apter 1991; Gamman & Makinen 1995)? When do we consider clothing a source of pleasure, what makes it a fetish and as a fetish, should it be thought of as a paraphilia or a perversion?

When clothes are specifically intended for sexual pleasure they can be fetishes (Steele 1996). But women's fetishes do not necessarily represent the same fantasies as fetishes men may use. Though both sexes may use black, metals, rubber, leather or other special clothing, the male use of the fetish as a guarantor of the integrity of the penis may not be echoed in the female use of the same objects. De Lauretis (1994) cites Freud's remark that half of all women are clothes fetishists and Apter's (1991) description of women's interest in clothes as a fetish. While Apter believes that this fetish stands for all the losses a female must necessarily endure, De Lauretis believes that the fetish clothing stands for the erotic female body as a whole. According to De Lauretis the image of her own female body as erotic becomes problematic for the oedipal girl when the mother refuses to leave the father's bed for the little girl's.

This paper considers some psychoanalytic evidence regarding the role interest in fashion plays in female psychology. It briefly outlines fashion a way of conceiving the erotic female body; as a covering for the intimacy of the body, as metaphor for the interior portion of the female genital. It also describes shopping for clothing as an activity particularly related to the female interest in clothing.

Fashion as Covering for the Erotic Female Body

Caper (1994) made dynamic use of one patient's attitude about clothing. His patient had a dream in which she was "looking at some silk blouses on a rack." In the dream her sister told her that cheaper blouses were just as good since they didn't show because they were worn under jackets and the good ones were almost as expensive as the suit itself. The patient had complained the previous day about a suit she was given by her mother. In his comment that she would prefer a sexier one, the analyst had hit upon something that changed the patient's view of herself. It countered the patient's unconscious fantasy that he had been trying to desexualise her. By allowing her to want what she believed others did not want for her, the interpretation also helped her to feel entitled to have her own ideas about other aspects of her life. Clothing was the relevant metaphor for that particular patient. For her, clothing was clearly connected with the female genital issues of sexiness, desirability and assertion of the positive value of female sexuality.

The use of clothing to heighten female experience of the body as erotic is celebrated in advertising and fashion magazines devoted to women's concerns about being sexually attractive.

While Donne's teasing poem expresses a man's cheerful impatience with his lover's coyness in covering herself when he wants her nude for lovemaking, the poem also tells of his honest lack of understanding of why she should cover herself any more that a man would. Why is it that we women cover ourselves?

One answer comes from a little girl who heard a song for children intended to teach them about sexual difference. The song says that "Boys are fancy on the outside; girls are fancy on the inside." The little girl was indignant. "No", she said, "That's not true. When I get dressed up, I'm fancy all over." To the male listener, this may sound like compensation for or defensiveness about penis envy. To this female listener, it sounds like an expression of whole body narcissism and pleasure. From the little girl's point of view, her whole body is a source of pleasure and an expression of beauty. By adorning herself, she is expressing her satisfaction with her body, calling attention to it, renewing it by calling attention to different aspects of it. Her erotic pleasure culminates in a shudder of the entire body.

It is only from the male point of view that the penis is paramount. The male emphasis on the penis seems to her reductionistic. Who cares that much about a body part she can only see and not feel? The boy's experience of his penis as the source of erotic pleasure makes him treasure it and pity the girl or fantasise that a girl must be consumed with envy of it. From my point of view, and that of the little girl, this is not such an issue. A woman in analysis feels misunderstood when she is told that her basic motivation is penis envy because that is not her experience, but a male fantasy of what his experience would be if he were deprived of his penis.

For women the female body is the erotic object (De Lauretis 1994). A grown woman experiences male envy and fear of her vulva as well as devaluation of her feminine fullness. Clothing serves as a barrier, allowing her to remove a bit at a time, testing whether the lover will be further attracted or repelled by her femaleness. Thus the removal of the clothing in stages is an important part of courtship.

THE EROTIC EXCHANGE

A woman in analysis described her pleasure in exchanging clothes with friends. She was delighted that her old clothes were new to her friends and theirs were new to her. They all put the things they no longer wanted in a pile and then each tried on the things that she liked. The fun of admiring each other in the new outfits they assembled was part of their experience she liked best. Other women have described shopping with a friend or a group of friends as a social activity in which they most enjoyed being told what was becoming to them. Giving this kind of judgement was sometimes seen as depleting, sometimes as affirming, but getting it was always pleasurable. The difference between sharing clothes and shopping for them in stores was important. Sharing avoided the aggressive power displays which are part of deciding whether to use one's financial resources to buy the clothing.

When financial resources are not available, not sufficient or conflictual, shoplifting can become the source of the feeling of power. As in the case cited by Winestine, the shopper may feel power in cheating the shopkeeper just as she feels belittled by not being able to buy limitless qualities of what is for sale. As a colleague pointed out to me (Mandlin 1995) women who shoplift may feel entitled to do so to make up for the emotional supplies they believe themselves to have been unfairly deprived of. Such women may feel that they deserve protection, attention and affection that they never got and may restore some sense of fairness by taking. Such women, like the shoplifter cited by Winestine, attempt to provoke authorities into setting limits in the hope of obtaining the protection from their own impulses that they have not experienced enough.

Erotic Shopping

The following case example illustrates several of these aspects of how clothing and shopping for it functions as salient to female psychology:

The patient, Patty, a tall, long-limbed blonde 30-year-old saleswoman in a high fashion optometrist's shop, had been in analysis for several years. One of her most puzzling symptoms was her need to 'improve' her looks constantly. She spent hours each morning on makeup, on selecting clothing and on doing her hair. While she was beautiful, she was convinced that she was "a dog." Having handsome boyfriends made her frantic because she believed that they were always looking for a woman more beautiful than she was. Clothing and make-up were disguises for her sense of herself as ugly and worthless.

She had been very agitated in the past week. After a disastrous love affair with what she called "a poor, dirty, low-class man," she had an abortion. She recalled an abortion she had concealed from her mother when she was 16 years old. When her mother found out, she slapped Patty and called her a whore. Patty was horrified, became docile, and stopped going to night-clubs. She followed her mother's advice on most things, spent much of her leisure time with her mother or with both parents and called her mother every day, sometimes several times in the course of a single day.

Shopping was their shared passion. Patty described these outings as teasing glimpses of a world of luxury. The shopping trips would consist of the mother asking Patty whether she "needed" something to wear. Patty would think of something. They would go to a boutique, Mother would try on clothes, Patty would try on clothes, and each would criticise the way the other looked in their outfits. Patty complained that her mother would insist on buying only the highest priced designer clothing while restricting Patty to lower priced items. A remark of her Mother's that Patty found chilling and believed to be true was: "Well you will never find a man who can give you as much as I can." Unfortunately, Patty believed her. This statement touched on her own fantasy of being her mother's beloved. The fantasy had been nourished by her belief, echoed by her mother's statements, that mother had held her marriage together for her daughter's sake, that she loved her daughter as much as she hated her husband and that her husband, Patty's father, was a detestable man who contributed nothing to the family. This belief was so strong that Patty had difficulty remembering that it was her father who earned all the money in the family. Patty knew and did not know this alternatingly over the seven years of her treatment.

Her mother doled out money to her grudgingly. She treated Patty as her husband treated her and with a similar result. Patty took money from her mother's purse or from her bank account whenever she was desperate for cash or wanted luxury items she could not afford on her own allowance (when she was not working) or earnings (when she had them). Money became the focal point of her guilt and her anxiety.

Several months before the abortion, Patty had moved her lover into her apartment. Her mother still paid the rent. With regard to her choice of men, she said that she was now aware that all the lower class, immigrant, and married men she chose were chosen in the image of her father. I reminded her of a family living in her parents' neighbourhood who had allowed their unmarried daughter to bring her baby to live with them. She had suspected that the baby was actually the result of the girl's incest with her father. By having the abortion, she had renounced having an incestuous baby. After all of this work, I was feeling quite pleased with her strides towards mature self-awareness. She then came in for her next session with a piece of startling news. Although she had been able to control her shopping lately, she had just bought clothes equal in price to a month's salary for her. She'd had so little time, she had not even tried anything on. In this context, we talked about the experience of shopping.

Her conflict over disapproving of her father was complicated by her sense that without her father she was destined to remain her mother's "Girl" forever. This reactivated her need to shop. She even felt an impulse to buy another one of a particular item her mother had bought for her years before. She was pleased that she had not been buying illicitly this time, but was also aware that she had been able to stop herself from buying something she already had. This was something she had never been able to do before.

The shopping spree that had at first seemed to me to be a regression or a negative therapeutic reaction now took on new meaning as an attempt to make some kind of restitution and to see herself as belonging to what she saw as my world. This shopping spree defended her from sadness and potential depression at her abortion. It also served to placate her self-condemnation about the fantasy incest and the disloyalty to her mother, as well as guilt about ending the potential life of her foetus. It also gave her a feeling of power, overcoming her self-induced helplessness. Because she had chosen to get pregnant with a man who could not support a child, and because she had not developed a career for herself which would enable her to support one, she had virtually ensured that she would feel helpless and have to rely on her mother's support. Thus, either having a baby or not having one would leave her feeling helpless. Only the shopping spree actually brought all of these issues to the fore. Her shopping was a clue to the dynamics of her abortion.

Similarly, Patty's attitude towards her clothing reflected her attitude towards her body. Early in the treatment she would buy many cheap pieces of clothing, be interested in them only for a few days and then want more. She frequently borrowed her mother's clothes and those of her friends. She seemed to be searching for another body. She was, I now think in retrospect, expressing with her clothes the restless disappointment with her own body and her wish to change her body back and forth, now thinner and more childish, now fuller and more womanly. Her more recent behaviour has expressed her stage in the menstrual cycle, from times when she thinks of herself and dresses as what she thinks of as "fat" and uninterestingly matronly to times when she feels and presents herself as lean and interesting. Her attempt early in the analysis to be very thin was fought against vigorously by her mother. Part of the mother-daughter drama was the wardrobe changes to match her changing bodily shape. As she lost and gained weight, she complained that nothing fitted her. She used this complaint to justify buying new clothes constantly. In this, she identified with her mother. But while her mother would change wardrobes only once a season, Patty changed constantly. In order to do this, she spent much of her time at weekends shopping. Shopping became her hobby, her passion, her constant companion.

She was ashamed of the erotic aspect of buying clothing even as she punished herself for the erotic pleasure she took in it by depriving herself of the other things she could have bought with that money. As she understood her shopping, it was "a release." She expressed it in highly charged language, more fully realised than any of her sexual encounters with men. "I choose the store. I like the ones where they let you sit there and they show you the stuff. I can hardly afford those. They are too expensive.

"But I get someone to help me in the other kind. I like them to want me to want it. I like to leave them with it. I like it best when it is just a little too expensive and I can't get it."

Earlier in her treatment she would go on shopping trips with both parents. A sadomasochistic pattern extending back to her childhood was repeated on these trips. As she described it: "When it's my birthday or something, they won't get me a present. But my Mom says I can have a new thing, whatever it is I want. So I go to a store and I find something. Then I go call my Mom and ask her. She won't let me have it. But she says: 'Okay. We'll go for a walk on Saturday.' My Dad comes on these trips with me sometimes. I hate it when she says: 'Yes' and he says: 'No.' I hate when they both do it. She says 'Yes'; he says 'No.' He can't stand it, but he's the one who says he wants to get me a present. They make me beg for it."

For this woman, the erotic interaction around buying clothes was part of a sadomasochistic character disorder of the sort Arlow (1971) described as a perverse character. In the earlier stages, it had been more in her character. In the analysis, it became dystonic and she became more aware of how it replaced all other forms of excitement and pleasure for her. She mourned giving it up even as she understood it as precluding pleasure in her erotic experiences with lovers.

Fashion Seasons

Mary, a very successful career woman patient reports: 'I went to the doctor yesterday. He told me I had started menopause. Not what I wanted to hear. Why does this have to happen now? Anyway, my first thought was to go and spend a thousand dollars on clothes. That kind of a spree would cheer me up. You don't have to worry. I won't actually do it. I would have four years ago. But now I just feel the impulse'. This woman is always afraid of losing her mother and father, both of whom have had life-threatening chronic illnesses since their daughter was 8 years old. Now in her fifties, she is still living in dread of her parents dying even though they are now in their eighties and have seen her through the decades of her childhood, adolescence and young adulthood. She stands at the brink of a transition into the last decades of her own life, still as frightened of their death and of her own as she was when a little girl. Knowing that she is no longer dependent on them is something that she is only attaining now.

Both she and her parents enjoyed an anniversary card she sent them recently showing a little girl saying 'This card is a miracle. I paid for it with my own money'. She has needed loans from them all her life. Often these loans went to pay for clothes she bought on her sprees. Although she has earned a lot of money in her life and complains that her closets are crammed with beautiful clothes she never wears, she has shopped for comfort at every hint that she could be getting more successful, more responsible or more secure in her relationships. I connected shopping for clothing with a fantasy she had talked of years earlier of having a rich and powerful father who would always be there to protect her. Thus, she was a dependent little girl in order to protect the fantasy from the encroachments of the passage of time.

She denied the passage of time by focusing on her spring wardrobe, her need for new clothes for summer and her feeling of anticipation for each new season. She kept herself very busy emptying her closets of the clothes of the last season, cleaning and relining her drawers, ironing, shortening, lengthening, taking in and letting out. It was crucial to her to have the exact new item featured in the latest fashion magazine. When all of her concern with seasons was interpreted as a wish to avoid the passage of linear time, she railed at me. But she was able to cut back significantly on the amount of time she spent in preparing her seasonal wardrobe, a gain which allowed her to spend more time in productive work in her career.

Refusal as Aesthetic

Elinor had a passion for shopping which usually eventuated in her buying nothing. Her weekend hobby was shopping for clothing and jewellery which she would return during the following week. She constantly yearned for clothes, felt satisfied when she was buying them and hated them when she "felt trapped" into keeping them because she had bought them. Old clothes, "antique" clothes were more acceptable. She enjoyed knowing that the antique dealers she bought them from would not accept returns.

Months after this patient had experienced some relief from her continual need to shop one of her uncles died. At the funeral the uncle's daughter thanked her for coming. The patient felt terribly sad. She reflected that she did not think that the death of her relative would make much difference to her own life. She then realised that the death of her own father had made little difference to her cousin. Her mourning for this relative was minimal, but she began shopping in a way she called an addiction. The pattern was so severe that she would get to know the salespeople in stores and would feel embarrassed for causing them so much trouble with her constant demands on their time and energy both to sell her the things and to issue the credits to her for returning them. Sometimes she would give the clothes away to relatives or friends rather than take them back to the store where she had bought them. Elinor wore the same winter coat for a decade while trying to find a substitute. She could not find anything that she felt comfortable in.

Her shopping pattern had been set when she was a little girl. She recalled being taken to a large city near her home town to buy new clothes for each new season. She and her mother would choose many things, but she would return most of them. In her analysis it became clear that both she and mother had been doing and undoing.

What was needing to be undone was related to the early death of mother's father. She was undoing what she feared, her own mother's early death. Her fear of the loss of her mother was concretely embodied in the buy and return cycle. It provided comforting proof that anything could be undone, nothing was final, nothing was irreversible, not even death.

When she had been in analysis for several years, she allowed herself more. Clothing now had to do with pleasure rather than seasonal fashion in the service of the denial of death. One day she came in and said: 'I bought a coat. It cost several hundred dollars. It's soft and classic. My kind of thing. It is amazing that I did it. And I'm keeping it. You probably don't believe it, but it was between two coats and this was the one I had wanted for a long time. I didn't need it. There were these two coats when it came down to it. The saleswoman said that the other coat was stunning. It would be great. She said people will stop you on the street in that one. It's more different. Has more style. But I knew I wanted the other one.' When I brought it home, my husband said it was elegant, just like me, but I think it's classic, simple.'

A: Your husband finds it elegant because he thinks it's essentially you—the elegance of renunciation.

P: No. That's saying too much. I was worried. What if I leave it in a taxi and lose X number of hundred dollars.

A: X number?

P: Preciousness. I feel childish and humiliated—small. You would think of a shopping spree as spending $5,000 in a day. I think of hundreds.

A: You can't see yourself as having more than I do. The older person has to have more. Like with your mother having all the dresses in her closet and you borrowing.

P: I have my own taste. I don't care about labels. I'm not stupid enough to be interested in that. I don't care about that.

The next day she came in and said: I had this disturbing dream. I was leaving my apartment, but there was something wrong with the lock. I could not lock the door. So I went back in and checked the apartment as I frequently do in real life. I looked under one bed, then I looked under another. Finally, I looked under the other bed. A hand and arm pulled me in. I woke myself up.

It has to do with the coat I bought yesterday. It has something about being single. Before Bobby moved in with me, I never worried about such things. Now when he goes on a business trip, I have to keep a light on at night. The thing is that I don't know how to understand it. Why should I feel vulnerable now? It has something to do with the voice I heard last Saturday. Both Bobby and I woke up and we both heard it, it wasn't just me. A woman was screaming. She was saying: 'Stop it. Stop'. I thought she was getting killed. I remember in our last apartment there was a woman who would scream every Sunday morning. I'd be home alone wile Bobby was at church. She'd moan and scream. I hated hearing it. I can't figure out what was so bad about it.

A: The dream and the fears are about being sexual. And how it is like being killed.

P: No. It is not like that. It is something else. Well, the thing is, it is something about being married.

A: Like being married makes you more vulnerable, but that seems not to make sense, after all a husband can protect you.

Later in that same session I suggested that she was afraid that I would pull her into my sphere from under the couch. The saleslady who wanted to sell her the wrong coat was like me in that I wanted to make her into someone she did not want to be.

She asserted that she believed I wanted her to be what I wanted, not what she wanted. For her, wearing clothes a woman would like was being attractive to a woman, something she fought against wanting.

The question of whether women dress for men or for other women may be answered differently for different women. For some women, competition is important, for others seduction is paramount, for still others the change of costume is a change of persona. For this patient, it was clearly related to the issue of object choice. It would seem almost obvious that this would be true for all women. To the extent that it is a sublimated expression of object choice, dress is part of culture. Yet no matter how far it is from overt sexual stimulation, dress is selection of that which touches the skin and therefore that which is closest to the body. Thus, it excites skin eroticism and lends itself to fetishistic use.

For another patient, Lola, torn or defaced clothing had great erotic meaning. She reported this dream:

I am in a room with my mother. I am wearing torn and ripped jeans and embarrassing people. My mother wants me to change. I decided to leave so I started packing. I was sweeping up the floor and I found little lumps of shit. It could be dog shit or human shit. It didn't matter which it was, I needed to sweep it up anyway. I did it frantically.

She recalled that she had actually had a similar conversation with her mother about a torn sweater she wore when she was visiting her parents' home and recalled that her mother had shamed her into changing it. She then recalled seeing one of her lesbian friends dressed as a 'drag king'. Saying that she thought her friend looked wonderful, the patient wondered whether she herself was aroused by the hypermasculine style regardless of whether it was affected by a biological male or a biological female. She recalled going to a party with a woman friend who had just broken up with a man. The patient worried that her friend might compete with her for a lover. Then she said "My new motto is sex, I want to have some."

For the rest of that session she talked about the themes of competition for lovers, sexually attractive clothes, and cleaning. These different themes reminded me of a story she had recently told me about coming home from college to find that her parents had moved their old bed into her room. She was indignant that the mattress cover still had her father's semen stains on it. Her mother had said that she shouldn't get so upset, by her age she should be aware that her parents had sex. I reminded her of this story and said that her mother had seemed to her to be parading her father's sexual emissions as a trophy to show her daughter that the mother was the winner in the oedipal war. The semen stains had been represented in the dream by the shit and by the torn clothing. In the dream she was embarrassing her mother while in the life event her mother had embarrassed her. For this woman, the clothing was a metaphor for sexual excitement in the drag king anecdote, and a symbol of shame in the ripped jeans.

DISCUSSION

Elinor's clothes shopping pattern was one of refusal. Lola refused in a different way, choosing ragged clothing as a refusal of everything her parents could give her. Their ways of being ascetic contrast with Patty's pattern of bingeing by buying more than she could reasonably use. Mary's seasonal shopping and refurbishing was also like a bulimia in that she used an excess in the service of her refusal to accept the reality of her aging.

It would be possible to see Elinor's and Patty's shopping pattern as a bulimia in which the pleasures are of gorging and vomiting. Both women wanted to have more of the mothering and of an erotic relationship with the mother than they were able to allow themselves. Both used clothing and shopping for clothing to express fantasies of loving and being loved by mother. Because shopping for clothes is such a female occupation in our culture, girls experience shopping with mother as sharing a closeness and acceptable erotic experience. This use of clothing as a female sharing is charmingly depicted by Beckerman (1995) in an elegy to her mother called *Love, Loss and What I Wore*. When there are fantasies about the mother-daughter relationship that cannot be expressed in words, they may be enacted in these 'perverse' scenarios.

Why do women develop this symptom? Clothing has an importance for women which goes beyond the meaning it has for most men. As decoration for the body, it calls attention to the features and proportions considered sexually attractive. As seen in the first case, it can serve many functions. Shopping for clothing can be a celebration of the body, as when Patty and her mother displayed themselves to each other in different outfits.

It can defend against sadness and loss as it did when Patty bought new clothes after her abortion. It can serve as a battleground for conflicting value systems as it did when Patty bought things her parents could afford and when she shopped in discount or 'off the truck' bargain places. That kind of shopping expressed her condemnation of her own greed when she consoled herself that she had spent less than the clothing was worth. It enabled her to indulge in the fantasy of having unlimited power when she bought without thinking of how she would pay for things.

She was able to use shopping as a strip tease in the dressing rooms she would share with her mother. The erotic aspect of showing herself was further enhanced when her father came along and when salesladies were consulted for their opinions on how she looked in the things she tried on. It became problematic for her when it involved the teasing game of pleading with her parents for things that cost more than they wanted to spend. It became debilitating when she substituted it for genital pleasures. Her statement that 'No man will be able to buy this for me' expressed her conflict. She could only allow herself to indulge in this form of erotic pleasure when she gave up men for mother as mother had for her.

Patty needed new clothes so often because she believed that her body was ugly. She was able to give up the very frequent shopping when she recognised that new clothes always seemed to her to offer hope of changing but did not ever really change the body beneath. Patty's analysis offers an illustration of the generalisation that clothes which conceal the body beneath them also take on the body beneath them so that patients who hate their own bodies will hate their clothes soon after they buy them.

When is shopping for clothing pleasure something worth thinking of as a paraphilia or perversion (Kaplan 1991)? Perversion is a term reserved for behaviour preferred to coitus, usually understood to have a large component of aggression in that it alienates the pervert from potential partners. Paraphilia is defined in the DSM-III-R (1987) as: "Arousal in response to sexual objects and situations that are not part of normal arousal-activity patterns and that in varying degrees may interfere with the capacity for reciprocal, affectionate sexual activity".

But this definition begs the question in that it does not describe what are "normal arousal-activity patterns". Is spanking normal? Is dressing up as a bunny normal? As a fireman? As a devil? Is a velvet glove normal? A whip? Is using one of these props normal? How about candlelight? Mirrors? Nipple rings? It seems that there is such a variety of possible means of arousal that no one could possibly categorise all of them as normal or abnormal.

In practice, I believe, clinicians think of a behaviour as a paraphilia worth trying to remove when the patient sees it as a symptom. We call the same behaviours perversions when they entail social opprobrium. For the clinician this variety has serious consequences. When a patient says that she prefers shopping to having a boyfriend, is that to be construed as a perversion? Is it simply a paraphilia or preference? From these cases and many others in my practice, I think it is the driven quality, the need, the constant renewal of a sense of need when there is no rational need that requires the understanding of this as a perversion, or, to put it more usefully, a perverse symptom. The advantage of thinking of it as a symptom is that it becomes a cue for analysis rather than for condemnation. Thus, clothing used for pleasure is not a symptom, used as a paraphilia, it replaces sexual pleasure and used as a perverse object it defies social convention as well as the human beings who would ordinarily be the objects of sexual desire. If a pair of black boots is worn for its sensual pleasure or to attract a lover, it is part of normal sexuality. If wearing the boots is more important than the other person, it is a paraphilia. If they are worn to harm or spite others and especially to deny their humanity, it is a perversion.

All of the women discussed in this paper used clothing for the "normal" purposes other people use it for. Clothing as costume is part of the embodiment or enactment of fantasy that keeps young children playing by the hour. For adults, fashion can be a fantasy of being a younger person or an older one, being a cowboy or an Arab, trying on in fantasy roles that will never be available in ordinary life. In this sense, dress is a clue to unconscious fantasy (Arlow 1969) and a part of enactment. For Freud (1907) this kind of fantasy was the kernel of creativity and the centre of psychic life. The reality created in such fantasy not only consoled the person, but also provided the basis for change and ongoing development.

As Freud put it in his early remark about all women being clothes fetishists (Rose 1988), a woman needs clothes to display that she has the female attributes. Here Freud speaks in a modern way about the entire body, not as a metaphor for the penis, but as what is important to a woman. Because the erotic body is paramount to a woman (De Lauretis 1994), the clothing which can alter, disguise, emphasise and even create body shape is valuable.

How does this analytic understanding match up with what has been done on this subject in other fields? Shakespeare took the economic view when he wrote: "Our purses shall be proud, our garments poor, / For 'tis the mind that makes the body rich." But Shakespeare here undervalues the use of fashion. For the woman who wants to use clothing to express other values, the cost is not the point. By dressing, a woman can use her mind to alter her body with clothing and cosmetics in ways that allow her to express her mind through her bodily appearance.

While Veblen believed that clothing is mainly used to provide evidence of the earning power of the householder, Bell (1967) discussed many ways clothing expresses values. Sumptuary laws show that dress can be used to display wealth. Rare or difficult-to-find materials and workmanship that need many hours of hand labour enhance the perceived value of the clothing. By dressing in archaic or avant-garde fashion, the wearer can make a statement about her place in society and her opinion on whether the good old days are preferable to the future. A woman can use clothing and grooming to display conspicuous leisure as shown in long fingernails, time-consuming hairdos, frequent changes of clothing and clothing that takes a long time to put on and adjust and by maintaining an attenuated body.

Artists have been paying attention to the role of fashion and clothing in the human experience. The visual arts have focused on clothing and fashion as expressions of feeling about the body in various ways. Zahm (1995) discusses the fashion of one designer who draws attention to the seasonal and timely aspects of fashion by refusing to change his clothing offerings every season. By recycling other people's designs from the past as well as his own past designs, he draws attention to the artificiality of having new clothes for each season and new clothes that are different from those worn in the corresponding season of past years. In addition, this designer takes the hidden construction elements of clothing and displays them. Thus, he undoes the clothing message that there are secrets contained in the body covering.

The idea of secrets in clothing was carried a step further by Leone & Macdonald (Meyer 1994). These artists shredded and made into paper their entire shared wardrobe. The wardrobe itself is memorialised in a hand-made book documenting the garments that went into the paper. By calling it 'foolscap' the artists recycle their clothing, changing it from the choice of images imposed on them by the fashion industry to an entirely self-chosen image, created to express their own needs for paper rather than body coverings. Another take on clothing comes from the artist Annett Messager (Conklin 1992). She used old dresses as relics, attaching pleas and prayers to them. She was pointing out the function of clothing to mark particular occasions or sequences of the life of the wearer and the effects on the spectator who may want some of the same. This use of clothing remarks on clothing as body part and relates to the aura of the person who wears the clothing as it attaches to the clothing itself. It seems to me to be parallel to my patient's use of clothing to change her body and particularly to her hatred of clothing that had already taken on her aura.

Clothes empty of wearers (Felshin 1993) convey another aspect of the role of clothing in female identity. While they may memorialise particular wearers, empty clothes, especially if they have never been worn, have another function as well. The empty clothes allow the viewer to "try on" or "fit" herself into the clothes. By taking the dimensions of the clothing as ideal, she can measure herself against what is expected or considered desirable.

Artists have shown, in sum, that clothing lends itself to make-believe, to secrets and to emphasis. All of these aspects of clothing are akin to the accessories of paraphilia. Clothes are disguises, but they also reveal the feelings of the wearer.

Clothes lie, but they tell the truth of what the wearer wishes she was. Clothes protect, but they put the fantasies of the wearer right out where the observer can see them and draw his or her conclusions.

Philosophers have taken up the question of why women value dress. Barthes (1993) subjected fashion to a structural analysis similar to that used for linguistic structures. He described the system of description of fashion and compared it with the structures of what was being described. Hanson (1993) alerts the reader to the concerns that philosophy has brought to the subject of dress. She asserts that dress has been devalued by philosophers for being superficial, concerned with change rather than with the unchanging, unable to withstand or defy the vicissitudes of death, based on the human body rather than the soul and passive rather than active in that it reduces the wearer to being the object of the gaze of the artist rather than the active subject. All of this is true despite Plato's equation of the beautiful with the good. Hanson concludes that female interest in fashion could expand man's appreciation of embodiment, being in a body and adorning it for pleasure, this could expand human consciousness and self-knowledge. This paper is an attempt in that direction.

Rather than ignore clothing, shopping for clothing and fashion interest as superficial and trivial, I suggest that we attempt to use our patients' interest in clothing as an important avenue to understanding their psychology. If clothing is intermediate between the body and the world, it speaks of what the wearer wants to convey of her body. It tells the observer something about the wearer's wishes, fears and moral judgements. It can express the power of the money spent on it and thus the power of the wearer or her supporters, parents or spouse. It can reflect much time and effort spent on selection and acquisition. It can be costume for a part the wearer is playing in her own life drama. I believe that seeing it in this way may enable us to see the compromise formation in degrees of pathology ranging from pleasure through neurotic symptom to paraphilia to perversion.

I am grateful to Janice Lieberman, Lynne Rubin, and all of the members of the RAPS Study Group on Female Psychology of the Association for Psychoanalytic Medicine for reading and generously contributing to this paper.

REFERENCES

APTER, E. (1991). *Feminizing the Fetish: Psychoanalysis and Narrative Obsession in Turn-of-the-Century France.* Ithaca, NY: Cornell University Press.

ARLOW, J. (1969). Fantasy, Memory and Reality Testing. *Psychoanalytic Quarterly* 38:28–51.

———— (1971). Character perversion. In *Currents in Psychoanalysis,* I. Marcus, ed. New York: International Universities Press, pp. 317–336.

BARTHES, R. (1990). *The Fashion System.* Berkeley: University of California Press.

BECKERMAN, I. (1995). *Love, Loss, and What I Wore.* Chapel Hill: Algonquin.

BELL, Q. (1967). *On Human Finery.* New York: Schocken.

BERGLER, E. (1953). *Fashion and the Unconscious.* New York: Brunner.

BERGMANN, M.V. (1985). The Effect of Role Reversal on Delayed Marriage and Maternity. *Psychoanalytic Study of the Child* 40: 197–219.

CAPER, R. (1994). What Is a Clinical Fact? *International Journal of Psychoanalysis* 75:903–913.

CONKLIN, J. (1992). Annette Messager. (Exhibition pamphlet) Ames, Iowa.

DALBY, L. (1993). *Kimono.* New Haven: Yale University Press.

DAVIS, F. (1992). *Fashion, Culture and Identity.* Chicago: University of Chicago Press.

DE LAURETIS, T. (1994). *The Practice of Love: Lesbian Sexuality and Perverse Desire.* Bloomington, IN: Indiana Univ. Press.

DONNE, J. & HERRICK, H. (1948). *The Love Poems of Robert Herrick and John Donne.* Louis Untermeyer, ed. NY: Dorset Press, 1994.

FELSHIN, N. (1993). *Empty Dress: Clothing as Surrogate in Recent Art.* New York: Independent Curators.

FLUGEL, J. (1930). *The Psychology of Clothes.* London: Hogarth Press.

FREUD, S. (1908). Creative Writers and Daydreaming. *Standard Edition* 9.

———— (1927). Fetishism. *Standard Edition* 21.

GAMMAN, L. & MAKINEN, M. (1994). *Female Fetishism.* NY: New York University Press

HANSON, K. (1993). Dressing down Dressing Up. In *Aesthetics in Feminist Perspective,* H. Hein & Korsmeyer, eds.. Bloomington, IN: Indiana University Press.

HOLLANDER, A. (1994). *Sex and Suits.* New York: Knopf.

KAPLAN, L. (1991). Women Masquerading as Women. In *Perversions and Near Perversions in Clinical Practice,* G. Fogel & W. Meyers, eds. New Haven: Yale University Press.

LURIE, A. (1981). *The Language of Clothes.* New York: Random House.

MANDLIN, H. (1995). Private communication.

MEYER, R. (1994). *Leone & Macdonald: Double Foolscap.* New York: Whitney Museum.

ROSE, L. (1988). Freud and Fetishism: Previously Unpublished Minutes of the Vienna Psychoanalytic Society. *Psychoanalytic Quarterly* 57:147–160.

SCHWABER, E.A. (1977). Understanding Unfolding Narcissistic Transference.

International Journal of Psychoanalysis 4:493–502.

SIMMEL, G. (1904). Fashion. *International Quarterly* 10.

STEELE, V. (1996). *Fetish.* New York: Oxford University Press.

WINESTINE, M. (1985). Compulsive Shopping as a Derivative of a Childhood Seduction. *Psychoanalytic Quarterly* 54:70–73.

VEBLEN, T. (1899). *The Theory of the Leisure Class.* New York: Macmillan.

ZAHM, O. (1995). Before and After Fashion. *Artforum.* March 1995.

****
****

Original publication of preceding chapter:

RICHARDS, A.K. (1996). Ladies of Fashion: Pleasure, Perversion or Paraphilia. *International Journal of Psychoanalysis* 77:337–351.

FREUD, PROUST, PERVERSION AND LOVE. **By Hendrika C. Halberstadt-Freud. Amsterdam/Berwyn, PA: Swets & Zeitlinger, 1991. 218 pp.**

Proust's great novel is called *Remembrance of Things Past* in English. The original French title, *À la recherche du temps perdu,* could be translated as *In Search of Lost Time.* This translation would make it clear that the book is an answer to Proust's parents' complaints that he wasted his life. Rather than devoting himself to some useful profession, as did his father and brother who were both physicians, Proust became a socialite, aesthete, invalid, and raconteur who also wrote (Painter 1959). Only after the death of his mother did he devote himself to writing full time, slowly and painfully producing his gigantic novel built on the experiences of his lonely illness and the empty pleasures of society (Hayman 1990). Proust's great book answers his parents' objection to their son's way of life by using his experience of society life to reach a deep understanding of human motivation.

Proust believed that love is longing, only sustainable when unfulfilled, only pleasurable insofar as one is able to enjoy pain. He believed that satiety can only produce dullness and boredom. Envy and jealousy prevent the dullness and boredom of satiety. Thus, he understood pleasure in inflicting and suffering pain as the inescapable dynamic of human existence. Sadomasochistic reversals of social status in which humiliation accompanies physical pain are the prototype of erotic excitement for Proust.

Above all, Proust saw and delineated in exquisitely fine detail the parallels between the psychological and the social, uniting in the form of fiction what has been divided, to the mutual loss of the sciences of psychology and sociology. He understood society as organized pleasure attained by inflicting pain. Like love, he thought, a party can give pleasure only as the participants are aware that they might have been excluded, that they are privileged to be invited. Part of the pleasure in belonging to a social circle is the pleasure of excluding others. In an ironic turn, worthy of Proust himself, it is only now, over half a century after he finished his great psychological novel, that psychoanalysts have attained a view of perversions that can intersect with his.

Halberstadt-Freud sets out to show that perversion is a defense against separation anxiety, dissolution of identity, overwhelming aggression, narcissistic anxiety, and fear of women. She includes the sadomasochism of everyday life in the perversions, thus widening her field of interest. She attributes the origin of perversion to the seductive mother.

Halberstadt-Freud appears to have overlooked Socarides's conclusions about the preoedipal origins and the role of early and ongoing disturbed relationships with the mother in generating the perversion (Socarides 1988). She believes that such a mother encourages the oedipal boy to develop the fantasy that she values him more than she does the father. The little boy responds by failing to accept the limits of reality, denying the value the mother attaches to the father's sexual potency and his power over the family. The situation can come about even in the presence of a patriarchal family when the mother conveys to the child that the father's authority is not real, not fair, or not what she believes in. This emboldens the child to defy authority by actually indulging in the forbidden pleasures which the neurotic might not even allow herself or himself consciously to dream of.

But how does this square with the observation that the person who develops a perversion is often the fearful adult who was a timid, overcompliant child? Suppression of anger and jealousy in the compliant child leads to splitting off of these feelings and channeling them into masturbation fantasies which become the basis for perverse enactments.

Halberstadt-Freud gives us a remarkable account of the similarities between Freud's thought and Proust's. She points out that Freud and Proust both depicted perversion as what Stoller (1975) would later call the erotic form of hatred. She draws a parallel between Proust's "involuntary memory" and Freud's "primary process." Both are timeless; both use condensation, displacement, and imagery. Similarly, Proust's "voluntary memory" is like Freud's "secondary process." Both use the laws of time, logic, and reality. Like Freud, Proust discovered that love is transference. Also like Freud, Proust viewed the state between waking and sleep as the dream state and as the access to the unconscious as well as to the thoughts and feelings of childhood. Both believed that jealousy is a necessary condition of love.

Halberstadt-Freud believes that Proust differed from Freud in a way in which she also differs from Freud: Freud paid relatively little attention to the role of the mother and never fully elucidated the genesis of the perversions. Actually, Freud's discussion of Leonardo does suggest that early oral seduction and sudden loss of the beloved mother may inhibit the capacity for heterosexual love. In Freud's view, however, Leonardo did not suffer from perversion, but managed a sublimation of heterosexual desire which may have allowed him the overt expression of homosexual wishes. Freud does not reconstruct a particular type of mother or style of mothering to be associated with sexual perversion. Both Proust and Halberstadt-Freud emphasize the role of the mother and her child-rearing practices in fostering the perversions.

Freud's earliest idea about perversion was that it was the fossilized version of the partial drive of the infant and young child. Perversion is the gratification of pregenital wishes, as in sadism, voyeurism, and exhibitionism. According to Halberstadt-Freud, his later view that the fetishist disavows the difference between the sexes is the key to all perversions. The manipulation of the object is the inevitable outcome of the child's having been used to satisfy the need of the mother rather than allowed to express and satisfy his own needs.

Halberstadt-Freud gives a series of vignettes from her own practice to show that patients with perversions are analyzable and to argue that deeper understanding of perversions can be derived from treating perverse patients with analysis. Among these are the following. A male cross-dresser feels relaxed and like himself only when in the guise of a woman. He comes to Halberstadt-Freud's office in drag. She feels no "real contact" with him. The treatment ends. A woman patient plays a game of tying her male lover to the bed and beating him to orgasm; he does the same for her. She gets no pleasure from intercourse. A supervisor advises Halberstadt-Freud not to continue the treatment because perversion is too gratifying to be dislodged by psychoanalysis. Halberstadt-Freud regrets taking the advice because she now believes that people with perversions have frustrated infantile needs which can be analyzed.

A male homosexual who engages in much teasing and rivalry with his partner develops a heterosexual transference to Halberstadt-Freud, gets married, and chooses a career he likes better than the one chosen for him by his step-parents. He had lost his own parents and had been shifted from one foster home to another before being adopted by a mother who, he believed, never loved him as much as she did her own daughter. The analysis was not complete, as he was never able to express anger toward his analyst.

A married woman enjoys her fantasies of having submissive lovers more than she does having intercourse with her husband. A married man has himself beaten and stepped on by his wife, but is afraid to attempt intercourse lest he be impotent. A homosexual man only enjoys anal intercourse after being beaten by an anonymous partner. He links this to his experience of being seduced in a humiliating way by his mother. For all of these patients, Halberstadt-Freud believes that the crucial dynamic of perversion is defying the parent in order to escape the symbiotic fantasy, forge a separate identity, and maintain it.

Proust's famous scene of the "goodnight kiss" illustrates a similar theory of the genesis of perversion. According to Halberstadt-Freud, Proust has encapsulated his theory of the genesis of perversion in the screen memory of the goodnight kiss. The mother indulges her child in a bedtime ritual in order to keep him close to her. The father wants him to be more manly, which to the father means more self-reliant. The mother needs her child as an ally against the father, as a substitute for him when he is away, and as a validator of her role in life. The child, in turn, sees his mother as all good and those who keep her from him as all bad. When the father refuses to allow the ritual one evening, the narrator suffers until the father realizes how terrible he feels and orders the mother to spend the night with him. He is to be allowed what he wants as long as he is sick and helpless. His fate is sealed.

Another scene of central significance in Proust's *Remembrance of Things Past* is the lesbian love scene. In it, cruelty is linked to the need for repudiation of the parent as the primary love object. Mlle. Vinteuil has been brought up by an overly solicitous father who wants her to be a dainty, feminine child instead of the sturdy mannish one she really is. She cannot love as a woman without giving in to the coercion of his idealized picture of her. The lover who helps her to deny the father by spitting on his portrait allows her to experience sexual pleasure of her own. The implication for Proust is that effeminate boys are equally misunderstood and pushed toward a masculinity unnatural to them.

Sadism is an attempt at liberation, but in Freud's view, the sense of guilt transforms it into masochism. Primary masochism, according to Halberstadt-Freud, was alluded to but never fully understood by Freud. The original dependence of the infant on the parent, with the consequent need to protect the parent even at the cost of pain and suffering to oneself, is what she posits as the origin of primary masochism. Primary masochism is then fostered throughout childhood and adolescence by the binding overprotection of the family. Pubertal sexual fantasies are colored by the idea that love and pleasure are a revolt against one's parents. The split-off hatred toward the beloved parents results in the paradoxical hyperesthetic traits of perversion. Proust believed that it is just these traits that are enacted in society: in the drawing room, domineering women are worshipped by frightened men; aristocrats hire servants to beat them; aesthetes torture rats for pleasure. Like perversion and social life, love is a revenant of that primary masochism which haunts everyone.

This observation leads Halberstadt-Freud to underline a clinical observation: perversion is not merely the enactment of a particular sexual scenario; perversion is also the defensive use of the perverse scenario in any situation which threatens psychological disaster. This generalizes erotic moment into character. Halberstadt-Freud seems to have missed Arlow's (1971) observation and elaboration of this same point.

Thus, Halberstadt-Freud concludes, the fascination of Proust's story lies in its evocation of the universal struggle of the growing child to free him/herself from the primary tie cherished from infancy. Freud and Proust both knew that the sufferer with a perversion is not so different from the lover and neither is he or she different from the artist. All long for what is not possible to attain.

Hate and love, sadism and masochism, go hand in hand in Halberstadt-Freud's conception. Perversion results from childhood events which the child experiences as cruel even when the parents inflicting the pain do not intend harm. While Proust introduced perversion in the context of a lesbian love, Halberstadt-Freud tells us that her theoretical understanding does not encompass female perversions, a topic on which she believes that more research is needed. I believe that some research is available and could have enriched her book (Grunberger 1966, Richards 1989, and Zavitzianos 1971). Yet when she presents clinical vignettes of six patients with perversions, four are men and two women. She follows what used to be the general pattern of using clinical material from women and making theoretical and developmental statements in which maleness is normative. Yet she triumphs over both the assumption that maleness is normative and over the once prevalent belief that perversion is not treatable because it is too pleasurable. Her point of view is ultimately that perversion is treatable precisely because it is excruciating and that the etiology of perversion is far more complex than was thought in the days when male fear of "female castration" (Bak 1953) was thought to be the dread against which perversion was the defense. For me, this book is very important because it gives clinical material from the actual treatment of patients with perversions and presents them in a light sympathetic enough to encourage other analysts to attempt to do the same thing.

REFERENCES

ARLOW, J.A. (1971). *Character perversion. In Currents in Psychoanalysis.* I.M. Marcus, ed. New York: International Universities Press, pp. 317–336.

BAK, R.C. (1953). Fetishism. *Journal of the American Psychoanalytic* Association 1:285–298.

GRUNBERGER, B. (1966). Some Reflections on the Rat Man. *International Journal of Psychoanalysis* 47:161–168.

HAYMAN, R. (1990). *Proust.* New York: Harper.

PAINTER, G. (1959). *Marcel Proust.* New York: Vintage, 1978.

RICHARDS, A.K. (1989). A Romance with Pain: A Telephone Perversion in a Woman? *International Journal of Psychoanalysis.* 153–164.

SOCARIDES, C.W. (1988). *The Preoedipal Origin and Psychoanalytic Therapy of Sexual Perversions.* Madison, CT: International Universities Press.

STOLLER, R. (1975). *Perversion. The Erotic Form of Hatred.* New York: Pantheon.

ZAVITZIANOS, G. (1971). Fetishism and Exhibitionism in the Female and Their Relationship to Psychopathy and Kleptomania. *International Journal of Psychoanalysis* 52:297–305.

****
****

Original publication of the preceding chapter:

RICHARDS, A.K. (1994). A Review of *Freud, Proust, Perversion and Love.* By Hendrika C. Halberstadt-Freud. *Psychoanalytic Quarterly* 63:804–810.

Perverse Transference and Psychoanalytic Technique: An Introduction to the Work of Horacio Etchegoyen

Books on psychoanalytic technique in English have been limited to a single point of view. For example, Glover (1955) explicates Kleinian technique, Fenichel (1941) structural-ego-psychological. Greenson (1967) is more object relational, while Bergmann and Hartman (1976) include essays by analysts of varied persuasions, but view the history of technique as a kind of ladder constantly approaching the heights of ego psychology. Etchegoyen's *Fundamentals of Psychoanalytic Technique* includes not only historical sources, but also current developments in these schools as well as the Lacanian and French non-Lacanians, Bionians, and others. He lays out their different points of view for comparison. Early in the book he sets out the problems that he is going to deal with. The problems are:

1. When, with whom, and how to start an analysis;
2. Problems in countertransference;
3. Interpretations and constructions;
4. Process of an analysis;
5. The beginning, midstage, and termination stages;
6. Analytic impasses, negative therapeutic reaction, and acting out.

Fond of paradox, and very playful in his thinking, Etchegoyen offers a salty commentary on the widely debated issue of whether the curative power of psychoanalysis lies in interpretation or in the analytic relationship. Describing the match of the couple in the analytic relationship, he remarks that the best match is the match with the best analyst. Like Brenner (1979), Stein (1981), and Curtis (1979), he argues for the good interpretation in preference to the good alliance. He is interested in the specifically analytic and he tries to interest the reader in this as well.

Wallerstein (1991) says in his introduction to Etchegoyen's book:

Etchegoyen points out repeatedly, and this is a major example of just how unstereotypically Kleinian he is, that although not everything is transference, yet transference exists in everything— which he emphasizes are not contradictions. And transference is spelled out in many, and to Americans, unfamiliar ways, like the following: of the distinction between transference as memory and transference as desire. Or the many variances of the transference neurosis, like the transference psychosis where he follows the English more sweeping usage rather than the American more restrictive focus; that is, he sees psychosis in many more places than an American would see. Or the transference perversion which is Etchegoyen's unique idea where the drives function not as desire, not as wish, but as ideology. Or the transference addiction with its genetic roots in masturbation called the primal addiction and reflected in the primal scene. Or the various permutations of the locus of transference, including the reverse Lacanian view which Etchegoyen characterizes as the emergence of the transference only when the dialectical process of analysis fails due to the analyst's resistance or counter-transference which is (called [in Lacanian terms] transference by entrapment) [p. xxxi].

This is a kind of road map of what the book is about. In it Etchegoyen introduces a concept which explicates technique as a response to a kind of patient most analysts would prefer not to treat: patients with perverse character disorders. In my view, his concept of perverse transference is the most interesting, original, and clinically useful part of the book.

Etchegoyen thinks that insight leads to change: insight and not relationship. Like Strachey, he concentrates on the transference interpretation as the vehicle of insight. What is unique to his view of transference is the idea of the transference perversion. This idea, parallel to the idea of transference neurosis, suggests that a stable pattern is developed in the transference which repeats a pattern outside the analysis and which, at least for a time, may replace the original symptom. Unlike the neurotic symptom in that it is ego syntonic, the perverse symptom usually causes more pain to others than it does to the patient. Similarly, the perverse symptom causes more pain to the analyst than to the patient.

Perversion has interested me particularly since I discovered that to understand a particular patient, I had to think that it was possible that what she had was a perversion. This 19-year-old woman had been treated by a psychotherapist since late latency for a very disturbing symptom: she was unable to get through the day without speaking with her mother several times. Her mother stayed at home waiting for her calls. This had been thought of as a separation–individuation problem. When she started treatment with me, she set herself a goal: she would only call her mother once a week. She then began to call me and her friends for the kind of comfort and reassurance that she had been accustomed to receiving from her mother. This allowed her mother to get out of the house, get a job, and pay for the treatment. Two years into her analysis, she reported that she had phoned a friend in another city in the middle of the night at her boyfriend's place. The friend said: "Why are you calling me in the middle of the night when I'm at a guy's house? What are you? Some kind of pervert?" She then hung up on the patient. When the patient reported this, I began to think of perversion.

It was then believed (Bak 1953, 1968) that perversions were the consequence of castration anxiety and only occurred in males. I searched through the literature to find mention of female perversion. There were a few examples, but the theory did not allow for the possibility of explaining it. Had I known of Etchegoyen's work, I might have understood from the quality of the transference that the patient was perverse. How could I have known that? One clue was that this patient had gotten the previous therapists to tell her school that she had to be allowed to make these telephone calls from school. Another was that she had convinced me that the "parameter" of telling her to compare herself to the other girls in the dorm was necessary. This coercive power suggests a perverse transference. I did not see it at the time, but when I read of the concept in Etchegoyen, I recognized the phenomenon and it clarified my understanding of this case and suggested a diagnostic use of the concept of perverse transference.

Perverse transference is one of those terms with a deceptively familiar feel. Perversion usually means some sexual act we disapprove of. Perverse transference sounds like a transference to be disapproved of, as my patient's friend disapproved of her phone call. But the person who practices the perversion believes it to be much more pleasurable than ordinary sexual intercourse. Another meaning of perverse in ordinary life is the equivalent of oppositional. We call it perverse when somebody is aggressively opposing the ordinary or the accepted. In this sense, we call a person perverse who always breaks the rules, regardless of what the rules may be. In psychoanalysis, the perversions have been traditionally defined by listing, for example, voyeurism, sadomasochism. Freud defined perversion as a fixed preference for other than genital sexual acts, or obligatory sex with an object other than another adult human being; that is, a child, thing, or animal. More current definitions of perversion take into account other meanings of perverse in ordinary language. Stoller identifies the importance of aggressive wishes in the maintenance of sexual excitement in the perversion (1975), but also in normal everyday sexuality (1985) where it appears as fighting before lovemaking. Etchegoyen believes that the perverse transference has to do with hostility and envy; that is, where the aim of the sexual impulse is aggressive rather than libidinal as with the rapist, the aggressive exhibitor, and/or the aggressive voyeur.

The perverse character has been defined by Arlow (1971) who widened the definition of what is perverse to include such character formations as the petty liar, the unrealistic character, and the practical joker. He defines perverse character as comprising an ego syntonic, long-term need to distort reality. Arlow traces the perverse character to fantasies in which aggressive impulses are predominant in a sexual context. Perverse character enshrines the need to deny the difference between the sexes and therefore to deny other basic realities. The petty liar needs to violate others' trust, and the practical joker needs to create an illusion which inspires panic or anxiety in another and to witness their humiliation when he exposes the hoax. Perverse characters range from mildly to seriously unacceptable to others, but their perverse characteristics are ego syntonic. The practical joker loves practical jokes. The petty liar loves to put one over. The unrealistic character loves dreaming: "Tomorrow I will be rich or my prince will come." The perverse act becomes a symptom when it leads to difficulties, either with one's own conscience or with social morals. In other words, if you have to go to jail because of exposing yourself, then it becomes a problem. But exposing oneself may be very satisfying. In the movie *Basic Instinct*, a woman suspected of murder exposes herself to a group of policemen. She exhibits. At the same time she smokes. Someone points out the No Smoking sign. She says: "What can you do to me?" and nobody thinks of anything to do. She sits in a room full of police, humiliating them by demonstrating how powerless they are. Exhibitionism is an erotic form of aggression in this scene.

Perversion is a prolongation of a normal infantile impulse. It is reversal, turning the tables. The child sees the adult as powerful and himself as powerless, and therefore imagines the situation exactly reversed. The child believes what a bright 3-year-old said to his mother: "Just you wait till you are little and I am big." This is the core of the aggressive side of perversion. Freud's earliest idea (1905) was that the perversions were remnants of infantile sexuality and that the neuroses were the negative of the perversions. This means that the neurotic symptom is the unfortunate outcome of incomplete or insufficient repression of the perverse impulse. But to the psychotic, according to Klein (1932), the early aggressive impulse is the source of psychopathology. Thus, Glover (1933), a Kleinian, believed that the perverse symptom is the result of incompletely or insufficiently suppressed early aggressive impulses of the sort that cause psychotic symptoms. In this view, perversion is the negation of psychosis.

The Kleinian view that perversion is the negative of psychosis, implies that perversion results when a psychotic impulse is insufficiently internalized. Kleinians see perversion as a defense against psychosis, while ego psychologists have regarded it as one of the degrees of severity of mental illness. Most severe is the psychotic, then the perverse, then the neurotic. And at the same time these are layers according to defense: the psychotic denies reality (has an ego defect), the pervert denies the rules of social life (has an insufficient superego), the neurotic represses and isolates (has an overly harsh superego). Etchegoyen says that perversion can be one of the causes of psychosis as well as a defense against it. This enables the clinician to observe the perverse transference and infer a perverse character trait or a frank perversion. Etchegoyen recognizes that perverse transference manifestations can occur in neurotics and believes that these reflect defenses against the psychotic aspects of the person.

From the point of view of scientific reasoning, the observation is the perverse transference, and the inference is the perverse ego. In my experience, the first observation is the countertransference to the perverse transference. The analyst experiences rage at the patient. From the rage, the analyst infers an intent to provoke on the patient's part. If, on inquiry, the patient is seen to be unaware of any intent to provoke, or does not see what is wrong with provoking, the analyst infers that the patient has a perverse ego. The perverse ego is similar to what Arlow has called the character perversion, namely, it appears in an analysis as flaunting the rules of the analysis and in everyday life as a flaunting of the accepted rules of behavior.

Etchegoyen discusses the work of Betty Joseph (1971) who believes that perversion can only be resolved by experiencing it in the transference. Erotization of the transference, silence, flooding with words, and passivity all may reflect the wish to attack the analyst, not merely defensively, but in order to destroy. Perverse aspects of the personality can appear in neurotic or borderline patients, according to Etchegoyen. The pervert seduces the analyst into scoptophilia or subverts the analysis so that the interpretations are surface "pseudointerpretations" which can destroy the analyzing instrument. Etchegoyen takes from Lacan (1956) the idea that the fetish is the incarnation of the female penis and at the same time veils the pervert's belief in the female penis by locating it (Rosolato 1966) apart from the body in the dress or accessory to the body.

Etchegoyen discusses a case to illustrate the concept of perverse transference. A young woman has come asking to be cured of her homosexuality and of her sense of emptiness. He takes her on. A pattern is set up in which she functions better and complains more. She returns from the first vacation of the treatment complaining of having lost a contact lens while the analyst was away. She tells a funny story of how she induced her mother to help her find it, and her mother stepped on one lens, which made her mother look like an idiot. In her session, she was wearing only one lens, only one eye sees well. She could not even tell her analyst that she had contact lenses before the vacation because she was afraid that he would envy her achievement at being able to wear them. Here Rosolato's idea about the fetish as female penis appears to have enriched Etchegoyen's understanding of the importance of the contact lens as a fetish. When she told him about this, she was also able to tell him that she was afraid that he was no longer a good analyst now that he was back from vacation.

The patient tells of a dream in which she is traveling on a bus with a man. Straddling his lap, facing him she sees his fly open and his penis out. They continue talking as if nothing was happening. Understanding this to be her view of the treatment, Etchegoyen believes that he and the patient are engaged in a pseudodialogue, a perverse transference. As she did better in her life, she also felt worse about the treatment. She believed that her analyst only wanted to humiliate her, to make her admit that he was right and she was wrong. Having previously had sex exclusively with women, she now began to engage in heterosexual sex.

The following session illustrates her polemical challenging tone. She had come from an examination and thought she had done well. She was still confused and had a tendency to become busy. She thought if the exam had been prolonged and she had been unable to attend the session it would be very difficult to do so on Monday and perhaps she would not come any longer. In other words, one missed session would end the whole treatment. She remembered that with her previous analyst, she had begun to miss sessions as the consequence of an exam and had later abandoned the analysis. Her all or nothing stance is similar to what is observed with borderline patients.

Etchegoyen reports the following interchange:

> A: Perhaps you wish to interrupt treatment and not come anymore? You fear that the situation with Dr. X. will repeat itself?
>
> P: You put ideas into my head that are completely strange to me. I do not feel anywhere that I do not want to come here anymore.
>
> A: We will see why you feel that these ideas are strange despite their being your own: you said that had you not come today it would have been more difficult to return on Monday.
>
> P: I tell you this, but I do not feel it, I think it, but I do not feel it.
>
> A: But this is a very equivocal argument: inasmuch as you decide that what you say you do not feel, I can no longer interpret anything.
>
> (Precisely because she places herself in that attitude, this interpretation is not valid.) [p. 193].

Etchegoyen sees this interchange as paradigmatic of the perverse transference. Whatever the analyst says is wrong because the patient refuses to engage with him in an affective way. She will talk, but she will not feel. Or she will not acknowledge what feelings she has. When the patient says, "You put ideas into my head that are completely strange to me," she is talking Kleinian language. Perhaps her analyst has told her: "You put things into me," when interpreting what he believes to be paranoid projective identifications. In the service of negating his interpretation she analyzes him; she says he is doing the projective identification. He says, we will have to see why you feel that these ideas are strange, despite their being simply your own. He is putting the idea back into her, and adding a sense of curiosity about why she should have these ideas. These are not ideas that he is condemning; he is curious about them. He says: You said that if you did not come today, it would have been more difficult to return on Monday. She says, emphatically, I tell you this, but I do not feel it. I think it, but I do not feel it. She is denying the affect. She is doing what in ego psychological terms would be called isolation. She is cutting off the affect from the intellectual understanding. "I think it, but I don't feel it," she says. Therefore, she doesn't have to own it. It's just a thought. And "I tell you this, but I do not feel it," defends against his interpretation. These are just words, she says. Then the analyst says: "But this is a very equivocal argument. Inasmuch as you decide that what you say you do not feel, I can no longer interpret anything." He says parenthetically, precisely because she places herself in that attitude, this interpretation is not valid.

If his first statement were recast as an interpretation of the affect in the transference, he might say: "You're afraid that you feel toward me as you felt toward Dr. X." Technically, a complete interpretation must include the interpretation of the impulse or the wish. It would have been possible, I think, to start by naming the affect as Brenner (1982) would in beginning to interpret a compromise formation. This way of working with the perverse transference has a certain advantage in that it brings the affect to the foreground immediately, thus allowing the analyst to deal directly with the aggression.

In his example, however, Etchegoyen describes how he actually accomplished a similar result:

> *Months later, the same polemical attitude appeared in connection with a dream but I was better able to understand. It was during the time when she alternated between homosexuality and heterosexuality with a lively fear of madness and of genital penetration, both of which are clear from the dialogue. In the dream, she was going to take an exam accompanied by her female friend who had slept at her house. Along the way, they encountered a popular uprising and returned home frightened. She remained dissatisfied at having been frightened. I interpreted that the dream seemed to express her conflict between homosexuality, the female friend who slept at her house, and heterosexuality, the exam. I suggested that the popular uprising must be the (feared) erection of the penis: she could not face it and took refuge in a secure place, the home, the mother, the girl friend* [pp. 193–194].

For Etchegoyen, the exam represented heterosexuality in that it was the representation of the patriarchal order. Here he was using the idea of conflict in a very different way than ego psychologists would understand it. We would think of a conflict as having a wish, a defense, and a compromise, or an affect, a forbidden wish and a prohibition. When his patient complained that there was more to her conflict than the hetero- versus homosexual wishes, ego psychologists would agree with her. Etchegoyen says: "I suggested that she treated my interpretation as a penis that was too small, that left her dissatisfied; but she insisted that I always left the social aspect out" (p. 194).

In this example of Etchegoyen's clinical work with perverse transference he uses the patient's tale about the exam before as an association to the dream, even though she tells the dream afterward. Why should the exam be heterosexual? Because it represents the norm and patriarchal society (Lacan 1953). She believes that another analyst could have interpreted something very different, perhaps that she had begged a social responsibility. Therefore, psychoanalysis seems insufficient to her. In other words, she gives him another Lacanian interpretation. Then he interprets her disappointment with his penis. This disturbance, he says in parentheses, is the opposite of vaginismus. He cites Garma (personal communication) as having noted it in women as well.

I suggested that she treated my interpretation as a penis that was too small and that left her dissatisfied, but she insisted that I always left the social aspect out. I replied that just as she criticized and even had contempt for my interpretation because it was small and insufficient, she also thought that I had contempt for her material, leaving things out. (I consider this interpretation as correct because it corrects the projection of her peculiar dissociation: Verleugnung, *dismantling).*

She admitted that she tended to think me sectarian and contentious. In another tone of voice she said that she thought the girl in the dream must be homosexual and added material confirming her fear of the erect penis [p. 194].

This session seems to me remarkably un-Kleinian. There is no mention of biting, spitting out, or poisoned milk. There is no mention of acting out. There is no mention of depressive position. There is no mention of splitting, or projective identification. None of the classical Kleinian ideas are mentioned explicitly either to the patient or to the reader. And where they are implied, they are implied in a very oblique way. The discourse is about the here-and-now between analyst and patient, and in the patient's current life.

After several years more of treatment, Etchegoyen's patient married and began to feel satisfied enough to think of terminating. Summarizing the gains, Etchegoyen tells us that: "After nine years of analysis, her symptoms had abated, her object relations were more mature and she no longer denied her depressive feelings" (p. 195).

Thus, the awareness of affect in the transference was a major accomplishment. But life intervened: her husband wanted a separation. The effect was catastrophic: she now believed that analysis was a farce, that she was homosexual, and only engaged in the charade with her husband in order to please Etchegoyen. It is to his credit, I think, that he was able to accept her complaint that he should never have agreed to treat her for homosexuality since it is not an illness. His acceptance of this criticism led to a new phase in the treatment.

After a homosexual affair which satisfied her, she again set a termination date. This time she was considering termination after having worked out with Etchegoyen the countertransference and transference implications of the perverse situation that she had set up from the beginning. The one thing they had never talked about was her complaint that she was homosexual. By accepting her definition of it as an illness, he was sitting with his penis out and his fly open, pretending to analyze.

She had set up an impossible choice. She could believe that her analyst could let her go only if she thought he wanted to get rid of her. But if he did not let her go, he was holding onto her for his own needs. Finally, she recognized her fantasy that the analyst would never let her go and the fantasy of being mad, crazy, so that he could never stop taking care of her; that is, she would merit tenderness and concern as long as she was depraved. With the expression of this seduction fantasy, the analysis terminated. By talking about it, it became more dystonic to her, until she was finally able to let go of it. Clinically, it should be noted that Etchegoyen used criteria for termination which included: improved object relations; abatement of her denial of her depressive affect; and a conviction that she had found her sexual identity. The perverse transference persisted to the end. Thus, the clinical correlate of the idea that perversion is the negative of psychosis is that a perverse transference is not converted into a transference neurosis.

Why coin a new term perverse transference to describe this situation? The term perverse transference serves to emphasize that the sexuality is in the service of aggression, the aggression appears in the form of opposition. The patient prefers humiliating the analyst to getting better. Thus, the negative therapeutic reaction in the perverse transference is motivated by humiliation rather than by guilt, as it is in the neurotic transference. The issue on which Etchegoyen's patient got him to feel stupid was homosexuality. He had agreed to treat her for something which he later agreed was not an illness. The patient was not making love with a woman because she loved the woman, but in order to humiliate men. The perverse transference was exactly analogous to the perverse behavior outside the transference.

We can consider other answers the analyst might give to her comment which would have led to other interactions. After the examination, she thought she had done well, she was still confused, she thought that if the exam had been prolonged she would not have been able to begin the session. It would be very difficult to do so on Monday and perhaps she might not come any longer. She admitted that with Dr. X, her previous analyst, she had to miss sessions as a consequence of an exam and later abandoned analysis.

If this perverse scenario involved castration anxiety, the interaction might have involved an interpretation of that dynamic. The patient might have believed that she had done well on her exam, felt guilty for succeeding in defiance of her analyst, and punished herself.

Her punishment for doing well is that she will no longer be able to allow herself the experience of an analysis. At the same time doing well brings her into new danger situations: the analyst might be someone who wants to castrate her and she needs to do poorly in order to placate him. By giving up the analysis she then punishes herself in order to prevent the analyst from punishing her.

An analyst who believed these suppositions might approach interpretation in a step-wise fashion. First, one would suggest that there was something dangerous about doing well on the exam that was causing her to react in this way, and perhaps this is something that is familiar to her. Focusing on the fear that she has to repeat what she has done before, one would emphasize, as Etchegoyen did in the second half of his interpretation, that "You fear that the situation with Dr. X would repeat itself."

An analyst focusing on object relations might focus on the tension between her wish to be close to the object and her wish to push him away. To an ego psychologist, that would be an interpretation up, one that supports the ego, that understands the person as self-protective. Going into the adaptive aspects of what the person is doing, one might predict what Etchegoyen found at the end of the analysis: that her fantasy of being crazy functioned to maintain her connection with him. A Mahlerian might emphasize how she was caught between her wish to get away and her wish to stay, and how this reflected her experience of the separation-individuation process when she was between 18 and 36 months old.

For Arlow, this might be an interesting fantasy to explore. If the patient is never going to come back, what would she be doing instead? What else will happen? He would want her to elaborate and develop the fantasy and understand what she is thinking of, why she would think it was horrible, it was wonderful, what was it? Are you going to die of it? Is she going to be happy and go read his books, or is she going to—the possibilities of what this fantasy would mean are endless. And see how much she can elaborate it and at some point the patient would then say, and that's like a dream I used to have, or that's like the way it worked out with my brother, or that's like the way it worked out with my mother, or whoever. But he would get to the genetic by means of spinning out the current fantasies as much as possible.

Brenner might look at affect. Starting with the fear that the situation with Dr. X would repeat itself, he might think: "Is this fear loss of the object? Is it fear of loss of the object's love? Is it castration fear? Which fear is most prominent here? Is it guilt? Is she saying that if she misses one session she is such a bad person that she doesn't deserve to have the rest of the analysis? Is this her cruel superego? Saying that if you make one mistake you're dead? So he would get her to talk about fear and elaborating on the fear aspect of it by saying "What are you afraid of?"

Klein might focus on the aggressive transference. She might say things like: "You want me out of your life." She might not acknowledge the importance of the libidinal aspect. A Kleinian might say that if you take care of the aggressive part, the sexual will take care of itself. An object relations view would take the position that her attachment to the analyst was the most important thing to interpret.

The concept of the perverse transference adds to the repertoire of understandings of a patient's seductive behavior. Rather than understand this seductiveness as sexual desire, one notices that the patient uses sexuality in the service of aggression to derail the analysis and mock the analyst. Perverse transference occurs in the person who has a perverse attitude, and the perverse character, or as Etchegoyen puts it, the perverse ego, means that aggression is expressed this way in every-day life. The person isn't bothered by this use of aggression. This is for Arlow a turning of passive into active. The person who does this has at some point experienced it. The need to humiliate comes from the feeling of being humiliated, which is inevitable, Arlow says, in the course of growing up. When a kid says "Wait till I grow up," it means turn the passive into the active. "Watch out, mom. I'm going to do it back to you." Arlow and Etchegoyen believe that the perverse ego or perverse character is an institutionalized defense against enacting a sexual perversion. That is, a person who is a practical joker may have sex in what looks like an ordinary way. That's the point of Etchegoyen's patient's homosexuality. She doesn't have a perversion. She never had one. She uses this against him to say: "I caught you. You're treating me for a perversion." And since he knows that she does not have one, he is in the wrong. But she has a perverse transference.

The point of the perverse transference is that it makes nonsense of any and all interpretations. With this kind of patient whatever the analyst says is wrong, beside the point, or has nothing to do with how she feels. Words are only words. The perverse transference fights against having to accept the gray everyday world. One more distinction between Arlow and Brenner and Etchegoyen is that Arlow and Brenner's interpretations would be directed to the perverse formation as it exists in the patient. That is, whether it may or may not be brought into what the patient was trying to do to the analyst—is not so central. Rather, the problem is inside the patient, and the resolution has to be inside, self-observation, understanding it as an intrapsychic conflict. Whereas I think Etchegoyen is suggesting, through the perverse transference, that the characteristics of the perversion are played out between the two of them and the communication in the transference is the signal.

When the patient comes in and says, I didn't feel like coming in today but I was afraid that if I didn't come, I'd never come again, Etchegoyen understands that as negative transference. He proposes the kind of responses that he has given. But these are examples of the kinds of responses he would use to try and get around it. He would talk about what's happening in the transference. He says, all right, if it's just words, then let's talk about words between you and me. And then it would liven up. That would make it alive in the transference. And then we would engage, and then we would have something that isn't just words.

He cites authors who recognize transference perversion to show how the perverse patient gets the analyst to feel that the analytic function itself is perverse. For instance, a patient who makes the analyst feel like a voyeur is pushing for an exaggeration of the analyst's role which expresses the patient's aggressive feelings toward the analyst and toward the treatment. The analyst can be read as talking as if he or she is really engaged with the patient when neither patient nor analyst is talking about anything meaningful, even when the patient is giving a whole series of early childhood memories and so on.

An example of this is the book, *Portnoy's Complaint* (Roth 1969), which ends with the analyst saying, "And now we're ready to begin." In other words, now we're ready to engage. Some patients who talk about their bad, abusive, or uncaring parents are engaged in this kind of perverse transference. The patient and analyst can agree day after day on the real shortcomings of the parents without any change in the symptoms or behavior of either member of the therapeutic pair. Etchegoyen cites French writers who emphasize perversion as an assertion that the father's rules are no good; that reality is not what tradition, religion, or the state declare it to be. In other words, that the perversion is a kind of social revolution occurring on a small scale. Thus both the Kleinians and the French see perversion as a challenge to authority but in very different ways. The Kleinians are much more concerned with the perversion in the transference. The Lacanians are much more concerned with the perversion of everyday life outside the transference.

The similarity to a transference addiction causes Etchegoyen to examine the differences. For addicts take the contradictory position in relation to drugs. The dependency on people triggers destructive hate toward the person on whom the addict begins to feel dependent. The outcome of this kind of dependency is that the analyst becomes addicted to the patient's cure. Here he agrees with Lacan that it is possible to become addicted to curing someone of something which may not need a cure. In this case it was homosexuality. Unable to give up the fantasy of curing the patient, the analyst must examine his or her own fantasies in order to make a decision to end treatment or allow it to continue. The parallel between an addictive transference and the transference perversion is split transference fantasy of the idealized all-good analyst and the terrifying all-bad analyst.

Is a perverse transference characteristic of people with overt sexual perversions? What does the concept of transference perversion add to what we already know about treating the difficult patient? It seems to me that it alerts the analyst to the possibility that a perverse wish exists when no perversion is mentioned. The perversion as the negative of psychosis implies a splitting of the world. One part is a world characterized by a sort of luminescence, filled with sexual tensions, anxieties, and attractions, one where there is no castration. It is a world filled with interest and excitement, and it is a world where women have penises. It is a world where gender differences don't matter. And then there is the world where women don't have penises and you have to trot off to work in the morning and you have to come back home to cook your own dinner. *Part of the difficulty of treating people with perversions is getting them to accept banality and boredom.* People with perversions enact aggressive wishes toward the analyst in the form of attacks on the analytic process, the person of the analyst, or the specific interpretation. In this sort of patient, the attacks never give way to a neurotic transference neurosis. No matter how much better the patient's life becomes, the attacks continue in the transference. With one of my patients who has a perversion, the perverse transference continued even after termination. Years after we terminated, she came back for a supportive psychotherapy. She reported having made very important life changes, progressing in both her career and her love life. She also reported having felt enormous rage toward me for terminating her treatment, having "forgotten" that she had insisted on the termination and that she had been able to get several other mental health professionals and a guru to listen to her tale of maltreatment in analysis. The perverse transference had never been altered. Interestingly, she resented all of her gains during and following the analysis, considering them ways in which I had manipulated her so that I could get rid of her. Thus criteria for termination with such patients may have to be different from the criteria we set with neurotic patients. I wonder whether definitive termination is even possible with these patients. And I wonder whether if it is not possible to terminate, some form of supportive psychotherapy may be appropriate after analysis.

The idea of sexuality in the service of aggression is, I think, a particularly useful one because it points up in the realm of analysis what has been denied even when there is much evidence for it. That women use sexuality to express aggression is clear in our experience with adolescents. Until recently adolescent boys expressed aggression by such behavior as fighting or stealing cars; while girls who were rebellious became sexually active, promiscuous, and/or pregnant (Armstrong 1977). The female flasher in *Basic Instinct* displays her power as follows: a group of tough policemen who are interrogating her lose all their initiative at the sight of her genital. The legend of Lady Godiva and the tales of Celtic queens who fought nude in battle in order to stun their enemies, as well as the Medusa myth, all speak to the same aggressive power of female sexuality. Etchegoyen's contribution has included pointing out how this power works in the analysis of female patients, and how confrontation and interpretation can alter the otherwise destructive impact of female seductiveness in the analytic situation.

REFERENCES

ARLOW, J. (1971). Character Perversion. In: *Currents in Psychoanalysis,* Vol. 1., ed. I. Marcus. New York: International Universities Press.

ARMSTRONG, G. (1977). Females under the Law. *Crime & Delinquency* 23:109–120.

BAK, R. (1953). Fetishism. *Journal of the American Psychoanalytic Association* 1:285–298.

——— (1968). The Phallic Woman. *Psychoanalytic Study of the Child* 23:15–36. New York: International Universities Press.

BERGMANN, M., & HARTMAN, F. (1976). *The Evolution of Psychoanalytic Technique.* New York: Basic Books.

BRENNER, C. (1979). Working Alliance, Therapeutic Alliance, and Transference. *Journal of the American Psychoanalytic Association* 27(Suppl.):137–157.

——— (1982). *The Mind in Conflict.* New York: International Universities Press.

CURTIS, H. (1979). The concept of the therapeutic alliance. *Journal of the American Psychoanalytic Association* 27(Suppl.): 159–92.

ETCHEGOYEN, R.H. (1991). *The Fundamentals of Psychoanalytic Technique.* New York & London: Karnac Books.

FENICHEL, O. (1941). *Problems of Psychoanalytic Technique.* New York: Psychoanalytic Quarterly.

FREUD, S. (1905). Three Essays on the Theory of Sexuality. *Standard Edition* 7:125–243. London: Hogarth Press, 1953.

GLOVER, E. (1933). The Relation of Perversion Formation to the Development of Reality Sense. *International Journal of Psychoanalysis* 14:486–503.

——— (1940). *An Investigation of the Technique of Psychoanalysis.* London: Baillière, Tindall & Cox.

——— (1955). *The Technique of Psychoanalysis.* New York: International

Universities Press.

GREENSON, R. (1967). The Technique and Practice of Psychoanalysis. New York: International Universities Press.

JOSEPH, B. (1971). A Clinical Contribution to the Analysis of a Perversion. *International Journal of Psychoanalysis* 52:441–449.

KLEIN, M. (1932). *The Psychoanalysis of Children.* London: Hogarth Press, 1975.

LACAN, J. (1953). Some reflections on the ego. *International Journal of Psychoanalysis* 34:11–17.

——— (1956). Object Relation. Unpublished.

ROSOLATO, G. (1966). Ètude Des Perversions Sexuelles À Partir du Fetichisme. In: *Le Desir et la Perversion,* ed. P. Autagnier-Spairani. Paris: Ed. du Seuil, 1967.

ROTH, P. (1969). *Portnoy's Complaint.* New York: Random House.

STEIN, M. (1981). The unobjectionable part of the transference. *Journal of the American Psychoanalytic Association* 29:869–892.

STOLLER, R. (1975). *Perversion.* New York: Pantheon.

——— (1985). *Observing the Erotic Imagination.* New Haven, CT: Yale University Press.

WALLERSTEIN, R. (1991). Foreword. In: *The Fundamentals of Psychoanalytic Technique,* by R.H. Etchegoyen. New York and London: Karnac Books.

****
****

Original publication of preceding chapter:

RICHARDS, A.K. (1993). Perverse Transference and Psychoanalytic Technique: An Introduction to the Work of Horacio Etchegoyen. *Journal of Clinical Psychoanalysis* 2:463–480.

Female Fetishes and Female Perversions: Hermine Hug-Hellmuth's "A Case of Female Foot or More Properly Boot Fetishism" Reconsidered

In reviewing the literature on perversions for the purpose of under-standing a case of what seemed to be a possible perversion in a women patient (Richards 1989), I read the work of Phyllis Greenacre on fetishes. Contrary to her usually meticulous scholarly habit, Dr. Greenacre (1955, 1960) twice mentions a case in the literature without giving a full cita-tion. Bak (1974), in a passage reflecting on Greenacre's work, actually cites this paper, by Hermine Hug-Hellmuth, in German. Colleagues I asked about the paper were interested in it because Greenacre and Bak mentioned it, but regretted that they had never read it. The case and the paper in which it was reported have remained unavailable to those who could not read German. My translation follows.

A CASE OF FEMALE FOOT— OR MORE PROPERLY BOOT—FETISHISM

As most of the literature on foot fetishism ordinarily concerns men, I am induced to report a case, though not to analyze it, of a female boot fetishism. Although it was almost 12 years ago, I recall it well because it was often spoken of in my circle of friends without our being aware of the true nature of this peculiarity. It concerned a then 30-year-old women who had been married to a general-staff colonel.

He had shot himself after a two- to three-year marriage, which was said to be characterized by disappointment and frustration. This lady came

Thanks are due to Mr. David Ross, Librarian of the New York Psychoanalytic Society Library, for helping me to find the article and to Ms. Gisella Tauber for help-ing me to translate it.

from a highly regarded general's family. As the youngest of three daughters, she was clearly her father's favorite from earliest childhood. She had clung to him passionately and took pride in going out with him in the streets of the garrison town in which he was, first as colonel and later as general, the most distinguished person. Early on she showed an unusual enthusiasm for the shiny high riding boots her father wore. Her dearest wish that she be permitted to wear such boots, at least in winter, was fulfilled on her tenth birthday. Later she became interested in military maneuvers and was better versed in military strategy than many an officer. As a half-grown girl, she coquettishly, and unfeelingly, accepted the admiration and flattery of the officers of the garrison, attention offered because of the amateurish zeal with which she worked on military matters, despite her lack of an official role. She was especially susceptible to dress promenade on horseback since "A man on a horse with high boots is the only truly manly man." She rejected numerous suitable marriage proposals until the age of 20 when she became engaged to a lieutenant colonel, 30 years her senior. To the objections of her family that he was too old for her, she had only one reply: "Yes, but if only he didn't have such enchanting feet" [referring to the high riding boots]. This fiance, who became aware of his bride's enthusiasm, gave her an onyx paperweight for Christmas with a pair of miniature riding boots on it, and being a person of a strongly sadistic nature, a dainty silver riding whip to place next to it. This gift made her fall madly in love with the giver. Despite her family's objections, she insisted that wedding plans be made. Luckily (for the family), the lieutenant colonel died before the wedding. As remembrances of him, the girl kept the paperweight and a pair of gloves, since she considered it impossible that his mother would let her have his enchanting boots.

After several flirtations with other cavalry officers, when she was almost 27 a colonel of the general staff came to the town in which the retired general and his family lived. The first sight of the colonel, mounted, in his high riding boots, was fateful. Despite his shocking ugliness, which was startlingly intensified by his scraggly beard, he was for the girl the embodiment of her ideal. "I am in love to the death with the most adorable riding boots I have ever seen," she excitedly told her girlfriend. She confessed that she did not know at all what the man looked like, only his feet: "The man is his foot" and "a person with a beautiful foot[1] one can

---

[1]The German word for "foot," as will be shown later, can be read as "boot" (Translator's note).

safely entrust oneself to," were her mottoes of love. She often repreated to her friend, "Do you think a civilian in low shoes is a man? A pair of riding boots can make one shiver so that one really falls in love."

Three months after their first meeting came their wedding. The marriage was unhappy. Two boys were produced by the couple, it is true, but the woman had sex unwillingly and found it "loathsome and degrading." Only the display of shining riding boots could bring her sexual pleasure. "Don't marry," she wrote to her girlfriend, "for a man with bare feet is a repulsive sight." Even as a girl she asserted the same disgust when questioned by her family about her passion for men's feet. "Yes, in shoes," was her answer, "but plain [naked], a man's foot is disgusting. When I even imagine the big toe, I am horrified. And the nails are always stunted, and the little toe that can never grow! That is a gruesome sight!"

A young officer to whom she had been attracted by the same sartorial charms when she was 20 suddenly earned her dismissal when he sat near her and she noticed him wiggling his toes in his shoes. Another man was rejected on account of bulges in the leather of his boots made by the toes beneath. In a third instance, she based her decision whether to break up an affair with a young officer whose heavy debts her father objected to on whether the young officer came to a rendezvous in high riding boots or low shoes.

I also wish to mention that the young girl, at 17 or 18, fell in love on the same grounds, although completely platonically, with her father's military valet, another time with a noncommissioned officer in the mounted archery unit. In reply to her sister's and girlfriend's reproaches, she countered, "What do you think? All men are the same to me. What gets me excited is their feet. Can't you allow me that?" And when the guardsman misunderstood her enchantment and pressed her, she asserted with indignation: "That simpleton—he believes I pay attention to him rather than his divine feet. Such a conceit is unheard of."

The boots had to be as shiny new as possible and not permitted to bulge out over the toes, with no hint of an impression of toes and no wrinkles in the fastenings. She loved best boots with Russian leather bindings because of their smell.

Her own shoes were important to her, yet she was not in love with either her own well-formed feet or her own shoes (except for the riding boots she got on her tenth birthday). For herself, she did not like low shoes but chose the highest possible little boots "for the smart appearance and pleasure of being tightly laced up." For puttees, leggings, and sportshoes, she had no use because "in them the shapes of the parts of the foot show indecently." High boots she considered "charmingly correct."

This case is very similar to the usual cases of men's foot fetishes. The correspondences in form and nature are so compelling as to suggest the same etiology of female fetishism as we speak of in men. These correspondences differentiate the preceding case from the mass of antecedents in the female gender that have come out where regard for one's own foot and its covering stems from narcissistic sources. That the general's daughter wanted high boots of her own as a ten-year-old and then admired herself in them probably came more out of identification with the beloved father and the passionate wish to be a boy (symbolic nature of the foot-penis) than out of self-love; this more likely came on after the child got possession of the high boots of the idealized father or got close to them. For the grownup, high riding boots were not merely a sign of lovableness nor a sexual symbol, as, for example, the heel in the case of Gerda's heel phobia;[2] the boots were rather the object of the erotic drive. I cannot say whether the characteristic mark of fetishism, the sexual manipulation of the fetish, is missing in this particular case or whether the strong repression of female sexual drives led to suppression of the evidence. The obvious erotic excitement, however, the "enchantment" aroused in the woman by the glimpse of her fetish, is clear in my memory. Furthermore, the situation partakes of the character of the true fetishist in that her full and only interest in men was in their footwear, that the man existed, one could say, only as an unavoidable backdrop for the fetish was actually expressed clearly in words. Not only does she resign from the normal sexual goal, but also makes use of the fetish to make sexual intercourse tolerable.

Her attitude toward naked feet, both before and after marriage, seems to be of particular importance. We consider that disgust always replaced special libido, that usually the foot is the symbol and substitute for penis, which gives us the correct connection. Perhaps the child was once directed to noticing the masculine or father's genital and then, through the sexual intimidation, the accompanying affect was repressed and displaced onto a less shocking body part—the foot. In its role as a substitute penis it must, however, be covered, and this covering is carried out in the service of the idealization of the object (Abraham 1911). This entails

---

[2] L. Binswanger, Analysis of an Hysterical Phobia.

special aspects like shiny newness (which probably means an undamaged state), spotlessness, and so on. From such a line of thought, we then also understand why the young girl found such intense enchantment in high riding boots. And only from such a line of reasoning can we understand why the young girl found the toes such an especially disgusting sight. I cannot say to what extent crippled toes and toenails implied castration to her. It is noteworthy that in this case there is no special focus on specific foot odors in contrast to what is often seen ultimately in other cases (except for the special taste for the smell of Russian leather).

On the other hand, the masochistic component in this case of shoe fetishism is clearly expressed: "In the presence of riding boots one trembles and must therefore fall in love with them." And when the girl laced her lace-up boots so tightly as to leave ridges in her flesh when she took them off, it became evident that to be attractive to her, the boots had to be laced up so that they clasped the calves of the man wearing them tightly.

As an overdetermination of this case on fetishism, I may not dare to omit that the father of this lady was a frank hand fetishist. Her evaluation of a person's character through his feet was doubtless analogous to the general's idea of the connection between character and the appearance of the hand (Hermine Hug-Hellmuth; First published in *International Zeitschrfit für Artliche Psychoanalyse,* Vol. 3, 1915).

DISCUSSION

Hug-Hellmuth implies several possible etiological factors for her subject's perversion. First, the woman's passion for her father was stirred by his seductive choice of her as his favorite. Second, his high shiny boots were associated with him as they walked together. Third, the father and the boots were highly regarded in their town so that she would have experienced enhanced self-esteem by being associated with such boots. Hug-Hellmuth points out that the girl's love for two lower-class men in high boots was completely platonic, that is, it was an ego interest rather than a frankly sexual passion. The absolute specificity of the choice of new, shiny, unwrinkled boots with the strong smell of Russian leather fits the requirement of a fetish as a guarantor of indestructibility. But in this woman, Hug-Hellmuth tells us, the fetish came not out of a narcissistic wish to preserve or magnify the importance of one's penis, but out of "identification with the beloved father and the passionate wish to be a boy." The presence of the masochistic satisfaction in her trembling and consequent attraction, in her tight lacing of her own boots, and in her willingness to accept the boots and whip as an engagement present shows the aggressive wish satisfied by this perversion. Her identification with her father in the belief that one can read character in the physical conformation of a part of the body only requires a displacement from the hand to the foot.

Greenacre (1960) commented on this case:

The persistent use of a fetish may occur in women of a less deviate sexual makeup than Hug-Hellmuth's case and in the setting of a neurosis rather than a perversion. As Freud pointed out, patients generally do not initially complain of the need for a fetish and bring it into the analysis only incidentally. In the cases I have observed in women, this was especially marked. Its apparent unimportance, however, might mask the tenacity with which its real significance in the whole neurotic picture was kept a secret. (p. 183)

This wish to cover up the sexual dysfunction may be what differentiates what Greenacre calls the neurotic use of the fetish from the more openly perverse use of it. Hug-Hellmuth calls this a case of perversion because the fetish replaced sexual intercourse as the goal of sexual activity. Greenacre, by contrast, sees use of the fetish as an adjunct to sexual intercourse as a perversion.

Freud (1905) defined fetish as pathological only when it replaces the sexual object, not when it is an adjunct to it. Similarly, he defined perversion as pathological only when it replaces the sexual aim completely and under all conditions. He allowed that much variability in both aim and object could be accommodated within the realm of normality. When, however, the fetish or the perversion replaces the object or aim entirely, the behavior becomes a pathological symptom.

Rank (1923) used a case of a perversion in a woman as his central example in his paper on perversion. For Rank, repression was only a cover for the underlying perversion. He described it thus:

Her principal dream was practically perennial, and had for years represented the only sexual satisfaction of this quite virgin girl; after great resistance she described her bodily position as a sort of "arche cercle," an arching of the back with protrusion of the genitals, accompanied by sexual orgasm and satisfaction. We see here, therefore, a fully manifest perversion as a manifest dream content; the conscious repression of the exhibitionistic impulse was so powerful, however, that the patient could only call up these changing dream situations in the course of analysis after the greatest resistances it is possible to imagine—silences lasting a quarter of an hour or like an inverted Salome after hiding herself under numberless coats and covers, etc. This truly exhibitionistic dream in contrast to the typical nakedness dreams of normal persons, but like those of perverts, contained no sense of shame and thus indicates that the desire to expose herself came to full expression in the dream (p. 276–277).

The emphasis on lack of shame and habitual or even exclusive use of the fetish as gratification is accompanied in Hug-Hellmuth's description by an emphasis on the masochistic component of the perversion. This emphasis is later expanded and developed by Greenacre in terms of the pregenital aggression repressed and bound by the fetish. The same connection was made by Rank when he remarked on the importance to his patient of memories of having seen boys urinate and having herself retained urine as prominent features of this case. Pregenital phallic aggressiveness was an important factor in the etiology of perversions for all three of these authors.

The issue of shame appears in Hug-Hellmuth's account in two ways: in terms of its absence when the young woman spoke openly of her passion, and in terms of the narcissistic component of her fetish. Here, Hug-Hellmuth rejects narcissism as an etiological factor and sees it, instead, as an outcome rather than a cause. The girl's interest in her own feet or footwear is denied. And the tight lacing of her own boots is taken as secondary to the fetish of tight-laced men's boots.

Thus, the possibility of narcissistic injury or narcissistic pleasure as a first cause of perversion is considered and rejected.

Perversions in women seem to have been more noted than analyzed and written about and the relative absence of consideration of perversions in females in more recent literature has been puzzling. Perhaps there is some simple reason for this, but if so, it is not, in Hug-Hellmuth's terms, "clearly expressed."

One possible explanation is social and historical. According to Morgenthaler (1988):

It is only under specific societal conditions that homosexuality gets stylized into an illness. The same is true with regard to perversions. The assumption, for instance, that fetishism or transvestitism as such belong to the psychopathology of human mental life is disproved by numerous customs and institutions of culture (p. 73).

In Morgenthaler's view, perversion is an innocuous form of self-esteem regulation in which a special sensitivity, which he likens to a talent or taste, is included in the self-image in order to insure self-regard. This idea echoes that of Bach (1985), who believes that perversion covers over perceived inadequacies in the self.

The historical point of view supports Morgenthaler's relativism. In America (D'Emilio and Freedman 1988), the 1880s are marked as the decisive era when sexual deviations began to be labeled as perverse and those practicing them as mentally ill.

> *In conceptualizing viable lives without motherhood, female couples offered an implicit challenge to the delicate structure of middle class morality. No wonder that apologists for marriage were beginning to attack these relationships as morbid and unnatural* (p. 201).

Thus, female perversions would be inadmissible to public discourse because they threatened the idea of motherhood and maternal purity more directly than perversions in the male.

Foucault (1978) considered the same historical process from the European point of view. He concluded that modern societies speak of sex constantly while at the same time treating it as if it were a secret. Seeing control of sexuality as a question of power, Foucault asserted that, beginning in the eighteenth century, there was a gradual progression in social control which ended in

> *. . . a psychiatrization of perverse pleasure: the sexual instinct was isolated as a separate biological and psychical instinct; a clinical analysis was made of all the forms of anomalies by which it could be affected; it was assigned to normalization or pathologization with respect to all behavior; and finally, a corrective technology was sought for these anomalies* (p. 105).

In the history of psychoanalysis, a series of shifts in the understanding of deviate behavior has occurred. Freud's early view in the *Three Essays* (1905) is more in keeping with modern thought than many of the ideas elaborated in the 80 years since then. As Compton (1986) pointed out, Sachs's early paper, "On the Genesis of Perversions," differs from modern psychoanalytic views more on the theoretical level than on the clinical descriptive level. Sachs depicted the origin of perversion as an overly strong drive bound up in a preoedipal experience that retains consciousness because it allows the oedipal elements to remain outside consciousness even while they are gratified through their association with the consciously indulged preoedipal elements.

Such a definition and psychogenesis for perversion contrasts sharply with the assumption by Bak (1953) and others that female perversions are impossible because females cannot have the castration anxiety that leads to the use of a fetish or similar substitute for genital stimulation. In the view of Bak (1974) and Greenacre (1953, 1955, 1960, 1969, 1970), the fetishist requires a substitute or representation for the female phallus to reassure the frightened male that he is not in danger of castration since females are not castrated either. According to Bak (1953), identification with the female disposes to fetishism because this identification carries a castration threat. The fundamental idea required for belief in female immunity to perversion is the idea that perversion is always a reaction to discovery, by the little boy, that the mother has no penis. Since this definition requires a little boy traumatized by the discovery of the female lack of a male genital, the conclusion that perversion is an exclusively male phenomenon seems logical but expresses a tautology. If adhering to this point of view requires ignoring the data of female sexuality, this appears to have been an acceptable choice. Perhaps this is due to the social forces adumbrated by Foucault, D'Emilio and Freedman, and Morgenthaler.

Greenacre (1953), for example, states that, of her few fetishistic patients, one is a female. Yet, in the same paper, she goes on to describe the development of the fetishist as a male with insecure body boundaries and consequent uncertainty about the possibility of castration as well as shaky masculine identity. She concludes, "From the material presented it is probably obvious why the fetish develops in a full state generally only in the male" (p. 28). By 1960, Greenacre had changed her mind on this issue, stating, "The relation of the fetish to the sexual life in women is less apparent than in men since the woman may more successfully conceal disturbances of sexual function, and frigidity can be covered up to a degree which is not possible with the disturbances of potency in the man" (p. 183). In this view, it is not the incidence but the obviousness of the occurrence of fetishism that differs between the sexes.

Greenacre (1968) later reconsidered perversions and fetishes. With no new data, she revised her view based on theoretical considerations. Now she stressed the role of trauma in the first year of life and of innate aggression, also in the first year. Here, Greenacre offered a new definition of what constitutes a fetish. It is no longer defensive, laid to castration fears, nor even sexual in its meaning. When this idea began to be thought of as similar to Winnicott's concept of the transitional object, she (1969) distinguished between the fetish, used for sexual purposes, and the transitional object, used for comfort. The fetish is hard, the transitional object soft; the fetish is taken up at puberty, the transitional object is given up usually before latency. The use of the fetish develops out of a traumatic exposure to the genitals of the opposite sex and/or to a bloody traumatic injury to another person or a pet; the transitional object is created in response to the normal separation experience. The fetish embodies the anger of the castration panic, the transitional object is part of a matrix of tender feelings. Thus, the transitional object is a normal phenomenon in contrast to the fetish, which is abnormal. Her final statement on the occurrence of fetishes is:

> *It* [the fetish] *generally remains an integral part of the equipment necessary for reasonably good sexual performance in the adult male and is also found in some adult female patients. In the latter it appears in a less obvious but very persistent form and represents an extremely severe form of the deviation* (p. 383).

The lack of obviousness, the secrecy is what distinguishes the female fetish.[3] Arlow (1971) showed that:

> *Essentially the perversion is the phantasy acted out. This accounts for the fact that so frequently perverse activity is connected with masturbation. The methods employed by the ego to attain reassurance against anxiety are varied and not mutually exclusive. It is not uncommon, therefore, to find several different perverse trends existing side by side in the same person. I would suspect that this is the rule rather than the exception* (p. 332).

Thus, the perversion is the outcome of a fantasy constructed to resolve a conflict and, in principle, analyzable in the same way other symptoms are analyzed. The analysis of the perversion was carried out successfully by Arlow in the several cases he cites in that paper. That analysis contributed to the understanding of the person being analyzed in a useful and perhaps even essential way.

Raphling (personal communication) has an unpublished case of fetishism in a woman similar to that of Spiegel (1967). Raphling believes

---

[3]Dr. Steven Rittenberg pointed out the crucial nature of the idea of secrecy as the hallmark of female perversions (personal communication).

that fetishism is more complicated in the female than in the male and that "subtle forms of the perversion may go unnoticed and may be more prevalent than previously realized" (p. 17). In his case, the woman used inanimate objects during masturbation and heterosexual intercourse to maintain the fantasy of having a phallus. The fetish was shown to have oedipal meanings, both positive and negative; it represented an oedipal baby. It also represented a hostile wish to destroy the man's penis in intercourse as well as a protection from bodily damage which the woman fantasized to be caused by penetration or impregnation. The fetish served as well to represent alternatives to affective involvement with men in her love life as well as with her analyst. The fetish is thus similar to Greenacre's final view—a necessary adjunct to relatively normal sexual intercourse. By Freud's definition, the use of the objects as adjuncts to intercourse or masturbation rather than as substitutes for genital satisfaction would qualify as a variation of sexual object, not as a true perversion.

It is possible to widen the concept of fetish to mean intense clinging to any object, as Hopkins (1984) did in her account of a foot and shoe fetish in a latency-age girl. But this is fetishism in the popular, not the psychoanalytic sense, since it has nothing to do with sexual potency or sexual perversion. It would be interesting to know whether Hopkins' patient eventually developed a true fetish. If not, it might be claimed that the early treatment might have helped prevent the formation of a fetish.

What difference does it make to uncover and analyze a perverse symptom? Unless one is open to the idea that perverse symptoms may occur in women, one is bound to miss such symptoms when they do occur. Recognizing the possibility of perverse symptoms can make the difference between ameliorating the symptom by analyzing it and driving it underground so as to remove the possibility of treating it. A perverse symptom is experienced as repulsive. It is all too easy to find the patient who has such a symptom repulsive as well. But so is a patient who does not respond to treatment. It may be in the interest of protecting women from social condemnation to think of them as never having perversions. But this protection also prevents their benefiting from treatment if it results in failure to analyze such symptoms. I believe that it is in our women patients' interests that we consider the possibility that they may have perverse symptoms. And if Hug-Hellmuth's paper helps us to do this, I am glad to have been able to bring it back into analytic awareness.

REFERENCES

ABRAHAM, K. (1912). Psychoanalysis of a Case of Foot and Corset Fetishism. *Jahrbuch für Psychoanalytische und Psychopathologische Forschungen* 3:557–567.

ARLOW, J. (1971). Character Perversion. In I. Marcus (Ed.), *Currents in Psychoanalysis*. New York: International Universities.

BACH, S. (1985) Narcissistic States and the Therapeutic Process. New York: Aronson.

BAK, R. (1953). Aggression and Perversion. In *Perversions: Psychodynamks and Therapy* S. Lorand, ed. New York: Random House.

——— (1974). Distortion of the Concept of Fetishism. *Psychoanalytic Study Child* 21:191–214.

BRENNER, C. (1982). *The Mind in Conflict.* New York: International Universities Press.

COMPTON, A. (1986). Neglected Classics: Hans Sachs's "On the Genesis of Perversions." *Psychoanalytic Quarterly* 55:474–492.

D'EMILIO, J., & FREEDMAN, E. (1988). *Intimate Matters: A History of Sexuality in America.* New York: Harper & Row.

FOUCAULT, M. (1978). *The History of Sexuality.* New York: Random House.

FREUD, S. (1905). Three Essays on the Theory of Sexuality. *Standard Edition* 7:125–221.

GREENACRE, P. (1953). Certain Relationships Between Fetishism and the Faulty Development of the Body Image. In *Emotional Growth.* New York: International Universities Press, 1971.

——— (1955). Further Considerations Regarding Fetishism. In *Emotional Growth.* New York: International Universities Press, 1971.

——— (1960). Further Notes on Fetishism. In *Emotional Growth.* New York: International Universities Press, 1971.

——— (1968). Perversions: General Considerations Regarding Their Genetic and Dynamic Background. In *Emotional Growth.* New York: International Universities Press, 1971.

——— (1969). The Fetish and the Transitional Object. In *Emotional Growth.* New York: International Universities Press, 1971.

——— (1970). The Transitional Object and the Fetish: With Special Reference to the Role of Illusion. In *Emotional Growth.* New York: International Universities Press, 1971.

HOPKINS, J. (1984). The Probable Role of Trauma in the Case of Foot and Shoe Fetishism: Aspects of the Psychotherapy of a Six-Year-Old Girl. *International Review of Psycho-Anaysis* 11:79–91.

HUG-HELLMUTH, H. (1915). A Case of Female Foot or More Properly Boot Fetishism. In *International Zeitschrfit für Artliche Psychoanalyse,* Vol. 3.

MORGENTHALER, F. (1988). *Homosexuality, Heterosexuality, Perversion.* Hillsdale, NJ: Analytic Press.

RANK, O. (1923). Perversion and Neurosis *International Journal of Psycho-Analysis* 4(3):270–292.

RICHARDS, A.K. (1989). A Romance with Pain: A Telephone Perversion in a Woman. *International Journal of Psycho-Analysis* 70:153–164.

SPIEGEL, N. (1967). An Infantile Fetish and Its Persistence into Young Womanhood. *Psychoanalytic Study Child* 22:442–425.

****
****

Original publication of preceding chapter:

RICHARDS, A.K. (1990). Female Fetishes and Female Perversions: Hermine Hug-Hellmuth's "A Case of Female Foot or More Properly Boot Fetishism" Reconsidered. *Psychoanalytic Review* 77:11–23.

A Romance with Pain: A Telephone Perversion in a Woman?

There didn't seem to be very many female perversions in that book. Perhaps because it was old. Perhaps women have developed these things more recently as a result of emancipation.

—MARGARET DRABBLE,
The Waterfall (p. 184)

A 20-year-old woman wearing black leather clothes and a very large hairdo came to me for treatment. She was in danger of being expelled from college because of her insatiable demands on faculty, and her inability to complete papers, and from her dormitory for unacceptable overuse of the dormitory telephone. She had a history of bladder and kidney infections since the age of six which her physician believed were secondary to urinary retention. Several operations on her genito-urinary tract had not helped. She had a history of erratic peer relations as well. She had gone from being president of her freshman class in high school to having no one willing to walk down the aisle with her at graduation. Although she described herself as wanting to be liked by her four older brothers, she also described constantly complaining to her mother about them. She was technically a virgin, although she had engaged in oral sex without orgasm. She denied masturbation. Her most prominent complaint was of "pain inside," her only method of self-soothing was telephoning her mother. She had been in psychotherapy since the age of eight.

At the start of the treatment she soothed herself by telephoning her mother at all hours of the day. I very gradually attempted to draw the symptom into the transference, encouraging her to call me instead and picking up her calls at least once a day. After six months, we agreed that she was to gain control by calling her parents on some schedule, not every time she wanted to. She inquired of other students in her dormitory. They called their parents once a week. She decided she would feel more like them and less babyish if she did the same.

Instead of calling her mother, the patient now called the analyst, friends, and neighbours when she became agitated. She moved often; she could not get along with any of the people she tried to live with; she had fist fights; she dropped out of school and worked at a series of jobs. Despite the turmoil she was able to tolerate the limit. She began using the analyst as she had used her mother—asking me to reassure her that the people she got into battles with had done her wrong. She was told that she wanted to hear that she was justified in her behaviour. Two years into the treatment she began to do better in school. She settled into a reassuringly impersonal institutional arrangement: an adult dormitory. After achieving this much autonomy, she made the telephone call that triggered a completely new conceptualization of the case for me.

The patient reported that she had called a friend very late the prior evening. The friend's roommate said that she was at her boyfriend's place. The patient got his phone number, called, asked to speak to her friend, and began her usual litany: "You don't know how much it hurts inside." The friend snapped: "What are you, some kind of pervert? You want to get in bed with us, or what?" She hung up. The question opened a new phase of the analysis; the patient went into detail about her feelings when she made such calls. She would become more and more tense until she achieved relaxation. The pain inside referred to her retention of urine until the bladder became painfully full and an orgastic shudder ended the tension and the content of the calls was a reflection of their form. If listened to in the light of a sexual experience, the repetitive quality, the stereotypic patterns, and the insistence on her inner body sensations were a precise description of her orgastic experiences. She was able to become aware of this as it was interpreted to her. Like many male obscene telephone callers, she involved the listener in her sexual experience only through the superego-dominated auditory sphere, not in the visual and tactile spheres of sensual enjoyment. Could this be a true perversion without awareness that the pleasure experienced was sexual? And could the lack of awareness be the specific hallmark of a female perversion (Freud 1919)? In order to understand the case, I re-read the literature on perversions, looking for what I could find on perversions in women.

FEMALE PERVERSIONS?

One of the most puzzling aspects of perversions has been the almost uniform depiction and theoretical understanding of perversion as a male phenomenon. From Freud's early presentation in the "Three Essays" (1905) to Chasseguet-Smirgel's current and theoretically rich consideration of the topic in *Creativity and Perversion* (1984), most psychoanalytic writers on this topic have dealt with the development and dynamics of male perversion. Few analytic accounts of female perverts are to be found in the literature. Even McDougall (1985) has described the treatment of female perversion only in patients whose perversion was homosexuality, a deviation of object rather than aim. The classical teaching case for female perversion had been Freud's "The Psychogenesis of a Case of Homosexuality in a Woman" (1920). But Freud himself had carefully differentiated homosexuality from perversion in the first of the "Three Essays on Sexuality" (1905). He called homosexuality inversion, reserving the term perversion for deviations of aim and for the choice of children, animals, parts of the human body, or inanimate objects as sexual partners. Later writers (e.g., Fenichel 1945); (Bieber et al. 1962); (Socarides 1968) blurred this distinction.

In the analytic literature only five cases of perversions in heterosexual women have been reported. Three of these reports were brief anecdotes. Grunberger (1966) briefly described a case of perversion in a woman.

For a long time she achieved an erotic pleasure in imagining, or when circumstances permitted, observing a little girl wanting to urinate but prevented from doing so. This sado-masochistic fantasy was for a long time the only form of sexual excitation at her disposal. This autoerotic act had once been highly invested narcissistically by her father who woke her up every night to urinate . . . an early erotic closeness in her relationship to her father resulted in a perversion (p. 165).

Khan (1979) described a patient complaining of agoraphobia. Analytic treatment uncovered two episodes of perverse behaviour in which she was tied up, gagged, and raped. She was able to attain orgasm in these episodes as she had not been able to do in her marriage. The episodes were initiated by her partners and ended when she left them because of life changes, apparently without regret. Chasseguet-Smirgel (1984) reported a case of a woman who submitted to her lover's perverse sado–masochistic scenario and dropped it when she dropped him. The author asks: "Was it a real perversion? She said that she did not enjoy it" (p. 132).

Two fuller case reports exist as well. Zavitzianos (1971) reported a case of a female fetishist and kleptomaniac who developed an exhibitionistic perversion during analysis, but he did not report whether the symptoms were ever resolved. Spiegel (1967) reported a case of a young woman whose fetish, a shoestring, alternated with masturbation by fingering either breasts or anus. After considerable work, the patient replaced the string with a "man on a string." She then interrupted treatment. While this is the most completely recorded case in the analytic literature of a female with a sexual perversion, it does not address the issue of whether such an analysis is terminable (Freud 1937).

The questions raised by this sparse literature are:

1. Why are female perversions so rarely reported in the psychoanalytic literature?
2. Are there analyzable females with perversions?
3. If so, can such an analysis enrich our understanding of the nature of perversion?

It is my hypothesis that female patients may have been considered as borderline or psychotic (Fliess 1973) rather than as perverts because neither they nor their therapists were aware of their erotic pleasure in their symptoms and therefore considered them bizarre eruptions of very early aggressive impulses. Freud (1919) asserted that only his male patients were aware of the crucial second stage of their beating fantasies. None of his female patients could recall them. Chehrazi (1986) summarized changes in the analytic understanding of female psychology as tending toward awareness of a specifically female sexual development rather than a variant of male development. As Bernstein (1986) has shown, the essence of the female genital is its hiddenness, its inaccessibility, and its diffuse sensations. Fisher[1] reports a study in which women showing physiological vaginal arousal to sexual stimuli did not report experiencing sexual feelings. Women could experience the excitement of the sexual tension build-up as anxiety. They could understand the shudder of discharge as 'someone walking on my grave', as one of my patients put it. With growing sophistication, at least some women experience orgasm as sexual even when it occurs outside the content of sexual intercourse or deliberate self-stimulation. For this reason it seems to me that it may now

---

[1]Charles Fisher, Personal communication.

be possible to obtain reports of perversions which had been inaccessible in the past.

According to Greenacre (1953, 1968), frequent observation of the genitals of the opposite sex increases the likelihood of a perversion. Perversions were thought by Chasseguet-Smirgel (1984) to be an expression of the anal-sadistic mixing of categories which children oppose to the adult separation of sexual, generational, and affective categories. Khan (1979) considered the perversions to be dramatizations of early memories of unsuccessful relationships with the primary objects. According to Bach (1985), perversion is an attempt to deal with a narcissistic fault by creating an idealized anal object. For these authors, object relations are the crucial element in the aetiology of perversions.

Bak (1968), Ferenczi (1911), and McDougall (1985) emphasized the instinctual drive in the perversions. For Bak, the perversion is an assertion of the female phallus. Eissler (1958) suggested that perversions which arouse guilt are the only ones treatable by psychoanalysis.

TELEPHONE PERVERSIONS

The specific perversion of obscene telephone calling has an analytic literature. The telephone has been understood as a fetish. Almansi (1985) pointed out that the telephone permits anonymous access for perverse as well as for compulsive and aggressive purposes. He described a patient whose perverse telephoning was precipitated by feelings of loneliness and abandonment; as a child he had seen his mother masturbate while listening in on a party line. Silverman (1982a) ascribed the importance of sounds coming from an unseen source to the voice of conscience and (Silverman 1982b) the institution of use of a telephone to defend against castration anxiety in a young boy. The use of the telephone as a phallic instrument was described in three cases by Harris (1957). In his cases telephone anxiety was a symptom related to oedipal conflict. Shengold (1982) described two cases in which telephoning led to masturbation. In both, overstimulation by the mother had marked the childhood primal scene fantasy.

Weich (1982) asserted that language as a fetish subverts the overt communication so that what is said is less important than the fact that the caller intrudes and the person called is intruded upon. Most notable is Bunker's (1934) description of the voice as a fantasy phallus, a symbolism supported by its functions in expressing emotion and allowing discrimination of the sex of the speaker. The female diva, the German Lorelei, and the Greek Sirens are such phallic-voiced women.

Lewin (1933) described two female patients, one of whom experienced her body as gradually stiffening through the day until relieved by the flow of words during the analytic hour, which was like an ejaculation. Another had a sensation of swelling, heat, and impulse to scream when she lay in bed. As a child the latter had witnessed adult coitus, developed enuresis, and later impulses to scream. A recent film, *Diva,* shows a singer refusing to allow her voice to be recorded. It is as if, understanding it to be her phallus, she will not allow it to be enjoyed detached from herself. She demands of her fans that she be present to enjoy them enjoying her. The patient I describe in this paper seemed to experience her voice as the phallus when she spoke over the telephone.

CASE ILLUSTRATION

The analysis was conducted four times a week for the first five years, five times a week for the last two years. All of the analytic work was on the couch. One telephone call, to be discussed in detail, added an element of action to the transference.

The patient was gradually able to understand her telephone calls as erotic. She had always known they were her only comfort, but in the analysis she began to understand the genital nature of her pleasure in them. Envy of the possessions of others led to expressions of her envy of the analyst. Seeing me wear a new pair of shoes started her on furious tirades about the fee. The money she was paying for the treatment enabled me to have them and deprived her at the same time. She was plagued by envy and spiteful wishes. Analysis of the fantasies involved included a consideration of her penis envy, denial of the female genital, rejection of any awareness of the penisless state of her mother, and fantasies of mastery attained through the giving and withholding of the urinary stream. The understanding helped her to give up the behaviour.

We were able to trace a particularly humiliating experience from the eighth year of life back to its roots in her early experiences as well as forward into certain adolescent forms of acting out (Arlow 1971). She repeatedly displayed her genital to other girls in the school toilet. They reported that to their parents, who complained to the school authorities. She was sent home in disgrace; expelled. Memories of having been exposed repeatedly to pissing contests between her four older brothers and of having constantly seen all the males in her family naked in the bathroom were recounted. The urinary stream may have gained particular importance as a result of this experience (Galenson & Roiphe 1976). The traumatic effect of all this male nudity was increased by the circumstance that her mother never undressed in front of her. The little girl had the choice of believing either that her mother was made the same as the men or that she was ashamed of what she had. She chose the latter idea, identified with the brothers and the father, and adopted a masculine attitude toward the mother.

This was reinforced by the father's repeated weekend absences from home, starting when she was 2 years old. Since the boys teased her when they were forced to baby-sit for her, the mother would take the little girl out with her, leaving the boys at home. She became her mother's escort, which increased her belief in her fantasy penis. When father was at home, however, he would accompany mother. The little girl was left at home with her brothers. They took revenge on her for having been left behind on other evenings, so she staged tantrums whenever the parents were about to go out together. Mother would telephone her to make sure she was all right. The telephone came to her rescue, gave her power over her brothers, symbolizing the fantasy penis.

Thus, despite the family constellation in which she felt extremely valued as a girl coming after so many boys, she had developed a conflicted masculine identification and a fantasy penis. These developments interacted with her identification with her extremely loving mother to produce a paradoxical and extremely problematic form of femininity. One could speculate that she attempted to resolve her conflictual bisexuality by reverting to a dependency on the mother characteristic of the little girl of the separation-individuation phase. By clinging, returning to home base by telephone, and demanding in an alternately whiny and threatening way, she retained the power of the toddler. It was a compromise in that she was feminine, dependent, and passive, yet secretly masculine and active in that she had the power to keep mother at home waiting for her phone calls.

This sort of understanding of her adolescent dilemma seemed helpful. It continued the themes of her previous therapies, but now in the context of the instinctual component. The other major symptom of her latency and adolescence had been insistent complaints of genito-urinary pain which led to several operations, starting at the age of 8, on her bladder, ureter, and urethra, after mechanical stretching of her urethra had not yielded the relief she demanded. She had abdominal scars from the bladder surgery as well as scars on her back from the kidney surgery. Pain in the genital area had been an important feature of her latency. In the course of the analysis it became clear that it had been libidinized and led to secondary narcissistic gratification. Opportunities to display her genital were part of the examination process as she went from doctor to doctor to seek a cure. The infections continued through the second year of the analysis when the urinary retention and its sequelae were uncovered and analysed. The relationship between the experience of painful intrusions and her later hostile aggressiveness was traced in the analysis. Her venom towards doctors extended to those who served her needs in other ways as well. Altercations with her dry-cleaner, dental hygienist, and the secretaries at school related to the pain, anguish, and humiliation she had suffered around the operations, examinations, and interviews with staff at both hospitals and doctor's offices. No genito-urinary infections were reported after that.

The infections and operations had required attention from the mother of a kind which reinstated the pre-oedipal ties. The mother, drawn once again into the pre-oedipal mode of nurturance and protection which the daughter's fantasies required, had been a virtual prisoner in the home throughout the daughter's adolescence. Since the telephone calls were restricted to once a week, however, the mother had developed a career of her own. With no treatment herself, she benefited from being relieved of the regressive demands of her daughter.

The positive oedipal conflict emerged only in the fifth year of treatment. She dreamt of a white horse. the dream and the telephone fantasy coincided in the associations. She remembered having called home from the nurse's office because she was sick in school one day when she was 10. Her oldest brother, home from college, came to pick her up at school. The nurse tried to cheer her up by saying, 'Here comes your Prince Charming on a white charger'. This memory condensed several ideas. She was entitled to sexual satisfaction only if desperately ill, an idea derived from early permission to sleep with mother if she was ill. She was to get up on a 'high horse' for this embodiment of arrogance. She was to become father's favourite when he came home unexpectedly. This fantasy was particularly dangerous since neither brother nor father was perceived as reliably law-abiding because both had displayed themselves to her. To protect her from fulfilment of the forbidden wish and to punish her mother for keeping father to herself, the mother had to be home at all times to receive her calls.

As she achieved in the field in which her father had achieved only a limited success, she became more able to tolerate heterosexual relationships. She was able to tolerate intercourse when she fantasied actively wrapping herself around the man's penis rather than experiencing it as penetrating her. This compromise was enhanced in the last year of the analysis when she found a lover who had not been circumcised. At last she enjoyed the sight of 'a penis that was not naked'. This modestly covered penis was not humiliating to her, it was not displayed as her father's and brothers' had been. The man became particularly important to her.

Much of the analytic work dealt with her narcissistic needs. For example, she began to develop more sense of self-esteem as she became able to tolerate the limits of her capacities. A cycle of testing and evaluating her own worth in terms of her achievements rather than her power over the people who represented her love objects was initiated. As this progressed, she was less vulnerable to fluctuations in self-esteem. She required less assurance to accept herself as worthwhile. This process was repeated in the treatment many times; increasingly stable self-esteem showed first in the area of work and only later in her love life.

As her life became increasingly satisfying, the patient began to experience the analytic sessions as interferences. She became increasingly able to tolerate impulses without acting on them and skilled at interpreting her own dreams, symptoms, and jokes. She wondered whether our work was done. We agreed on a termination and, after talking about it for several weeks, she was able to set a date. She chose one six months from that time.

By this time she had more of a sense of cohesion than she presented early in the treatment. She expressed this sense of lowered vulnerability to stress by saying, 'The glue is sticking'. The underlying sense of superiority was no longer detectable. Other people could choose what they wished to give her. Her need to be the favourite sibling was no longer so prominent. She no longer needed to focus on her brothers' shortcomings but could differentiate and value their individual traits. Her envy and resentment of the achievements of others abated. She no longer needed to compete with the analyst. While she was prey to envy of her colleagues, she could curb its expression. Her sense of being an exception because of early suffering moderated as she became able to forgive her parents for their mistakes in terms of modesty and in handling her fears of separation as well as in allowing her to substitute for her father in her mother's social life. The sense of entitlement moderated down to a willingness to work for what she believed she deserved. She was also able to express gratitude.

The limit on telephone calls to her mother was analysed shortly after the decision to terminate treatment, but before setting of the date, the patient's grandmother died. In the week following her death, daily calls between the patient and her mother precipitated a crisis which was a miniature of what brought her into treatment. Again she was whining, her mentor began complaining that she was demanding too much time, and she began to be afraid that her parents would entangle her in what she believed to be their shady finances. All of this was related to her guilt over the greedy wishes to have her mother to herself in a sexual way as well as having her mother's love for her as the special child. It was also related to the frustration of those wishes and her fury at her father, who frustrated them. She became aware of the sadistic control over her mother's mobility she had exerted by forcing her mother to stay at home to receive her calls. She also saw how angry her mother's over-indulgence made her. She decided she was better off sticking to once-a-week contact with her parents. She began mourning the loss of her grandmother-analyst, a saintly person who never intruded or demanded things for herself, but only accepted confidences and gave support to one's efforts.

With the transference in this unrealistically sunny state, she left an apologetic message. She would not come to her session because she was constipated. She was really sick. She was doing the best she could but she could not come in. She felt feverish although her temperature was not elevated. She was nauseous (*sic*). The doctor had prescribed two quarts of liquid a day and exercise. She was desperate. If I wanted to, I could call her back at the time of her session. The unnecessary elaborateness of the message alerted me. Had she simply not wanted to come in because she felt ill, that would have been enough. The complaints were very close to those of seven years before. And the telephone calls, which had been limited to very occasional communications about schedule changes, were now to be extended into a substitute for a session.

She was incredulous when I pointed this out to her. She had completely forgotten. So I recalled it for her, using her exact words, which I had no difficulty remembering after hearing them so many times. The pains inside. The pressure. The conviction that only her mother could possibly soothe her. The desperate need to be soothed. The assurance that she would not have called unless she were desperate. She was, however, able to remember having had exactly those thoughts this very morning. She had intended to call her mother later. As I connected the thoughts to the sexual excitement, she settled down. I said that her forgetting had to do with the sexual use she had made of those calls. At this point, she excused herself to go to the toilet. When she came back to the phone, she had discharged the sexual excitement by urinating in what she described as a heavy, phallic orgastic stream from a full bladder. I interpreted her action as exhibiting herself seductively to me as she had exhibited herself in the school toilet.

The meaning of the use of the telephone on that one occasion years after the regular use of telephone calls had ceased was discussed in the following sessions. The themes of the overwhelming excitement, the desperate need to be soothed by the mother, and the need to be absolved by the mother were repeated and understood as part of an elaborate fantasy. She understood that call as a last attempt to actually penetrate me—to make me see—to make me understand—to get into my head. She understood that she had to use the telephone for this because the telephone was the only way she could get through to me. It was, in other words, her fantasy penis. On the couch she did not have it, so she was reduced to talking—which she had believed could never get through to me. Her magical belief in the telephone and its power to "get to you," as she put it, could only be tested by actually trying it. This last attempt to prove that she had a phallus, could use it effectively, and could penetrate me with it and thus gain relief herself was the focus of the remainder of the analysis.

Analysis of this fantasy on the couch in the ensuing weeks produced evidence that she understood the telephone as a phallus. With the telephone in her mind, she felt powerful. The concrete object was important. She was not just talking, she was "getting through to you." Although she was enraged at the idea that this assuaged her envy of those, like my husband, who had a penis, could go on vacations with me, and could "get through to you," she eventually acknowledged it in the context of a memory. Talking about the telephone as a phallus led to a recall of a nightmare which had recurred several times a year since her childhood. In this nightmare she was being suffocated. She wanted to fight back but was helpless in her panic. Her nightmare was a castration-rape fantasy; the rapist was a witch, punished by castration. She was relieved as she understood her fear as related to her obsessional question of whether she or another person was at fault. She saw this as the problem of the couple formed by herself and her mother. Whoever had the penis was innocent; the person without the penis was the witch, the criminal, at fault. She was terrified because she was alone, helpless, penisless, and a criminal; all the fears of her infancy coalesced in this nightmare (Brenner 1982). She expressed gratitude after the analysis of this dream. Her appearance, which had gradually softened during the seven years of treatment, now attained a look of satisfaction, a look she had long begrudged the analyst, the look she had earlier bitterly called smug.

DISCUSSION

The question of why female perversions are so rarely discussed in the literature seems to me to be capable of illumination from this case. The perverse-system was hidden, as female sexuality generally has been hidden from scrutiny because it is anatomically hidden (Peto 1975). It was hidden also because it gave evidence of aggressivity which was unacceptable to her because it was a too-masculine threat to her feminine wishes. It was hidden as well because the patient's shame and guilt frightened her—she expected disgust and rejection from the analyst because of it. She could hide the behaviour and its associated affect so well because she is a woman. She was motivated to do so by her socially motivated feminine modesty, her superego condemnation of her own aggression, and her projection of this condemnation on to the analyst.

A male patient who was fired from his job for persistently exhibiting his penis to his female supervisees reported that he was frequently unaware of his condition until alerted to it by the startled look of the woman to whom he was exhibiting himself. His pleasure consisted in the eye contact, the woman's anger and humiliation, and, as we discovered in his treatment, his previously unconscious thought that women are aroused by the sight of the penis because they have one which can be aroused also. The central issue in this man's perversion was not his awareness of what he was doing, but the denial of the differences between the sexes. His idea that women have hidden penises which can be aroused by the sight of a man's penis was an absolute precondition for him to have sexual intercourse. The psychological difference between this man and my woman patient seems to lie in the degree of awareness of the specifically erotic nature of the excitement and satisfaction, which I believe is the crucial difference between male and female experiences of sexuality.

An early example of female urinary eroticism appears in Freud (1894):

During this erotic reverie she had the bodily sensation which is to be compared with an erection in a man, and which, in her case—I do not know if this is always so—ended with a slight need to urinate. She became greatly frightened by the sexual sensation (to which she was normally accustomed) because she had resolved within herself to combat this particular liking as well as any other she might feel, and the next moment the affect had become transferred on to the accompanying need to urinate and compelled her after an agonizing struggle to leave the hall. In her ordinary life she was so prudish that she had an intense horror of anything to do with sex and could not contemplate the thought of ever marrying. On the other hand, she was so hyperaesthetic sexually that during erotic reverie, in which she readily indulged, the same voluptuous sensation appeared. The erection was each time accompanied by the need to urinate, though without this making any impression on her until the scene in the concert hall. The treatment led to an almost complete control over her phobia (p. 56).

Here Freud presents a symptom which he calls a phobia, but which, were it to be described in a man, would very probably be called a perversion. The need to urinate as a substitute for sexual contact with an eligible and interested member of the opposite sex, the tension, the enjoyment without awareness of the sexuality, and repudiation of the behaviour all find parallels in my patient. A man experiencing an erection with need to urinate and accepting this in place of sexual contact with women would surely be considered a pervert.

The difference between a diagnosis of perversion and one of symptom neurosis in Freud's case seems to me to be a result of his consistent tendency to be more forgiving, more indulgent, and more protective towards women than towards men. And the subsequent literature has followed his lead in this respect. Kramer[2] put it this way:

As far as the paucity of female sexual perversions is concerned, I have felt for many years that all of female sexuality is under-reported, and my women analyst colleagues agree with me. We find it interesting to note that we recognize a much higher incidence of female masturbation than do our male colleagues. Virginia Clower and I discussed this and feel that many male analysts have what we

---

[2]Selma Kramer, personal communication.

call the "sugar and spice" attitude toward their female patients. Surely nice girls don't!

A more recent formulation by Stoller (1987) focuses on the predominance of hostile aggression in perversions, a view which resurrects the disapproval and rejection of compromise formations labelled perversions.

For my patient the urinary stream was idealized, as anal products were idealized by the Marquis de Sade (Bach 1985). Her telephone calls condensed her fantasy of her father's phallic intrusion on her mother with the patient's auditory intrusion on her (Chasseguet-Smirgel 1984). The sadistic quality of her transference behaviour was clear. Through it she constantly mixed up affects, giving pain for pleasure. She disavowed the differences between the sexes, between generations, and between pleasure and unpleasure (Greenacre 1968). At the same time, she was dependent for her sexual pleasure on the use of the telephone and on the power and narcissistic enhancement of the urinary stream. Genital sensation was available only through this deviant scenario which had to be acted out in reality, compulsively, frequently, and with a sense of being driven that prevented her from experiencing actions of her own. Was this a perversion?

Freud first defined perversion as persistent preference for fantasy which punishes and ensures forgiveness. Some later writers have focused on the fetish, others on sadomasochism, and yet others on narcissistic reparation. The case described here shows all of these features. It could be the female analogue of what would be called a perversion in a male. Stoller (1979) defined perversion as the ability to remain excited while aware of one's sexual activity. As Michels (1980) has pointed out, this definition would include normal sexuality as one of the perversions. Thus awareness may be a necessary aspect of sexual activity if it is to be called perverse, but it cannot be sufficient. Awareness may not even be dichotomous.

Sachs (1986) dealt with the issue of consciousness in the perversions. His clinical data showed a mixture similar to that of the present case. He described it this way:

During the rather lengthy drawn-out repressive process which had not begun until after puberty, as well as during that portion of the analytic work during which the repression was being lifted, there were intermediate states where one could not be sure whether what one was dealing with was a neurotic symptom or a form of perverse gratification (p. 480).

From this observation he concluded that: "Thus with the insertion of addicts as a connecting link, it is possible to construct a continuum with perverse gratification at one end and the neurotic symptom at the other" (p. 482).

The relation between awareness and unconscious fantasy is complex. Arlow (1969) took the position that unconscious fantasy goes on all the time. "Unconscious daydreaming is a constant feature of mental life. It is an ever-present accompaniment of conscious experience. What is consciously apperceived and experienced is the result of interaction between the data of experience and unconscious fantasying as mediated by various functions of the ego" (p. 23). Beneath a conscious scenario there may thus be an unconscious one as well. The pervert acting out a scene acts a variant or derivative of the unconscious fantasy. In this sense, a perversion is like any other symptom. All that distinguishes the perversion from other symptoms, in my view, is the social condemnation of perversion as contrasted with the social evaluation of the symptom as nonvolitional and therefore morally neutral (Lydston 1889).

If one wishes to preserve a distinction between perversion and neurotic symptom, awareness of the pleasurable aspect of the symptom which is attained in the course of analysis constitutes the conversion of that symptom into a perversion and it is only the analysis of the libidinal aggressive wishes, defensive manoeuvres, and internal prohibitions attached to that symptom, together with reconstruction or recall of the original fantasy behind that symptom, which removes the perverse symptom.

On the other hand, it seems more fruitful to consider both symptoms and perversions as compromise formations and use Brenner's (1982) criterion of more or less successful compromise formations as the indications for analysis and the criteria for analytic cure rather than continuing to make a distinction between perversions and ordinary symptoms.

This case was analysed to a conclusion which not only resolved the symptom but convinced both the analyst and the patient that the patient was now free to continue the work on her own and satisfied that she had received enough. Her naive but liberated friend provided a clue—to call her symptoms a perversion. While her friend did not mean by the term exactly what is meant by it in the analytic literature, she did raise what I believe to be an analytically fruitful issue.

Having dealt with the question of why female perversions are reported so rarely in the literature and the related question of whether analysis is possible with such a patient, I will turn now to the third question: Can this analysis enrich our understanding of the dynamics and genetics of those compromise formations which have been called perversions?

While inference from male psychology to female has been traditional, only in the area of perversions has the reasoning from female to male been suggested in the past. In speaking of extreme submissiveness in women, Annie Reich (1940) states:

> *I think that such extreme submissiveness in women is a clear-cut clinical picture which may best be regarded as a perversion. It is found in men as well as in women, but since my clinical material happens to comprise only female cases I will restrict myself to discussing the mechanisms at work in women. It is possible that the mechanisms in men are similar* (p. 86).

On the basis of the analysis of this case, I believe that the issue raised by Greenacre's (1968) formulation can be addressed. Greenacre suggested that the earliest pregenital identification with the mother is responsible for the male pervert's difficulty in feeling certain that he retains the penis when faced with the terrifying female genital. The female is in a state of confusion similar to that of the male in that she believes that her genital is identical to the male's. Her identification with the mother is conflicted as an outcome of this belief, but this patient needed to consolidate the identification with her father in her work before she could achieve an identification with the oedipal mother, and thus attain a heterosexual, genital love life. It appears that in the female it is not only the primary identification with the mother which can cause the confusion which leads to a compromise formation likely to be labelled a perversion, but also the failure of the later identification with the father.

Since many of the persistent, clinging, repetitive telephone calls made to therapists are made by women patients, it may be that exploration of the possibility that the telephone is being used as a fetish may enhance our understanding of such patients. In turn, such exploration could also enhance our understanding of the perversions.

SUMMARY

The patient repeatedly and compulsively made stereotyped telephone calls to her mother and other female protective figures. She had a history of genito-urinary infections and operations consequent to urinary retention. These symptoms were relieved gradually in the course of analysis, in which this was interpreted as a sado-masochistic perversion based on a central fantasy of phallic intrusions on the mother. The fantasy was related to turning passive viewing into active exhibitionism, actively seeking to inflict pain on herself and others in an attempt to overcome early painful medical intrusions, misplaced identification with the father, complementary relationship with the passive, compliant mother, and consequent failed identification with the oedipal mother. In the analysis, she attained a gradual reorganization of adaptive functions which allowed identification with the father through her work, reconciliation with the rivalrous siblings, and enjoyment of her female sexuality in heterosexual intercourse with the use of a fetishistic requirement that the man be uncircumcised.

The hypothesis was developed that whether called a symptom or a perversion, the treatment was the same so that it was most useful to think of it as a compromise formation rather than attempting to preserve a distinction largely based on moralistic considerations.

REFERENCES

ALMANSI, R.J. (1985). On Telephoning, Compulsive Telephoning, and Perverse telephoning. *Psychoanalytic Study of Society* 11:217–235.

ARLOW, J. (1969). Unconscious Fantasy and Disturbances of Conscious Experience. *Psychoanalytic Quarterly* 38:1–27.

——— (1971). A Type of Play Observed in Boys During the Latency Period. In *Separation-Individuation: Essays in Honor of Margaret Mahler.* J. McDevitt & C. Settlage, eds. New York: International Universities Press.

BACH, S. (1985). *Narcissistic States and the Therapeutic Process.* New York: Jason Aronson.

BAK, R. 1968 The Phallic Woman: The Ubiquitous Fantasy in Perversions. *Psychoanalytic Study of the Child* 23:15–36.

BERNSTEIN, D. (1986). Female Genital Anxieties: Conflict and Mastery. Paper read at the American Psychological Association, Division 39, February 1986.

BIEBER, I. et al. (1962). *Homosexuality.* New York: Basic Books.

BRENNER, C. (1982). *The Mind in Conflict.* New York: International Universities Press.

BUNKER, H.A. (1934). The Voice as (Female) Phallus. *Psychoanalytic Quarterly* 3:391–429.

CHASSEGUET-SMIRGEL, J. (1984). *Creativity and Perversion.* New York: W.W. Norton.

CHEHRAZI, S. (1986). Female Psychology: A Review. *Journal of the American Psychoanalytic Association* 34:141–162.

EISSLER, K. (1958). Notes on Problems of Technique in the Psychoanalytic Treatment of Adolescents with Some Remarks on Perversion. *Psychoanalytic Study of the Child* 13:223–225.

FENICHEL, O. (1945). *The Psychoanalytical Theory of Neurosis.* New York: W. W. Norton.

FERENCZI, S. (1911). *On Obscene Words in Sex in Psychoanalysis.* New York: Basic Books, 1950.

FLIESS, R. (1973). *Symbol, Dream, and Psychosis.* New York: International Universities Press.

FREUD, S. (1894). The Neuro-psychoses of Defence. *Standard Edition* 3.

——— (1905). Three Essays on Sexuality. *Standard Edition* 7.

——— (1919). A Child Is Being Beaten *Standard Edition* 17.

——— (1920). The Psychogenesis of a Case of Homosexuality in a Woman *Standard Edition* 18.

——— (1937). Analysis Terminable and Interminable. *Standard Edition* 23.

GALENSON, E. & ROIPHE, H. (1976). Some Suggested Revisions Concerning Early Female Development. *Journal of the American Psychoanalytic Association* 24:29–58.

GREENACRE, P. (1953). Certain Relationships Between Fetishism and the Faulty Development of the Body Image. *Psychoanalytic Study of the Child* 8:79–98.

——— (1968). Perversions: General Considerations Regarding Their Genetic and Dynamic Background. *Psychoanalytic Study of the Child* 23:47–62.

GRUNBERGER, B. (1966). Some Reflections on the Rat Man. *International Journal of Psychoanalysis* 47:160–168

HARRIS, H.I. (1957). Telephone Anxiety. *Journal of the American Psychoanalytic Association* 5:342–347.

KHAN, M. (1979). Alienation in Perversions. New York: International Universities Press.

LEWIN, B.D. (1933). The Body as Phallus. *Psychoanalytic Quarterly* 2:24–47.

LYDSTON, G.F. (1889). Sexual Perversion, Satyriasis and Nymphomania. *Medical and Surgical Reporter* 61:253–258.

MCDOUGALL, J. (1985). *Theaters of the Mind.* New York: Basic Books.

MICHELS, R. (1980). Sexual Excitement by Robert J. Stoller, M.D. In *Women, Sex, and Sexuality,* G. Stimpson & E.S. Person, eds. Chicago:

University of Chicago Press.

PETO, A. (1975). The Primal Scene in Perversions. *Psychoanalytic Quarterly* 44:176–190.

REICH, A. (1940). A Contribution to the Analysis of Extreme Submissiveness in Women. In *Annie Reich: Psychoanalytic Contributions.* New York: International Universities Press, 1973.

SACHS, H. (1986). On the Genesis of Perversions. *Psychoanalytic Quarterly* 55:477–492.

SHENGOLD, L. (1982). The Symbol of Telephoning *Journal of the American Psychoanalytic Association* 30:461–470.

SILVERMAN, M. (1982a). The Voice of Conscience and the Sounds of the Analytic Hour.*Psychoanalytic Quarterly* 51:196–217

——— (1982b). A Nine-Year-Old's Use of the Telephone: Symbolism in Statu Nascendi. *Psychoanalytic Quarterly* 51:598–611

SOCARIDES, C.W. (1968). *The Overt Homosexual.* New York: Grune & Stratton.

SPIEGEL, N.T. (1967). An Infantile Fetish and Its Persistence into Young Womanhood. *Psychoanalytic Study of the Child* 22:402–425.

STOLLER, R. (1979). *Sexual Excitement.* New York: Pantheon Books.

——— (1987). Perversion and the Desire to Harm In *Theories of the Unconscious and Theories of the Self.* R. Stern, ed. Hillsdale, NJ: Analytic Press.

WEICH, M. (1982). Language Fetish. Paper read at American Psychoanalytic Association meeting, December 1982.

ZAVITZIANOS, G. (1971) Fetishism and Exhibitionism in the Female and Their Relationship to Psychotherapy and Kleptomania. *International Journal of Psychoanalysis* 52:297–305.

****
****

Original publication of preceding chapter:

RICHARDS, A.K. (1989). A Romance with Pain: A Telephone Perversion in a Woman? *International Journal of Psychoanalysis* 70:153–164.

Loneliness used to seem to me to be encompassed by the ideas of: longing for a specific other; longing for a kinship group; longing for a lost twin-ship with the mother of infancy and; longing for recognition and appreciation from the other. Now I think it also means longing for oneself as one used to be, longing for one's own body as it used to be, longing for the possibilities for the future as one would like to imagine it.

To the ideas of longing for a specific object (Brenner 1974), longing for an empathic object (Kohut 1959), longing for acceptance in an elite group (Proust 2003) and longing for a national or racial group's acceptance, Almodovar (2011), in his movie *The Skin I Live In,* has added longing for oneself. This idea is implicit in Freud's assertion that narcissistic love can be longing for one's former self, longing for one's ideal self, or longing for one's mirror image. But Almodovar gives us a picture of someone longing for his former sexual and gender identity that was not possible in Freud's time because the possibility of surgery was not available. The closest that could be achieved was adopting the gender role of the opposite sex in life and the sexual role of the opposite sex in love making. So a psychological change was possible. Castration was possible, but transsexuality like that of Tiresias only became possible with modern surgery.

How does this work in the clinical situation? A patient who is disappointed with her present life and afraid to try to break out of her self imposed aloneness dreams and daydreams about going to far away places and doing daring deeds. She is longing for another self. Maybe it is the self of her early toddler years when she was running free and happy. Maybe it is the self she yearns to create but cannot because she feels too weak and too defective to succeed in her present modest goals. She feels lonely even in the presence of her family and friends, but especially lonely when they have other agendas rather than being with her. Feeling that she is too small and too defective to compete with her many older siblings leaves her feeling unable to compete in the larger world. I think that her longing for a place far away and a profession that will surpass those of her older siblings has led her to conceive of a world far from her siblings and the realm of her parents. She sees the world as herself versus all the others; she is alone. When I convey this way of thinking about why she has to keep herself alone, she becomes resentful. If I am so smart, why don't I help her to do the things she really wants to do?

I remind her that her mother has always told her she can do anything she really wants to do. I say that I want to be an opera star, but I cannot even carry a tune. It doesn't matter how much I want it, it can never happen. By reaching for what I cannot have, I would be ignoring the satisfying career that I can have. By normalizing her frustration and modeling contentment with realistic goals, I hope to allow her to see that she can get satisfaction and self esteem from developing her own talents. I join her; she is no longer alone.

I now see loneliness as ameliorable by therapy simply by being the patient's other in a reflective way. By truly hearing what she is saying and truly responding from my own point of view, I get the patient to live in a two-persons-working-together world. When she rejects me, as she often does, I join her in rejecting my comments. Wrong again I cheerfully say. Wrong again! A gesture of knocking on my own forehead makes it funny and playful.

REFERENCES

ALMODÓVAR, P. (2011). *The Skin I Live In*. (Spanish film: *La piel que habito*) New York: Sony Pictures Classics.

BRENNER, C. (1974). On the Nature and Development of Affects: A Unified Theory. *Psychoanalytic Quarterly* 43:532–556.

KOHUT, H. (1959). Introspection, Empathy, and Psychoanalysis—An Examination of the Relationship Between Mode of Observation and Theory. *Journal of the American Psychoanalytic Association* 7:459–483.

PROUST, M. (2003). *In Search of Lost Time*. (6 volumes; Transl. C.K.Scott-Moncrieff & T. Kilmartin; revised by D.J. Enright). New York: Modern Library.

PAPERS IN SECTION III
(All papers in this section are coauthored by
Arlene Kramer Richards and Lucille Spira)

Chapter 13
Proust's Novel, A Clinical Case, and the Psychological and Social Determinants of Snobbery, Prejudice, and Love
[Originally Richards, A.K., & Spira, L. (2012). What We Learned from Proust: Psychological and Social Determinants of Snobbery and Prejudice. *International Journal of Applied Psychoanalytic Studies* 24:

Wiley Online Library, http://dx.doi.org/10.1002/aps.1307
(DOI: 10.1002/aps.1307).]

Chapter 14

(2006). Proust and the Love of Longing. Presented at American Psychoanalytic Meetings January 21, 2006.

Chapter 15

(2003). The "Sweet and Sour" of Being Lonely and Alone. *Psychoanalytic
Study of the Child* 58:214–227.

Chapter 16

(2003). On Being Lonely: Fear of One's Own Aggression as an Impediment to Intimacy. *Psychoanalytic Quarterly* 72:357–374.

Proust's Novel, A Clinical Case, and the Psychological and Social Determinants of Snobbery, Prejudice and Love

Proust's original contribution to understanding social exclusion is the focus of this paper. Proust's psychological novel, *In Search of Lost Time* is used to show how social exclusion is related to early feelings of exclusion from the parental couple in the family. Proust's addition shows how a child who wins his mother's attention by acting as a victim suffers from both guilt and humiliation which he may resolve by defending another victim or by excluding others if he identifies with the aggressor. This paper shows how excluding others from events, opportunities, and equality under the law can be an attempt to repair the humiliation and attenuate the anger of having been excluded. We include a case vignette that shows how Proust's work complements and expands Anna Freud's idea about identification with the aggressor.

A CASE VIGNETTE

A therapist is getting anxious. Her patient Jonny, is telling her that he was anxious because his girlfriend was pissed with him. The couple had met in high school and began seriously dating in college. He presented himself as helpless; he could not convince his parents to invite her to their holiday party. He explained that his parents did not want her there because she was an outsider whose presence would upset some of their guests. He knew that his relationship already upset his father; he ignored her. His mother had been cordial toward her as long as she thought that she was just a friend. But, as it became clearer that the young woman was his girlfriend, the mother was reportedly cooler toward her.

Why was the therapist anxious? She thought she was being set up to see him as a victim, being forced to empathize with his sense of powerlessness, with his presentation of himself as a child of powerful parents rather than as the highly achieving competent young man he was in the world. Was this a discrepancy between his self- image as a member of his family and the image he presented to the world? Was he trying to set up a triangle with the therapist opposing his mother? Or his father? Or opposing his ethnic group? He knew the therapist to not be one of them. The therapist knew that in their native land, before Jonny was born, his family had seriously suffered because of their status as an ethnic minority. His therapist wondered if unconsciously Jonny was allowing his girlfriend to be excluded for being different because of the oppression and cruelty wrought on members of his family and ethnic group. He saw himself as the victim not the girlfriend.

The theme of someone being excluded as in the example above appeared in a number of different ways with Jonny. Soon after he began treatment, he said with a smile that he was going to tell the therapist something about himself that he had not shared with his former therapist with whom he had worked several years. That therapist moved his practice and Jonny was referred on. The way he began to tell the story, the smile and his telling the therapist that she was going to be given a special secret seemed seductive. As this was explored, what emerged was that being excluded was a theme in Jonny's life. He had a way of becoming a favorite of women: teachers, to the exclusion of other students; his female boss, to the exclusion of his colleagues; and earlier his mother to the exclusion of his father. Jonny got noticed and rewarded while others got ignored. His male friends envied him for being sought after by "babes"— the hot, sophisticated young women.

He believes that he captured his mother's attention more than his father since he was about twelve years old. He remembers his private school teacher telling his mother that he was very intelligent and talented and from that point she began to take a special interest in him. He enjoyed her attention and would go out of his way to please her in order to maintain her interest.

From then on he was the one who accompanied her to cultural events, visits to relatives, and to her friends, always leaving the father home. This pattern of the father being excluded, or excluding himself, is dramatically illustrated by the following: When the Jonny was a mid-teen one summer he slept in the parental bed with his mother while his father moved into the Jonny's room. The bed was a large one and according to Jonny there was no physical contact of any kind between mother and son; each just slept. Jonny believed that he went into his parent's room to sleep because of the poor air conditioning in his room; he could not tolerate the heat and he believed that he went into his parents' room intending to sleep on the floor. His attempt to sleep on the floor reportedly upset his father who turned his side of the bed over to Jonny and went himself to sleep in the uncomfortable room. This exchange of sleeping quarters continued until the air conditioning was repaired some days later.

Jonny did not recognize feeling any guilt about any possible discomfort this might have caused his father but volunteered that he was ashamed of sleeping in the bed with his mother at the age he was then–others might think of him as babyish. Jonny's history of chronic anxiety and sense of being a fraud began somewhere during that period although he had not made the connection to the bedroom episode. His self-esteem was fragile and highly contingent on winning love; often, soon after he won the sought after person's love he became disillusioned and felt imprisoned.

How would a psychoanalyst understand the theme of exclusion—either being the excluded one or excluding an other? Psychoanalysts have many theories to bring to such reports: oedipal conflict, separation individuation conflicts, fear of their own aggression projected into the other, or some combination of these dynamics. Sometimes great artists can add dimension to psychological understanding.

Proust's *In Search of Lost Time* (1913–1927) focuses on social exclusion in his delineation of the psychology of character. He describes in affecting detail how the painful experiences of childhood motivate adult social behavior. Jonny's therapist believed that she could understand Jonny better after reading Proust's accounts of how his hero, and other characters in his novel act out variations of early painful situations.

Social snobbery springs from psychological roots—the adult assures himself that rather than be excluded he can exclude others. How does this come about? Here we turn to Proust and his novel.

Barbara Probst Solomon (2001) pointed out that Proust is the first major twentieth century writer to make prejudice a central theme in his work. His memoir-like novel, conveyed as if it were seen through the eyes of a narrator, stimulated us, among other things, to think about how the social and psychological intertwine.

His depiction of the social mores of characters from all walks of life and different developmental stages suggests one root of why a person might find pleasure in excluding others or casting them as dangerous outsiders. Psychoanalysts found much in Proust to elaborate on and expand their psychological theory. Poland (2003) concentrated on Proust's view and demonstration of reading and writing as sublimation that can remake one's world. Miller (1956) and Halberstadt-Freud (1991) were interested in analyzing the author from the evidence of his imaginative productions. Halberstadt Freud's developed her theory of perversion by way of an analysis of Proust's work. Kohut (1977) saw the hero of *In Search* as suffering from a fragmented self: tragic man, one in search of a self. Kohut differentiated tragic man from classical guilty man who suffers with the residue of his oedipal resolution. More recently, Fried (2008) creatively used Proust's portrayal of the hero's treatment of Albertine to illuminate the impact of the analyst's planned absences on both patient and analyst.

Proust's novel shows how continuous longing for love, though painful, might be more satisfying than requited love (Richards and Spira 2012). How a child and his parents negotiate the challenges of the time when we are longing for the exclusive love of one of our parents while in the throes of ambivalence toward the other parent has psychological impact and wider social ramifications as well. But so does what happens to us and to our loved ones in the broader environment.

Is excluding other people a social or psychological phenomenon? It depends on how you look at it. That being excluded can be painful is obvious; that the excluder suffers may be less apparent. The pleasure in excluding is the sense of power, but power implies exercising free will and therefore leads to responsibility and its handmaiden: guilt. Social norms play a role in what is shameful and what is a source of pride. Excluding another person serves a defensive purpose as well. Often the impulse to exclude arises from the shame and sense of being degraded by the experience of having been excluded. Campbell (2011) elaborated this idea by asserting that the different are excluded and subordinated to the established power structure. He pointed out that the subordinated are at risk for psychological damage. We see those who subordinate as also at risk as they are subject to feelings of persecution.

Proust's memoir-like novel, *In Search of Lost Time* develops understanding of social and psychological aspects of social exclusion. His rich character portrayals depict heroes, heroines, and anti-heroes from all spheres of society. He describes in affecting detail how the painful experiences of childhood motivate adult social behavior. His work shows how social snobbery can spring from psychological roots. The adult assures himself that rather than be excluded as he was as a child, he can exclude others now that he is powerful. Snobbery excludes others. To rationalize this exclusion the snob irrationally attributes negative characteristics on the basis of class, race, religion, gender and/or sexual orientation. Jonny in the situation with the girlfriend and the holiday party, was seeing only his parents as the excluders. He did not consider his own ambivalent feelings as playing a part in his girlfriend being excluded.

PROUST AND HIS NOVEL

Proust's hero-narrator, sometimes referred to as M or Marcel, eagerly sought his mother's love in a way that appeared successful. The narrator shares many characteristics with the author Proust though there are major differences unlike the historical Proust, his character is heterosexual and an only child. Proust's hero is not explicitly a member of any excluded group.

The novel introduces the theme of exclusion when we are told about a young boy suffering in his bedroom because he is exiled from his parent's dinner table. The boy's parents are entertaining their rich neighbor Swann; Swann's wife, Odette, has not been invited because of rumors about her sexual past. She is excluded from their social circle because she had been kept by rich lovers. Her sexual choices give the bourgeois family the right to exclude her from society. But what did the young boy do to be excluded? This night the young boy does not get his good night kiss, his sexual wish gets him into trouble just as Odette's sexual behavior earned her social obloquy.

Unhappy about not getting the kiss he desires, he sets out on a campaign to get it. He solicits the maid to give his mother a note asking her to come to his room. Before handing over the note he realizes that this maid is too protective of his parents to casually interrupt them. To counteract what he sees as her servility, he tells her that his mother is expecting to hear from him. He hopes to make her feel as if she is acting on his mother's request rather than his own. The boy's plan works in that the maid sees to it that his mother gets his note. Believing that the note will bring his mother to him, he calms down. But when he gets word that his mother has said that she has no reply, he sees that his ploy did not work and once again feels painful longing. He provokes exclusion by trying too hard to get included in his mother's attention.

Proust's boy longs for his mother's kiss. He believes that he can avoid the pain of being excluded by pursuing her until she gives in. He knows that dinner will eventually end and his mother will have to ascend the staircase to get to her room. He chooses to wait on the staircase to catch her. When she sees him there, she attempts to encourage him to go back to bed. He experiences her as being annoyed with him. His father enters the scene and seeing the boy's suffering becomes alarmed that his son will become sick if he does not get his mother's attention. He urges his wife to stay with their son. She does so reluctantly and spends the time lying beside him reading him stories.

One story she reads is about a young orphan boy befriended by a woman named Madeleine who acts like a surrogate mother. When the child in the story grows up, he falls in love with Madeleine, and eventually persuades her to marry him. The boy wins his "mother" and lives happily ever after. Is Proust implying that a child who hears such a story and gets his mother to sleep with him can take it to mean that he can also get to marry his mother when he grows up? Does the boy in Proust's story, feel content or powerful? Not as he tells it.

The Aftermath of That Night

Proust's hero sees beyond the moment when his wish was gratified. What little Marcel's persistence has gained humiliates him. He recognizes that his mother did not want to stay but did so only because the father asked her to. The father feared the boy would make himself sick; reader surmises that he felt pity for Marcel. Marcel realizes that he has caused his mother pain; he sees that she looks sad and deduces that it is because she perceives him not to be strong enough to manage growing up. He feels guilt about causing his mother pain and shame about eliciting his father's pity. The next morning he feels regretful. The narrator writes of the young Marcel's regret: "And if I had dared now, I should have said to Mamma: "No I don't want you to, you mustn't sleep here" (Proust 1913/2003), vol. 1, 51.) It is from this time that the boy thinks of himself as a sickly child.

As an older man Marcel happens to see a copy of Francois le Champi and recalls that crucial night of his childhood. He says:

> . . . *during the night that was perhaps the sweetest and saddest of my life when I had alas! won from my parents that first abdication of their authority from which, later, I was to date the decline of my health and my will, and my renunciation, each day disastrously confirmed, of a task that daily became more difficult* (Proust 1927/2003, vol. 6, p. 287).

This recalled moment comes after the reader has already witnessed the growing adolescent and the adult man only achieving pleasure at the cost of great pain. His Oedipal victory left him full of guilt and shame for the rest of his life.

Proust's Lesbian Lovers

Proust also shows a woman who suffers from oedipal victory. Mlle. Vinteuil, brought up by her adoring father after her mother dies when the daughter was still a young child. Clearly an oedipal victor, she becomes an adult who loves women and feels spiteful hatred for her father which she acts out with her lover. The young narrator looks through an unshaded window to see Mlle. Vinteuil dare her lover to threaten to spit on a picture of her father, in a sado-masochistic love ritual. Love and aggression are linked as is typically the case in life. Could it be that the aggression allowed Mlle. Vinteuil to withstand the village ostracism that she suffered for being a gay woman? Or, as Halberstadt-Freud (1991) suggests, the inclusion of the sado-masochistic love ritual may be Proust's way of having his character dis-identify from her masochistic father. Her open sexual play with her lover makes them a topic of gossip; members of the community pity her father. The narrator describes himself as a child passing the home of M. Vinteuil while on a walk with his parents. The little boy was aware that:

> People said: "That poor M. Vinteuil must blinded by fatherly love not to see what everyone is talking about a man who is shocked by the slightest loose word letting his daughter bring a woman like that to live under his roof! . . . He may be sure it isn't music that she's teaching his daughter" (Proust 1913/2003 vol.1, p. 207).

Mlle. Vinteuil and her lover are excluded from the society of the narrator, his family and their friends. They are excluded from the social life of their little town. Prejudice against lesbians forces them to find another context for their lives. Mlle. Vinteuil and her lover become part of a group of lesbian artistic women who share camaraderie, creativity, and love not unlike the situation of a number of lesbian women during Proust's time (Souhami 2005). They exclude the heterosexual world that excluded them. This is an example of how one gains power by excluding others. We see with the situation of Mlle. Vinteuil, one of Proust's contributions to understanding social exclusion—how the psychological and the social are intertwined.

PROUST AND SOCIAL DETERMINANTS OF LOVE

The social definition of a character's status determines personal choices as well. Proust's haughty intellectual character Baron Charlus is homosexual. He takes an uneducated and unscrupulous tailor as his lover and closest companion. Does knowing that he would be rejected if society knew that he was homosexual cause him to choose a lover who is degraded? Even though Swann has a Jewish mother, he has entrée into aristocratic circles where ladies of the nobility are interested in him. Rather than choose one of them, he falls in love with the degraded Odette with whom he had a tumultuous courtship. Does he choose a beloved who is as socially unacceptable as his mother would have been to many in society portrayed in the novel?

Social Snobbery and Class

Proust exquisitely depicts social snobbery based on class as well as sexual orientation. He shows snobbery within and among all levels of society. Proust's Duchess de Guermantes, behaves contemptuously towards anyone whom she considers less sophisticated, clever, aristocratic, or cultured than herself. That includes almost everyone. A matron at a public toilet excludes an indigent woman while toadying up to bourgeois patrons. The narrator likens the matron's condescending behavior to that of a duchess: the society dinner is the duchesses' social realm; the matron's toilet is hers. Housekeepers are also snobs: one bullies an inexperienced kitchen helper.

But the social snobbery is not simple disdain for those lower on the social scale. The bourgeoisie exclude the aristocrats: the hero's grandmother initially resists overtures made to her by an aristocratic acquaintance whom she knew from childhood. The grandmother believes that nice people associate only within their own social class. Her grandson, M, is determined to break down barriers. He is the same character who got his mother to sleep the night in his room. As a young man he uses that same persistence to ingratiate himself with the aristocratic Guermantes set. Proust himself crossed the barrier from a bourgeois family into the society of aristocrats and great artists when he was a young man. He used his wit, observational acuity and entertaining skills to make himself a desirable companion for people of greater achievement and social status than he himself had at that time. Kristeva (1993) sees this blending of fact and fiction as an overarching theme in Proust's work and as an example of the fluidity of barriers. Under certain circumstances, social barriers expand and contract as time compresses.

Social Snobbery and Prejudice

As Proust mixes fiction with fact, he provides insights into the nature of prejudice. He uses the Dreyfus case as part of his narrative. Dreyfus was a French military officer convicted of treason. This became a cause célèbre in France. One faction claimed that he was framed because he was a Jew while the other side believed he was guilty of spying against France for Germany. Proust's characters clash: Dreyfusards versus anti-Dreyfusards. The Dreyfusards are M, Swann and the young noble St. Loup. In the real world the Dreyfus affair separated those of the Jewish "race" from the old aristocracy of the army officers. Even those like Proust who had been baptized and others who had converted to Christianity were seen as of the Jewish "race." French artists like Zola and other people who shared the values of hard work, learning and the philosophy of liberty, equality and brotherhood sided with the Dreyfusards. The French old guard, many aristocrats and peasants, some under the thrall of the dominant religious establishment, wanted the conviction to stand because they believed that reversal would upset the social order. Proust has an anti-Dreyfus character assert that you cannot be both a Jew and a Frenchman. Proust uses the Dreyfus affair in his novel as a metaphor. Rose (2012) highlights the importance of Proust's emphasis on the need to transcend barriers driven by nationalism in finding a fair outcome for Dreyfus. She takes from his work how failures of memory and empathy by some Israeli's impact current Israeli-Arab relations. To her dire consequences arise when the group sees only their own victimhood and forgets how they have transgressed against the other. In Proust's novel this is represented by M in his relations with Albertine and by those who denied Dreyfus a fair trial. In life, we see this pattern with Jonny as he rationalizes that it is others, not he himself, who take pleasure in someone else being excluded.

Most interestingly, Proust alerts us to the ironic capriciousness of prejudice. Odette Swann had not been welcome at either aristocratic or bourgeois homes even after marrying the wealthy Swann. When she allies herself with the anti-Dreyfusards she suddenly finds herself welcome in aristocratic circles. Just as Odette becomes acceptable to St. Loup's aristocratic relatives, St. Loup, Swann and the narrator fall out of favor with those aristocrats who had formerly welcomed them. Having similar prejudices serves to draw otherwise disparate people together. He shows how social barriers can give way when they conflict with racial prejudice. The viciousness of ethnocentrism and religious bigotry is on a continuum with the viciousness of the small town attack on the lesbian lovers.

DISCUSSION

If Freud taught us that the Oedipus myth is a story of exclusion from the loving couple, Proust shows us that exclusion from the social group is the heir of oedipal conflict in the social sphere. Social exclusion can be seen as a way to mitigate the pain of oedipal humiliation. By turning passive exclusion into active exclusiveness, the social snob does to others what she felt had been done to her.

Proust shows little Marcel longing for his mother while she is at dinner with adults. The dinner guest Swann becomes the barrier between little Marcel and his mother with the Oedipal rivalry displaced from his father to the visitor who represents the intrusion of society into the family. Thus Proust links the social scene with the oedipal rivalry and longing. In this way he establishes the link between the oedipal exclusion and the social exclusion that later gets played out when the adult M wants to keep his lover for himself and away from her social circle.

Freud showed how the child who was not the oedipal winner suffered from revenge fantasies. Proust shows the child who wins by suffering spending much of his life having fantasies of winning by losing. The side effect of Marcel getting his father's permission to have his mother stay the night with him is accepting as his identity the sufferer from illness, the child who is no threat to the father or any other man, the mama's boy who can only suffer at the hands of women whom he loves. As an adult he becomes a torturer of his beloved, Albertine, because he cannot allow himself to be excluded from her presence. He keeps her prisoner so that she would have to cheat on him in order to have any life of her own. He repeats the triangle of himself with his mother and father but transforms it into the triangle of his love, himself and other women. Here again Proust transforms the personal into the social when he describes M's jealous fantasy that his beloved is actually having sex not with a single other person, but with a whole group of lesbians. He is jealous of the group of women, not simply of another woman. His torturing behavior can be ignored.

A second way in which Proust develops a Freudian idea is the extension of identification with the aggressor into the social realm. Proust shows how the excluded Mlle. Vinteuil and her lover create a social circle of lesbians and exclude the villagers who excluded them. Once again the sexual and the social are linked in the psychological realm and use the same adaptive strategy. For M, identifying with the aggressor was not adaptive. He tried to become the excluder with his lover, but it only bought pain on himself. It worked for him when he found his way into the Guermantes set where others were excluded. It also worked for Odette when she joined the anti-Dreyfusards who had excluded her and were now excluding Dreyfusards.

Another original idea in Proust is the power of identification with the victim. While Anna Freud (1936) later described the defensive use of identification with the aggressor, Proust used his own understanding of human nature to show the defensive use of identification with the victim. M defines his place in a social realm by identifying with Dreyfus. Since Dreyfus was disempowered and humiliated, M could see him as a fellow sufferer who was also weak, fragile and unable to cope. By supporting Dreyfus M attempts to undo being a victim, but at the same time becomes a member of a group that identifies itself with the victim. Being a member of a group gave him power; being a member of the group enables him to transform weakness into power. In the novel, such groups are comprised of homosexuals, lesbians, Jews, and intellectuals.

Social Snobbery and Prejudice in Contemporary Life

Do officially sanctioned humiliation and exclusion still pervade our institutions? Corbett (2009) reported on a school that holds a senior prom for the African American students and another one for its white students. The students say that they want one prom with all students invited. Some say it is harmless tradition to hold two proms.

By dividing the students according to race, the white parents were exercising the power of the dominant culture. By claiming that each group would prefer to be separate they were ignoring the students' feelings. Not having one's feelings understood about not being included can sting; not having one's feelings about wanting to be inclusive can sting also. However we categorize this exclusionary behavior, early experience and the intertwining of the psychological and social play a role. The excluders are identifying with the parents who did not include them in their adult pleasures. Understanding that the impulse toward excluding comes from the experience of having felt excluded oneself is beautifully exemplified in Proust's adult pleasures humiliates the child but replacing the parent as the parent's best beloved makes the child an Oedipal victor. Being an oedipal "victor" comes at a great price to adult development (Lasky 1984; H. Gil 1987; Halberstadt-Freud 1991). It inhibits growth by provoking guilt. When such victory is gained by acting like a victim it produces humiliation.

Humiliation can either propel a person to humiliate others by excluding them or to oppose the humiliation of others. Proust himself opposed the humiliation of Dreyfus as his hero M did in the novel by defending Dreyfus. Becoming an adult requires accepting responsibility for participation in society. It also requires that each person finds a way to satisfy her/his loving and aggressive impulses without hurting him/her self or others. That some of us lose this struggle is unfortunate.

It seems that Proust found a way to undo his humiliation by embracing his creativity and contributing to society by standing up for justice in the Dreyfus affair. Poland (2003) concluded that Proust undid his humiliation finally by writing his great novel.

Jonny, after many years in psychoanalytic treatment, eventually married a young woman who differed significantly in style and personality from his mother. As he saw his new wife as unlike his mother, and that she had his father's approval, his anxiety and guilt lessened. She did not see him as a victim and expected him to perform as an adult male. He had to own his aggression and sexuality and could no longer hide under the umbrella of being weak and helpless.

The point of this paper is that including the social along with psychological understanding (Hamer 2002; Campbell 2011) better enables us to understand our tendencies to exclude others and our responses to being excluded. Including the social along with psychological understanding also makes our interpretations to our patients more applicable to everyday life.

REFERENCES

ACIMAN, A., ed. (2004) *The Proust Project*. New York: Farrar, Straus & Giroux
BEGLEY, L. (2009). *Why the Dreyfus Affair Matters*. New Haven: Yale University Press.
BLOCH-DANO E. (2007). *Madame Proust: A Biography*. Transl. A. Kaplan. Chicago: The University of Chicago Press.
CAMPBELL, D.B. (2011). Oppression of the different. *International Journal*

of Applied Psychoanalytic Studies 8:28–47.

CORBETT, S. (2009). A Prom Divided. *The New York Times* March 24.

FRIED, W. (2008). The Sweet Cheat Gone: Here and There—Elation, Absence, and Reparation. *Canadian Journal of Psychoanalysis* 16:3–22.

FREUD, A. (1936). *The Ego and the Mechanisms of Defense.* New York: International Universities Press Inc., 1966.

FREUD, S. (1921). Group Psychology and the Analysis of the Ego. Standard Edition 18:65–144.

GARELICK, R. (2011). High Fascism. *New York Times* March 7.

GIL, H. (1987). Effects of Oedipal Triumph Caused by Collapse or Death of the Parent. *International Journal of Psychoanalysis* 68:251–260.

GREEN, A. & KOHON, K.(2005). *Love and its Vicissitudes.* London & New York: Routledge.

HALBERSTADT-FREUD, H.C. (1991). *Freud, Proust, Perversion and Love.* Berwyn, Pa.: Swets and Zeitlinger.

HAMER, F.M. (2002). Guards at the Gate: Race, Resistance, and Psychic Reality. *Journal of the American Psychoanalytic Association.* 50:1219–1237.

KOHUT, H. (1977). *The Restoration of the Self.* New York Int. Univ. Press Kristeva,

KRISTEVA, J. (1993). *Proust and the Sense of Time.* New York: Columbia University Press.

LASKY, R. (1984). Dynamics and Problems in the Treatment of the "Oedipal Winner." *Psychoanalytic Review* 71:351–374.

LEHRER, J. (2008). *Proust was a Neuroscientist.* New York: First Mariner Books.

POLAND, W.S. (2003). Reading Fiction and the Psychoanalytic Experience: Proust on Reading and on Reading Proust. *Journal of the American Psychoanalytic Association* 51:1262–1282.

SOLOMON, B.P. (2001). Citizen Proust: on Politics and Race. *The Reading Room* 1:97–111.

PROUST, M. (1913–1927). *In Search of Lost Time.* (6 volumes, Transl. C.K. Scott-Moncrieff & T. Kilmartin), New York: Modern Library Edition, 2003.

——— (1956). *Marcel Proust; Letters to His Mother.* (Transl. and ed., G.D. Painter) New York: Citadel Press; Westport, CT: Greenwood Press, 1973.

——— (1997). A Race Accursed. In *On Art and Literature 1896–1919.* S.T. Warner, Transl.; Introduction by T. Kilmartin. New York: Carroll & Graf Publishers, Inc. pp. 210–229.

RICHARDS, A.K. & SPIRA, L. (2012). Proust and the Lonely Pleasure of Longing. In *Loneliness and Longing: Psychoanalytic Reflections on a Crucial Aspect of the Human Condition.* (Brent Willock et al., eds.), London: Routledge.

ROSE, J. (2012). *Proust among the Nations.* Chicago: University of Chicago Press.

SAND, G. (1850/1977). *The Country Waif. (Francois le Champi).* E. Collis, Transl.; Introduction by D.W. Zimmerman. Lincoln: University of Nebraska Press.

SOUHAMI, D. (2005). *Wild Girls: Paris, Sappho, and Art: The Lives and Loves of Natalie Barney and Romaine Brooks.* New York: St. Martin's Press.

TADIE, J.Y. (2000). *Marcel Proust: A Life.* Transl. E. Cameron, New York: Penguin Books.

WEINSTEIN, A. (2004). *A Scream Goes Through the House: What Literature Teaches us about Life.* New York: Random House, Inc.

WHITE, E. (2009) *Proust.* New York: Penguin

WILSON, E. (2004). Marcel Proust. In *Axel's Castle A Study of the Imaginative Literature of 1870–1930.* Introduction: M. Gordon. New York: Farrar Straus & Giroux. 107–151.

****
****

A version of this paper originally appeared as:

RICHARDS, A.K., & SPIRA, L. (2012). What We Learned from Proust: Psychological and Social Determinants of Snobbery and Prejudice. *International Journal of Applied Psychoanalytic Studies* 24: Wiley Online Library: http://dx.doi.org/10.1002/aps.1307 [DOI: 10.1002/aps.1307].

Proust and the Love of Longing

Freud chose Oedipus, Narcissus and other characters in both visual and verbal arts to illustrate psychological concepts of motivation, character, and personality. We hope to look at Proust's novel *In Search of Lost Time* to understand love and longing in the Freudian tradition.

We assert that Proust denuded romantic love, the great ideal of the nineteenth century, of its major illusion: the importance of possessing the object of love. In this Proust comes very close to Freud's idea that the object is the least fixed part of the wish. For Freud (1905), the source of the wish is more fixed and more stable than the choice of an object. Yet what distinguishes love from the sexual perversions or simple lust is the longing for the object and the fixity of that longing. As Proust shows us, a person comes to stand in the real world for the ideal because that person is unattainable. It is the longing that is prized, not the fulfillment.

> *In her heyday, she would like to think, she could have given winged Eros himself cause to pay earth a visit. Not because she was so much of a beauty but because she longed for the god's touch, longed until she ached, because in her longings, so unrequitable and therefore so comical when acted on, she might have promised a genuine taste of what was missing back home on Olympus.*

> From *Elizabeth Costello,*
> —J.M. Coetzee (2003)

What is love? What is longing? Are they the same, or are they different or overlapping? In this paper we intend to examine Proust's presentation of erotic love as the central problem and greatest motivator of life. Erotic love is not just tender affection, but a state of sensual excitement and a belief that the beloved is the only one who can satisfy. This

Presented at The American Psychoanalytic Meeting, New York, January 21, 2006. Thanks are due to Dr. Sidney Phillips M.D. and Stephen Kerzner.

kind of love includes idealization and leads to a tendency to identify with the beloved. It is intense, involving ecstacy, elation and euphoria and on occasion pain. Longing is the state of wanting but not having the remote or unattainable beloved. How can it be that Proust, like Coetzee, believed that longing is such a prize? One possibility is that longing allows one to have the object in one's fantasy and that this is not spoiled the way having the beloved person in one's life and being exposed to the torments of jealousy, fear of loss and recognition of the demands of the other person.

Freud chose Oedipus, Narcissus and other characters in both visual and verbal arts to illustrate psychological concepts of motivation, character, and personality. We hope to look at Proust's novel *In Search of Lost Time* (1913–1927) to compare his view of love and longing with that of the Freudian tradition. We follow the precedents of literary critics who have focused on different themes in Proust's novel (White 1931, Wilson 2004; Aciman 2004). Rose (1997) takes a historical perspective when she traces parallels between the mores of her own social group and those of Proust's time and place. Proust has fascinated psychoanalysts as well as literary critics. Poland (2003) concentrates on Proust's view of reading as a sublimation that can remake one's world. Miller (1956) and Halberstadt-Freud (1991) were interested in analyzing the author from the evidence of his imaginative productions. We were interested in learning from his work and using his observations of character and motivation to illuminate some of the struggles that we have seen in our patients.

In *Search,* Proust depicts the inner life of his narrator and the varied lives of characters who expose human passions and human fears and agonies. This story is seen through the eyes of Proust's narrator. At first the narrator is telling us about a young boy: Marcel. The narrator, also called Marcel, struggles with love, with passion, with fragile self-esteem, and with getting his sexual needs met. The narrator Marcel describes the young boy's journey over love's terrain. According to the narrator the young Marcel's passion for his mother was all pervasive. In a poignant scene he longs for his mother to come to his bedside and kiss him good night. When he gets the kiss and permission to have her stay the night, he hates it. His father had urged his mother to stay when he saw how much his son longed to have his mother. In this scene the narrator hints that the father was seduced by his son's distress. What the young boy fantasizes would be a delicious experience, turns out to be a bitter humiliation that becomes a pattern for his life and for the lives of other characters in *The Search*. Fulfillment of the wish to possess the beloved leads to regret.

The child Marcel recognizes that his father's indulgence will ultimately cost him dearly. Marcel believes that his father gave his mother to him out of pity, thus depriving him of the respect and equality that would be due to a rival. The father's willingness to step aside for his son is like a screen memory that organizes Marcel's experience of himself as weak, passive, and uncertain of his role with women. The gratification deprives him of the chance to master his conflict by finding his own solution to temper his frustration. His mother attempts to soothe him by reading to him. She chooses a novel *Francois le Champi* by George Sand (1850). The heroine of this book is named Madeline and the plot involves her nurturance of a little boy of six—near Marcel's age—and her eventual marriage to him when he grows up. Such a story would exacerbate longing. Madeleine will turn out to be the name of the cookie that sets off the train of memory that is the novel. This coincidence of names underscores the centrality of love and longing set forth in this work.

What could match the anticipation he felt as a boy awaiting his mother's kiss? Would he come to believe that he was entitled to have other men's women? Would winning love be equated with weakness? Or would tender love be equated with the suffering prototype of the sadomasochist (Halberstadt-Freud 1991). Marcel may have been an oedipal victor, but one doomed to suffer in love.

Proust shows us a world in which love is longing, only sustainable when unfulfilled, only pleasurable insofar as one is able to enjoy pain. In this world satiety can only produce dullness and boredom. Envy and jealousy prevent the dullness and boredom of satiety. Thus, pleasure in inflicting and suffering pain is the inescapable dynamic of human existence. Sado-masochistic reversals of social status in which humiliation accompanies physical pain are the prototype of erotic excitement for Proust.

Above all, Proust saw and delineated in exquisitely fine detail the parallels between the psychological and the social, uniting in the form of fiction what has been divided, to the mutual loss of the sciences of psychology and sociology. He understood society as organized pleasure attained by inflicting pain. Like love, he thought, a party can give pleasure only as the participants aware that they might have been excluded, that they are privileged to be invited. The central tenet of love is exclusivity. The lover must be faithful; the beloved is believed to be the only person who can ease the lover's longing. Part of the pleasure in belonging to a social circle is the pleasure of excluding others. In an ironic turn, worthy of Proust himself, it is only now, over half a century after he finished his great psychological novel, that psychoanalysts have attained a view of perversions that can intersect with his.

Freud and Proust both depicted perversion as what Stoller (1975) would later call the erotic form of hatred. A parallel can be drawn between Proust's "involuntary memory" and Freud's "primary process." Both are timeless; both use condensation, displacement, and imagery. Similarly, Proust's "voluntary memory" is like Freud's "secondary process." Both use the laws of time, logic, and reality. Like Freud, Proust discovered that love is transference. Also like Freud, Proust viewed the state between waking and sleep as the dream state and as the access to the unconscious as well as to the thoughts and feelings of childhood. Both believed that jealousy is a necessary condition of love.

In Search of Lost Time portrays characters yearning for love to be requited. Proust shows us the complexity of object choice as he takes his heroes and heroines through their love lives. We are struck by how much his characters are driven by the same passions that influence the patients in our offices. Proust's co-mingling of actual events such as the Dreyfus affair with his fictional characters and circumstances, makes his characters more real and captivating to the reader.

Proust not only got around in social circles, but saw what Freud saw. Just as patients recount their experience, so Proust used his experience to create a narrative that illuminates love. He takes us to a French aristocrat's drawing room in the late nineteenth century, to seaside resorts on the North Atlantic coast and to a house of sado-masochistic male prostitution. Despite these exotic settings the affects, wishes, fears and social mores his characters present recur. His vivid descriptions heighten our sensitivity to the links between the familiar and the new. He makes dramatic use of free association and lets us see the bittersweet experience of appreciating for the first time that which was painful when it happened but later understood as precious and lost. He uses the concept of time to illuminate the transitoriness of human relationships. Proust shows the power of sensory experience to awaken repressed affect and the connection to memory that is awakened by that affect. He tantalizes us with the idea that the experiences of earlier time could be regained and life could be continuous. He promises us that memory makes it possible to gain some control over the ephemeral nature of life. As memory preserves time it also makes us aware that time has passed, the tragic nature of life with its inevitable losses is balanced by the recreation through memory. Love and hate, and the many affective tones in between, are the glue that bind the themes of our repressed memories. If this sounds to you like the experience of psychoanalysis, it sounds that way to us too.

LOVE AND JEALOUSY

Proust's multi-dimensioned characters provide variations of the vicissitudes of love that expand the boundaries of Freud's ideas. Freud thought that lovers are brought together by memories of the earliest beloved parents and early caretakers, or by wishes to be loved by images of oneself at early ages or what one dreamed of being in those early years or an image of what one is now. Proust shows how these images of the beloved are transformed as later experience shapes and distorts them. Love starts with jealousy. The child loves his mother, but suffers jealousy because she belongs to his father. He loves his father and suffers jealousy because he belongs to his mother. Love caused jealousy, but later loves are triggered by jealousy. What makes love exciting is the jealousy that keeps the lover in a state of anxiety. The pain caused by jealousy penetrates and permeates the victim. This pain is the experience of falling in love in Proust. Cupid's arrow hurts, but is cherished because it recalls the painful jealousy of infantile love. For Proust erotic love is always narcissistic and sadomasochistic. His characters also interface across social boundaries but what appear as insurmountable social barriers give way more easily than emotional ones. Here we will use Proust's cast of characters to flesh out our ideas about the dynamics that drive not only the choices made by some of his exciting lovers.

In Search of Lost Time

A wealthy aesthete; a young man who wants to be a famous writer; a courtesan; a man of the nobility who acts ignoble; as well as one who is brave; doting parents, and a bourgeois couple; these are some of the characters who touch us emotionally as Proust's narrator Marcel (1992) unfolds their lives. His characters often are caught between yearning to have their love requited and struggling with love's vicissitudes. Being in longing is a major theme in Proust's work as it is in the life of many lonely people. These people echo Brenner's (1974) view that loneliness is the longing for a specific object to return. We believe that this mental object may be created out of images of the early caretakers commingled with images of oneself.

Idealized Love

The first adult love the narrator sees is that between Marcel's parents. As he describes it, their marriage is simply a comfortable, convenient one. Never passionately angry, passionately loving or even flirtatious with one another, never shown in nightclothes; even their bedroom is never mentioned. Their life is depicted as always accompanied by other family members and friends. They dine; they walk; they converse. All of this is done gently, fondly, but never romantically or sexually.

Swann and Odette: Lovers Who Long

Swann is the first passionate adult lover depicted in the book. His attraction to Odette and his developing obsession with her reprises the young Marcel's obsession with his mother. Swann is known as a man who has dined with the Prince of Wales and is cherished by haute society for his charm, wit, sensitivity to art and for his intellectual understanding of it. He is also admired in society for being very rich and very generous with his money.

Odette depends upon the generosity of the many men, and sometimes women, who give her gifts and money in exchange for sex. She lives on the borders of society somewhere between making her living as a courtesan and being a prostitute. She had been married to a provincial lesser aristocrat whose money she squandered. After she left him he lived in the country being supported by friends. Swann's reaction to finding out about this was to give him an allowance. Odette had never been accepted by society though she longed to be; what attracts her to Swann is his entree into that world. In this he eventually disappoints her. Despite all that Swann has and is, his place in society is not powerful enough to bring Odette along. Society will never receive her. How Swann and Odette feel about each other, how they will resolve their relationship, as well as what drives it intrigue the reader.

A courtesan would seem to need to keep her customer happy; yet throughout their affair Odette treats Swann badly. Odette seems to know that making him jealous is the only way to keep him. She behaves secretively, is openly seductive toward other men, and often unavailable to Swann. He knows that she uses his money to entertain his rivals. She even excludes Swann from outings and parties that he pays for. Later we learn that Odette had been genuinely attracted to Swann; she used these tactics to keep his passion alive.

Love Found and Lost

In *Search*, love evaporates or disappears. Did Swann's apparent devaluing and suspicious attitude toward Odette turn her against him? Was it his failure to bring her into society? Was it his jealousy? He would question her about ostensible affairs and on occasion stalk her. She saw that by mistreating him, she had captured him. He was no longer exciting. That made her the object of his love but prevented him from being the object of hers. The theme is established. Passionate love is longing. Requited love is destroyed love.

As Proust saw it, jealousy feeds passion. Swann's passion for Odette was at its height when he imagined that Odette was having sexual pleasure with someone other than him. She was exciting to him when he believed he could not control her; what appears out of reach entices. The involuntary memory is like love; its power is derived from the impossibility of control. Pleasure is achieved only when one cannot exert control. It appears by serendipity. Only involuntary memories and experiences have power. Cupid's arrow hits a mark when the target is not grabbing it. Poland (2003) shows that how one uses a recovered memory is what counts; the capacity of a person to turn passive into active creates a new world for that person.

Odette captivates Swann despite his strong insistence that he finds her neither beautiful nor interesting, nor his type. Ultimately, he collects her as one might collect a work of art; their affair was sparked when he associated her with a woman in a Botticelli painting. As he associates Odette with this masterpiece, she becomes desirable to him because he believes others would want her as they want the painting. Swann understands that he will pay a price for marrying Odette: his social standing will decline. This choice shows his character: he is willing to tolerate losing the esteem of the society ladies whose esteem others want. Swann's independence is further illustrated by his taking up a cause that most of his upper class friends do not support; he becomes an advocate for Dreyfus because he believes him to have been condemned unjustly. He wants what he cannot not have: Odette. What he has, he does not want: the esteem of high society. Socially as well as romantically, longing is more valued than satisfaction. This theme, begun with Marcel's longing for his mother, carries through the novel to other lovers and other loves.

Love of the Elusive

After their tumultuous affair, Swann and Odette have a crashingly disappointing bourgeois marriage. The sadomasochism that shot through their affair disappears; each of the couple appears less anxious. Odette gives up her lovers for the secure and luxurious lifestyle provided by Swann. She even gives up her friendship with the wealthy and status-seeking Verdurins. They had encouraged Odette to spend time with other men. They had not believed that Swann was welcomed by the very upper crust people who would not accept them. Out of loyalty to her husband, Odette gives up her friends.

Jealousy was the driving force of Swann and Odette's affair, but they marry only after their daughter Gilberte is born. The gossip has it that Odette uses Gilberte to manipulate Swann into marrying her by limiting his access to his daughter, creating the longing for her that he had once felt for Odette. Once married, each longs for something that the other cannot provide: social status for Odette and Gilberte. Odette wants to be accepted by the aristocracy; Swann wants his daughter to be welcomed by the pinnacle of the aristocracy: the Duc and Duchess de Guermantes. Swann attains pleasure and narcissistic gratification from watching Odette develop her own salon with his help. But the hope that some time in the future their daughter, Gilberte might become a member of the best society is only fulfilled after Swann's death. Though the Guermantes did not accept Odette, Swann had continued his relationship with them. He may have thought that if they accepted him, they might be more likely to eventually come to accept his daughter. What makes acceptance by the aristocracy so precious is that it is withheld.

Swann is the essential link between love and social life. He takes pleasure in what he has because it is exclusive. He wants Odette exclusively. He wants the relationship with the Guermantes because they are exclusive. They are seen as discerning. What makes them valuable is that not everyone can have their company. Just as love is kindled by the idea that the beloved is unavailable, so membership in a social circle can give pleasure only as the participants are aware that they might have been excluded. It is the exclusion of others that makes membership a privilege. There is pleasure in excluding others, a situation that leaves those who wish for invitations pressing their noses to the window, like the child who observes the primal scene, feeling left out.

Love Among the Excluders

Swann and Odette bond as outsiders; each sees in the other an outsider who longs for acceptance. The Duc and Duchess de Guermantes are insiders. They are cousins and they do not have children. He contains the sexuality in his love affairs; she is cultured and abstinent. They function as one person, each supplying the missing part of the other. There is no hint of eroticism between them. The Duc's affairs serve to protect his sense of masculinity. He prides himself on wife's wit and exceptional taste. He champions her by acting the bumbler; setting up the circumstance for her to tell a story, or make a witty remark. Through the young Marcel's idealizing eyes they seem to be sophisticated and desirable as companions and as models. The narrator Marcel notices that the Duc is a social conformist with no capacity to discuss ideas. In contrast to Swann's support of Dreyfus, the Duc professes not to understand why the affair needed to be re-examined. Like most of his class, he believes that justice was served by the first tribunal. He is a shallow, an ill-informed gossip.

The Duc's esteemed social position ensures that the Duchess, will be able to exhibit her goods where it counts. Her narcissism matches her regal beauty. She holds court as if she were the lead actress in a play. She is fun to watch and seems to enjoy herself. In her, Proust has created a character who believes that everything that she is, or that she had been, or has, is the best. Both her taste in the arts, and the ideas that she professes about painting, music, and life, have been influenced by Swann. Self love prevails, she appears to long for nothing and no one.

Bars to Love: Narcissism, Envy, and Jealousy

If the Duchess has everything, how can she be envious or jealous? She is smug. Her grandiose self and pride allow her to seem above it all. Her biting humor hides her submissiveness toward her husband. Each time the Duc ends an affair he asks his wife to invite the discarded woman into her salon, and she acquiesces. She complies despite her stated policy of only entertaining women who are relatives: women whom she could not exclude. The reader is left to wonder whether she did not enjoy the company of women because they did not admire her the way men did or because they were potential rivals for the attentions of the men or so as to avoid being an unwitting procurer for her husband. She creates longing in others: she even denies Swann his dying wish that she would invite his daughter to her home. She had no daughter of her own. She might have envied Swann that. She was not the person Swann loved the most.

She might have envied Gilberte that. (Ironically, after Swann's death, circumstances converge that place both Odette and Gilberte on a more equal footing with the Duchess.)

Proust used the characters of the Duchess and the wealthy-bourgeois Verdurins to show love overcoming a hostile environment. The Duchess does not approve of Swann and Odette's relationship nor that of her nephew with a young actress. Robert de Saint-Loup the nephew of the Duc and Duchess, was notified that he was being transferred from his military post near Paris to a distant location that would make it impossible to continue his affair with his love and mistress, Rachel. The Duchess refuses to help her nephew when he is posted away from Paris. She rationalizes her selfish refusal by saying that she is protecting Saint-Loup from a relationship with a woman whom she sees as ridiculous.

Later we find Saint-Loup married to another woman. While married, he has affairs with both women and male prostitutes. Eventually, he falls in love with a man. His erotic interest in men is portended early on when he accused Rachel of flirting with and desiring most of the men with whom they had come in contact. As it turned out, it was he rather than Rachel who desired the men. Fighting with her over her ostensible flirtations allowed him to experience his longing as longing for her love rather than longing for the men. The longing was both painful and pleasurable; it allowed him not to make a commitment to either a man or a woman.

Same Sex Love

Proust's exploration of where Cupid might shoot his arrow includes many examples of love between characters of the same sex. Edmund White (2004) believed that Proust saw men who loved other men as inverts: in their souls women. White believed that Proust would take a position on an issue, but he also would make the case for other possibilities. Men who loved men could also be masculine themselves. The character of St. Loup is an example of a man who loves men but is also masculine. Proust shows him to be devoted to his military career; brave in battle; a lover of the camaraderie of his fellow officers; and well respected by the men in his command. Yet he is also a romantic. He quotes poetry. Though attractive to men, he also is considered dashing by many women.

Proust had introduced same sex love with a scene of what he later came to understand as sadistic love between two women. She makes love with a lesbian; while making love, Mlle. Vinteuil encourages her lover to say that she will spit at the image of Mlle. Vinteuil's father, an act observed by Marcel, and one that he understood as a desecration of her deceased father. The narrator understands this act of cruelty as necessary for the overly scrupulous Mlle. Vinteuil can only allow herself to enjoy the pleasure of sex.

If the sadomasochistic aspect of Mlle. Vinteuil's character is in the service of separation (Halberstadt-Freud 1991), then Mlle. Vinteuil needs the sadism of her lover in order to disidentify from her masochistic father. Evidence for this idea is that Mlle. Vinteuil and her lover spent their lives painstakingly resurrecting and promoting his music. They are responsible for his posthumous fame. Thus debasing him was partly a way of freeing Mlle. Vinteuil from her too close identification with him. The sadistic love scene was a reaction formation masking her longing for her father.

Sado-Masochism and Erotic Love

Another character who reflects the many dimensions of love in Proust is wealthy Baron Charlus, the brother of the Duc de Guermantes. He is a widower. The narrator comes to see him as effeminate; his demeanor is like a woman's. M. de Charlus covets Morel, a talented musician who looks like an angel. Charlus values Morel's youth and beauty; Charlus longs to be thought beautiful by other men. He sees in Morel the musician he might have become if his social position had not made it necessary to give up a career as a musician. He maintains his scholarly appreciation of other people's performances. The Baron is longing to be loved by a lover who represents himself as he had been and would like to be. Effeminate himself, he makes a narcissistic object choice, a kind of choice that Freud (1914) illustrated with the example of a homosexual man, although he did not restrict it to this kind of love, and that Proust shows us to be usual for both men and women, homosexual and heterosexual as well.

Morel's choice of Baron Charlus is a multidetermined one; narcissism is meshed with ambitious opportunism since Morel desperately wants to be received by the aristocracy as if he were one of them. As we consider what drives their relationship, we can see how object choice influences the tone of what goes on between a couple. Baron Charlus admires Morel, even if he is not loved by Morel. Morel envies Charlus social position, Charlus envies Morel's youthful looks and potential. The envy each has toward the other, exacerbated by idealization, sets the stage for sadomasochism. The Baron is not above being sadistic to Morel as he was to others even though he loves him. When he fears that Morel is straying he coerces him to spend more time with him; he tells Morel that he was arranging to fight a duel over him. Charlus knows that a duel would humiliate Morel by bringing attention to the sexual nature of their relationship. Charlus succeeds in getting his lover's attention. But coercion is not love; fear is not love. Coercion can force the beloved to behave as the lover desires, but it engenders hate.

The narcissism of these characters is in their concern for their own aims and their utter disregard for the feelings of others, even the feelings of those they profess to love. This concern for the self arises not from self love, but from self hatred. The need for love from others is the main thing that motivates them. They need to be loved because they cannot love themselves. Charlus and Morel each have an antipathy for an aspect of the self which they try to hide from certain others. Charlus hates and tries to hide his own homosexuality; Morel hates and tries to hide his own lower class origins. Fear of how others might perceive them if they knew the secrets that they wanted to hide causes them to require reassurance of the kind that Kohut (1977) called the function of the self-object. Morel's self-hatred is displaced onto another object and given life in the scenario in which he acts out his fantasy of causing pain to a lower class young woman. The Baron is unable to tolerate Morel's indifference to him and is driven to be being beaten by lower class men. Why does he seek pain? Is being beaten a punishment? Does he seek pain to counter the pain of his loss? Is he angry at himself for the wishes that drive him to love men? Choosing lower class men preserves the aspect of Morel that he loved and Morel hated. Ironically, his social position is what caused him to lose his music, being lower class is valuable because it is what Charlus cannot have. Can allowing himself to be beaten be understood as a way to feel less powerful and more like the powerless Morel? If so, being beaten allows him to hold on to the lost beloved by feeling onself to be him. Here unbearable longing is converted to pleasure by being encapsulated in physical pain. Pain becomes pleasure, longing becomes having by being and the beating (Freud 1919) is sexual pleasure.

[Charlus calls the shots while he is tied down and being beaten. He gets the control while putting the other person in the apparent role of the sadist relieves any conscious guilt he feels. Being less guilty and being able to tolerate physical abuse sustains an illusion of being strong and masculine. In this scenario we see a variation of Freud's (1919) idea about beating fantasies. For the boy, the beating fantasy has the father in the active role; he administers the beating and as such is a source of erotic pleasure. Here the baron is an example of a masochist sadistically enacting his own fantasy. If the beater represents the father, then the father is as a devalued object, able to be controlled.]

Longing: Pleasure, Pain and Resolution

The reader has followed Marcel's life until he becomes a middle-aged man, through the course of which Proust has taken us through a myriad of settings including the drawing rooms of aristocrats, the homes of the wealthy bourgeoisie, and houses of prostitution. Though the narrator was neither an aristocrat nor wealthy he gained entry into the world of the elite through his family connections. His beloved grandmother started his climb up the social ladder by introducing him to her aristocratic elderly friend. He impressed his grandmother's friend with his intelligence, curiosity about life, and knowledge of the arts; she invited him to her salon where he got to know the Duchess de Guermantes, who invited him to her salon. He was eventually welcomed at many other exclusive soirees. He appeared pleased to be in these elegant surroundings and among such prominent hosts and hostesses. Observing how others lived and got along, Marcel formed opinions about what he had observed.

Throughout the work, Marcel always seemed to be hungry for love, admiration, or sexual excitement. His romantic interests were fleeting; jealousy, or an idea that his object of desire might be unattainable, as well as his need to gratify his sexual urges, led to his interest in many different women. We see him imagine how nice it would be if one of them desired him. Marcel is excited by the fantasy of being loved by Gilberte, the Duchess de Guermantes, Madame Swann, a milkmaid, a fisher girl, and, in turn, various members of what he describes as a band of girls whom he meets at the seashore. With the exception of Albertine, his love affairs exist mainly in fantasy, though sex with prostitutes is implied.

He falls in love with Albertine, a young woman cyclist who appears strong, tough and athletic, and who he imagines to be the girlfriend of a cyclist. His sense of himself as sickly and weak makes her physical strength and toughness appealing. She is what he wishes himself to be. He becomes obsessed with her comings and goings. While he admires her, he is also ambivalent because she is not educated or sophisticated in the way that he is. Despite his ambivalence toward Albertine, he persuades her to move in with him as his mistress. Once Albertine appears to love him, he spoils the relationship by obsessing about whether or not she is betraying him with by having sex with one of a number of women.

He is possessive of Albertine, acts jealous and has her spied on. She is treated as a captive.

Albertine feeds Marcel's suspiciousness by behaving secretively and allowing him to catch her in a number of lies. She had shown signs early on that she was sexually excited by women, yet Marcel believed that he could win her by showering her with gifts and keeping her under his watchful eyes. Eventually, Albertine is unable to tolerate his controlling behavior. She resents his constantly questioning her loyalty, and since she doubts that he will ever marry her, she leaves Marcel. In this act she wrests control from him and rekindles his interest in her; once more he falls under the thrall of longing. Recognizing his ambivalence, he attempts to comfort himself and regain control by having an affair with one of her friends and telling this to Albertine. He hopes to make her jealous, then she would be the one wanting him. He finds comfort in a trip with his mother and sex with a prostitute.

By the end of *Search* Marcel comes to realize that what he has learned about himself and others is worth preserving in the form of a novel. He sees that for him the sweetest pleasure was the anticipation of what might be—the sensation of longing. The excitement that comes from unrequited love provided the juice that would allow him to succeed in his goal of becoming a writer. At this moment Marcel, the hero of the book becomes the narrator who has been telling Marcel's story from the beginning of it. Marcel needed to create his novel more than he needed to possess a lover or have a family. Here he becomes the novelist, Proust. This turn integrates the hero, the narrator and the author.

DISCUSSION

Why is longing so valued? Longing engenders excitement by allowing the fantasy of perfect gratification in the future. Leavy (1990) examined a novel by a contemporary of Proust: Alain Fournier. He asserted that longing is a wish for an ideal desexualized object. In Leavy's view the object does not have to be desexualized, but is always idealized. Phillips (2001) builds on Leavy's idea; for Phillips longing is the repudiation of unavailability of what is desired. Longing allows the "no" to be magically undone in fantasy even as it is accepted in dull reality. For Phillips longing is failure to grieve the impossibility of fulfilling a wish. The granting of the child Marcel's wish deprived him of the opportunity to grieve the loss. The result, as Phillips sees it is a feedback loop in which the defenses of undoing and disavowal operate against the integration of the pain of the loss.

Our contention that longing is what makes the object desirable for Proust is corroborated by Doubrovsky (1986) who sees the incident of the madeline as the core of the novel. Longing for the madeline makes the whole experience of the place where Marcel first tasted it come to vivid life. The madeline evokes the fantasy of longing, the longing the little boy felt for his mother's kiss. We note that the madeline is also the name of the motherly lover in the story Proust's mother read to him on the night she stayed in his room rather than letting him find a way to soothe himself.

Longing is a state where closure has not yet occurred so that a person in longing has the experience of being in motion, going toward the desired object. Marcel's experience of longing for his mother's kiss is more satisfactory than having received the kiss because in the state of longing he did not realize that gratification would come at the price of guilt; the price was the loss of self esteem. He lost the fantasy of his father seeing him as a powerful rival. Longing is associated with innocence, a time before gratification. Longing for the mother's kiss comes before the superego is fully formed and prohibitions solidify, a time where anything might be possible: paradise. Later longing represents a fantasy of a return to paradise or to a state of omnipotence. In Freudian terms, it is before the resolution of the Oedipus conflict, when one is in the thrall of love and allowed any object for its aim including the self. Longing allows one the fantasy of control; if you have no contact with another person you never have to experience aggression toward or from the object (Richards and Spira 2003). Proust's work elaborates the link between masochism and omnipotence which has been described by several analytic authors (Novick and Novick 1996; Bond 1981; Bach 1991) in their study of masochism. They point out how for the masochist a happy ending results in loneliness and a sense of vulnerability; pleasure that depends on other people is a threat to the masochist's need to control. But, as with all compromises, longing causes pain as it also provides gratification. The pain in longing is masochistic precisely because it is more valued than satisfaction.

Proust's understanding of human relationships is that longing for love is longing for fulfillment, for happiness. But since the longing comes out of oneself and one's own experiences, the only one who can know what to do to fulfill one's desire is oneself. The other is irredeemably different, irredeemably alien, altogether motivated by different wishes and needs. The extreme of this view is embodied in the incident in which Charlus pays lower class men to beat him (Wilson 1931). He realizes that they are only doing it for the money. Not even viciousness can call out the same feeling in another person, the other will always be doing things for his own reasons. Even when love is gained for a moment, it changes with time as the beloved changes and the lover's needs and wishes change also (Beckett 1931, 1999). This change and particularity of viewpoint is highlighted in Aciman's (2004) compilation of twenty-eight literary critics' responses to the question: "What is your favorite passage in *Search?*"

Shattuck (2000) hypothesized that Proust's insistence on the value of what is unattained comes from Montaigne's assertion: "I attach too little value to things I possess, just because I possess them and overvalue anything strange, absent and not mine. . ." (p. 83–86).

According to Shattuck, Proust believes this because he does not value himself so that any one or any thing that comes close to him loses its value. But we note that the character Marcel does value his gandmother, scenery, social life and many other peopleand things. It is only in the field of romantic love that devaluation follows attainment.

Romantic love, the great ideal of the nineteenth century, stands denuded of its major illusion: the key importance of possessing the object of love. In this Proust comes very close to Freud's idea that the object is the least fixed part of the wish. For Freud (1905), the aim of the wish is more fixed and more stable than the choice of an object. Yet what distinguishes love from the sexual perversions or simple lust is the longing for the object and the fixity of that longing. As Proust shows us, a person comes to stand in the real world for the ideal because that person is unattainable. It is the longing that is prized, not the fulfillment.

Psychoanalysts of various persuasions have commented on Proust's views of what constitutes love in *The Search*. Tobin (2006) suggested that the tension of little Marcel's painful longing might have been relieved if his mother had left him alone to devise his own soothing by masturbating. This classical drive understanding is one way of reading *The Search* as if it were the patient on the couch. Another way of understanding the same onset of painful longing was put forth by Kohut (1977). He saw little Marcel as the victim of parental lack of empathy. Because his parents could not see that what he needed was not the presence of his mother, but her understanding that he longed for her and her confidence in his ability to overcome his misery, he was left with a deficit that Proust called longing for love. Yet another way to see this onset of longing

(Kerzner 2006) is from Winnicott's point of view. Here little Marcel suffers from a lack of early oneness with his mother that prevents his development of mature sexuality by leaving him with a deficient ability to connect with others. In this same tradition Halberstadt-Freud (1991) saw Proust himself in little Marcel as the victim of a failed separation-individuation process because his mother was too intrusive to allow him to become a separate self.

Our point of view is different from all of these because we see Proust as adding something to the understanding of love by his depiction of the many characters with differing childhood experiences, different mothers and different life stories who all suffer from the same longing and who are insatiable. Here we second Freud's assertion that he lays down his arms before the artist. What Proust adds to these psychoanalytic views is the idea that longing itself is the value that cannot by blunted by satiation, cannot lead to de-idealization of the loved one, cannot lead to boredom or dullness. The state of longing is not confused with love, it is valued above it.

REFERENCES

ACIMAN, A. (2004). Preface. In: *The Proust Project,* A. Aciman, ed., New York: Farrar, Straus and Giroux.

BACH, S. (1991). On Sadomasochistic Object Relations. In: *Perversions & Near; Perversions in ClinicalPractice.* G. Fogel and W. Meyers, eds., New Haven: Yale. pp.75–92.

BECKETT, S. (1931/1999). *Proust and Three Dialogues with Georges Duthuit.* London: John Calder.

BOND, A.H. (1981). The Masochist is the Leader. *Journal of American Academy of Psychoanalysis* 9:375–389.

BRENNER, C. (1974). On the Nature and Development of Affects: A Unified Theory. *Psychoanalytic Quarterly* 635–654.

COETZEE, J.M. (2003). *Elizabeth Costello.* New York: Penguin, p. 191.

DOUBROVSKY, S. (1986). Writing and Fantasy. In *Proust la Place de la Madeline.* (C.M. Bove with P.A. Bove, Transl.) Lincoln, NE: University of Nebraska Press.

FREUD, S. (1905). Three essays on sexuality. *Standard Edition* 7:125–245.

———— (1914). On narcissism. *Standard Edition* 14:73–102

———— (1919). A child is being beaten. *Standard Edition* 17: 175–204.

HALBERSTADT-FREUD, H.C. (1991). *Freud, Proust, Perversion and Love.* Berwyn, PA: Swets and Zeitlinger.

KOHUT, H. (1977). *The Restoration of the Self.* New York: International Universities Press.

LEAVY, S.A. (1990). Alain Fournier: Memory, Youth and Longing. *Psychoanalytic Study of the Child,* 45:495–532.

MILLER, M. (1956). *Nostalgia.* New York: Houghton Mifflin.

NOVICK, J. AND NOVICK, K.K. (1996). *Fearful Symmetry: The Development and Treatment of Sadomashochism.* New Jersey: Jason Aronson Inc.

PHILLIPS, S. (2001). The Overstimulation of Everyday Life: New Aspects of Male Homosexuality. *Journal of the American Psychoanalytic Association* 49:1235–1267.

POLAND, W.S. (2003). Reading Fiction and the Psychoanalytic Experience: Proust On Reading And On Reading Proust .*Journal of the American Psychoanalytic Association* 51:1262–1282.

PROUST, M. (1913–1927). *In Search of Lost Time.* (6 volumes, Transl. C.K. Scott-Moncrieff & T. Kilmartin), New York: Modern Library Edition, 2003.

RICHARDS, A.K. and SPIRA, L. (2003). On Being Lonely: Fear of One's Own Aggression as an Impediment to Intimacy. *Psychoanalytic Quarterly* 72:357–375.

ROSE, P. (2000). *The Year of Reading Proust: A Memoir in Real Time.* Washington, DC: Counterpoint.

SAND, G. (1977/1850). *The Country Waif (Francois le Champi).* E.Collis, Transl., Lincoln NE: University of Nebraska Press.

SHATTUCK, R. (2000). *Proust's Way: A Field Guide To In Search of Lost Time.* New York: W.W. Norton & Company, Inc.

STOLLER, R. (1975). *Perversion: The Erotic Form of Hatred.* London: Maresfield Library

WHITE, E. (2004). A Race Upon Which a Curse Is Laid. In: *The Proust Project.* A. Aciman, ed., New York: Farrar Straus and Giroux.

WILSON, E. (1931). *Axel's Castle.* New York: Farrar Straus and Giroux, 2004.

****
****

Preceding chapter originally presented by:

A.K. RICHARDS & L. SPIRA (2006). At the Meeting of the American Psychoanalytic Association, New York, January 21.

The "Sweet and Sour" of Being Lonely and Alone

This paper explores the question of why some lonely people seem to forget what goes on in their treatment when they are away from the analyst's presence. The authors look at loneliness from the perspective of a female patient using the transference to attempt to undo a childhood trauma of early abandonment and neglect. This woman appeared child-like and helpless while she resisted using insight. A dream highlights the unconscious wishes and fantasies that fueled her stance in treatment. The premise is that by not allowing herself to use her insights when out of the analyst's presence, she was maintaining herself as the lonely abandoned child that she had been. Using her treatment in this way seemed to assuage her pain while she waited for the father of her fantasy. The price she paid for waiting was loneliness, loss of self-esteem, and a life with few adult pleasures. Her fantasy of cure followed a sequence from a deficit model, to a model of internalization of bad objects, to a conflict model. The authors believe that sequencing the view of her troubles in this way had a therapeutic effect.

W hat makes some lonely patients act as if they do not remember what went on in sessions after they leave the office? One such patient, Ms. A, maintained continuity from one session to the next, but recalled her insights only vaguely, and only when she was with her analyst. Having arrived in New York from the South a year before, Ms. A was in her late twenties when she began treatment. Dissatisfied with her office temp job, she could not see her way to a career that might

The patient was treated by Lucille Spira. The discussion is a collaboration between the authors. We wish to thank Doctors Martin Widzer and Jane Kupersmidt, and members of the discussion group of the American Psychoanalytic Association "Towards an Understanding of Loneliness and Aloneness in Women" for generously sharing ideas and clinical material that has enriched our understanding.

satisfy her. Worried, and neglectful of her appearance, she seemed like a fearful and fragile teenager who was large and overweight. To soothe herself she would overeat or smoke. She was lonely and without friends, which she attributed to her large size, lack of sophistication, and a chronic rheumatoid condition. While she reported being unhappy about being alone, she avoided potential friendships as she held on to a belief that no one whom she would value would be interested in her.

Almost everything made her anxious and advocating for herself aroused intense anxiety. When she began treatment, she said that she wanted to feel less anxious and in better control of her eating. She also wanted a college degree and a career. Later, we came to see that she wanted something else even more; she wanted to be the favorite child of her father. After years of treatment we came to believe that keeping herself alone preserved her fantasy of becoming her father's favorite as she had imagined herself being as a little girl.

The following vignette typified her behavior. She had not been given her recent paycheck because the woman who usually gave her the check had been absent. Although she needed the money, she could not ask her male department manager for it because she feared that he might be annoyed by such a request or think that she was rude. She said that she would die if the manager reacted toward her as she imagined that he might. I asked if she were scared to ask him for her check because he was a man. She said that she thought his age and position intimidated her. I said that fear might be related to other experiences when she had asked something from an older powerful person. We could not understand why her fear was so intense. Because I thought that she wanted me to confirm or disconfirm her belief about what might happen with the manager, I told her that while I could not guarantee how he would react if she asked for her check, I would be available to help her with her feelings, whatever might happen. She decided to wait for her check rather than chance the result that she feared. She waited several days. Over the years she kept longing ineffectually for most of what she wanted.

Ms. A acted as if she had all the time in the world. The issue of time came up while trying to understand one of her self-abusive behaviors. She was surprised that I thought it had been a long time, adding that she herself had not thought about time, since she did not know how long treatment should take. Then she had been in treatment for about nine years.

MS. A'S HISTORY

Ms. A is a middle child; she has a sister two years older and another two years younger. She was subject to a number of traumas and misfortunes, which included her mother leaving home for a year when Ms. A was three. Ms. A has no memories of having missed her mother during that time. She did not blame her problems on her mother's leaving. During her mother's absence, a nanny, with whom Ms. A became embroiled in a struggle over bowel habits, cared for the children. As Ms. A reports it, the nanny believed that her failure to defecate on schedule meant that she was withholding her feces; Ms. A believes that the nanny punished her by isolating her.

Ms. A was criticized for her weight since she was four years old and offered bribes to reduce. She was messy in her appearance and with her belongings throughout childhood. Her mother had the task of seeing to it that she met the father's standards for attractiveness and neatness. The fact that Ms. A did not in fact conform in these ways caused her father to criticize her mother; Ms. A later decided that she was guilty of causing the breakup of the marriage during her own adolescence.

Ms. A also suffered from her mother's alcoholism. Ms. A said her mother constantly criticized her unfairly, did not love her, and was meaner when she was drunk. Her successful father worked long hours. The care of the children was provided by a series of nannies and maids who her mother told her disliked her because she was loud and messy. But mostly she and her sisters were left to their own devices. Ms. A idealized her father and believed that she was his favorite because he granted her requests for toys and other things. Her sisters too saw her as the favorite, as they felt that they received even less of his attention than she did. Her requests seemed to have been few. She did not report having taken care of her mother or siblings, nor did she describe herself as a pseudo-companion to her father. She was the child who mirrored his tastes and interests, that is, for particular foods and music. She tried to live up to his wish for her to be a singer despite a sense of hopelessness about her ability.

While she remembered being lonely and scared in childhood, the painful reality of her life had not kept Ms. A from having friends at school. In adolescence, she felt less a part of the group because she tried to avoid dating; so scared was she of the pressures that she saw went with it. She avoided being admired by boys by making herself obese.

When she was about 14, her father separated from her mother and took up residence with a woman reputed to have been his mistress. Eventually they married and moved out of her home state. No one in her family had had any inkling that her father was leaving; she remembered being scared when he did not show up for a week. As a college senior she transferred to a school in his new community, losing credits in the process. She felt humiliated when he showed little interest in her. But because her sisters had not been offered this "opportunity," to live near her father, she concluded that she was the favorite; this perception evoked guilt as it had in her childhood.

Ms. A had her first sexual encounter when she was in her early twenties. She allowed a handyman to seduce her, only to have him leave her when his previous lover returned. Shortly after this brief affair, she became ill with a rheumatoid condition that she learned would be chronic. For years she believed that her illness was caused by her relationship with the man. She saw her condition also as a punishment for choosing someone of so much less status than her father. The illness clinched her belief that she could never be a performer. If she were not to be a singer, however, she wondered how she would be able to recapture even her father's lukewarm interest.

TREATMENT

Her symptoms were persistent and witnessing her suffering was painful for the analyst. Each of her traumatic experiences contributed to her fear of failure and frequent claims of being the victim of other people's rudeness or inconsistencies. The analyst told her that she was neglectful toward herself not only because she was unsophisticated, as she claimed, but also because she was treating herself as she had been treated, turning passive experience into active. Rather than complain about the loss of her mother, her concern was to hold onto her father's love.

Through many years of treatment Ms. A avoided opportunities that might have provided her with comfort or pleasure despite her wishes. For years she resisted buying a comfortable bed. She did not complain enough to her doctor to receive adequate pain management. Despite her suffering, she was rarely tearful when discussing her history or current situation. Her empathy toward others did not extend to herself.

She did not alienate her peers at work, nor did she report not liking them. She once generously gave a peer a computer for his child; she gave to collections for office parties. She reported waiting to be asked to join peers at lunch; she did not take social initiatives like asking to join social groups at work. Thus her loneliness was due to her passivity rather than exclusion by others.

She believed that she was greedy and messy because she could not be any different. The small steps she took toward her career goal led to modest successes, although she did not feel empowered, nor did she seem to build on these successes. For example, she would get her hair cut so that it was neat, but then not cut it again for a year so that she looked increasingly messy again. When her boss criticized her messy desk, she cleaned it up, but did not keep it clean. In therapy she made an effort to be what she thought of as a good patient: never missing sessions, always paying her bill on time, and being polite. The greediness she reported as part of her history and her current life was absent. She never criticized the analyst. Characterized as "bad," she acted "good" in treatment. At work she enacted her mother's view of her, so that her bosses experienced her oppositional characteristics.

She had first insisted her troubles were due to personal deficit, then accepted that neglect had a role, and about ten years into treatment, we saw how conflict played a role in her compromises. Remarking that the only job she was fit for was to be a street cleaner, she stated that this was a job for an "ex-con." This self-perception contributed to her slow progress. While she berated herself for past "crimes" like her overeating, which she saw as greed, we eventually came to see that she had other reasons for her guilt. Previously, her taking responsibility for all that was bad had been understood as a way to defend against helplessness by defensive omnipotence. Fantasies of revenge were persistent, in the form of fears that someone she knew might be killed in a transit accident. It was always someone with whom she had been angry. Eventually, she connected this fear to one she had had in childhood of her mother dying in a car crash. Later she was able to talk about her fear that my plane might crash when I left for vacation. In this way we began to talk about present feelings and fantasies that might be contributing to her guilt, rather than only those from the past.

Oedipal interpretations resonated with Ms. A since she could connect with feeling envious, fearing envy, and being angry when she thought she was being excluded. Her long-held guilt for stealing sweets and thus depriving her mother and sisters was eventually interpreted as a displacement of her fear of having stolen her father from her mother and sisters.

She expressed fear that her mother would envy her if she were to have a richer life.

Her fear of being envied showed up in the transference as well. Once she kept her raincoat on during a session just before she was to meet her father. Her step-mother was not going to be there. Under the coat was a nice dress. The analyst interpreted her fear of the analyst's envy. Her usual messy teenager-like style functioned as a compromise that allowed her to hold on to her father while not exciting the envy of other women. Following that interpretation she adopted a less messy but plain style.

Eventually, we were able to understand what made it so difficult for her to use their collaboration when they were not together. She related a very dramatic fantasy that illustrated how her relationship to her father sustained her isolation of her insights. She reported feeling frustrated by spending endless weekends alone in her apartment. She added that it was particularly uncomfortable when it was warm because she could not open her windows because she did not want a pigeon to fly in and hurt her. When she was about nine she had left the kitchen door open and a bird flew into the oven. Her father was called home to handle the "crisis." She remembered that he told her afterward to keep the door closed, because if birds fly in, she could get hurt. This memory seemed to be not only a screen memory but also the kernel of an organizing principle by which Ms. A tried to lead her life, a magical solution for safety. Being open and taking anything in is dangerous. This fantasy might explain why she was not open to the interpretations that came from her treatment. While this idea did not work magic, it did open a dialogue in which we could consider how she was allowing her father to impact her life.

Ms. A's idealization of her father had been maintained in the face of constant disappointments. Several events occurred that resulted in her father being idealized less. She came to trust her analyst. Once her father set her up with a date by giving her phone number to a man from New York who had visited his country club in the South. Ms. A fantasized that the man was the "one." She felt humiliated when they met because the man seemed shocked that she was ten years older than he. She felt hurt by her father had set her up for rejection. Before this date, the analyst had opened up the possibility that the man might not be what she imagined. Later, she told me that our discussion had, to some degree cushioned the pain that would have resulted had she gone in cold. She began to consider that her father could be sadistic and withholding.

Seeing some of her father's negative traits seemed to increase her investment in herself. She began to see the analyst as more connected to her and to her reality than her father was. While she still wanted him to see her as mirroring him, she began to see her own ideas as valid. She also overvalued the analyst.

About two years ago and after many years of treatment, a poignant moment allowed her to consider how she might be overvaluing our relationship at her own expense. On returning from vacation, the analyst noticed that she had laryngitis, and wondered if she had been neglecting her health. When asked how long she had been suffering with the chest cold and laryngitis, she tearfully said that when the analyst is away she has no need for her real voice, the one that talks about her feelings; it was as if she herself were not reason enough to take care of herself. It was the first time she had cried about anything that occurred between them. The theme of others denying her voice began to appear when she believed that she was being excluded. When she imagines others to be more powerful than herself she narrows the range of her voice by excluding the part that tells her to take care of herself.

Now we return to the question: Why do some lonely patients act as if what went on in therapy does not exist for them outside of the therapeutic relationship? Thus far, we have touched on a number of factors that we understood as contributing to the way that she used her treatment: the early history which likely made it difficult for her to trust, the anal aspects of her character, her guilt over her wishes, and her relationship with her father, both real and fantasied. These factors kept her locked alone in her past. A dream she had after thirteen years of treatment added to our understanding of why she seemed to forget the therapy collaboration when she was alone. It suggests that Ms. A consciously wished to be a baby with her father as she unconsciously wished to be my favorite baby.

MS. A'S DREAM

Patient: I had a dream. You were in it. We went on a trip together—but it was to my family, dad and Mary [step-mother]. Dad was playing with a baby [Her father and Mary do not have children]. I said to myself: I feel so jealous. Then we had to do this presentation. Yours was really good, and it was amazing how you put it together with very little effort—colors and miniature figures. It was really good. Then, we are leaving and you are going on your way. You left carrying your portfolio with you. That's it.

Analyst: What do you make of it?

Patient: In the beginning we met and you had to persuade me to go, in a neutral way. Maybe in the dream you are helping me to get to another someplace. But, I'm not doing well, just an observer—watching it all—not participating. I brought you to meet my dad because maybe I wanted you to see how many problems I have because of my family. Dad was playing with the baby. I said to myself I wish I could be that baby, that's why I was jealous, I wanted to be the baby. I was bringing you to the root of my problems. I have been worried that I can't job hunt well. You might think I'm not doing everything I can.

Analyst: Is there something that I did that makes you feel that way?

Patient: No, I think I wish I could report more progress. I want to be doing everything I can. I want to get on with things. I may also want you to think I'm the best patient. But, instead I think: all these years, and I throw things out. I'm quick to avoid what I can't easily do. I take things in from here, but I take the far road to get there. It feels like a long wooded forest and I get lost sometimes and I forget about reality a little bit; space out denying myself and punishing myself. Sometimes I think I forget that when I think I am indulging myself I may actually be denying myself something else. When we talk about it here, I get it but, when I'm alone and have to think it out, I think it's a struggle. I have to make decisions by myself; that's why we went on the journey so I could do that, it's hard. The presentation in the dream, it was weird. I was surprised how good it was pulling a rabbit out of a hat. It was as if you were performing magic, but I knew it wasn't magic. I was impressed and confused. There was a slanted board you could display pictures on it like panoramas. You were in it and shrunk down walking across it. I said oh my god and you used lighting also, wow cool then over.

Analyst: Is there a fantasy about what I do?

Patient: I think you have a perfect but difficult job. Perfect because no boss, you are your own boss, nice setting the hard part is always having to deal with the human elements instead of like with paper work that I do. You don't know what they will bring to the table. You met my father in the dream, weird but you didn't really since there was no interacting. Mary was peripherally there on the side, some others too but can't figure that out. I wished I could be that baby, but that's a sweet and sour wish. What are the chances of my father being able to do better? Very very iffy, and I'd have to grow up and that wouldn't be so good either. No new beginning. This dream was different, but the same too as some of those dreams that have a supernatural quality, those are where evil things are out to get me. But not this dream, but I knew it might be lurking in the background, never really safe. I'm going to get working on my job hunt. I didn't need to take time out to go to Janet's get-together, would not have made a bit of difference if I had not shown up. I used the party as an excuse not to work on my stuff.

Analyst: Does the dream say anything about that?

Patient: Tells me I avoid, wishing someone else could do it for me. That's a wish in the dream: if I could follow someone, not have to think for myself, you know like a baby. I think I have a wish to recreate the past and have it come out so I would feel better. When I stop being active I fall back. I hang on to staying passive. Being active takes me a universe away from the possibility of the fantasy. I need a magician, give you that job.

Analyst: Maybe you want me to know not only how painful it was when your sister was born, since it felt like you lost your dad, but how you try to avoid the painful reality that you can't get him back by giving all the awe to me. Maybe I fall into it, and that doesn't leave you confident.

This dream was her story of her treatment. I was the one in awe reversing the dream—since she had not reported many dreams nor had she taken an active role in analyzing her productions. She was newly willing to recognize what she had achieved in her treatment. Beyond the two degrees and her six-figure salary, she had learned to use a process that enabled her to feel in touch with herself, rather than lost. She now understands her defenses and why she needed to take the "far" road. She was demonstrating that she could hold on to her insights.

After she told me the dream, I chose to let her take charge rather than to refocus her on each dream element. What's new here is her readiness to mourn the fact that "you can't go home again." Her use of the metaphor "sweet and sour" shows that she is recognizing the conflict inherent in her wish. In other words, if you act like you know how to get along in the world, you have to give up on the idea that you can still get the family that you never had in childhood. As we can see from Ms. A's resolutions, it may be that you can only let go of the wish in tiny stages, as you come to realize bit by bit that it was a fantasy maintained at the price of self-esteem and adult gratifications. Interestingly, "sweet and sour" also refers to a favorite dish she and her father enjoyed together.

Since Ms. A's parents had never acknowledged their role in her difficulties, I said that I was doing too much. I could see how I overwhelmed her, which left her feeling misunderstood and alone. The painful affect in the dream is represented by her standing in my shadow. It is also represented in the form of the lurking danger. This danger is superego anxiety: punishment for rivalrous feelings toward the baby, toward Mary, (perhaps standing in for her mother), and less consciously toward me.

Over a year later Ms. A told me that when she doesn't stay on her track, she is choosing to ignore what we have done. She is aware that she can call upon her inner resources if she so chooses. After 15 years Ms. A, now over 40, has become able to make more favorable compromises that allow her friendships and more pleasure. She has her career and an advanced degree, has traveled, given up smoking, and controls her eating. She allows herself pleasure from a pet. Most importantly, however, she can own her skills and accept the fact that conflict plays a role in her life. How does she use our collaboration when we are not together? Recently, she put a world map in her office to symbolize that she never has to feel lost again. At an office event she recalled my idea that she overeats when angry with herself. Although she was not sure if she were in fact angry, she decided not to binge in case she was. Later, we could explore what she had been feeling. Her thoughts about her treatment? She has told me that I cannot retire for at least five years. We have yet to understand how she arrived at that time frame.

DISCUSSION

The following formulations derive from discussion by the authors. The ideas developed as we analyzed the clinical material and from our reading and experience with other lonely patients. To return to our original question: Why do people act as if what went on in therapy does not exist for them outside of the therapeutic relationship?

Abend (1979) showed how a patient's unconscious fantasy, as it interweaves with his/her theory of cure, can act as a resistance in treatment. He believes that it is important to analyze a patient's fantasy of cure as early as possible. In this case understanding the many layers of fantasy has taken many years and still goes on.

Ms. A's original goals were: to control her overeating (weight); position herself for a career; and reduce the anxiety that made such goals seem impossible. These wishes were associated with getting her father's love. While she was telling her analyst what she wanted, she was enacting something else; her theory of cure—to be re-parented by her analyst.

We believe that her wish for her analyst to see her as good prevented her from using her treatment outside of her sessions. She had to be the obedient little girl and get praise more than she needed adult success. To rely on her insights outside of her sessions, even when they derived from her therapy, was in conflict with this wish to be a good girl. Using her mind on her own would mean being assertive. She equated assertiveness with greed, aggressiveness, and being bad. To act more adult by relying on her inner resources would mean giving up the hope of regaining her father—the father of her fantasy, where there were no rivals. Her wish to be loved had to be disguised as a wish to be a baby because it was less anxiety provoking for her to imagine being her father's baby than being his lover.

By trying to acquire what she missed in childhood, Ms. A was avoiding mourning. Her reluctance to use her insights reinforced her sense of helplessness as it determined her need for her analyst. This was a paternal transference; in the past she had made her father too important, now she needed her analyst for the same thing. The fact that her esteem suffered by her adherence to remaining child-like meant less to her than the fantasy that she could return to and correct her past.

Paradoxically, when Ms. A persisted in depending on her analyst's presence, she created her scenario of loneliness. Our understanding of this dynamic differs from that of Silverman (1998), who believed that her patient held on to his negative objects to avoid loneliness and from that of M. V. Bergmann (1985), who believed that her patients avoided marriage and children so as not to repeat the relationship with the draining helpless mothers of childhood. Her self-neglect and her compulsive eating was an identification with her neglectful alcoholic mother (Anna Freud, 1946). She numbed anxiety by compulsive eating just as her mother had numbed her feelings by drinking. Like many neglected children (Jarvis 1965), she had used compulsive behaviors to mitigate loneliness. The sequence we hypothesized was the wish for closeness and being loved, the prohibition of this wish when it caused loss of her mother's love, turning to father for this love and defensive turning toward compulsive eating to soothe her anxiety and depression. In her adult life this pattern cut her off from other people because it made her fat and unattractive and because it sapped the energies she would otherwise have had available to engage with them.

The major way in which Ms. A had attempted to deal with the loss of her mother and of her mother's love was to turn to her father for maternal nurturance. It was only later when she got into analysis that she experienced the analyst as nurturant in a dependable way that she could understand her loneliness as a child and see that her current loneliness was a recreation of a fantasy characterized by manic overoptimism (Klein 1963) in which her father would come to rescue, nurture, and admire her. This, in turn, allowed her to attempt to get something from her current environment that made her feel loved.

By understanding her loneliness as a longing for a specific lost object (Brenner 1974), she was enabled to assuage it with people in her current life. This differs from Fromm-Reichmann's (1959) formulation that those with "real" loneliness forget past objects and do not believe that there will be others in the future. By her forgetting the therapeutic relationship, Ms. A created a fantasy that mother was absent and father would have to rescue her. It allowed her to mute her analyst or abandon her for not being omnipresent, as she herself been abandoned. That she put her analyst in suspension only when she was not with her, and acted engaged in her presence, may explain why her analyst did not feel alone when she was with her, as others have found who work with some isolated patients (Greene and Kaplan 1978; Cohen 1982; Schafer 1995). By forgetting her analyst, was she imagining that she was lonely when away from the patient (Anna Freud 1967)?

Her current reluctance to pursue a mate seems designed to protect her from being hurt as she had been in the past (Kohut and Wolf 1986). She fears humiliation from a man as she had it from her father. If she were to seek out a man, it is not clear to what degree social factors like being overweight in a culture that values slimness (Hirschmann and Munter 1988) and the scarcity of suitable men (Lieberman 1991; Rucker 1993) prevent her finding a mate.

Despite Ms. A's conflict about moving on with her life, and the fact that her analyst did not fully understand the depth of what was being enacted in treatment, Ms. A has been able to form new compromises that are more compatible with her adult ambitions, ones that leave her in less pain. What helped? We think it was a sequence of the analyst's hope, her initial acceptance of Ms. A's view of herself as a victim, her interest in listening to her feelings, and her understanding the defensive value of Ms. A's oppositional erasing of the interpretations. She needed to gradually become stronger, less guilty, and more sure about her analyst so that she could mourn the loss of her fantasy. The analyst's patiently waiting for Ms. A to establish her own schedule that finally allowed her to use the analyst's formulations to change her view of the world so that she could exercise her own power to form new relationships outside the analytic one.

Many analytic contributions helped in understanding this patient: the idea of fantasy formation (Freud 1907); the unconscious fantasy (Arlow 1991) as the discovery that leads to freedom from the unsatisfactory compromise formations (Brenner 1983); a developmental perspective including the way one symptom can reflect conflict from more than one psychosexual stage (A. Freud 1965); the various routes through which masochism can be traced through development (Novick and Novick 1996). M. S. Bergmann's (1966) idea of the dream as a communication led to focusing on what might be new in the patient's dreams and associations. Like D. J. Cohen (1990) we found that the patient who had suffered early loss could not sustain a sense of personal value. Our case corroborates his idea that for such patients the relationship with the analyst, although it is resisted, is necessary for the acquisition of such a sense of personal value.

REFERENCES

ABEND, S. (1979). Unconscious Fantasy and Theories of Cure. *Journal of the American Psychoanalytic Association* 27:579–596.

ARLOW, J., with Beres, D. Fantasy and identification in empathy, 217–234. In *Psychoanalysis*. Madison, CT: International Universities Press.

BERGMANN, M.S. (1966). Intrapsychic and Communicative Aspects of the Dream. *International Journal of Psycho-Analysis* 47:356–363.

BERGMANN, M.V. (1985). EffecT of Role Reversal on Delayed Marriage and Maternity. *Psychoanalytic Study of the Child* 40:197–219.

BRENNER, C. (1974). On The Nature and Development of Affects: a Unified Theory. Psychoanal Q. 43: 532-556.

———— (1983). The Mind in Conflict. New York. IUP.

Cohen, D.J. (1990). Enduring Sadness: Early Loss, Vulnerability and the Shaping of Character. *Psychoanalytic Study of the Child* 45:357–375. New Haven: Yale Universities Press.

———— (1982). On Loneliness and the Ageing Process. *International Journal of Psycho-Analysis* 63:149–155.

FREUD, A. (1946). *The Ego and the Mechanisms of Defense.* New York: International Universities Press.

———— (1965). *Normality and Pathology in Childhood: Assessments of Development.* New York: International Universities Press.

———— (1967). About Losing and Being Lost. *Psychoanalytic Study of the Child* 22:9–19.

FREUD, S. (1907 [1906]). Delusions and dreams in Jensen's Gradiva. *Standard Edition* 9:3–95.

FROMM-REICHMANN, F. (1959). Loneliness. *Psychiatry* 22: 1-15.

GREENE, M. & KAPLAN, B.L. (1978). Aspect of Loneliness in the Therapeutic Situation. *International Review of Psycho-Analysis* 5:321–330.

HIRSCHMANN, J.R. & MUNTER, C.H. (1988). *Overcoming Overeating.* New York: Addison Wesley.

JARVIS, V. (1965). Loneliness and Compulsion. *Journal of the American Psychoanalytic Association* 13:122–158.

KLEIN, M. (1963). On the Sense of Loneliness. In *Writings of Melanie Klein 1946–1963.* New York: The New Library of Psycho-analysis, 1984.

KOHUT, H. & WOLF, E.S. (1986). The Disorders of the Self and Their Treatment: an Outline. In *Essential Papers on Narcissism.* A.P. Morrison, ed. New York: International Universities Press.175–196.

LIEBERMAN, J.S. (1991). Issues in the Psychoanalytic Treatment of Single Females over Thirty. *Psychoanalytic Review* 78(2):176–198.

NOVICK, J. & NOVICK, K.K. (1996). *Fearful Symmetry: The Development and Treatment of Sadomasochism.* Northvale, NJ: Jason Aronson Inc.

RUCKER, N. (1993). Cupid's Misses: Relational Vicissitudes in the Analyses of Single Women. *Psychoanalytic Psychology* 10(3):377–391.

SCHAFER, R. (1995). Aloneness in the Countertransference. *Psychoanalytic Quarterly* 64:496–516.

SILVERMAN, D.K. (1998). The Tie that Binds: Affect Regulation, Attachment, and Psychoanalysis. *Psychoanalytic Psychology* 15(2):187–212.

****
****

Original publication of preceding chapter:

RICHARDS, A.K. & SPIRA, L. (2003). The "Sweet and Sour" of Being Lonely and Alone. *Psychoanalytic Study of the Child* 58:214–227.

CHAPTER 16

On Being Lonely: Fear of One's Own Aggression as an Impediment to Intimacy

This paper considers loneliness from the point of view of compromise formation and the development of fantasy as a means of defending against painful affect. Our idea is that at least one strand of loneliness derives from longing for an ideal object with whom one would never have to feel aggression and from whom no aggressive actions would have to be tolerated. The development of such a fantasy in a middle-aged man is traced to early loss of a parent with missed mourning, and is shown to be ameliorated by psychoanalytic treatment that allowed the mourning to take place.

> *Loneliness razors into each sunup, every sunset,*
> *and, like a pitiless sword, with its victim—my heart*
>
> —GORDON PARKS
> (2000, p. iii)

Loneliness is limited neither to those who come to psychoanalysis or psychotherapy complaining about it, nor to those who are alone. Although many patients who complain of loneliness are women (Lieberman 1991), we want to show that loneliness is an equal-opportunity misfortune, available to men as well as women.

Some people complain that they cannot find the right person to share life with; others do not want to share their space; others believe that no one could stand being with them full-time—but not having someone may leave all of them feeling lonely and/or ashamed (Gillman 1990). We offer the idea that loneliness protects against the dangers of loss of control of aggressive impulses toward the person who represents the ideal object, and that interpreting the fear of aggression toward a loved one may alleviate the need to defend against this fear.

CLINICAL CASE

While sociological studies (Weiss 1973) and psychoanalytic ones (Lieberman 1991; Rucker 1993) document the statistical chance that a woman is more likely to be alone than a man, the experience of loneliness is not limited to women, as mentioned above. Many men, single and married, suffer from isolation and fear of intimacy.

One such man taught us a great deal about both aloneness and loneliness when I treated him for several years.[1] Mr. A was a political scientist and an activist on behalf of oppressed poor people. His days were filled with meetings and productive interactions with his constituents and colleagues. He had a loyal, long-term staff. He had never been married when he came for analysis at age forty.

The analysis succeeded a twenty-year psychotherapy with a male therapist, who retired and suggested to Mr. A that he would benefit from more intensive treatment. Mr. A longed for a family, and in spite of his professional success, which he attributed to his own hard work as well as the benefit of his long psychotherapy, he considered himself a failure in his personal life. He entered a four-times-per-week analysis on the couch, which continued for five years, with the stated goal of "getting a personal life."

In the second year of his analytic treatment, Mr. A reported that since his teen years, he had spent a lot of his free time playing a private game of imaginary baseball. This consisted of being alone and imagining a baseball league with teams and players whom he made up in his head. The players all had batting averages, the teams played on a regular schedule, and he enjoyed watching their season unfold in his mind. This activity kept him company during long, lonely weekends, and often in the evenings as well. We talked about his baseball league very often. At first, it seemed to make up for his lack of friends, but as time went on, he recognized that he preferred it to getting too close to people. He was capable of working closely with others, but only in groups and when there was a project to accomplish together.

Before the specific session to be described, Mr. A had been thinking that the baseball league pleased him because he was in complete control. His father had died when he was three years old. He and his younger

---

[1]This patient was treated by one of us (A.K.R.), but the discussion reflects the views of both authors.

brother had grown up with their widowed mother, who had been subsidized by her own family of origin so that she could stay home to care for them. He recalled always having felt the lack of a father. He thought that their family was poorer than the neighboring ones because of the lack of a father. Thus, he came to analysis seeing himself as the victim of a social system in which women did not work and therefore had less money than men, and in which children of single mothers were poorer than children of two-parent families. In the early sessions, the analyst refrained from challenging these ideas. They veridically described his experience. Pushing him to see that there were more personal reasons for his isolation, or even that he was isolated, would have been too great a blow to the self-esteem he derived from his belief that he was mastering his loss by seeing it as a social problem. What appealed to him about this compromise was his belief that he could be a savior to disadvantaged youngsters who had not had a fair start in life because of this social inequity.

In the course of treatment, Mr. A began to complain that the sessions were boring. The analyst agreed with him too much; the sessions were not challenging. He was not learning anything new; he was only hearing himself reflected back. He recalled his earlier therapist, who had confronted him more, made more challenges of his rationalizations. At this point, I thanked Mr. A for his supervision and began to ask what else his social isolation might mean for him personally in relation to his own development. I said that the exploration of more personal meanings would supplement and deepen his understanding, without replacing or denying the social problem that he so clearly saw as important for any young man who had grown up without a father.

The patient's stories about himself featured ways in which he had escaped his home: by staying in friends' homes, by going away to camp in the summers, and eventually by leaving home to be on his own in a very adventurous way that furthered his social activist goals. I asked whether he had substituted more neutral, nurturing contact with social groups for the highly charged emotional atmosphere of his home. In this context, he began to talk about how his mother beat him when he was a little boy. Now he emphasized the event that had brought him into his first treatment: the day late in his adolescence when he had first hit back. Hitting back ended the abuse, but frightened his mother; she had then sought out a therapist for him.

In a way that was similar to the patient's discussion of his use of neutral social group settings and social theories as better for his development than his home environment, I suggested that he had used his first therapist as a protection against his rage at his mother and her rage at him. He had begun to utilize that therapy to explore his own options—but mostly, he wanted the therapist to act as a father to protect him from his mother's beatings.

Mr. A gradually began to see that he had needed a father for protection against his mother's seductive intrusiveness as well as her physical abuse. We explored his resentment of his mother's insistence on inspecting his stools until he was six years old. We came to understand his need for control as a reaction to the feeling that she had too much control over him. We saw this in the transference as well, as he refused to come for morning sessions and frequently requested rescheduling. Later, he described his brother's inexplicably fond memories of their mother; he believed that his brother was never beaten. Why would she treat them so differently? He recognized that he himself must have had something to do with it.

The gradual nature of Mr. A's change was indicated by these progressive reframings of his early life and of his current defensive patterns. In both the earlier treatment and in the current analysis, he continually attempted to understand how he had managed to survive with the bad mother he believed her to have been. He had alternating views of his mother: sometimes he saw her as all bad, while at other times, he saw her as attempting to be a better parent in a self-defeating way.

A Key Session

At a time when the patient was seeing his mother as abusive, and her abuse as the major case of his distancing himself from other people, the following hour took place:

PATIENT: Oh, did I give you the check?
ANALYST: Yes. On Tuesday. Or was it Wednesday? No—Tuesday.
And I gave you the insurance form that day. [Here I am thinking that I should recall the exact day and that Mr. A might feel wounded if I do not. Confused, I think that he wants me to focus. He has been talking about insurance all week. It seems to me that he is asking for reassurance about the safety of the analysis in testing my memory. I am relieved to recall the day and want to reassure him.]
PATIENT: I continue to feel relaxed. It's strange. I have nothing to feel relaxed about. I brought my car in to be fixed. It hasn't been fixed

since the accident. Not that it will take much fixing, but they never give you the right time. So I didn't get to the dentist. That's the other thing I was going to do this morning. I never know how long it's going to take. This is a simple cap. I can't tell whether it's his fault or the people who made the cap, his lab. If I can't have any idea how long I'm going to be at the dentist . . . What right do I have to miss a couple of hours of work? I pressure myself. It all started with the car accident. I was hurting myself then.

ANALYST: Mmm-hmm. [I am thinking that Mr. A is unused to being annoyed without having a tantrum, as with his annoyance at the car mechanic and the dentist.]

PATIENT: I went to the office. It was all decorated for Christmas, and I was aware that the staff did it to please me. I really love to have that. There was a new, big tree and all the office doors were covered with gift wrap. And lots of wreaths. I do it so well every year. And this year they did it for me. All these people want is my praise. Where do I miss their needs?

ANALYST: Am I missing it?

PATIENT: What? What does that have to do with it?

ANALYST: Am I missing your need for praise from me? [Here I am trying to find out if he can experience anger at me while in my presence without having a tantrum.]

PATIENT: Well, not as much as I need or want. You don't do enough, maybe. Barry wanted me to meet people from Boston who do videos of interactions. Everything revolves around asking what I'm doing right, not what I'm doing wrong.

When I was training, I had a professor in urban anthropology who was always asking what went wrong, not what went right. I was a good researcher—I worked with young adolescents. There was this kid in the group, Frankie. Everybody made faces at him. They hated him because they were rough kids and he was this goody-two-shoes. He was a big kid, bigger than them, and he went to parochial school and got good grades. Even I hated him because he was always so nice to me—an ass licker. I went to this group and I helped the group tell Frankie what they didn't like about him. It was good that they put it into words. So this professor called and said Frankie's mother had called her and wanted to know what I did that made Frankie fall to pieces.

So they kicked me out and I had to go to another place to do field study. And my professor there, I showed her my first report, and she said,

"What do you think of it?" She wanted me to pick out what I was doing that was helpful. It charmed me. After two or three of those comments, I asked her what was wrong in what I did, and she told me to criticize it myself, ask what I didn't like about what I had done. It charmed me and disarmed me. I knew it worked on me, so I did it when I worked with the kids. And when I taught.

I was replaced at my first placement. I had to go to the dean and my mentor told me to go in there and say it was all my fault and I would not do it again. But I said I should just stay there and shift my major to social advocacy or political policy and fix up the organization. My boss there said she'd hire me tomorrow. The dean said something that changed my life: "Mr. A, when are you going to take responsibility for your actions? It's up to you to survive to take care of the kids you care for." Later, I got to teach unskilled minority students and I just did what my professor taught me. I used to help my research assistant when she worked with the gangs and I showed her how to do that. I don't need that video bullshit. I know I don't praise my staff enough.

I hated the psychoanalytic bullshit that used to go on in school. When I was in the group home, it didn't work. The whole life of the home was analyzed every day. I took the model from Redl—there were no rules. We decided what to do in each situation as it happened. There was this multicultural, multiracial staff trying to do everything. The staff was furious at me. I finally said to myself: "Look, they're the ones who have to be there at 3:00 a.m." The staff was scared; the kids were out of control. This nice staff person got a black eye. I had told them they had to put their body between the kids when two kids start to fight. She did it, but she waited too long, so she got hit. I know it's very hard to be a child care worker. Psychologists and social workers and even anthropologists look down on them.

After that, I changed everything. I had the workers make a set of rules themselves, only I insisted that they show them to the kids. I would side with the kids, but then I saw I had to understand the staff too.

ANALYST: Just as I make the mistake of siding with you against your mother when she was on duty twenty-four hours a day, seven days a week, all alone. [Here again I am attempting to enable Mr. A to safely experience his anger at me. Is this too confrontational? I think that he has almost made the inference in his remark about the house parents.]

PATIENT: No. The staff was not like my mother!!!

ANALYST: Neither was your mother. [Bingo. He is expressing his anger at me toward me, without displacing it back onto his mother. I push him a bit farther, and he is angry but does not explode.]

PATIENT: Yeah? Like Tammy [his chief of staff]. I was provoking her; I see it now. It was subtle, but she reacted to it. I could apologize, but I did it again. I would just forget some of the people she told me to call, or I wouldn't do it when I was supposed to. She's weak in meetings; she needs me to be there. I've tried very hard in the past two weeks. She's been warmer in response. I had a professor once who was a gentleman. He'd ask me how I was doing and tell me about his life. I knew he was interested in me.

When Tammy gets down to business right away, I feel down. She does this thing where she puts me down by saying: "Did you do this yet? Did you do that?" Then she finds something I didn't do. It's inevitable— there's bound to be something. Then she can put me down.

My staff could be videotaped and see themselves and ask, "What did I do wrong?" I know Jason needs more praise. He showed me a sports trivia game he made up. It's good to teach reading and study skills; he's got the idea.

I remember a time with my mother when I was older—I wouldn't do it when I was younger—but my mother wanted to take me to a Greek restaurant up the hill for my birthday. I wouldn't go. She used to take us there for a treat. Then she would make us order the most expensive thing, even if it was not what we wanted. When I said no, I saw her hurt. I felt bad because she did care for me and wanted to do something nice for me. I feel mad at what you said. [He cries.]

I can't forget all the terrible things she did. She threatened to throw me out and give me away.

ANALYST: So you provoked that in school and at your jobs. You got yourself thrown out.

PATIENT: [Sobs] What? What?

ANALYST: When you see her as all bad, you protect yourself from your longing for her. [Here I wonder whether I have it mixed up. Is the anger defending against the longing or the other way around? I decide to think provisionally that each defends against the other.]

PATIENT: [Sobbing] When?

ANALYST: Now. Here. With me.

PATIENT: [Sobbing] When I was nineteen—when I knew I had to get away from her. I was better off that she died. And with Dr. L. He helped me by not saying, "You are a bad person." While I was seeing him one day, I got angry at my mother and threw jelly beans all over the house. I knew it was good. Other times I had hit her or hurt myself. But she called Dr. L and demanded to see him, only he refused. Good technique! He knew it was not right to do family work and individual together. She was so paranoid. She'd say, "What's going on between you and Dr. L?" In the session, he asked me what happened. When I told him, he was shocked. He said, "That's all?" I'm so angry with you right now—I'm this little kid who'll never get over what my mother did to me. I don't want to give it up, and you're telling me to give it up.

The other night, I was with Mollie on the subway and I saw this little girl crying because she didn't know where her mother was. Then we saw her mother; she was stoned. All made up, looking a little like a prostitute. But she didn't care that her daughter was crying—she didn't care, no. I said, "She's stoned." Mollie was just like my brother: "How do you know?" I said, "I know! She's a fucking piece of shit. She's stoned." I was angry at the kid for clinging to her mother. But how could she know? She's looking for her mother when she isn't stoned—when she's good, when she takes care of her.

ANALYST: Good. Have a nice weekend. See you Monday.

My intervention about whether I was included in Mr. A's feelings about his staff surprised him at first, but on reflection, he was able to realize that he had also been talking about himself and me. The patient could then notice that he was not praising his staff enough because of a feeling that I did not praise him enough. In that intervention, I understood that he saw me as the mother-boss. This interpretation introduced a new dynamic in the session, eventually leading to material that opened the view of his mother as not all bad. This engendered an affective connection: there were now two people in the room, collaborating.

Achieving such a rapport is the first goal with isolated patients like Mr. A. Although rereading the account of this session leads me to think in retrospect that I may have been too active, or that I crowded too much into one session, it came after many years of preparation and did lead to fruitful interchanges.

Most important in my mind at this point was Mr. A's expression of rage toward the bad mother. This was to prove to be the theme of the next phase of treatment. We elaborated and specified the rage expressed in his uncharacteristic expletive, "She's a fucking piece of shit." The conviction that this stranger was stoned on drugs was likened to his impression that his mother had been depressed, evidenced by her smoking and engaging in compulsive card playing. His comment that the stranger's makeup was "like a prostitute's" expressed rage at his mother's sexuality. The subway was a place of dirt, noise, and danger. The whole vignette was used like a dream, as a nodule for associations.

The Ensuing Treatment

This session included themes that echoed other sessions, and that were important in the analysis even though they were barely represented in this single session itself. Interpretations were intended to link the session to preceding ones, deepening the meaning of what had already been understood about the patient's need to keep away from any intimate relationship—whether with a man or a woman. The major interpretation was the statement that "Not even your mother was your mother," which pointed to his fantasy of his mother as all bad.

Mr. A described his mother as bad in this session, using the woman in the subway as a metaphor for her (and for the analyst), although he knew that she had wanted to do something loving for him in taking him out to dinner. Both earlier and later sessions focused on the bad analyst who wanted to give him something bad. The image of the bad analyst was interpreted as a way for Mr. A to keep his original mother in mind, even though she was no longer present in reality, and as a way to understand the world he had constructed as a child. How did he come to see his mother as bad? The interpretation that the person in reality was not as bad as the bad mother of his fantasy had value; he cried when he heard it. She had become bad in Mr. A's mind when she left him by being depressed, and again when she left him by dying. Losing someone bad seems less painful than losing someone whom you loved and who loved and valued you.[2] While the analyst understood this in Mr. A's case as a fantasy, a Kleinian analyst might have considered it an integration of the good and bad objects, which healed the split and resulted in achievement of the depressive position (Klein 1963).

The preceding vignette encompasses a hypothesis that would be elaborated in later sessions: that the patient's picture of his mother was colored by an even deeper anger at his father, who had abandoned the

---

[2]The bad mother is a fantasy that Arlow and Beres (1991) discussed as one created to defend against loss.

family when Mr. A was a toddler. Thus, the longing for love from a father was a compounding factor, rendering insatiable his longing for his mother's love. At the same time, his rage at his father intensified anger at his mother for imposing limits on his autonomy and for failing to provide him with a father, as well as for her inattentiveness during her mourning over the loss of her husband.

As Mr. A came to understand the extent to which his feelings toward his mother were colored by the displacement of rage from his father onto her, he began to see women in his current environment differently. He was surprised to notice that his deputy, a woman who stood by him through decades of political battles, was not the weakling he had thought her to be. He noticed that she was sought after for meetings and negotiations, and that her silence and reluctance to confront people were perceived by others as tact and empathic understanding. He saw that he had relied on her in the past to heal the wounds he had caused with his rougher, confrontational style. He reported that other members of his staff remarked on the change in his behavior. Gradually, he began to tell me about more contacts with friends and how much he enjoyed them.

The groundwork for this change in the patient's object relations had been laid by his identification with his previous longterm therapist and by his experience with his current analyst, and, most important, it was codified by a series of key interpretations. These interpretations were that: (1) his childhood transgressions were actually attempts to reengage his mother after she became despondent over the loss of her husband; (2) his image of his mother had been skewed by his fantasy, rather than being simply a veridical picture of her as a parent; (3) this fantasy was colored by his rage at her for being unavailable when she was depressed; (4) his displaced rage from his father to his mother reinforced his view of her as bad; and (5) her behavior toward him was acknowledged as unreasonable and provocative.

Mr. A's fantasy of his mother was thus modified by analytic interpretation. I think that my interpretations of the affective or drive aspect of his object relations were much more meaningful than the understanding put forth in his first therapy—that is, their development as a reaction to his truly bad mother of infancy. This view was also more accurate than my first understanding of Mr. A's fantasy of the bad mother, which was as a defense against sadness at her loss. It was the understanding of his fantasy in terms of his rage at his father for abandoning him that provided the impetus for change in Mr. A's current object relations.

Another important aspect of the treatment that followed the session presented here was a prolonged series of attacks on the analyst. The patient came late, forgot appointments, claimed that his effectiveness at work was being sapped by the emotional demands of the analysis, and generally evoked a concerned and sometimes intense worry. When the analyst recognized that her rescue fantasies were being mobilized by this apparent regression, the fantasy of the all-powerful mother came into the treatment. Mr. A had made his mother out to be omnipotent in order to protect him, the way other children had fathers to protect them. He made a constant effort to show both himself and the analyst that the analyst could not force him to come to his sessions, highlighting that it was the convergence of her rescue fantasy and his fantasy of being rescued that had previously fueled the treatment, but that now needed to be made explicit, let go, and mourned. He was able to relinquish and mourn this only very slowly—perhaps as mourning at last for the early loss of his father, while also mourning the loss of his belief in a rescue fantasy.

Expression of his rage and elaborations of its meaning alternated with descriptions of how the patient was increasingly able to deal more realistically with various people in his life. For example, he could now fire incompetent staff members without needing to humiliate them, and he could support certain constituents without starting fights with other constituents. He could do what he had earlier marveled at in other people: make up after a quarrel instead of cutting off the relationship forever.

A rage like Mr. A's has been described as characteristic of children who lose parents early in their development (Cohen 1990; Wolfenstein 1969). This kind of rage may appear when mourning for the lost parent has not taken place. Theory based on the absence of mourning asserts that children cannot mourn until they have achieved adolescence. However, it appears that later mourning in treatment is possible, and child analysts have asserted that even young children can mourn the loss of a parent if they are allowed and encouraged to do so in treatment. As Cohen (1990) describes, there are some adults who have lost parents as children, missed the mourning, and consequently developed destructive rage, but who can mourn later in treatment what they did not mourn as children.

Mr. A's treatment focused on the modification of his rage, succeeding in modifying it as mourning began to replace the rage. I believe that it was this process that allowed him to see himself and others in a new way. No longer afraid that he would destroy others with his rage, no longer needing to see them as potentially dangerous provocateurs, he was capable of becoming more comfortable with and more generative toward others.

This patient's treatment followed an indirect and sometimes seemingly meandering path. For a period of time, the analyst needed to accept the patient's view that the reality of his commitment to his career barred his finding a mate. He used this reality in a way that women patients sometimes use their minority status, weight, age, infertility, or commitment to career as rationalizations for remaining alone. An intermediate stage in which the patient understands him- or herself as unwilling to settle for a less than ideal object can lead to the position evidenced in the session described above, when the patient comes to see that the fantasied mate is the perfect object who will never stir up the patient's aggression.

Mr. A's idea that he could have relationships only when they were governed by the rules of the game was a theme evidenced by his constant, obsessive, imaginary game of baseball. That theme was echoed by the idea that he could arrange for trainers to come to his office and teach his staff rules by which they could interact with one another. His observation that he could interact well with co-workers, but failed in his personal life, was one that the analyst related to the patient's fear of being abandoned by her, by his mother, and by other women in his life, as well as by his father. He was observed to counter his fear of abandonment by isolating himself, so that he did in an active way what he feared might happen to him, thus turning passive into active. His longing for closeness was expressed in the baseball fantasy, which turned his aloneness into a world peopled with many competing men and an admiring audience.

Brenner's (1974) idea of loneliness as a longing for the return of a specific lost object implies that Mr. A's refusal to marry can be seen as an act of loyalty to his mother, who might return to him if he were to keep waiting for her; this view illuminates as well his having remained in the family home for decades after her death. Fantasies of resurrection surfaced at this point in the analysis in the idea of termination. If his mother could come back, his father could, too. His fantasy was of a blissful return to the time before his father's death, before his brother's birth—a time when it was just he, with both father and mother adoring their little boy.

Being angry at his mother and seeing her as all bad could easily have had its roots in the early loss of his father. As Mr. A progressed in analysis, the theme of the loss of his first therapist, a male, and the loss of his father became more prominent. The best way to understand Mr. A now seemed to be Wolfenstein's (1969) observation that rage predominates in the affective life of children who have lost a parent early and were unable to mourn the loss successfully. The interpretation of the woman whom Mr. A had seen on the subway as not so bad, and the statement that even his mother was not so bad, were elaborated so that he could then see how he had displaced his rage from his father to his mother. He understood his need to displace it onto her as a way of avoiding the loss of what little good feeling he might have had toward his father after experiencing his death as abandonment.

Mr. A's persistent quest for the lost parent was expressed primarily in his experience of his first therapist as a parental figure, and secondarily in his repeated election contests at his work, in which he won his constituents' votes, thus giving him a job that he experienced as sustenance. Yet the initial long psychotherapy with no resolution proved that no one could help—a characteristic fantasy seen in those who have been unable to mourn early loss (Cohen 1990).

While the patient's rage was a defense against the utter despair of losing his father, achievement of this understanding took a long time, having gone through the route of first coming to an understanding of his mother's temper as a defense against her depressive affect at the loss of her husband. Once Mr. A was able to understand her as struggling to cope with her unmanageable feeling of loss, he observed that he felt less furious with her. This led to my remarking that he might feel less worried about whether I would accept his rage if he saw that I could understand it as a defense against his grief. Eventually, this in turn led to his accepting his own rage as a defense against his grief, and to the realization that he had controlled that grief for years and no longer needed to worry that he would not be able to keep it in check. This allowed the patient to build increasingly intimate relationships, both with people at work and with those in his social life. He was finally able to fill his life with individuals he truly cared about and who cared for him.

SUMMARY AND CONCLUSIONS

This case illustration shows one way of working with a patient who comes for analysis to deal with the symptom of loneliness and the sometimes concomitant feeling of inner aloneness. Loneliness transcends diagnostic categories, but it is most profoundly painful when experienced as inner aloneness. Both people who are alone and those who experience inner emptiness can be lonely, despite leading apparently full social lives. Loneliness can result from a longing for a perfect object with whom one would never have to feel aggression. This dynamic is related to the early loss of a parent when mourning is missed and rage becomes the predominant affect. The interpretation of fear of aggression in relation to a beloved other may free the patient to try establishing intimacy with another, and the experience of the contained aggression of the analytic relationship contributes to the ability of the patient to discover, accept, and use such an interpretation. In the clinical example provided, the gradual working through of this insight via remembering, forgetting, refinding, and making discoveries in new situations was a long and painful one, but one that, according to the patient, was ultimately worthwhile.

Acknowledgment: The authors wish to thank the members of the American Psychoanalytic Association Discussion Group, "Toward an Understanding of Loneliness and Aloneness in Women."

REFERENCES

ARLOW, J. & BERES, D. (1991). Fantasy and identification in empathy. In *Psychoanalysis,* ed. J. Arlow. Madison, CT: International Universities Press.

BRENNER, C. (1974). On the Nature and Development of Affects: a Unified Theory. *Psychoanalytic Quarterly* 43:532–556.

COHEN, D. (1990). Enduring sadness. *Psychoanalytic Study of the Child* 45:157–178.

GILLMAN, R. (1990). The Oedipal Organization of Shame. *Psychoanalytic Study of the Child* 45: 357–375.

KLEIN, M. (1963). On the Sense of Loneliness. In *The Writings of Melanie Klein, 1946–1963.* New York: New Library of Psychoanalysis, 1984, pp. 300–313.

LIEBERMAN, J.S. (1991). Issues in the Psychoanalytic Treatment of Single Females over Thirty. *Psychoanalytic Review* 78:176-198.

PARKS, G. (2000). A Star for Noon: An Homage to Women. In *Images, Poetry and Music.* London: Bulfinch.

RUCKER, N. (1993). Cupid's Misses: Relational Vicissitudes in the Analyses of Single Women. *Psychoanalytic Psychology* 10:377–391.

WEISS, R.S. (1973). Loneliness: The Experience of Social and Emotional Isolation. Cambridge, MA: MIT Press.

WOLFENSTEIN, M. (1969). Loss, Rage and Repetition. *Psychoanalytic Study of the Child* 24:432-460.

****
****

Original publication of preceding chapter:

RICHARDS, A.K. & SPIRA, L. (2003). On Being Lonely: Fear of One's Own Aggression as an Impediment to Intimacy. *Psychoanalytic Quarterly* 72:357–374.

Perhaps I have been influenced by my many years of co-leading a study group on loneliness at the meetings of the American Psychoanalytic Association that I pay so much attention to the experience of longing for another while being alone. It has always seemed to me that the trust inducing situation of psychoanalysis is the regularity of the analyst being available to hear the person's feelings that enables that person to trust the analyst. It came as a great flash of insight when I first read Warren Poland's (1996) *Melting the Darkness.* It was the equivalent of saying: "Oh, now I see what I was breathing. It is air." Being with the person—as a mother is with her baby, as a teacher is with her students, but even more intimately than either of these roles because I was focusing on what the person feels at the moment—was the essence of therapy.

I thought of how a baby learns over and over again that she is alone, that the limits of what she always has with her are defined by her own skin. The experience of falling asleep, the moment of refusal to do the mother's bidding, the tantrum, the rush away to reach a toy or another person, the pain of falling, all of these jolt a toddler into the awareness of her own boundary: her skin. The urge to cuddle, to hug, to keep close soothes the pain of separateness. But being able to put that longing into words is the closest one can come to experiencing comfort while retaining adult separateness. Translating this longing into words is the work of psychoanalytic therapy. The inevitable refusal of the other who is too busy, too tired, too involved with a need of her own or too involved with the need of another to pay full attention to the refusal of the needy infant or toddler is the prototype of loneliness. The rage it induces, the tantrums it precipitates further distance the toddler from the caretaker's closeness.

Looking at psychoanalytic therapy in this way makes it clear that it can be used to treat a wide variety of patients. Some are called narcissists because they seem vulnerable to loss of self-esteem or even a cohesive sense of self. Others are called neurotics because they seem to suffer from guilt when they have committed no crime. Others experience guilt, shame and/or disgust at their own bodily functions and are called depressives.

But anyone experiences relief when she can talk about what is bothering her and believes that her listener understands her without condemning or becoming disgusted at her. It is the intimacy of this being listened to and heard that is healing. Being heard can mean being told what the patient's story means to the listener, it can mean being echoed, it can mean being silent together when something that seems important to both people has been said.

REFERENCE

POLAND, W.S. (1996). *Melting the Darkness: The Dyad and Principles of Clinical Practice.* New York: Jason Aronson.

PAPERS IN SECTION IV
(All papers in this section by Arlene Kramer Richards)

Chapter 17

(1997). The Relevance Of Frequency Of Sessions To The Creation Of An Analytic Experience. *Journal of the American Psychoanalytic Association* 45:1241–1251.

Chapter 18

(2001). Talking Cure in the 21st Century: Telephone Psychoanalysis. *Psychoanalytic Psychology* 18:388–391.

Chapter 19

(2010). Training Analysis and Training Analyst Status: Where Are We Now? (original version: *Psychoanalytic Review* 97:955–969).

The Relevance of Frequency of Sessions to the Creation of an Analytic Experience

An all-day panel organized by Arnold Rothstein discussed the topic of the relevance of frequency of sessions to the creation of an analytic experience. Rothstein, crediting Arnold Goldberg with having suggested the topic, posed a series of questions for the panel. The primary questions were (1) Can analysis take place at a three-times-per-week frequency? and (2) Under what conditions might such a frequency result in analytic treatment? A number of subsidiary questions followed: What is essential to a therapeutic experience to call it analytic? What is the relationship of frequency to the creation of that experience? How does one distinguish psychoanalysis from psychoanalytically oriented psychotherapy? Also to be considered was the relationship between the personalities of patient and analyst in setting the frequency.

Two cases were presented in the morning and two in the afternoon. Each case was discussed directly after presentation. For reasons of confidentiality the cases will not be presented in detail here. To provide a coherent account without the detailed cases, the discussions are organized by presenter rather than by case.

Milton Viederman presented a case with a specimen hour. The work had initially been conducted twice weekly and now continues at three times. Another case was presented by Alan Z. Skolnikoff. That case, also initially conducted twice weekly, was increased to three and then four times a week. A case presented by Howard Levine went from a once-a-week frequency to two and then three times a week. He also presented two verbatim hours taken from the three-times-a-week period. Lewis Kirshner presented a case with a frequency of three times per

Panel held at the Spring Meeting of the American Psychoanalytic Association, Los Angeles, May 4, 1996.

Panelists: Arnold Rothstein (chair), Lewis A. Kirshner, Howard B. Levine, Alan Z. Skolnikoff, Milton Viederman. Discussants: Philip Bromberg, Charles M.T. Hanly, Milton H. Horowitz, Estelle Shane.

week. One interesting aspect of these presentations is that the analysts generally believed that greater frequency produced greater intensity and that this produced a better analytic process. When crises arose in the treatment, the analysts typically suggested increasing the frequency, a recommendation the patients generally accepted.

Skolnikoff discussed frequency requirements for meeting standards for training analysts in the San Francisco Psychoanalytic Institute, a consideration that persuaded him to forgo the added income he could have earned by charging a higher fee for fewer hours.

The discussants were Estelle Shane, who introduced herself as a relationalist / self psychologist analyst; Milton Horowitz, a classical Freudian analyst; Philip Bromberg, an interpersonal/relational analyst; and Charles Hanly, a philosopher and classical analyst. Each of the discussants responded after each case was presented. They agreed that an analytic process could be seen in every one of these treatments conducted two or three times weekly, yet they also agreed that greater frequency would have been better in each of the cases. Since these were not training cases, issues of educational value were put aside: clinical usefulness was the sole criterion.

Horowitz set the stage for the discussions to follow by distinguishing "psychoanalytic atmosphere" from "psychoanalytic experience" and "psychoanalytic process." He regards the atmosphere as the tone of respect and acceptance set by the analyst. He believes that this tone is conveyed by allowing the patient to tell what the patient wants to tell and to do so at the pace the patient wants to set. This contraindicates a DSM-IV initial interview. (Viederman concurs that a DSM-IV initial interview is always contraindicated.) The "analytic experience" is the patient trying to free associate and examining the barriers to doing so as the analyst tries to listen while neither judging nor intruding on the patient's experience. The analytic experience can come at any phase of the treatment. The "analytic process," by contrast, can be evaluated only over time. It consists in the shifts of points of view and in alterations of symptoms associated with changes in transference and resistance/defense. Reviewing his own clinical practice, Horowitz compared frequencies of three to six times per week and concluded that greater frequency leads to greater intensity and more process changes, especially with regard to issues of sadism and aggression. Though limitations of frequency attributed by the patient to cost and available time were cited in each of the cases presented, Horowitz asserted that in every case the fear of intimacy and object loss was in fact the most important unconscious determinant of the limitation.

Horowitz remarked that Skolnikoff's case demonstrates that as frequency increases so does the tendency to relive rather than merely talk about the past. This tendency requires even greater frequency, so that patient and analyst may find ways to interrupt enactments by verbally expressing affect and thereby attaining insight. Fear of intimacy on the analyst's part will derive from similar early losses and from current disruptions in the analyst's life that threaten to interfere with a capacity to safeguard treatment boundaries.

Horowitz noted, in the case presented by Levine, the fear of intimacy and the danger of object loss it presents. In that case, castration fears were linked to fear of object loss in that the patient believed that only his sister was truly loved by his mother. He recalled threats of punishment that he believed to be castration threats, and, most tellingly, the transference included the idea that just as his parents had caused his illness in the first place, his analyst was responsible for making him sick now. Of particular interest was the observation that sessions spaced out over the week had less intensity than sessions three days in a row. In this connection, Horowitz mentioned that in general he recommends to his supervisees a three-days-in-a-row schedule in preference to a Monday, Wednesday, Friday arrangement. Time can represent time spent with the mother, as in this case, an instance of object ties being directly related to the analytic schedule. In the case reported by Kirshner something similar occurs.

That case was dominated by fear of an object tie to the father rather than to the mother. The patient experienced the analysis as a threat to his defenses against his longing for a loving reunion with his lost father and an attendant castration fantasy. His fear was so great that once he achieved some symptom relief he left treatment without fully understanding his longings. Horowitz concluded from this that wishes to limit contact reflect complex problems in object relations that are expressed through the metaphor of time spent with the analyst.

Charles Hanly took up the question of the criteria for analytic process. He proposed becoming conscious of formerly unconscious memories and fantasies, and improvement in psychological functioning. These criteria could be used by different schools of analysis, even though different memories and fantasies would be privileged by each. Hanly argued that it cannot be concluded, on the basis of anecdotes, that more sessions per week would have been more therapeutically effective, because the result of increased frequency cannot be known where it has not been attempted. But he did believe that analysts could pool the results of their clinical judgments and thereby approximate an answer to the question. Hanly did not believe that psychoanalysis could be differentiated in principle from psychoanalytically oriented psychotherapy, but he did propose that "we can in practice make the differentiation if there are real and consistent variations in the factors specified by the criteria caused by couch, chair, and frequency." In his discussion of Viederman's case, Hanly asserted that the frequency may have limited the affective involvement of the interchange, given that the conversation was very intellectual and removed from raw feeling. Idealization of the analyst and the presence of associations illustrating defenses against castration fears, both present in the session itself, were sufficient to demonstrate analytic process. The question Hanly raised is whether the analysis could be brought to a satisfactory termination at that frequency. He believed that an increase to three or four sessions per week would increase that likelihood.

In discussing Skolnikoff's case, Hanly argued that the four-times-a-week standard for psychoanalysis has been idealized because it is the standard of the IPA for training analyses and control cases. However, since treatment at four times a week does not necessarily produce an analytic process, it is insufficient as a criterion.

Levine's case seemed to provide evidence that the patient had experienced with his analyst the same traumatically impoverished state he had previously experienced over the loss of a parent. Though the transference was clearly established, Hanly questioned whether the loss was ever remembered and worked through. The analyst's uncertainty about the patient's motives, fears, and moral prohibitions, Hanly thought, speaks to a need for further treatment; the question remains, however, whether the patient undergoing treatment three times a week can eventually use the established transference repetitions to gain enough therapeutic advantage to make the analysis successful.

With regard to Kirshner's case, the intense anxiety aroused by treatment may have been useful: understanding the anxiety would alleviate the patient's unpleasurable affect. While the anxiety was aroused and discussed in a twice-a-week treatment, it was not clear whether the infrequent sessions were sufficient to liberate the patient from his fears. It was particularly uncertain whether he had eventually made a sexual object choice and had embarked on a life in which he experienced anxiety of the everyday sort rather than the terror evident at the beginning of treatment. In all, Hanly detected the analytic process in every one of the four cases, from which he concluded that the process is possible, though the outcome doubtful, even when there are fewer than four sessions per week.

Estelle Shane described her theory as two-person and dialogical; it acknowledges the influence of the analyst's preconceptions on the patient's associations. Shane asserted that coming to agreement about analytic process is fundamentally impossible. She stated that both theoretical and idiosyncratic ideas of the analyst influence the course of treatment. For her, self psychological and attachment theories provide the framework of interpretation, with oedipal issues less important than difficulties in attachment. Further, "the analytic relationship provided for the patient a development enhancing new experience involving a view of the analyst as a novel other, not based exclusively on unconscious models from the past." Shane's sense is that this relationship provides new patterns of interrelating that allow further development. She proposed that the construction of a consistent life narrative is an essential part of the reparative effect of psychoanalysis. Any frequency of treatment that allows the construction of a narrative and the ameliorative effect of a new object would be enough to produce an analytic process. Though Shane would accept a once-a-week treatment, she believes that more is always better and that the greatest frequency tolerable to both analyst and patient is optimal.

In discussing Viederman's case, Shane pointed out that the narrative appears to be oedipal, yet lacking the bisexuality inherent in Freud's view of the oedipal drama. She considered the process analytic because it displayed an affective convergence that she believes the analyst to be feeling with his patient, and she expected that the patient would benefit from the experience of being understood in a profoundly affective way.

Shane suggested that Skolnikoff's case was a more modern presentation than the others, as it presented countertransference directly and in detail. In particular, she cited Skolnikoff's dilemma over whether, in order to achieve training analyst status, he should accept the lower income often attendant on seeing patients at a four-times-a-week frequency. Since he knew that this patient could afford only a set amount per week, to meet the institute's requirements he would have to see her four times for the price of three sessions. How much to reveal to the patient of the reasons for this arrangement was an issue for her, as were patient attachment and self-revelation in general. Shane noted the possible danger of idealizing the four-times-a-week frequency to the point where the patient could not "accord to the analyst the benefit of the doubt and view his interest in preserving the analysis as more to the analyst's benefit and well-being than to the patient's. . . ."

Use of the couch for the thrice-weekly sessions was a focus of Shane's discussion of this case. She considered this a way to tap into procedural, nonverbal memory of the earliest infantile experience and thus provide feelings of safety, comfort, and being cared for that foster curiosity, self-reflection, and mutuality.

Shane considered Levine's case to be one in which issues of insecure attachment are predominant. She saw the patient's childhood and adult losses of important people in his life as formative. She believed that analytic work was done on the attachment issue in the four years of once-weekly treatment that preceded the increase of sessions to three times a week. When the emerging themes were interpreted as relating to the frequency of sessions and the degree of attachment the patient could tolerate, he was able to enter into more frequent treatment. Whereas Levine considered the period of greater frequency to be "the analysis," Shane believed that the analytic work in the once-a-week sessions was crucial in resolving the issues of attachment sufficiently to allow work on other issues. That Levine believed that the greater frequency allowed the real analysis to begin indicated to Shane that this belief was communicated to the patient, thus allowing them to work together at a deeper level. Despite the emergence of oedipal themes in the thrice-weekly sessions, Shane asserted that attachment themes still predominated and needed to be addressed.

Kirshner's case presented other issues. Particularly important for Shane was the issue of how pressures coming from the analyst for greater frequency might have influenced for the worse the analytic work in this case. She noted that Kirshner did not pressure his patients and appeared satisfied to work on a three-times-a-week schedule. Had the analyst believed he was doing anything short of real psychoanalysis, he would perhaps have inadvertently conveyed this conviction to the patient. The fact that the patient had experienced the analyst as accepting the patient's view of frequency may, according to Shane, have provided an unintended corrective emotional experience. She argued that because the patient had seldom had experiences in which his ideas were valued and respected, such an experience in the analysis would have been unusual and effective for him. The patient then engaged in a transference repetition in which the analyst was experienced as a father who was pushing him to be masculine. Shane noted that although the patient did not experience a transference repetition of the relationship with his mother, analyst and patient were able to construct a narrative of that relationship. Shane regarded this as demonstrating "a full and rich analytic process" that addressed both dyadic and triadic developmental issues.

Philip Bromberg began his discussion by stating that the relevance of frequency is tied totally to what in a particular analyst's opinion accounts for the power of the analytic relationship. Within an interpersonal-relational model, the transferential intensity that leads to genuine analytic experience is co-created through the real, not "implied," interaction between the participants, and it is the analyst's ability to observe his or her contribution to an enactment that is the critical element in enabling patients to see themselves through the analyst's eyes and make use of interpretations. Bromberg argued that although more rather than fewer sessions is probably a useful rule of thumb, the creation of analytic process does not depend on the number. He used the Japanese film *The Woman in the Dunes* as an allegory for the relational process that leads to mutative growth in analysis. The protagonist of that film, encapsulated in a relationship that began as a means to an end, slowly became involved in the here-and-now relational experience as an end in itself. Linear time became irrelevant, and his psyche was freed through what could be accomplished relationally at any given moment. What was possible depended not on frequency but on the evolving relationship and its potential for cognitive creation of new meaning in the here and now.

Bromberg illustrated this perspective in his discussion of Viederman's case. What Viederman said to his patient about the interaction with his woman friend could best be understood in the context of the interaction taking place between patient and analyst as the interpretation was being made. Because Viederman addressed only the patient's transferential act of "setting him up" as an authority, he failed to make sufficient use of his own experience of annoyance with the patient's passivity. That annoyance, Bromberg believed, had motivated Viederman to himself take on the role of authority figure using the transference interpretation in part as a form of paternal rebuke.

Skolnikoff's twice-weekly psychotherapy that later became a three-times-a-week analysis was credited by Bromberg as having in itself been a genuine analytic process. He believed that the intense affective involvement of patient and analyst during the two-times-a-week phase, and their processing of it in the here and now, created genuine structural growth. Bromberg commented particularly on the patient's unanalyzed experience of "mystification" when the analyst became more silent—and, Bromberg believed, more affectively uninvolved—as the patient got on the couch and began three-times-a-week treatment. Bromberg agreed with Skolnikoff's interpretation of a warded-off erotic transference, but felt that the failure to addressed the patient's experience of sudden, "mystifying" change in the analyst's relational style deprived interpretations of their impact. Bromberg argued that what is traditionally conceptualized as a "fear of intimacy" that leads to flight from analysis or a refusal to accept increased frequency of sessions is more usefully understood as a fear of being unable to regulate the traumatic flooding of affect (autonomic hyperarousal) that patients come to associate with feeling trapped in a relationship and unable to escape psychological traumatization from some unilaterally imposed situation that is offered as being in their best interest.

Levine's case was of interest to Bromberg as an example of a patient who is willing to increase frequency of sessions not as a result of a "successful" interpretation, but of one that made him feel worse. Bromberg argued that the patient felt more secure when he noted that his analyst's reaction to his feeling worse was to offer him more frequent contact. Thus the "degree of control over insecure attachment" that the patient gained by being offered more sessions allowed him to accept greater intimacy with a feeling of personal safety. Here frequency was more powerful as content than as structure. From Bromberg's perspective, greater frequency provides the opportunity to analyze enactments as close as possible to the time they occur. In general, he remarked, greater frequency is most important with patients for whom trauma and dissociation are central and for whom genuine intrapsychic conflict is a developmental achievement yet to be attained. In the course of analysis such patients show increased tolerance for affective hyperarousal to the point where intrapsychic conflict becomes bearable and the issue of frequency is less critical in maintaining an analytic experience.

Responding to Kirshner's presentation, Bromberg asserted that the patient's fear of proactive aggressiveness had paralyzed his development; he was afraid that "self-change" was equivalent to psychic death. It was particularly important, Bromberg thought, that the transference work take place increasingly in the here and now of the treatment; the patient had to become able to confront the reality that the very process of change in which the analyst had the greatest investment was in fact what the patient unconsciously feared above all else.

The general discussion was lively. Viederman remarked that his work with his patient was not all as intellectual as was the particular session he presented. Some sessions were full of affect. He asked of Bromberg how he could have interpreted the patient's wish for him to be authoritative without in fact being so. Bromberg replied that the point is not to avoid the role of authority but to recognize that such moments not only cannot be avoided but in fact offer profound opportunities for structural growth if the relational context is made explicit as close as possible to the time they occur. Regarding Skolnikoff's case, discussion centered on the degree to which his personal motive for increasing the frequency of sessions was discussed with the patient. Rothstein drew attention to the agreement among three of the four discussants that the initial twice-a-week psychotherapy seemed to embody a genuine analytic process. He also noted that the two relationalists, Bromberg and Shane, would have analyzed the increase in frequency, while the more classical analysts would have accepted the increase as evidence of the efficacy of the process. Skolnikoff said that he had told the patient that he wanted the increase in frequency because he wanted to do analysis, but not that he needed more four-times-a-week experience to become a training analyst. He believed that the work might have been successful even if it had all been conducted at a twice-a-week frequency. Each of the decisions to increase frequency of sessions, he noted, was taken seriously in context. He added that the patient had later undertaken four-times-a-week treatment and had fled the analysis after a few years. She returned years later and worked on the delayed mourning that she had not been able to complete earlier in the treatment. He said that the outcome was satisfactory in that she was not as prone to fear of loss or fear of attachment as a possible setting for loss.

Kirshner stated that he believed that on commonsense grounds one might assume that four-times-a-week frequency would lead to greater intensity, but that for many patients this may not be so. He agreed with Shane that insisting on four or more sessions a week might have been counterproductive. Not infrequently, such demands precipitate difficult-to-analyze anal struggles and control battles, as well as fears of intrusion.

Comparing Viederman's and Skolnikoff's cases, Arlene Richards asked whether the therapeutic effect of being a confident, experienced senior analyst working at lower frequency was different from that of an aspiring analyst who needs the greater frequency to obtain a credential. Richards wondered whether the effects of greater frequency on the analyst are important. Specifically, she asked, what are the implications for analytic training? Rothstein thought that the panel should keep to scientific rather than political questions. Richards clarified her remark by saying she thought the panel was a way of doing science in that it was a presentation of several different analyst-patient pairs. By collecting instances, we could see which factors seemed general and which seemed particular to each pair. Viederman regarded frequency as an educational issue. He had been much less flexible at the start of his career, he reported, but was now much more willing to experiment because he had greater confidence in his clinical judgment.

Leon Hoffman posed a question about the negative results so rarely reported in the literature. What could we conclude from negative results in analytic treatment conducted at a lower frequency per week? Would we determine that a lower frequency would not work in certain cases?

Levine replied to Bromberg's comment on his case that the patient seemed to have accepted increased frequency as the result of an interpretation that caused him pain. Levine said he did not think that interpretations are successful if they soothe the patient. Rather, they are successful if they break things up, "like a cue ball." By this he meant that interpretations may be successful when they cause pain because they ring true to the patient or have some other impact, unintended, that disrupts the dynamic status quo or impresses the patient with the power of the analyst's words.

Gerald Fogel asked Bromberg and Shane what their criteria would be for recommending analysis at a four-times-weekly frequency. Bromberg responded that when the patient is surrendering dissociative mental structure but is as yet unable to experience intrapsychic conflict, more sessions may be indicated when the patient finds it intolerable to be alone between sessions, or when the patient is not satisfied with sessions. Shane said that increasing the sessions would be important when the patient is not talking freely. Patients themselves will suggest greater frequency when they are dealing with trauma or loss. Sometimes in such instances she may see a patient five or six times a week. She sets the sessions on successive days, rather than spreading them out over the week, even when the patient comes only twice a week. Fogel stated that increased frequency may be useful also with less traumatized patients, as this would prevent avoidance of the patient's "private madness."

Viederman's case raised the issue of whether a patient's establishing an intimate relationship with a lover should be a criterion for successful treatment. Should the intimacy fostered by frequent sessions be viewed as preliminary to establishing intimacy with a lover? Horowitz cautioned that patients might choose a life in which they are not intimately involved with a lover and that this might be a satisfactory analytic outcome.

****
****

This chapter originally appeared as:

RICHARDS, A.K. (1997). The Relevance of Frequency of Sessions to the Creation of an Analytic Experience. *Journal of the American Psychoanalytic Association* 45:1241–1251.

Talking Cure in the 21st Century: Telephone Psychoanalysis

Is psychoanalytic treatment by telephone a standard practice for psychologists? If it has value, in what situations is it effective? A survey of 120 members of Division 39 of the American Psychological Association showed that 83% had used it over the previous 2 years: 84% said they found such sessions usually productive, and 98% found them productive at least some of the time. Geography was the most frequent indication. A therapist or a patient moving to a new location and a patient traveling for work were the usual causes. Case studies showed that telephone work was especially useful in uncovering patient need for emotional distance and patient shame about physical characteristics.

This symposium posed several questions about treatment conducted on the telephone. One implicit question was whether this modality is standard practice for psychologists. Another question was whether it has a place in the treatment armamentarium. Finally, a third question was whether any value could be shown regarding treatment conducted over the telephone. The attempt to answer these questions consisted of a research report and three clinical papers on the subject of psychoanalytic therapy conducted by telephone. The survey reported by Franklin Goldberg was jointly constructed by Goldberg (as a representative of Section 5) and myself (as a representative of Section 1). Of the 120 respondents to the questionnaire, 74% reported conducting therapy by telephone currently, and 83% had used it in the 2 years prior to the survey. Those using telephone therapy reported that they used it with only some of their patients: 58% of therapists interspersed the sessions with face-to-face sessions often, and 35% did so sometimes. Only 3% said they never interspersed them. More than 84% of respondents said that they found telephone sessions usually productive, and 98%

found them productive at least some of the time. Of those who had never used telephone sessions, 50% said they would use the telephone if geography or contingency made it necessary. Thus, 86% were willing to use the telephone when it was the only alternative to disrupting treatment. These findings make it clear that the use of the telephone is currently standard practice when it is indicated by circumstance. Does this somehow affect the treatment? The clinical papers attempt to answer this question.

Martin Manosevitz, the panel organizer, reported on a case in which the telephone was used because the analyst moved away. The patient was a recovering alcoholic who had felt abandoned many times in his childhood. He had been raised by an alcoholic mother and by a father who had to leave home on business trips. Before his analyst moved, he had used gestures frequently to indicate bodily states. The analytic work consisted of connecting his verbal statements of bodily states with the emotional states he was not able to put into words. The patient talked about his body in order to get nurturance, especially when he was afraid that his analyst would abandon him or thought he had abandoned him. What was most surprising to the analyst was his patient's satisfaction with telephone sessions when the patient went on a business trip just prior to the analyst's moving away. Later, the patient's intense transference reaction when his analyst took his customary two-week vacation showed the analyst that the telephone sessions were much more emotionally engaging for the patient that he would previously have thought possible.

Linda Larkin presented a case in which a patient in psychoanalytic psychotherapy moved to a city far from her therapist. The patient's intense ambivalence about being in treatment at all found expression in her refusal to meet a new therapist in the city she had moved to. Instead, she insisted on telephone sessions. She believed that on the telephone she was more comfortable because she was not being scrutinized and criticized. She had lost both parents suddenly to illness just before becoming ill herself and therefore sought desperately to maintain control in her current life. She believed she had more control of the treatment because she chose the telephone as the modality. Prior to the telephone work, she had a history of needing rescue and feeling intense gratitude toward the rescuer and attachment to him or her. She had married her husband after he noticed that she was ill on a date and taken her to a hospital even though she was denying that there was anything seriously wrong. She had needed emergency surgery that saved her life. She had responded well to psychotherapy and decided to leave after remission of her presenting depression. Three years later she returned with a recurrence of the depression, now consequent to learning that she would not be able to have children. The analyst believed that the first experience of leaving therapy without destroying the analyst or their relationship was itself therapeutic. She developed a serious illness just after losing her job in the new location. There were several telephone sessions in which she repeatedly complained of authorities whose word she could not trust, a boss who did not know how to manage, and doctors who recommended treatments that might not do any good; she became able to explore her doubts about the therapy not doing any good, to express her rage and disappointment at her parents, and to reevaluate her wish to be taken care of. On the telephone she was able to accept treatment while still rejecting the idea of treatment in person. The modality worked for this patient because it allowed her to express her pent-up feelings and maintain a therapeutic relationship without feeling that she was in danger of becoming too dependent.

The paper by Sara Zarem was a clinical exploration of the potential of telephone therapy as an adjunct to face-to-face work. She chose to use the telephone as an alternative to face-to-face treatment for therapeutic rather than logistical reasons. In her case no one had moved, and the therapeutic couple was not too far away to allow meeting in person. Her patient was a large African American woman who was dealing with intense grief over her husband's alcoholism. The physical contrast between the obese black patient and the slender white therapist would be something to talk about, but would be difficult for the therapist to bring up. It seemed particularly important that the analyst not see the body that sat in the chair. Dr. Zarem was aware of the countertransferential problem. She was not to see what she saw. The patient brought in her fantasy of being "blond, blue eyed, and big titted." She joked that she was at least one of these three. Initial supportive work on her concerns about her husband's out-of-control body led to talk about her own out-of-control body. Her husband's alcoholism stopped, but with the emergence of his cancer, she binged and put on more weight. Telephone sessions were necessary when the husband's illness made her too despondent to come for treatment. But they turned out to serve another crucial purpose. On the telephone she was disembodied. This patient specifically wanted her therapist to recognize her voice, not her body. Her voice represented her fantasy self, the slim white woman that her voice represents her to be. Dr. Zarem's recognition that her attitude toward and mental image of the patient were different when she spoke on the telephone than when she was in the room was the key to understanding her patient's dilemma. Here the telephone clearly facilitated the understanding.

In sum, the use of the telephone in these cases was clearly in the patient's interest. The papers as a whole constitute a breakthrough in reporting and evaluating the use of a relatively new modality of treatment. This modality has been shown by the survey to be widespread and to have a history in analytic work, and it was shown by the case reports to be effective both in situations where the geography requires it and in situations where it provides a special situation for the analysis of otherwise too humiliating interpretations dealing with the patient's appearance.

****
****

This chapter originally appeared as:

RICHARDS, A.K., (2001). Talking Cure in the 21st Century Telephone Psychoanalysis. *Psychoanalytic Psychology* 18:388–391.

Training Analysis and Training Analyst Status: Where Are We Now?

ATTEMPTS TO DEAL WITH PROBLEMS OF TRAINING ANALYSIS

Training analysis has become the most contentious and most central part of the process of education to become a psychoanalyst. It is the most expensive, time consuming, difficult and painful part. Because of the confidentiality necessary for openness in analysis, it is also the most difficult part of the educational process to evaluate. Schachter (2011) researched it by asking analysts about how satisfied they had been with their training analyses and whether they had later analyses to deal with issues not sufficiently dealt with in the training analysis. His study remains the landmark in this field. In an attempt to revise the training analyst selection procedure for the New York Freudian Society, I read the history of training analysis and found some startling discussions of how and why the training analysis was invented and adopted by training institutes.

Balint (1954) summarized the history of the first generation of training analysis as follows:

A person interested in Freud's ideas read his works and uses his ideas in understanding his own and other people's unconscious.

This led very soon to traveling to Freud for a short analysis in order to achieve an experiential understanding of repression and of analytic technique in addition to the intellectual one attainable by reading. Pressure from Ferenczi led to lengthening the training analysis so that it lasted at least as long as any therapeutic analysis in order that the analysand both know and be able to control his own character weaknesses (p.158).

Ferenczi wrote in 1928: "... the analyst himself. . . must know, and be in control of, even the most recondite weaknesses of his own character; and this is impossible without a fully completed analysis."

Freud (1937) replied:

> *The effect upon the patient has been so profound that no further changes would take place in him if his analysis were continued. The implication is that by means of analysis it is possible to attain to absolute psychical normality and to be sure that it will be maintained.*

But Freud believed that such super-normality was not possible. He knew that many analysts graduated from institutes and sought further analysis either with the same analyst or a new one.

Balint regarded the post-training analyses as either continuations of the training analyses or evidence that the original analyses or selection procedures were inadequate. Either way, the absolute psychic normality did not exist.

Yet Balint asserts: "All the modern 'progressive' institutes are profoundly influenced by the idea of the 'supertherapy' . . . and I know of some training analysts, at least in London, who in verbal communications advocate 'research' as the true aim of their training analyses, but I have not yet seen this idea in print" (p. 158) nor did it appear in print to the present day. According to Balint, the supertherapy idea came about when senior analysts confronted their dissatisfaction with their own mental health, and since they could not find analysts senior to themselves in their institutes, began to travel to other countries to seek further analysis. He believed that this was prevalent from about 1920 to 1935. To prevent the losses and disruptions caused by migration training analyses were lengthened and became "super-therapies." The central focus of these new super-therapies was pre-verbal experience. Transference and counter-transference were examined very closely; aggressive wishes were addressed in detail and negative transference was regarded as the seat of analytic transformation of the personality.

This was revealed to be a direct consequence of Ferenczi's complaint that Freud had not analyzed Ferenczi's negative transference.

In "Analysis Terminable and Interminable" (1937) Freud asserted that it was not useful to attempt to elicit aggressive wishes towards the analyst or to provoke the negative transference when it was not evident in the discourse because such a procedure would either make the analyst act like a cranky critic or stifle the patient's development of anger towards the analyst. The annoyance or irritation interpreted too early as transference aggression would convince the patient that the analyst had to protect himself from the intense anger and aggression that would develop in the course of an analysis if it were to be allowed to go forward without consistent interpretation of every instance of anything that could be seen as aggressive. This stance led to the splitting off of the object relations theorists—of which Balint was a leader, from the Kleinians who were interpreting aggression early and often. Balint believed that the consistent interpretation of aggressive wishes would lead the patient to idealize the analyst as someone who faced aggression courageously and accepted its ubiquity. The analyst would be introjected as a whole rather than subjected to a selective identification with admirable traits and rejection of traits less appropriate to the candidate.

Balint thought that this was relatively harmless for the patient who would finish analysis and have no further contact with the analyst, but disastrous for the analytic candidate who would be recruited into a faction.

The factions in Britain were led by Anna Freud and Melanie Klein. In a general way Anna Freud followed her father's view that negative transference should not become the focus of all analytic work, but should be seen in balance with positive transference and that love and hate should be examined as evenhandedly as possible. Klein and the Kleinians found this attitude unsuccessful and followed Ferenczi's suggestion that interpretation of negative transference was what changed personality and even character. Analysts tended to side with whichever position their own analysts espoused. Thus the British Society split into factions Since they disagreed completely both could not be right. By forming a third group and examining as closely as possible what effect their interpretations of both kinds of transference had on their patients, the group that formed in the middle considered that they were different from the other two in that the others accepted dogma while they did "research."

Ferenczi expected that the introduction of the technique of prolonged and negative transference focused super-therapy would end the era of factionalism in psychoanalysis. Armed with self understanding all graduate analysts would come to the same conclusions about what worked and what did not work in analysis. The British experience showed the reverse.

Balint concluded:

As we all know, to deal with aggressive impulses, with hatred, has always been one of the unsolved, and perhaps insoluble, problems of mankind, causing troubles far beyond the fields of psycho-analytical training. It is a platitude to state that we training analysts have not *found the solution either. The danger is that some of us, proud of the success of our new techniques, might think that we are near the solution. As a warning I wish to quote the device of the Unitarian Church of Hungary, which ought to be the device of our training regulations too—*semper reformari debet—*or, as translated by a friend of mine, 'reform unremittingly'* (p. 162).

Reforming continued with a 1954 conference on the problem at the International Psychoanalytic Association (IPA). Bibring led off with a succinct statement:

Anna Freud is said to have formulated the problem as follows: "A training analysis is characterized by the analyst's having social contact with his patient and making the major decisions for him." These major decisions are furthermore aggravated by the fact that . . . the analyst not only interferes with the analysand's own decisions, . . . and turns into the dreaded judge. His expected criticism is anxiously circumvented by the candidate and he is constantly suspected of hostile reactions which may destroy the candidate's training opportunity. Kubie felt that this problem can hardly be solved within the didactic analysis, but may have to await a later, second analysis, after graduation and membership have already been secured. It is certainly correct that the second analysis often proves infinitely easier and may under the circumstances described yield important material which had remained repressed—or even hidden—during the first analytic process; but it does not solve the problem as long as we cannot achieve the paradox of beginning the training with this second analysis.

This problem seemed insoluble at that time. But Schachter (2011) actually found that second analyses after the candidate had graduated were rated as satisfying but not statistically more satisfying than the training analysis. Waiting for the second analysis before graduating the candidate would subject that one to the same drawbacks as the first. What has happened meanwhile is that analyses are longer, candidates graduate while still in analysis and the new analyst can be free to reveal less attractive traits, desires, fears and moral issues that were not apparent while the analyst appeared to be the judge of whether the analysand would be a good analyst.

In the 1954 conference Heiman (1954) tried to redefine the training analysis in order to minimize the potential difficulties caused by using the analysis for training as well as therapeutic purposes. Issues arising from the clashes between different schools of analysis were intruding on candidates' analyses. She proposed using these issues to deepen the candidates' understanding of her own thinking and feelings "by consistently analysing the external interferences from the training course, by turning difficulties into instruments . . . " She also cautioned the training analyst to "adhere to purely analytic procedure" and to "recognize and master his own problems so that they do not obscure his countertransference."

Nils Nielsen (1954) wrestled with the issue of how much the candidate tells the training analyst what he knows the training analyst wants to hear. He believed that analysts should use information from relations, friends, colleagues and others. He asserted that information could "be elicited without undue interference with subtle analytical mechanisms." His ideas were in fact put to the test as he had wished them to be. Informal networks of information about candidates were and are always working. A committee meets to talk about a candidate's progress. An analyst absents herself. Other members of the committee see this and judge the candidate as likely to be well analyzed if they respect the analysts, not if they do not. The same kind of informal and unavoidable thing happens with supervisors and course instructors. Even knowing who the candidate's spouse or friends are affect the way the analyst sees the candidate. But most analysts regard this kind of information as leading to bias, not good judgement.

As an alternative Nielsen suggested selecting "aneurotic" candidates and going back to the idea of the short didactic analysis originally advocated by Freud. But Nielsen had the example of Ferenczi who had complained that his own analysis with Freud had been too short to teach him about his own character flaws and other candidates could well have the same reaction to a short and relatively superficial analysis.

Nielsen concludes:

My points of view are mainly theoretical, but my aim is practical. There can be no purpose in defining or criticizing standards of psycho-analytic training if they are not constantly referred to experience. No theoretical construction can be so perfect that we can or must not ask ourselves: "How does it work?"

Within the American Psychoanalytic Association at this same time a fierce discussion was going on as reported by Tower and Calef (1954). All the participants in that discussion agreed that a training analysis should be therapeutic and that obstacles to this goal must be removed.

But the participants disagreed on whether the training analysis should be flexible in scheduling and on the extent the training analyst should participate in judgements about the analysand's career progress. Windholz (1955) struggled with the idea that the training analysis should be therapeutic, yet should also create an identification with the analyzing function so that the analysand acquires the analyst's skills via the transference. He regarded the self analyzing function as the necessary outcome of training analysis but not necessarily of therapeutic analysis.

Szasz (1958) saw the history of psychoanalytic education as a gradual process of systematization. The power of judgement gradually shifted away from the candidate and toward committees, institutes and associations of institutes. Training got longer and more uniform. But future development of psychoanalysis as a scientific discipline could go in the direction of teaching by example and offering the student the opportunity for learning what she herself wants to learn. Szasz concludes:

> *Analytic training began as a short period of apprenticeship and rapidly evolved into a complex social structure, the modern training system. In the latter, the system and its representatives have great power over the selection of candidates and their fate. It is held that the psychological implications and effects of this sociological change in the analytic training system have not received the attention which they deserve.*
>
> *Indeed, to focus on the content of psycho-analytic training (e.g., training analysis, seminars, supervised analyses, etc.) while disregarding the total structure of the educational system is grossly misleading. It is reminiscent of the traditional parental attitude about raising children, according to which parents 'tell' all the 'right things" to their child and are later full of indignant 'surprise' at the human end product which results.*
>
> *'If you want to find out anything from the theoretical physicists about the methods they use,' said Einstein, 'I advise you to stick closely to one principle: don't listen to their words, fix your attention on their deeds'.*
>
> *Have we any reason to assume that this principle is any less valid for our understanding of the methods of education?* (p. 609).

Bernfeld (1962) wanted to eliminate: (1) requirements as to previous training; (2) committees on admission, education, and students; and (3) the category of "training analyst." Instead an analyst would bring someone who seemed talented and interested to meetings of the Society, to meet other analysts, perhaps read a paper, and receive supervision of psychotherapy. After courses and supervision the group who would decide whether or not to accept that person as a member. Bernfeld suggested that this informal procedure would eliminate "extra-analytic considerations." What emerged from this controversy was an idea similar to that of Szasz and Bernfeld but articulated by the conservative Kairys (1964) as well as by Nacht (1954) and Nacht et al. (1961) and van der Sterren & Seidenberg 1974). This solution was a complete separation between the training analysis and the educational process. The TA no longer reported anything to the institute about the analysis. The TA was not to teach or supervise the analysand nor was the TA to sit on any committee that decided anything about the candidate's selection, progress or graduation. But this institutional solution left a further problem: being a training analyst can result in an idealization of oneself as an analyst and of one's own analytic style. The only way of dealing with this issue that came up in the IPA pre-congress meeting on the role of the training analyst was remaining in touch with colleagues who do not share in the idealization (Pffeffer 1974).

Another problem of training analysis is the question of termination. When is a training analysis complete? As we have seen Freud's original view that it could be brief had been superseded by an insistence on more and more completeness. Yet in a panel on the termination of the analyses of adults (Firestein 1969) reported that almost all analyses were relatively unfinished and that the analysands often ended without achieving more in the way of resolution of the transference than expressing gratitude to the analyst. Thus the training analysis could be expected to end with the transference still relatively active and the inevitable contact between the training analyst and the new analyst would be bound to be colored by remaining transference.

THE THIRD GENERATION

A current (1995–2009) battle in the American Psychoanalytic Association (APsaA) concerns the issue of who is fit to be a Training Analyst. Beginning as a critique of the Certification system by which the central organization vets analysts who wish to become Training Analysts at their local societies, the issue has grown into a controversy since applications for training at Institutes of APsaA have diminished. The local analytic institutes which are not members of APsaA are attracting those who are already in analysis with analysts who are not certified by APsaA and therefore not appointed Training Analysts at their local institutes. The prospective candidates find that their analysts are acceptable to the non-APsaA institutes and therefore choose to go where they can continue in their satisfactory analyses. Some institutes of APsaA have chosen to allow people already in analyses with analysts who are not certified by APsaA and to urge these candidates to seek a further analysis with a Training Analyst after their current analysis is terminated. This arrangement has brought objections from the Board of Professional Standards of APsaA. They believe that the Certification procedure is necessary to preserve "standards."

Kirsner (2000) investigated four American Psychoanalytic Association component Institutes: New York, Los Angeles, Boston and Chicago. He concluded that psychoanalysis claims to be a positivist science, but operates in as authoritarian model. Knowledge and standards are transmitted from one analytic generation to another through the training analyst system as truths, but do not present supporting empirical evidence. He advocates that in order to preclude this anointment process to a powerful and privileged status, that the title of training analyst should be eliminated.

An indication of how serious a rift has been opened is the fact that a recent president of APsaA who ran on a platform of eliminating the TA system never mentioned it again after she was elected. The issue may now seem too divisive. Some members of APsaA believe that if a local institute does not submit to the dictates of APsaA, it can be thrown out of the national organization. Furthermore, some of the members of the Board of Professional Standards have warned that such institutes would not be able to join the International Psychoanalytical Association either because they would not meet the standards for IPA Training Analysts.

On the other hand, *The American Psychoanalyst* (*TAP*), the newsletter of APsaA, printed the following:

THE URUGUAYAN MODEL

This model is, in part, a reaction to what was felt to be a previously existing excessive concentration of power in a group of training analysts. It represents an attempt to ensure that training becomes a more democratic, free, and equitable endeavor. It attempts to do so by allocating training functions to four different groups of analysts, each charged with organizing and conducting one specific aspect of training: admission, supervision, personal analysis, and teaching. **A graduate analyst can choose to which group he or she wishes to belong.** *A considerable amount of personal analysis is required* *(usually three years or more) before admission and is expected to continue during training, usually another five years. Personal analysis is conducted at a minimum of three times a week with intensification of frequency during periods of significant regression. The analyst needs to be a member of the IPA.*

In the course work, there is emphasis placed on a great deal of written work and numerous presentations (Jacobs 2007; emphasis added).

Dan Jacobs (2007) continues:

THE FRENCH MODEL

The personal analysis of the candidate is placed strictly outside the realm of training. The French model does not recognize a "training" analysis and has no position of training analyst. Any analyst who is an IPA member can do the candidate's analysis. One of the major goals of the personal analysis is to clarify and work out the unconscious motivations behind one's wish to become an analyst. This analytic work takes place, for the most part, prior to the candidate's application for admission to training. There are no training requirements governing the frequency of personal analyses. Patient and analyst, based on clinical indications, decide upon the number of visits per week (Jacobs 2007, emphasis added).

The controversy continues, as a current candidate for office in APsaA has written:

Some of our institutes are asking for the option to appoint training analysts without national certification . . . let's respect the IPA's carefully considered procedures and give our institutes that local option as soon as possible, in whatever way is most expedient. It won't solve all our problems and differences, some will be unhappy with it, but I believe in the end it will move us forwards (Jaffee 2011).

Dr. Jaffee's statement came in response to a statement from Judith Schachter, a past president and now treasurer of APsaA, she wrote:

Since the necessity for a training analyst position in our APsaA institutes is considered such an essential part of our standards, now being discussed by two task force groups, I believe we should recognize that the two other IPA accepted models do not demand our version of the analyst of candidates and ask for comments by those running for office in APsaA (Schachter 2011a).

Meanwhile first the New York Freudian Society and then the Institute for Psychoanalytic Research and Training have significantly altered their procedure for becoming a Training Analyst. For 30 years, each member became a training analyst by virtue of being a member for 5 years. Joining the International Psychoanalytic Association required a change to a formal process. An initial simple interview was later supplanted by a more formal, rigorous and rigid set of guidelines. Members began to experience the ordeal as unpleasant or even harmful, although a small minority were pleased with the process: applications for TA status decreased. A year long process of meetings of the membership initiated by Jane Hall and carried out by Arlene Kramer Richards allowed members to co-write a new set of criteria for TA status. A series of objective criteria for attaining the status of training analyst was written cooperatively through open discussion amongst all members of the society. These are:

- Membership for five years.
- Four analytic cases seen four times per week.
- Participation in study groups and/or seminars.
- Attendance at analytic meetings, writing and/or presenting papers and/or teaching.
- Service to the Freudian Society on committees or the Board.
- Supervision experience with psychotherapy cases.
- Experience of a seminar in supervision of psychoanalysis for one year.
- A statement of not being under investigation for ethical issues.
- After meeting the above criteria and designation as a training analyst, the new Training Analyst presents a case, either orally or in writing to two Training Analyst colleagues chosen by the new Training Analyst.

Instead of examining prospective Training Analysts, the existing TAs participate with them in seminars to prepare them for special problems of training analyses and supervision of analytic process. Each new training analyst has had seminars in supervision, ethics and termination. Thus, the new training analyst has had an education in the specific work of a training and supervising analyst. The new form of interview provides a chance to participate in a collegial discussion. Everyone has been pleased by this welcoming meeting. Its emphasis on candidate choice of group members, of what to present and when to present it leads to a greater sense of individual voice as a psychoanalyst and less dependence on others to validate what is often uncertain and unsettling.

To determine the effectiveness of the new procedure (Hall et al. 2008), a committee composed a research questionnaire that 82% of all members of the New York Freudian Society completed. 2/3 of the TA members are in favor of the Newly Revised procedure. Of the group of TAs appointed by the Newly Revised method, 83% are satisfied with both the standards and procedures. However, several TAs wanted to return to the less restrictive 5-year rule.

At IPTAR (Institute for Psychoanalytic Training and Research), as at many societies of APsaA, self nomination for the status of training analyst replaced the older model of invitation, but the testing model continued. Different theoretical orientations became officially acceptable as the logic of analytic treatment. Thus these societies participated in the overall trend toward opening this category of analysts to more people than had been training analysts before the 21st century.

It is my own observation that the more testing, the more hierarchical levels of organization, the more restrictions on admission, training and graduation a psychoanalytic community imposes on its potential candidates, its members and its graduates, the less creative, less adaptive and less viable it becomes. It is not only the training analysis as a separate part of the training, but also the whole array of requirements, "standards" and regulations that defeats the ultimate purpose of analytic training. That purpose seems to me to be to develop a person's ability to listen with a truly open mind so as to learn from the person in analysis what that person wants and how she attempts to protect herself from her own worst nightmares on the road to getting it. Listening that way and learning from the patient that way are fostered not by attempts to meet the standards of examiners, but by the experience of having been listened to and taken seriously. This is the sense in which Einstein's comment about taking note of what we do rather than what we say we intend to do is relevant to analytic training and to the training analysis in particular.

Another problem of training analysis is the requirement that all training analyses be conducted by one of the training analysts of the same institute as the candidate takes courses and has supervision. This arrangement can easily lead to the "halo" effect through which a candidate is favored because she has an analyst who is particularly respected as a teacher or supervisor. Conversely, a candidate may be considered tainted by being the analysand of a not so well respected analyst. Graduation may be accelerated or retarded by this kind of circumstance. Schachter's (2011) study found that most analysts believed that they had been "convoyed" by their analysts through their training and afterwards during their careers. And the candidate may choose an analyst on the basis of whether being in analysis with that person will promote her career. Choosing an analyst with that in mind will inevitably affect what the candidate chooses to say in analysis. It can only taint the process. In addition, the covert and even unconscious collusion with the analyst's theoretical positions is bound to go along with the understanding that agreeing with the analyst can only do the candidate good. By having the analyst from a different institute, the candidate may be freed to be less pleasing and more reliant on her own efforts to graduate. This would imply an opening up of the requirements that would lead us towards Bernfeld rather than Ferenczi.

Yet another current issue is whether training analysts should only be allowed to function as such for a limited period of time. This idea has been proposed as a way to deal with the impaired analyst. After years or even decades of functioning as a training analyst, a person may become too overburdened, suffer physical or mental deterioration or just have not kept up with the current thinking in the field. Would it be good to guard against these eventualities by having term limits? Or is it the case that at least some analysts may become more skilled with experience and may open their minds to the ideas and needs of specific patients rather than following the theoretical positions of their own training? And is that to the good or to the bad?

The idea of term limits had had a partial endorsement in the requirement of some institutes that the candidate choose an analyst who is less than a certain age. But this limit is illegal in the United States where it is considered age discrimination. The age of the training analyst has not been shown to correlate with outcome of the analysis. Putting an arbitrary limit on the age allowed may open institutes to lawsuits. Yet instituting some other form of regulation is problematic as well. Should there be a consultative process in which colleagues evaluate each other? Should that be mandatory after a certain age? Or after a certain term of functioning as a training analyst?

Are we leaning toward Bernfeld's open model or is this just a minor retreat from the ever more restrictive model promulgated by Ferenczi? And will the newer institutes with no restrictions on who is a training analyst win the day by recruiting most of the potential candidates? The training analyst question vexes us today as much as it has over the past century of psychoanalytic training.

REFERENCES

BALINT, M. (1954). Analytic Training and Training Analysis *International Journal of Psychooanalysis* 35:157–162.

BERNFELD, S. (1962). On Psychoanalytic Training. *Psychoanalytic Quarterly* 31:453–482.

BIBRING, G.L. (1954). The Training Analysis and Its Place in Psycho-Analytic Training. *International Journal of Psychooanalysis* 35:169–173.

FIRESTEIN, S.K. (1969). Problems of Termination in the Analysis of Adults. *Journal of the American Psychoanalytic Association* 17:222–237.

FREUD, S. (1937). Analysis Terminable and Interminable. *Standard Edition.*

HALL, J., RICHARDS, A.K., SLOATE, P., & TURO, J. (2008). On Becoming A Training Analyst: Working Through. In *Group Examination to Self-Evaluation at the New York Freudian Society* (unpublished).

HEIMANN, P. (1954). Problems of the Training Analysis. *International Journal of Psychooanalysis* 35:163–168.

JACOBS, D. (2007). Three Models of Training. *The American Psychoanalyst* 41(2):11,19.

JAFFEE (2011). Personal communication.

KAIRYS, D. (1964). The Training Analysis—A Critical Review of the Literature and a Controversial Proposal. *Psychoanalytic Quarterly* 33:485–512.

KIRSNER, D. (2000). *Unfree Associations: Inside Psychoanalytic Institutes.* London: Process Press.

NIELSEN, N. (1954). The Dynamics of Training Analysis *International Journal of Psychooanalysis* 35:247–249.

NACHT, S. (1954). The Difficulties of Didactic Psycho-Analysis in Relation to Therapeutic Psycho-Analysis. *International Journal of Psychoanalysis* 35:250–253.

——— LEBOVICI, S. & DIATKINE, R. (1961). Training for Psycho-Analysis. *International Journal of Psychooanalysis* 42:110–115.

PFEFFER, A. (1974). The Difficulties of the Training Analyst in the Training Analysis. *International Journal of Psychooanalysis* 55:79–83.

REEDER, J. (2004). *Hate and Love in Psychoanalytic Institutions.* New York: Other Press.

SCHACHTER, J. (2011). Comparison of Satisfaction with Training Analysis with Satisfaction with Second Analysis. Presented at a meeting of the American Psychoanalytic Association, New York, January 2.

——— (2011a). Personal communication.

SZASZ, T. (1954). Three Problems in Contemporary Psychoanalytic Training and Therapeutic Analysis. Panel Report *Journal of the American Psychoanalytic Association* 2:175–178.

TOWER, L.E., & CALEF, H. (1954). III. Training and Thereapeutic Analysis. *Journal of the American Psychoanalytic Association* 2:175–178.

VAN DER STERREN, H.A. & SEIDENBERG, H. (1975). The Problem of the Training Analysis. *Annual of Psychooanalysis* 3:259–267.

WINDHOLZ, E. (1955). Problems of Termination of the Training Analysis. *Journal of the American Psychoanalytic Association* 3:641–646.

****
****

A version of the preceeding chapter originally appeared as:

RICHARDS, A.K. (2010). Training Analysis and Training Analyst Status: Where are We Now? *Psychoanalytic Review* 97:955–969.

A rlene Kramer Richards and I, at some point early in our friendship, discovered our shared love of movies, and our love of
writing, talking and thinking about psychoanalytic meanings conveyed
in movies. I have learned a great deal from her writings on movies.
They have both deepened and broadened my understanding of the
human condition—covering a wide range of what being human entails
on both a conscious and unconscious level. Her movie reviews (as
well as her other writings) deepen our understanding of developmental stages in girls as well as gender issues in both males and females.
In addition, she illuminates the contexts that we are immersed in. These
contexts include the womb, the family, the impact of religion, politics,
and the mores of our culture and country, as well as historical and generational factors of the present and past world in which we live and
die, and the knowledge of our own mortality and how we face, ignore
and deal with that knowledge.

All these movies are rich, complicated, multi-dimensional works of
art. It is noteworthy that these are the movies that Arlene has chosen to
delve into, and she explores them in a profoundly stimulating and infor-
mative way. Just as the movies themselves reveal their rich and deep
meanings upon repeated viewings, her reviews benefit the reader most
when they are read more than once. This is to say, her reviews are
works of art in their own right, as well as original psychoanalytic writings which forge new and important territory.

The movies that Arlene has written about include: *Pan's Labyrinth,
Basic Instincts, That Obscure Object of Desire,* and *Munich.* In addition,
she and her husband, Arnold Richards, have written about a trilogy of
Las Vegas movies (*Bugsy, Casino,* and *Leaving Las Vegas*).

Arlene's movie reviews are groundbreaking and remarkable in that
she not only applies existing psychoanalytic theory to these movies, but
she also advances psychoanalytic theory in her discussion of female development and gender issues in men and women. Thus, in the three movies
in which she focuses on gender issues (*Basic Instinct, That Obscure Object
of Desire,* and *Pan's Labyrinth*), developmental sexual issues are studied

in an original way—in which the body, the socio-cultural context and myths are viewed as interrelated in how they all shape and reflect fears, desires, beliefs and behavior.

The movies that Arlene has studied cover a rich and varied spectrum of the human condition. They explore the following areas: the knowledge of our own mortality and how we (or some of us) face, ignore and deal with that knowledge (Las Vegas movies and *Pan's Labyrinth*); issues of ethnicity and religion—as matters of pride or shame (Las Vegas movies); gender issues: i.e., how sexuality and power are experienced and dealt with—in and between men and women (the Las Vegas movies, *Basic Instinct*, *That Obscure Object of Desire*, and *Pan's Labyrinth*); developmental issues—especially in girls (*Pan's Labyrinth*); murderous rage and revenge, both personal and political, as well as the relative importance and power of religion, nationality and family in a person's comfort and welfare, including the extreme matter of life and death (*Munich*, and the Las Vegas movies).

Gender Issues

In both *Basic Instinct* and *That Obscure Object of Desire*, Arlene focuses on men's desire, fear, longing for, obsessive infatuation with, and terror of the desired woman. In both films, the woman is the leader and is also dangerous in relation to the man: she is a man-eater. In *Basic Instinct* she is strong, bisexual, and captures men by the image of her exciting, yet dangerous vulva. Arlene focuses astutely on the attraction and fear that engulf men regarding the powerful, sexually passionate and uninhibited woman. This woman is portrayed as either sexually exciting and then killing the men in her life [power], or tantalizing and then abruptly depriving and frustrating the men who desire her.

In *That Obscure Object of Desire,* the heroine's strength lies in an image of purity, represented by her intact hymen. Her fascination lies in her elusiveness, her tantalizing hints of sexual consummation, always ending in frustration and rejection of the man who pursues her and longs for her. The woman's elusiveness and seductiveness is crazy-making for the man: he is obsessed with her while also viewing her with disgust and degrading her. Like the male protagonist's friend "who loves women very much and thinks they are bags of excrement," these men try, unsuccessfully, to regain their own dignity and value. It seems to me that they are projecting onto women their own self-loathing for desiring the "obscure object of desire," who, according to Arlene, remains valued only as the virgin, fertile woman (the mother); while the sexually active woman is portrayed as sterile and childless.

The breadth of Arlene's psychoanalytic and literary reservoir of knowledge creates a rich mosaic for the reader to ponder upon regarding an understanding of the complicated issues for woman and man in their relationship to their own sexuality and to the quest for power vis-à-vis each other. Arlene's discussion of these two movies draws on symbolic explications, literary references, Greek mythology, along with references to psychoanalytic theories of gender issues for and between men and women; these all contribute to how fascinating and richly thought provoking these reviews are. Arlene's movie studies underline my conviction that there is unquestionable power in using the medium of movies to deepen and broaden our intellectual, emotional and artistic understanding of these human issues. I believe Arlene's movie reviews have the potential to speak to everyone—as well as sharpening our psychoanalytic understanding of the human condition—and in the instance of the films discussed above—of gender issues within and between men and women.

In both of these movies, attractive, educated and powerful women are both feared and denigrated. They toy with men's affections and desire for them, taunting, promising, teasing. Arlene sees these movies as promulgating a hateful message by artful means. In her analysis of *Basic Instinct* she notes: "Educated women are dangerous, blood-thirsty lesbians. Even the ones who seem to love men are at best unethical, and, at worst, murderous. The most attractive and openly sexual ones, like Catherine, are the most deadly. Powerful women who achieve things like writing books or getting a degree in psychology are the worst. Beautiful woman are the enemy; men attracted to them are doomed." Movies, a medium that can and often does reach a global audience, feed and draw on deep-seated conscious and unconscious perceptions and fears of women through how they are portrayed.

Arlene comments that *That Obscure Object of Desire* emphasizes that men can only trust men; the butler is a better friend than any woman can be. This also implies that by avoiding beautiful young virgins, men can avert death. This movie reassures women that their power is in their protestation of virginity, and that they can get away with any kind of behavior as long as they maintain the illusion men want so much to believe in. *That Obscure Object of Desire* shows the power of the sexually abstinent, but reproductively capable woman, while *Basic Instinct* shows the power of the childless, sexual woman.

Arlene's emphasis is on men's fear and hatred and longing of the sexual, educated, powerful woman—as well as their fear, hatred and longing for the pure, virginal woman who they put on a pedestal. Either way, women cannot be both respected, loved and penetrated emotionally and physically. In these two movie reviews, she powerfully illuminates these complex views of women as they are so ingrained in so many men and women. I found that her insights into these two movies, which she compares and contrasts in a powerful, erudite way, gives us much to think about.

Female Development

Arlene's dedication to understanding female sexuality continues in her analysis of the film, *Pan's Labyrinth.* She is also sensitive to other themes in this film such as the Spanish Civil War and the quest for freedom and self-determination, as well as the fairy tale involving the tasks necessary for the pubescent girl to reunite with the lost father (killed in the Spanish Civil War). It is also a story of nature—both natural and supernatural, its trials and rewards, its beauty and its ugliness.

And yet Arlene's primary focus is on the coming of age of a young girl, Ofelia. Arlene comments on trials and tests that confront Ofelia in her journey towards becoming a woman. Arlene's interest in female gender issues (about which she has written several original theoretical and clinical papers) enriches her discussion of this movie. Can Ofelia be strong, adventurous, nurturing, and passionate in her appetites on all levels? What are the tests she must pass to achieve these goals? What are the barriers? On the one hand there is Pan, who represents hedonism and pleasure, but also prescribes tests of inner restraint and willpower that she must pass. As they are in fairy tales, the tempting obstacles and trials of the journey are portrayed concretely by grotesque monsters and terrifying places and tests. This image is a metaphor for what is necessary for becoming a mature, fulfilled woman.

Arlene emphasizes that the mother in this movie is practical, and focused on survival, which she believes entails submitting to the wishes and power of a man. On the other hand, her daughter, Ofelia, has a vivid imagination and loves reading fairy tales, and physically enters these fairy tales where she must experience the necessary tests to becoming a woman. Arlene emphasizes the paradoxes and contradictions in objects, events and journeys presented in this movie—what is ugly is also beautiful; what is familiar is also uncanny; what is desired and longed for is also scary:

"Sexy is scary . . . menstruation enters the world of a girl as both natural and unfamiliar . . . . The first menses is the crucial moment" (chapter 22, p. 386; this volume).

On the one hand the mother submits to the brutal, powerful, fascistic man, who gives her the gift of a son, and then discards her, ignoring her while she is bleeding to death. On the other hand, the rebellious, strong woman, the servant Mercedes, is shown as a single woman—loving and caring for Ofelia and her newborn brother, and a courageous freedom fighter against the fascistic political forces. The journey toward being a strong mature woman is fraught with terrible tests and trials—and these are shown as parallel to the dangers and courage involved in the quest for independence and political freedom.

What is remarkable about Arlene's exposition of this movie is its deep and exquisite understanding of the conscious and unconscious conflicts, desires and fears involved in the transition from childhood to adulthood in a female. And in this movie, as in the two discussed above, political/cultural/family influences affect and parallel the individual's personal journey through life.

Images of Violence and Immortality

In the four remaining films that Arlene has analyzed (*Munich,* and, in collaboration with her husband, Arnold Richards, the trilogy of Las Vegas movies) there is a multi-dimensional perspective that includes historical, political, national, familial, religious identity, and sexual longings for the other—and longings to procreate.

Speaking first about *Munich,* Arlene helped me understand the movie as well as understand why I did not like it when I saw it. She compares *Munich* to a Rorschach—an ambiguous portrayal that, depending upon the viewer's psychological, ethnic, religious, political and esthetic affiliations and sensibilities, evokes strong love/hate reactions, and sometimes these are overridden by confusion about what is exactly going on at various points of the movie. The film is so complex and confusing that the viewer is enabled to project his or her conscious and unconscious feelings, desires, fears, and conflicts onto it. Although this is no doubt true to some extent of all movies, the complexity and multitude of vectors in *Munich* make it especially true of this film.

It is a tribute to Arlene that she was able to parse out her own subjective reactions or prejudices to understand this complex film. This is not a simple movie about revenge by the Israelis for the Munich Olympic massacre. Arlene homes in on the multiple vectors and pulls presented in this film: family ties, national loyalties, and personal and national power expressed by revenge through brutal killings. The way these vectors conflict with each other—and the way that the political, machismo determinant destroys the tender tie and loyalty to family (wife and child) is made painfully clear and well-illuminated in Arlene's analysis of Munich. I think her work is groundbreaking in how she links socio-political, family and psychoanalytic perspectives in a complex understanding of one film. (This is also true of all the other films she has written about, but in *Munich,* for me, the film was made much more accessible after reading her paper.)

Moving on to the three Las Vegas movies there are significant insights into three dimensions that most people deal with: issues and conflicts regarding family ties (to wife and children), one's own cultural and religious identity (specifically being Jewish), the quest for both omnipotence and self-destruction, and the phobic and counter-phobic ways of dealing with one's own mortality.

The three movies, *Bugsy, Casino,* and *Leaving Las Vegas* show, successively, three generations of Las Vegas. Although, in these three generations Las Vegas and the mob are different in striking ways, the mentality of the protagonists in all three movies are eerily the same. There are parallels between the Las Vegas movies and Munich as they are analyzed by Arlene and Arnie. There are conflicting pulls on the Jewish protagonists in all these films. In pursuing their quest for power and revenge family values and ties are sacrificed.

Although these movies were difficult to watch, especially *Munich,* which I found confusing, after reading Arlene's write up of *Munich,* (and Arlene and Arnie's papers on the Las Vegas movies), I had deeper insights into all four of these films and I especially understood why I did not like *Munich.* Arlene helped me understand the multiple levels that these film portrayed and the complex issues they were addressing. In *Munich,* Arlene discusses family ties and loyalties, historical referents to earlier persecutions of Jews—the Dreyfus case and the importance of family (his brother) in his being deemed innocent of treason, the Munich putsch, the betrayal by Chamberlain in his giving Czechoslovakia to Hitler in return for the promise of peace with England, Golda Meier's mission of revenge after the massacre of the athletes in the Munich Olympics. In the Las Vegas movies Arlene and Arnold discuss three generations of the development of Las Vegas and the men who were instrumental in its growth. Las Vegas is a gambling Mecca in the desert. Arlene and Arnold helped me understand the allure of Las Vegas and gambling in particular. In gambling some people entertain the myth that they can beat the odds, not only in connection with winning money, but defy that odds that they will die: "The hope of life everlasting is conveyed by the lights that never go out as the gamblers search to beat the odds" (chapter 20, p. 367, this volume).

Reading Arlene's exposition of these complex films enriches our understanding of the multi-determined mixture of love, sex, quest for power, greed, autonomy, brutal violence and revenge and immortality. In all four movies, she points out—not without compassion—the darker side of the Jewish male, who is both at the same time strong, driven and powerful, and weak, envious and self-hating.

What is remarkable is Arlene's (and in the Las Vegas film reviews—Arnold's) courage and insight in delving deeply into the darker side of the human condition—and thereby deepening our understanding of men and women.

It is a pleasure and honor to have the opportunity to study, discuss and introduce Arlene Richard's rich contribution to understanding film through psychoanalysis and psychoanalysis through film.

REFERENCE

RICHARDS, A.K. (1999). The Terrifying Woman: Latin and Anglo View of Female Sexuality in *Basic Instinct* and *That Obscure Object of Desire*. *Projections* 12(2):35–52.

(All other references cited in the preceding essay are found in the chapter-list below and appear in the present volume.)

PAPERS IN SECTION V
(All papers by Arlene Kramer Richards except chapter 25, written *with* Arnold D. Richards)

Chapter 20
RICHARDS, A.K., & RICHARDS, A.D. (1997). Gambling, Death and Violence: Hollywood Looks at Las Vegas. *Psychoanalytic Review* 84:769–788.
Chapter 21
(2009). Review of the Movie *Munich*. Sept. 6.
http://internationalpsychoanalysis.net/2009/09/06/review-of-the-movie-munich-by-arlene-kramer-richards
Chapter 22
(2008). "Girl Into Woman: Growing Strong" Review of *Pan's Labyrinth*.

http://internationalpsychoanalysis.net/2008/08/22/arlene-kramer-richardss-review-of-pans-labyrinth

Chapter 23
(2004). *Matchstick Men:* Psychological Thriller and Therapeutic Paradox. *PANY Bulletin* 42(2):Summer.

Chapter 24
(1998). Woman as Medusa in *Basic Instinct. Psychoanalytic Inquiry* 18:269–280.

Chapter 25
(2009). Gambling and Death. In *Greed: Sex, Money, Power and Politics* E. Ronis and L. Shaw (eds).

Gambling, Death and Violence: Hollywood Looks at Las Vegas

AN AMERICAN DREAM

Las Vegas has been the focus and locale of several big Hollywood movies in the past decade. We have chosen three of these movies to represent Las Vegas as depicted by Hollywood. They seem to us to tell the story of the place, the activity it was built to house, the people who created it, and the people who go there to gamble. The three movies are violent. Two of them end in the death of their hero, and the remaining one begins with a death scene and ends with the death of an era. The point here is violence and violent death. Violence in the movies is arresting. Bottom line, violence is about dying. Movies tell us that death is only temporary. The actors who die do not really die. All of these movies about Las Vegas present heroes who have much in common with the hero of the conventional Western, just as Las Vegas has much in common with other Western towns. The stories follow a form parallel to that of the Western as well. They all feature the hero coming into town on a quest or at random, working out his meeting with destiny, and accepting the outcome. In this respect, they parallel the experience of the visitors who come to Las Vegas to gamble. The visitors to Las Vegas thus see themselves as like the cowboys who came to the frontier to seek their fortune.

According to the Las Vegas Chamber of Commerce, the modal age of people coming to Las Vegas to gamble is between 55 and 65. They are people who are facing the waning of sexuality and imminent death. To these people, Las Vegas is the last promise of the American Dream. It declares that you can beat the odds. You don't have to give in to statistics. You can win. Even though the odds on your dying are perfect in the long term—no one has ever succeeded in not dying—even though the odds on your losing in the long term in casino gambling are perfect—no one lives to walk away with the profits except the casino—

still the casino gives you hope. The parallels are amazing, and it took movie makers only a couple of decades after the founding of Las Vegas to figure it out.

The first of the movies we will consider is *Bugsy*, the story of the founding of Las Vegas as a mega gambling city in the 1940s. The second is *Casino,* the story of the industrialization of Las Vegas in the 1960s. The third, *Leaving Las Vegas* depicts the city as an existential locale, a setting for death in the 1990s. Taken together, they offer a kind of film history of the city as a site for gambling from the start to the present. Taken together, they all describe heroes who go to Las Vegas in search and find the individual meanings it has for their lives. One way to see these movies is as a generational saga: They are about one generation apart. The hero of *Bugsy* could have been the father of the hero of *Casino* and he, in turn, could have been the father of the hero of *Leaving Las Vegas*. Another way to see them is as a description of changing American attitudes toward ethnicity, race, and social class and unchanging American attitudes toward gender. All of these have a place in a psychoanalytic consideration of these movies. But the major focus of our discussion has to do with violence in the movies and its relationship to the fear of death and the fantasy of immortality.

All three movies begin with an intimation of violence. An early scene in *Bugsy* shows the hero, Ben, committing murder. The man he kills dies for a reason. Ben tells him that he has broken the laws of the mob by cheating on the money he pays them. The opening scene of *Casino*, that of a man being blown up in his car, makes the same essential point. The voice over tells us that this happened for a reason: some people ruined their "paradise on earth." Paradise, after all, is the place where there is no decay, no aging, no death. Death is something to be terrified of and you can avoid death by gambling. Similarly, the opening scene of *Leaving Las Vegas* is a scene of decay. As the cheerful hero collects liquor bottles from a supermarket aisle and loads them into his cart, he slips as if he is starting down a slippery slope. A generally cheerful, even manic affect pervades all three of these scenes, as if to say that death is not so bad, only a joke, only a silly mistake. All three movies set the scene for a place where death is not terrifying, only a joke, and even in the case of *Casino,* reversible.

The movies about Las Vegas tell a story. The first of them is a movie about the founding of Las Vegas: *Bugsy*. In this tale of a founding, the mythical nature of the beginning is emphasized by the mythical stature of the founder. He is the father of an idea. The film begins economically with an introduction to the heroic founder. In an early scene he is selecting clothes with exquisite taste while reciting an elocution exercise. This narcissist is also a perfectionist. He works hard on sounding and looking the perfect gentleman. His elocution exercise is ironic and will provide a leitmotif for the movie. "Twenty dwarves took turns doing handstands on the carpet." It describes lots of effort toward an absurd end. The man reciting it is making a great effort. The exercise, the movie implies, will lead to an absurd end. The suspense in the movie is what this end will be.

He goes on to meet with a businessman while his partner waits in a limousine in the street below. Ben tells the man that he knows the man has been cheating on him in a business deal, gives the man a gift of some shirts, which he calls "the shirt off my back," and shoots him dead. This scene makes death absurd. By giving him something new and beautiful to wear before he kills him, Ben mocks the man he kills and reduces the dignity and seriousness of death itself. He introduces a split in our perception of death in the movie. It is serious, but at the same time, not serious, irreversible, yet playfully reversible. The man could wear the ties and shirt to his grave.

One of Ben's partners remarks that he could have relied on a hit man they had hired to do the killing. His other partner replies that Ben has never really cared about money, implying that he is doing the killing himself for the pleasure of it. The hero is violent, yet he is playing by a set of rules of honor. This is a murder, but it is also a rule-governed act of justice. The rules say that if you cheat a business partner, the wages of that sin is death. The scene establishes the hero's likeness to us—the audience that believes it is wrong to kill—by implying that the hero has a different rule, yet is also impulse ridden, not just tough as his partners are tough and not just venial as his partners are venial.

If Ben is not just motivated by money, what does he care about? We know that he cares about family and values his role as the provider for his family when he tenderly asks his children what presents they want when he comes back from a trip. On the train he agrees when a friend asks him for money to pay off investigators. Ben gives him the money and advises him to: "Bend your knees when you jump from the train." Again, money and life are equated. If a person cheats or loses or gets into debt he cannot repay, the code of honor demands his death in return.

Death in this movie is not the result of natural processes, not the outcome of rage or aggression, but a chip in the game of life, a counter to be paid for a debt.

Ben's train is met by his friend the Hollywood star. He watches a tough guy scene being filmed. He asks a starlet to let him light her cigarette; his friend tells him: "That's Virginia Hill." He tells Ben that she is the girlfriend of a very jealous mobster. She repeats the warning. When he plays with her he plays with fire. He makes an overture, she asks him if he will divorce; he says that he is loyal to his wife; she blows him off. He is motivated also by sexual desire. This moment contrasts with an earlier scene in which he meets a woman in an elevator, seduces and abandons her. She is just a passing moment, a trifle, to him. Women may tempt him sexually, but his family comes first. He still values being a husband and father even though he has moved far away from his family. But Virginia is a tough woman, independent and fiery and experienced. She wants security. We can see that he will have to give up a lot to get her.

In a parallel scene, his friend Georgie shows him celebrity houses. Ben demands to go into one he fancies. Georgie tells him that it belongs to Lawrence Tibbet, an early Hollywood opera star. When Tibbet calls him Bugsy, Ben gently but sternly reproves him for calling him a bug, buys his house, and gives him keys to a bungalow at the hotel. Ben insists on his name, Benjamin, a name from the Old Testament. Throughout the movie there are strong and insistent reminders of his Jewishness. He speaks Yiddish with Mickey Cohen and with his old friends. He has kept his roots in Yiddish culture. The scene establishes Ben's relation to High Culture as well as his pride in his Jewish roots. He wants what the swells have, but his loyalty to a nonreligious ethnic identity is important to him. Throughout the film, the Jewish gangsters are shown having special loyalties to each other, protecting each other from their Italian partners. Ben lives on the boundary edge of the worlds of organized crime, of Jewishness, and of art as well as celebrity. The scene further establishes his impulsiveness and his proneness to violence.

Next Ben sets himself up in business. Ben goes to see Jack, the current boss of L.A., and offers him a deal. Jack will now work for Ben, Meyer Lansky, and Lucky Luciano. When Jack protests, Ben offers him only one alternative: He can kill Ben. Jack caves in, then agrees, but consoles his guys by saying that they will eventually kill him. The scene establishes the identity of the men in the smoke-filled room and the power they have to intimidate even the toughest opponents. It also reinforces the theme of death as a part of business, equating money with life and loss of money with death. This grandiose view of business is underlined in the next scene.

Having established himself in a home and in business, Ben goes out to a nightclub. His grandiosity is established when he meets an Italian count who is a friend of Mussolini. Another theme of the movie, the theme of Ben's grandiosity and passionate intensity to the point of madness, continues. He is outrageous enough to believe that he can rid the world of these dictators. Grandiosity is built into Las Vegas by its founder. The whole of Ben's life is governed by his grandiose sense of being entitled to do whatever he chooses.

Ben is in the nightclub for pleasure. He sees Virginia dancing with another man, sends her a piece of jewelry, and buys her interest. Virginia comes to his house as he is on the phone with his wife; he asks to kiss her, she says Joey would kill them, but would have to worry about which one first. Money is not only what staves off death; it is also what buys love. The obsessive theme returns: "Twenty dwarves took turns doing handstands on the carpet." Money mediates the tension between love and death. This theme echoes through all three of the movies. The women loved by the heroes are all whores. They sell love for money. In *Casino* a variant on the theme emerges. The beloved sells not only love but also children, the hero's fantasy of immortality.

Conflicting values are shown to be a source of conflicting loyalties in all three movies. In *Bugsy* this is shown in Ben's relationship with Mickey Cohen. Mickey Cohen, a Los Angeles mobster, has stolen money from Ben's partners. Ben does not kill him for this. Instead, he confronts Cohen in a steam bath. Ben gives Cohen a job in return for the restitution of money he stole from Jack. Ben is thus breaking the rules of their game: The wages of the sin of stealing from the mob is death. As in the other tense scenes of the movie he repeats "Twenty dwarves took turns doing handstands on the carpet."

Back home with Virginia, Ben taunts her about former boyfriends; she throws an ashtray at him, cutting his forehead. With the blood still wet on his face, Ben confronts Jack again, tells him he was trying to rape him by stealing from him. In contrast to his treatment of Cohen, Ben humiliates Jack, making him crawl, bark, and oink like a pig. Meanwhile Ben is still bleeding from Virginia's blow. They are both excited by Ben's sadistic humiliation of Jack. They have passionate sex.

The next scene is in an airport. Ben wants to show Virginia a place in the desert. She is too afraid to fly. The pilot says: "Let's go. Time is money." Again the movie underlines the equation between time of life and money. Ben, Virginia, and Mickey Cohen are driving in a car. They go across the desert to the tune of "Ole Buttermilk Sky." They visit one of Ben's gambling spots in Nevada. He closes it down because she thinks it is ugly. Ben quarrels with Virginia about his loyalty to his family in Scarsdale. He leaves the car; she drives off, leaving Ben and Micky walking on the road in the desert. Ben gets an idea. He opens up his world with an image of a desert. To the audience, the desert is a place of desiccation and death. To Ben the desert is a place of infinite possibility, an opening in nature. The duality of the metaphor weaves together the place of death, of skulls and skeletons, with a magical place where mirages can stand for hallucinations of all sorts, even the mirage of winning a fortune.

The Las Vegas mirage turns into Hollywood in the next scene. In another nightclub Ben talks with the countess who offers him a chance to meet Mussolini. He sees Virginia with someone else, goes across to Virginia who is with a guitarist. She leaves saying he is not divorcing his wife. He promises to do it. Micky and Ben eat breakfast, Mickey reads a story about the stool pigeon, the man who Ben gave money to on the train when he was going to Los Angeles. Ben says he's going to New York to get a divorce. Micky says he is sorry.

We next see Ben decorating his daughter's birthday cake. His partners come in and meet with him while he is still in the chefs hat he wears to decorate the cake. The partners are angry that Ben closed their gambling place in Vegas because it produced money every month, Ben tells them he plans to replace it with The Flamingo, a place for sex, romance, money, and adventure, the American dream. It will be a place where gambling is allowed, where everything is allowed. His partner Meyer Lansky says "A good place to get people's money." Ben says the casino will be beautiful because the Hoover Dam will provide enough electricity for air conditioning and lighting. Ben's manic genius has hit upon the perfect use for the gigantic new source of electrical power in the desert. The manic quality of his thinking is conveyed in a series of rapid cuts: Ben chases after Virginia by phone; Ben rushes back into the meeting; Ben chases after his angry children. Ben's mania will be translated into Las Vegas. The city will embody his brilliant idea and his madness.

Ben apologizes to Joey for taking Virginia away from him. "I know you were in love with her." Joey says "I'd never let myself fall in love with a slut like her." His wife asks Ben for a divorce; he refuses. We see him as a man torn between three loyalties: his family, his business, and his love. The whore is contrasted with the mother. All of the themes of the movie are in place.

Ben's anger frightens Virginia in a scene that sets up the reason for her later betrayal. When he returns to Los Angeles, he finds Virginia in pyjamas with a man. Ben throws him through a window in a defenestration that is a subtle castration. He doesn't believe her when Virginia insists that he is her brother. When the man proves that he is, Ben offers him a red Cadillac convertible. He uses money to make reparations for his anger.

Ben's old friend Harry Greenberg arrives. Harry is the man who ratted on Ben and his friends to the police. Ben offers him a bedroom for a nap. Harry says "If I was anywhere else I'd be dead."

Ben: "You talked."
Harry: "I talked. So what should I do?"
Ben: "Take a drive with me."

Virginia insists on coming along. Harry asks Ben about Virginia's boyfriend. He asks about Esta. He is Ben's dearest friend, his alter ego. Ben and Harry go into the woods. Ben comes back to the car. Virginia asks him what happened. The audience knows Ben has killed Harry. Ben chants to himself: "Twenty dwarves took turns doing handstands on the carpet." Ben's mantra covers his conflict. He has upheld the moral code at the cost of his best friend's life.

Ben kicks Joey to a pulp for calling Virginia a whore. Luciano and the others dance while the beating is going on. Honor is important; violence is not important. Ben sees his wife and daughters leaving him through a rain splashed restaurant window. Cutting his tie to his family echoes his killing his old friend. When his family matters less than Virginia and his friend matters less than his business associates, violence replaces order in his life. He is depicted as slowly cutting his ties to all of his love objects. Each loss is a step toward his own inner death and leaves him more dependent on his grandiosity to replace the lost objects.

Honor extends to money as well as silence. Not keeping one's word about money is punishable, but Ben is heroic in his disinterest in money. When faced with cost overruns, Ben sells his shares in the Flamingo. Meyer warns him he will wind up with nothing. Ben says "The Flamingo will be there. That's not nothing." Both Ben and Virginia are seen to be increasingly irrational, prone to tantrums, and distrustful of each other. Mickey tells Ben that Virginia has two million dollars in a numbered bank account in Switzerland. Joey insists Ben knew about Virginia's stealing. Meyer says Ben did not know about the stealing. He gets the men at the meeting to wait for the Christmas opening. If the casino succeeds, Ben will pay off, if not "I'll handle it myself."

When he gets a telephone call summoning him back to Los Angeles after the hotel's opening night fails, Ben knows he is going to be killed. Ben walks into his house, runs his screen test in which he says that a woman doesn't make a wife for a right guy. Ben is shot to death. Lansky's men take over The Flamingo. Virginia Hill is seen standing in the wind, her chiffon dress and scarf blowing behind her. A black-and-white page on the screen tells us that she returned all the missing money to Lansky within a week. Another screen tells us that she committed suicide in Austria. The final screen says that the original six million dollar investment has returned over one billion dollars in revenues by 1991. Love loses. Death wins. Money wins more. The ironic ending is actually the American dream ending. No one escapes death. The odds are always the same. No one beats them. But life in Las Vegas is about living as if one can beat the odds. The only winners are those like Lansky who accepted that and bet on death, and those like Ben who accept death.

The story of *Casino* echoes that of *Bugsy*. *Casino* traces Las Vegas' history through several decades after its founding. In *Casino*'s opening scene, the hero talks about love as trust and walks into his car. The car explodes. Flashing lights dissolve into flames with figure falling through them. While this goes on in the background, titles appear written neatly over the violence. The title sequence foreshadows the movie's theme of rationality superimposed on violence. The hero's sidekick describes the paradise they had in the desert before they fucked it up. The wife appears briefly. They represent Adam, Eve, and the Serpent in Eden. The movie will tell the story of the fall that ends in the flaming inferno that opens the movie.

The hero of *Casino* is Ace. Like Ben in *Bugsy*, he is a smart Jewish guy with a gangster look. But he is another breed. Dour, cool, calm, and calculating, he comes to Las Vegas looking to work the odds. He is not at all grandiose in the way Bugsy was. Nor is he creative. He is the continuation of Meyer Lansky's attitude: Players don't stand a chance. Everything is arranged to get the money from the people who bring it there. Romance is a dream used to promote the goal. Now Las Vegas appears in a religious light, where the religion is the worship of money: The scene is the room where the money is counted. This room, the count room, is, the voice tells us, the "Holy of holies." The reference is to the Ark of the Covenant in the ancient Hebrew Temple. The religious theme is broached, but blasphemously.

The name "Ace" was chosen for the movie although the character on which the screen version is based was called Lefty. The name "Lefty" would have referred to his body, his humanity. Ace is the name of a card, establishing his identity as part of the system, inhuman and a tool. At the same time Ace is also the winner, the highest card. In the gambling world, Ace is called "The Gold Jew." Back East, Ace is shown as working with a mobster, a criminal who is capable of violence and irrationality as well as clever thievery. It is as if the character of Bugsy was split into two people: One is the calm and rational Ace; the other is his violent and unpredictable friend, Nicky.

Ace is the fisherman who keeps the whales coming. He keeps them playing and keeps them coming back. He pretends that a heavy winner cannot get home because of weather. By the time the man has spent another night in the casino, he has lost back all that he had won. As the voice of a casino owner tells us: "We get it in the end." The voice tells us that problem in Las Vegas is that everyone knows that lots of money is being circulated, and everyone wants some. In Vegas, everybody has to watch everybody else to see that they are not being cheated or robbed. Ace is constantly watching for cheating. He is clearly honest with his bosses, even though he is playing the casino game. This man has no life outside of his work. He is the ultimate nerd. In this, he is the antithesis of Bugsy. He is a professional, unimaginative, obsessional, cold.

Once Ace is established in Las Vegas as the best casino manager, he looks around for more. The scene of his choosing a lover is completely in character for him. A glamorous blond woman who is betting for a gambler wins a lot of money for him while skimming. The man who is using her to bet for him refuses to give her a share of the winnings, pointing out that she has already taken some of it off the table. She gets even with him by throwing all his winnings to the crowd. Ace sees her and becomes fascinated. She is a hustler, but with a code. For her, love is a business. She tips the guys who park the cars. She knows how to control everyone. She is slick and powerful, but sticks to a code of understanding other people's rights and needs. She is fair. Yet she has a tragic flaw as well. She has a relationship with a man who takes her money: a pimp. With everyone else, she can be tough. With him she is weak. Needing to pay money for love is a pathetic weakness she shares with Ace.

In a hilarious scene, a counterpart to the love between Ace and Geri, Nicky, Ace's old buddy from back East, is shown with his wife going through customs. Nicky's luggage is being searched. Next, they are at home, at the kitchen table. Nicky's wife is shaking diamonds out of her hairdo, having outwitted the customs agents. She and Nicky are clearly a team in crime. Having established his family values, Nicky is next seen in Vegas strong-arming bookies; then he appears watching his son at Little League. The contrast is clear: He is a family man, but will do anything to anyone outside his family.

Next we see Ace supervising the crushing of a cheater's hand in his casino. He then proposes tenderly to Geri, the tall blonde beauty, tells her that he knows she does not love him, and that what he wants from her is a family. Ace is like his friend Nicky in that they both share an ethic of family as the ultimate value. The wedding scene shocks us twice. First, we see the bride wearing a veil like a nun; then we see that she wears it over a mini-dress. In this scene, religious values are presented and mocked. The bride has kept her part of the bargain; she has a baby already. Ace keeps his bargain; she comes home to a surprise wedding gift of an elegant house and lavish wardrobe. He even accepts her telephone call to her lover during the wedding party. He overlooks her alcoholism. He forgives anything and gives everything in exchange for a family. Like Ben in *Bugsy*, Ace chooses a woman who is a prostitute. Also like Ben, he trusts his wife, showing her where he keeps his money and giving her exclusive access to it while the sound track plays the music of "What a Difference a Day Makes."

Nicky is shown to be stopped from going into the casinos because he has a criminal record. By the 1960s the gambling in Las Vegas is an industry under government regulation. No longer an unequivocally mob operation, the casinos are at least nominally lawful businesses. Frustrated, Nicky set up a ring that begins a series of robberies. As a cover and for the pleasure of it, he invests in a restaurant that will be outside the casinos and therefore accessible to people like him who are not allowed in the casinos because of their criminal records. Despite his devotion to his family he begins to date showgirls. We see one of them giving Nicky a blowjob in the parking lot. He chews out an employee who gambled instead of paying for his home heating. In a scene very like that of Ben in his chefs hat, Nicky makes his son pancakes. In the very next scene he tortures to death a man who killed a member of their mob against orders. He has his code and he lives by it. Even though he is a much tougher and less sympathetic character than Ace in some ways, he has a kind of liveliness and energy that could make him attractive to a woman like Geri.

We next see Geri asking Ace for twenty-five thousand dollars. She will not tell him what she wants it for. He refuses but accepts that she will go to the bank vault in Los Angeles and take it. He gets Nicky to follow her. She gives the money to her lover. Nicky beats the lover in front of her. She screams. She is clearly excited by Nicky's feverish punishment. Nicky asks her what she expects, he tells her to take care of herself, they clinch. Nicky has the romantic violence Geri saw in her former lover. Despite her initial aggressiveness, she now appears to be a masochist.

By contrast, in the next dramatic scene Ace is in his office, dressed as elegantly as he always is. This time he is in shades of powder blue with pale blue shoes to match. But he is without pants. His outfit is ridiculous because he tries too hard. This is a man without humor or a sense of proportion. He takes a call, asks his receptionist to hold the visitor and puts on a perfectly matching pair of perfectly pressed trousers. He is dressed in the best, groomed like a racehorse, perfectly self satisfied. His visitor is the sheriff. He has come to ask Ace to rehire his friend. Ace refuses to rehire the incompetent employee. The sheriff tells him that this is his town and he will run Ace out of it. Ace is now overconfident and overextended, as much in thrall to his grandiosity as Ben was to his.

Ace's grandiosity breeds trouble on all sides. His wife takes pills, drinks, and cries. He screams at her. She promises to try to reform. The bosses complain that their skim from the casino is being skimmed by someone else. Ace gives an interview saying that he is the real boss of the casino. The sheriff gets the gambling board to kick Ace out of town—retaliating for Ace's firing of his brother-in-law. Ace's life is spinning out of control.

The bosses decide that he should walk away. Desperate to ward off loss of status, Ace meets with Nicky, who tells Ace he is the mob guy there and Ace is only his cover. Nicky leaves Ace in the dust of the desert. The scene repeats that in *Bugsy*, when his girlfriend Virginia leaves Ben in the desert. She left Ben to die in that scene and in the eventual ending of the story. Is the parallel to continue? Is Nicky going to leave Ace to die?

Nicky makes his move. He enters the casino even though he knows that his presence could cost Ace and the casino to lose their license. He fights. Like the sheriff, he makes anti-Semitic comments. He is attacking Ace in his career and in his identity. Ace's marriage is breaking up at the same time. Geri sues for divorce and goes back to her lover, taking her child with her. She calls Nicky to get help. Nicky goes to Ace, sits in his car and hears "You can go your own way" on the car radio. These scenes show Ace losing his tenuous relations to people just as Ben lost his.

Ace gets a call from Geri saying that she wants to come back. She tells him that she spent some of his money. He asks: "What's the number?" She tells him it is twenty-five thousand dollars. He says: "More I couldn't live with." His obsessional interest in the amount of the money is all that matters. Neither one of them talk about disappointment or betrayal. It might as well have been a suburban shopping spree rather than an attempt to flee with a lover. They talk it over in a glamourous restaurant. Ace doubts her accounts of what she could have spent on suits or her lover. Ace, realizing that she is relating to him as she did to the men who paid for her company when he met her, denies what he sees. He says that he is not a John; he expresses his anguish by berating her about money. By saying that he is not a John, he is denying what he accuses himself of being. He is a person who trades money in the hope of getting love in exchange. The realization is his final loss.

Unlike Ben, however, he retains his connection to his child, so that he is not totally at the mercy of his own grandiosity. When Geri leaves, Ace throws money at her, gives her the car keys, but refuses her the child. He will give her money and the things money can buy, but he wants his family. She gets in her car, leaving their child behind. She comes back; she sleeps in his bed. He sends their child to school. He then gives wife a beeper, telling her that he needs to be in touch with her at all times. He tightens his control.

Geri goes to Nicky, asks for someone to help her get the jewelry out of their bank vault. Nicky agrees to do that. She says she could have taken Ace's child to Europe. Nicky says "That's one thing you don't do. You don't take a guy's kid." Geri does not know the code both Ace and Nicky live by. She does not understand the absolute value of family to them. Geri weeps. "He scares the shit out of me. I never know what he's gonna do." The scene resolves into love making between Geri and Nicky. The song lyrics on the soundtrack go: "My only sin was I loved you much too much."

The love scene in the motel is followed by a scene in the boss's home. Rumors have spread. The courier who carries the skim to Kansas City lies, telling the boss that Nicky isn't sleeping with Ace's wife. Cocaine sniffing and random murder establish an atmosphere of menace. The courier is reporting back to Nicky: "He asked me again about you and the Jew's wife." They talk outdoors, hiding their faces behind handkerchiefs. They discuss killing "the Jew." Now Ace's ethnicity is that of the outsider. The Italians have a loyalty to each other deeper than the friendship between Ace and Nicky. The scene echoes that in *Bugsy* in which Meyer Lansky vouches for Ben Siegel when the Italian partners refuse him credit. Both movies make the point of ethnic loyalty within the larger organization. The loyalty to one's own ethnic group within an overarching loyalty is an American ethic first noted by De Toqueville.

As was the case with *Bugsy*, almost all of the major characters are dead by the end of the movie. Ace's voice tell us: "Geri died with bikers in L.A. They gave her a hot dose. In the end all she had left was thirty-six thousand dollars in mint condition coins." The connection between death and money could not be made more clear. Nicky is shown beaten almost to death, but buried while still breathing. Ace turns out to have survived the bombing. But the Tangiers casino and hotel was exploded. After the Tangiers, the sound track tells us, it was all Disneyland. After the Teamsters got knocked out of the box, the corporations took over. Now whales could be asked for their social security number by twenty-five-year-olds. In the final moment, Ace handicaps, makes people money. In the last scene of the movie he has glasses, a pencil, a desk, knowledge. He is still a nerd, still not feeling, still surviving, but still not alive. Ace has remained an obsessional. He is the middle generation, the one who may not live himself, but is intent on passing life on to his children. In that way also he is the embodiment of the American dream.

Leaving Las Vegas takes place roughly one generation later than *Casino*. Its hero is named Ben, like the hero of *Bugsy*. We first see him in a supermarket, pushing a wire grocery cart down the aisle, loading it up with liquor bottles while the soundtrack plays "*L.A. Love Song.*" At first he looks carefree, but when he drops a bottle, he looks careless, maybe even frantic. As we watch him, we realize that this is not a man preparing for a party, this is an alcoholic preparing for a binge.

We next see Ben in a restaurant meeting one person at a table where two couples are having dinner together. He approaches one of the men, who reluctantly introduces him to the others. The men have Jewish names. Their blonde ladies do not. They are talking about movies. One blonde says that the cool thing about the movie was they use real guns in it. She introduces the theme of violent death. As they talk we see that the man Ben went up to wants to get rid of him. Ben agrees to leave when the man gives him all his cash on the promise that he'll never ask for anything again. Ben was part of this world, but makes a bargain with the devil. Like Faust, he will have pleasure now and accept death later. The bargain is made even more clearly in the next scene where Ben agrees to leave his job when his boss gives him a check on the condition that he never come back again.

The same bargain is made a third time when Ben hits on a woman in a bar, and comes on too strong because he is drunk and unpleasant. The bartender buys him a drink and asks him to never come back again. Being ejected from a bar is the last straw. We next see Ben in a supermarket, buying plastic bags. Then he is in his home, burning papers. A picture of a woman with a little boy curls and burns. Is this his wife and child? Is it himself as a child with his mother? In any case, it is his family. The scene corresponds to scenes in *Bugsy* where Ben loses his wife and children and in *Casino* where Ace loses his wife but keeps his children. Because it comes so much earlier in this movie, we understand that this is a story with no middle, just a long fall to the end. Immediately following this scene Ben gets into his car; he is leaving for Vegas.

The first image of Las Vegas is a dark traffic-filled street in front of a casino. A beautiful, seraphic-looking blond, dressed in silver walks the street. Her blouse, cut square and low across her chest and her miniskirt give her the look of a Botticelli angel or heavenly page. Ben picks her up and pays for an hour of her services, takes her back to his miserable motel, and falls asleep with her. Like Ben's Virginia and Ace's Geri, Sera is a whore. She spells her name out for him: ... S ... E ... R ... A.

Her name is the first four letters of the word seraph or angel. Sera then appears in the room of her pimp: Yuri. Yuri (You or I) berates her. She has not made enough money for him that night. He roughs her up. She bends over a table to let him cut her haunch to punish her and relieve his rage. She does this sweetly, sorrowfully and deliberately. Is she, like Geri, able to love only the man she gives money to? Is this her masochism? Or is she an angel? No mortal woman could be so selfless.

Yuri and Ben appear in the same pawnshop. Yuri is desperate to sell his jewelry, bargaining with the pawnbroker. Ben gaily accepts five hundred dollars for a 1993 Rolex Seafarer watch. In the perfect Las Vegas metaphor, time is converted into money. But Ben does not care that he is being given so little for what is worth so much. He is letting himself be abused just as Sera was letting herself be abused in the previous scene. Yuri's indignant reaction to the pawnbroker's offer of so little money for his jewelry is more like what you or I might feel. The pawnbroker who sells time for money drives a hard bargain. Ben's carelessly throwing it all away makes him like Sera, selfless. His attitude echoes that of Ben in *Bugsy* in that he does not care about what everyone else in Las Vegas cares about passionately: money.

Sera finds Ben, who asks her to dinner. She regrets that she cannot. She has to work and bring the money back to Yuri. In a confrontation in his room Yuri tells Sera never to come back. As she leaves, she sees gunmen come to kill him. He has welshed on something, perhaps on paying protection money, perhaps some other kind of deal. His watch is worth nothing. His time is up.

Sera comes back to Ben's miserable motel room to ask him to dinner. She no longer needs to work that night. They go on their first date. He can't eat, tells her about how awful his drinking gets, warns her not to expect him to be acceptable. Sera hears his warning but asks Ben to move in with her anyway. We have the sense that she is terribly lonely, terribly frightened, and determined to be with Ben. He packs his booze, leaving his clothes behind. He comes to her prepared for death, not for life.

Sera comes to the gate of her garden apartment. Lush landscaping alerts us to the middle-class status of her environment. We see her land-lady and landlord waiting for her. The camera centers on Ben passed out on the sidewalk in front of the compound, head on his suitcase. Sera defies the nasty landlady and leads Ben into her house. She gives him presents: new clothes, a silver hip-flask. He gives her all his money. In their parody wedding only the emotion is real. They give each other what they have to give. The groom is carried over the threshold. They are married, not for life, but, the silver hip-flask says, for death.

They go to a casino. They are gambling. He gets too drunk, too loud, too sloppy. They get thrown out. This is a repeat of what happened to him in Los Angeles. He is cast out once again. Sera won't give up. She takes him to her favorite inn in the desert. They drink at the pool, he drinks underwater, she pours booze on her nipples, he drinks it. In this scene she becomes liquor, an ecstatic moment of drinking peace and comfort from the breast makes even a nondrinker understand the fatal pleasure. But Sera looks the soul of innocence in this scene. She is the giving mother. But she is the mother who gives the poisoned milk of death. Life can end no other way. In the movie Ben crashes a glass table at the pool side, leaving shards of broken glass where it can cut the bare feet of the bathers. The landlady cleans it up, refuses payment, and asks them to leave and never come back. Ben has been thrown out a second time in Las Vegas.

Ben and Sera are driving back to Las Vegas. Sera goes to work, Ben goes gambling, gets drunk, and brings a hooker home to Sera's house. Sera comes home. The hooker is telling him that he gets her hot, giving him the lines Sera gives her customers. Sera cries and throws him out. He is out for the third time in Las Vegas. Sera then picks up a gang of drunken young men, full of menace. She gets gang-raped and beaten, bruised and robbed. Ben is alone, Sera searches for him. He calls when she is waiting in her pale green, sterile room. She goes to him and Ben agrees to go with her. In a death scene she stays with him until he drinks himself literally to death, keeping him company for his last hours.

DISCUSSION

Bugsy, Casino, and *Leaving Las Vegas* are three movies about violent death. By the violence of the deaths of the characters in these movies, the audience is to understand death as the result of people's malevolence and/or self destructiveness. Like all movies that depict violent death, these movies are strangely comforting. Death is not something that happens to everyone as a result of natural processes, these movies tell us. Death is sudden, unexpected, and going to happen only to people who somehow deserve it. This leaves people the hope that immortality is somehow available for those who have luck, for the elect. The elect behave well because they are the elect. But this Protestant ethic is worshiped at the gambling table instead of in a church.

In the Las Vegas shown in these movies death and immortality are at center stage. The hope of life everlasting is conveyed by the lights that never go out as the gamblers search to beat the odds. Death is represented by the idea that in the end the casino always wins. Cheating is the prime crime, enforced by the casino. Death is the wages of the sin of cheating. This is the ethic of the mob presented in the opening scenes of *Bugsy*, depicted in the early scene in *Casino* where Ace has the cheater's hand smashed and the cheater accepts that as just, and shown in *Leaving Las Vegas* when Yuri is killed for not having met his commitment.

The heroes of all three movies have accepted death. They are the ones who cannot be intimidated because they are ready for it and expect that it will happen to them. Ben Siegel, the hero of *Bugsy*, goes willingly to his death at the end of the movie. He has no fear, no bitterness. He does not expect any reprieve, nor does he try to get out of being killed by repaying the money Virginia has stolen. The hero of *Casino*, Ace, is not perturbed by having his car bombed. He makes no gesture of retaliation. He accepts what happens. But even before the car explosion, he has shown his wife Geri what to do in case he is kidnaped and how to pay ransom for him. He makes these arrangements in a matter-of-fact way. Life is dangerous, so you prepare the best you can. The extreme form of acceptance of death is shown in *Leaving Las Vegas* when Ben plans his own death and commits a long, slow suicide with no reprieve. It is just by their acceptance of death that all of these men become heroes. Like the cowboys of earlier Westerns, these men are willing to die. They are not the Las Vegas gamblers trying to cheat death, but men who stand up and live until they die, never allowing fear to weaken them.

The currency of Las Vegas is money and sex. The women all start out working at sex work. Taking the three movies in sequence, the hero's woman becomes more clearly a hooker and becomes the ultimate cause of the hero's death. All three heroines in these movies are hookers. The man chooses a hooker to link money to sex. After the mother and before the angel of death, each of the heros chooses as the lover a woman who trades sex for money. The lure of the woman who sells sex in the context of Las Vegas is that you can buy life. This is clearest with Ace, who marries his lover in exchange for a continuation of his life: children.

Paying for sex is gaining power. If you pay for it, you are powerful, you are in command. If you buy a woman, you are not dependent on her wanting you. The only woman before whom a man can be powerful and not dependent is the whore. Passivity is death. The alternative to buying it is taking it, forcing by violence. This is emphasized in a fourth movie about Las Vegas, *Showgirls*. In that movie all of the sex is in exchange for money except one scene where the woman wants the man and then he rapes her. The point is that the man is not passive, not the victim, not dead.

Freud (1912) suggests that myths and stories about the woman in a man's life shed light on man's attitude toward death. He discusses stories involving choosing between three boxes. In these stories, the man must choose between three boxes: One is gold; one is silver; one is lead. The correct choice, the one that wins the chooser the hand of the princess in marriage, is the lead box. Why lead, asks Freud. Because the golden box represents the mother of infancy, the most valuable woman in a man's life. The silver, Freud tells us represents the lover, the Goddess of Love. But the third box, that of lead, represents the Goddess of Death. She is related to the Great Mother Goddess of the east. She is the destroyer as well as the creator. In western mythology the goddess is simply mother. But the myths bring in the three faces of the goddess so that she is won only when man accepts death as the inevitable consequence of birth and love. The myth of Las Vegas is that one can beat the odds. All three of these movies end with the hero's acceptance of not beating the odds, with his acceptance of death. For Bugsy, it is the acceptance of going back to Los Angeles to be killed for having cheated on his partners. For Ace, it is acceptance of the threat to his life by having his car blown up. For Ben, it is the consequence of having lost the picture of his family. All of the heroes accept their death, even walk toward it knowingly. This allows the death to have the heroic quality that the gamblers in Las Vegas feel if they accept the odds, know they will lose and choose to play anyway.

Gender and race are given only the most cursory treatment in all three of these movies. All have a hero, not a heroine; all have no non-White characters. All expect the viewer to identify with the white male protagonist as Everyman. Children are depicted as the objects of their parents' adoration, but not as people with needs or desires of their own. All of these movies see the problem of death as so overriding that it overcomes any differences between people. Since we all die, we are all interested in the passage to death.

In *Leaving Las Vegas*, the early scene in the restaurant is the only scene in which Jewish ethnicity is even hinted at. In *Bugsy*, Ben Siegel joked with his friends in Yiddish and was loyal to and got loyalty from the Jewish partners above and beyond what he got from or gave to his Italian partners. In *Casino*, Ace Rosenthal was not shown to have any special ethnic loyalty to Jews, but when the chips were down his partners called him "the Jew." Ben, whose last name we never learn, has no special ties or loyalties to Jews. He only comes from a Jewish world. Ben Seigel left his Jewish family for a non-Jewish woman. Ace Rosenthal married a non-Jewish woman. Neither Ben's wife nor Ace's understood their codes of honor, and both betrayed their husbands in ways that violated that code. In *Leaving Las Vegas*, Ben's family is shown only in a photo that he burns when he is leaving his home. He will not marry his lover, but she wears a black cross on a black cord around her neck. Not only is she blond, she is labeled by the cross as someone who wants to be recognized as a Christian. If she is Christian, she is the angel of mercy, the transporter of life into death, but death as the promise of eternal life.

All three of these movies were made independently of each other. In this article we have treated them as if they had been a trilogy. The reason for this is that they cover the time span of the birth, growth, and industrialization of Las Vegas to the present day. Together they give a chronological picture of Hollywood's relationship to Las Vegas and the evolution of the American Dream as well as that of the Western. Most important, they show the particular relation between gambling and death that has formed the need for a Las Vegas, the expansion of it, and the evolution of it from a place for the hope of life to the place for the acceptance of death. Las Vegas movies show that the only winners are those who accept the necessity of death, give up the dream of beating the odds, and choose to set the odds for others to lose. In this way, they illustrate Freud's tale of three caskets and elevate it to the ultimate fable.

REFERENCE

FREUD, S. (1912). The Theme of the Three Caskets. *Standard Edition* 12: 289–301.

****
****

Original publication of preceding chapter:

RICHARDS, A.K. & RICHARDS, A.D. (1997). Gambling, Death, And Violence: Hollywood Looks At Las Vegas. *Psychoanalytic Review* 84:769–788.

Munich—The Movie

*M*unich made a great splash for a moment. It drew criticism from both the Israeli side and the partisans of Black September. It angered Jews who saw it as a call for a return to the pre-Holocaust Jewish pattern of being too holy to defend themselves. It angered Arabs who saw it as a movie where the Jews always killed righteously while the Arabs were shown killing innocent civilians. The film buffs saw it as gratuitously violent, the movie goers saw it as too preachy. No movie that irritates so many can be one-sided. The very controversy may mean that the film serves as a sort of blank screen on which the audience can project its own prejudices or it may mean that both sides are presented in such a balance that the viewer matches the ideas in the film to his or her own preconceptions, or yet again, it may mean that the film presents the ambivalences and defects of the compromise formations that allow action so as to expose the inevitable costs of any compromise.

The advertising for this movie makes clear the macho intent. It is about guns and desperation. But the title makes unclear what the macho picture says about the violence it shows. Munich means different things to different generations. Historians recall the Munich *putch* when Hitler came to power in a Germany still reeling from economic depression caused by the enormous revenge in the form of reparations demanded by the winners of World War 1. They believe that the punitive vengeful peace agreements that brought Germany to poverty in the 1920s and 30s led to despair and vengeful hatred for the European powers that imposed it. For a generation that remembers World War 11 calling the picture *Munich* calls up the image of Chamberlain giving Czechoslovakia up to the Nazis in exchange for "Peace in our time." The deal was notoriously bad. Compromising with the Nazis destroyed and maimed; it did not promote peace anywhere for any time. Far from buying peace, capitulation led to a war in which all of Europe grew weaker as Germany built planes, tanks, bombs and guns with which to destroy European governments. It brought the world perilously close to destruction and ended up costing the lives of millions, the destruction of the Jewish culture in Europe and the brutalizing of a whole generation of young soldiers. Vengeance clearly did not work; neither did giving in to the aggressive threat. For a younger generation *Munich* calls up the images on television of the horrific murders of Israeli athletes by a band of Palestinian assassins. And the movie takes these stories to a new generation by showing the story of the Israeli response to the murders of their athletes. What the movie looks like to a psychoanalyst is affected strongly by the memory of Zionism as a political response to the Dreyfus case in France. The response of Theodore Herzl to this case in which a very patriotic French Jew was accused and wrongly convicted of collaborating with the Germans who were enemies of the French at that time was to theorize that the only way the Jewish people could live in the world was to have a state of their own. Baron Rothschild, a French Jew, began sending money to support the pioneering Jews who started agricultural production in Palestine at the end of the nineteenth century. Other French Jews and non-Jews rallied to Dreyfus' defense, but, in the end, it was only his own brother who got him a pardon and saved his life. The crucial importance of family and the secondary importance of national ties became clear to Jews.

At the same time the Dreyfus case exposed the very weak bonds of patriotism in a land where one is an outsider, an immigrant, an "other." All of this background becomes part of the film as it unfolds in the constant juxtaposition of family loyalty and political process. Beginning with a montage of the names of European and Middle Eastern cities deeply affected by World War II, the title shot of the word Munich evokes this history. It goes from there to the filigree iron gates in shadowy darkness. Athletes carrying gym bags meet a group of American athletes who have been out in the beer halls after curfew. The Americans help the others over the fence and into the compound. As the "athletes" enter a dormitory, they strip off their gym suits, take machine guns out of their "gym bags," put their arms around each other, hug each other and push into a dormitory room where an older man is slicing bread for toast. The terrorists are ready to kill; the athletes are living like a family in a dormitory where they want to do ordinary things like eat toast. This contrast introduces what will be the major theme of the movie, contrasting family loving care with murderous terrorism. Irony appears when one of the victims uses that bread knife to defend himself by killing one of the assailants.

A television broadcast cut into the kidnapping scene informs the audience that we are at the "Peace Olympics" at the Olympic Village in Munich in 1972. We see Israelis watching in horror on a TV in a coffee bar, and we cut to Arabs cheering in front of a TV in a village square. We see the world watch in horror and the German army and police attempt to appease the Black September, the Arab group that claims responsibility for the kidnapping and massacre. Appeasement has the same outcome that it had when Chamberlain used it; appeasement whets the appetite for death. We see the kidnappers kill their bound and defenseless victims. They use machine guns and grenades to destroy them. Scenes of the massacre are intercut with scenes of the revenge throughout the movie. The rest of the movie deals with the horrific experience and how the Israelis react to it.

A young couple watches the TV coverage of a false hope that the athletes were rescued and then the pictures of the dead as they had looked when they were going to the Olympics only a few days earlier. Intercut with the pictures of the athletes are photographs of the leaders of Black September. The young couple cry. The pregnant wife voices her fear for her husband: he is Mossad. Golda Meir, the prime minister of Israel at the time appears at a meeting where the pictures of the terrorist leaders are displayed. She likens the deaths to those of Jews in Germany thirty years earlier. Bitterly, she says that the Olympic games are going on—the world is playing, no one cares. This time she will not depend on world opinion. She chooses revenge on the terrorists. One of the men at the meeting demurs; they have already bombed Palestinian refugee camps where the terrorist have their bases. Sixty people have been killed. Meir takes the responsibility for the new targeted reprisal on herself. She is the military leader; she chooses revenge. We find out that Avner, the young expectant husband has been chosen for the job when he is escorted into a car and driven to a meeting with the prime minister, generals of the army and served a cup of coffee in a delicate gold banded china cup by the Prime Minister herself. She hugs him, recalls his heroic father and asks him to take part in a plan that will take him away from his family for years in which he will not know his unborn child. At the same time she reminds him of the importance of family. She describes her own choice not to attend the funerals of the slain athletes because she chose to attend that of her sister instead. As he makes his choice, Avner makes love to his wife, accepts her bitterness at his not being there for the birth and accepts her statement that she will go along with this "Until I don't." The irony of family values preventing the Prime Minister from attending a state funeral while asking a young father to abjure being at his child's birth embitters the scene. Avner walks along the beautiful boardwalk on the Tel Aviv shore while children play and adults stroll in the sun. His boss in the secret service feeds him baklava, an Arab sweet, and tells him that he will have backup but he will be the killer of the eleven men who started Black September and planned the Munich massacre. He agrees. Ironically this lovely country and peaceful scene is to be protected by leaving it and killing the people who plan its destruction. On the plane to Europe where the terrorists live and are to be killed Avner sees in his mind the terrorists and how they killed the first hostages who tried to resist or get away from them. He takes off his wedding ring. He has chosen country over family.

Yet the country becomes his family as he gets the money for his team out of a safe deposit box, and provides for them by cooking—they will eat as a family. But they introduce themselves to each other not by name but by the job they will do in the team. A dignified older man is an antiques dealer. He will forge the documents they need; a middle aged serious looking man is the cleanup person. He will make sure they leave no clues. A young curly headed boy is the bomb maker. A tall burly blond man is the driver and bodyguard. Avner explains that he learned to cook in the kibbutz. Again the ironic mixture of peaceful providing for a family contrasts with the reason they are together; they are a new family: a family of assassins. The assassins get information about the whereabouts of one of the Palestinian Black September planners. He is a poet who has translated *The Arabian Nights* into Italian. He gives a reading, saying that he is fascinated by the connection in the text between narrative and existence. This resonates with the Palestinian narrative and its advocacy of the destruction of Israel. The competing narrative of the Israelis is more like that of the beautiful wife who tells stories to prevent her destruction. The assassination team follows him, waiting while he buys milk and other groceries. As he stands in the lobby waiting for the elevator, Avner and the youngest team members come at him with guns. They ask his name, making sure they are targeting the right man. Yet even after he admits who he is they hesitate before shooting him. Their reluctance is palpable. They do not find it easy to kill a man. They do it reluctantly, not with the fury that the kidnappers displayed when they kidnapped and killed the athletes. When they do, his blood mixes with the milk spilling from the bottle he just bought. The Jewish taboo on killing is broken, the Jewish taboo on mixing milk and meat is broken. The team has just done something they recognize as taboo. Afterward they have a conversation about whether to celebrate their success and use the Passover narrative to say that the deaths of the Egyptians were sad, but were also a warning to those who would destroy the Jews.

Now in Paris, the team looks older and less hesitant. Avner strides purposefully, wears a peaked cap, introduces himself with a German name. His contact in France is Louis, a short man in both stature and conversation. He recognizes Avner as a Jew, jokes that if they start bargaining over fees, a Frenchman and a Jew, they will bargain forever. He says that he is simply in the spying business for the money; will not deal with governments; is not ideological. Avner displays his knowledge of food as they shop together in an outdoor market; Louis claims that his father knows food, but he does not. They come to an agreement. When Avner gets back to the team apartment the TV blares the news that three of the Munich kidnappers have been freed by the Germans in exchange for a plane which had been hijacked by Black September. As the television coverage shows and one team member says out loud, the Arabs have no trouble rejoicing. Killing innocent athletes does not offend their consciences. At no time in the movie do we see any Arabs showing regret.

In the next scene, the young toymaker poses as a reporter. He asks the Palestinian leader whether he has any qualms about the Munich kidnaping. Sitting in his elegant Paris apartment, sipping coffee from a gilt edged china cup similar to the one Golda Meir offered Avner, flanked by his elegantly dressed wife, the Palestinian claims that his people have been impoverished by the Jews. His wife is more outspoken. Putting on jewels carefully matched to her couture dress, she justifies the killings because the Jews have been, she says, killing her people for 25 years. Impoverished? Not judging by the way they live. Killing and oppressing her people? She is living well while her people suffer. Ironically, she and her daughter are driven in a chauffeured Mercedes in their elegant Paris neighborhood. The toymaker places a call "to his editor," meanwhile copying the model number and drawing the outline of the phone. Later he explains to the team the way he will detonate the plastic explosive in the replacement phone that they will plant in the elegant apartment. The wife and daughter enter their limousine on their way to their days' activities. The moment for calling the Palestinian spokesman has come. But the daughter runs back to the apartment and happens to pick up the phone. The team is horrified, aborts the call and waits for another opportunity. They will not willingly kill innocent bystanders. But they do kill the Black September plotter: the child's father.

Another ironic turn follows: Avner goes to Israel to sees his wife and new daughter. His mother waits outside the labor room. She reminds him that his father was not there at his birth. "No," Avner says bitterly, "He was in jail." His mother says that she is proud of what he is doing, yet in the next breath says that she no longer visits his father. The deed is for the state and pride, the man is not loved for doing it. Seeing his daughter Avner jokes that she is ugly. His wife retorts "She takes after you." The loving dialogue contains a bitter truth. He has become ugly. He tells his wife that he needs her to live in New York so that he can see her sometimes. She protests that she wants her family and his around to help her. He insists that his family made him the mess that he is. Moving on to Cyprus to eliminate their next target, the older team member congratulates him on becoming a father, and then on the death of the man they bombed in Paris: that other little girl's father. They plan to set a bomb in the bed of their target in Cyprus despite the fact that the man's room is next to that of a honeymoon couple from Israel who had to come to Cyprus to marry because Israeli law will not permit a Jew to marry a non-Jew. Avner takes the room on the other side of that man so that he can signal the team when the man goes to bed. Is he being careful with the mission or careless with his own life? When the target goes out on his balcony, chats with Avner about the noise the honeymooners make at night and offers him a pill so that he can sleep through the night he becomes a person. Avner refuses his pill but hesitates giving the signal to kill him. After he does give the signal and the explosion turns out to be much stronger than they had planned Avner helps the honeymoon couple get out of the hotel. His cleanup man has to lead him out of the hotel. The question of whether he is risking his own life unnecessarily becomes the center of the next scene. The bomb maker insists that Louis has provided much stronger explosives than and that they were mislabeled.

Back in Paris, Avner looks longingly at a display of a lavish modern kitchen in a shop window. Louis comes up behind him. Is Louis for them or against them? Louis will not allow his information to go to any government. But he offers the location of Abu Youssef, the planner of West Bank terrorism and two other important Palestinian terrorists. They are in Lebanon. Avner's boss comes to Paris. He does not want the team operating outside of Europe. The team insists: "Let us get on with our job." They will not give Louis' name up. They want to use his information for the next targets also.

The team appears in Lebanon. Now in the company of a larger force, they leap off boats, dress in women's clothes and wigs, stroll up to the guards on the dock and machine gun them to death. They run into the hotel, find the targets in their rooms, push the women they are in bed with aside, compare their pictures to their faces and kill them. The team has become a war machine. But their very success makes trouble; it is unbelievable that they could have pulled off a landing in Lebanon and a quick, faultless assassination of the three terrorists and their bodyguards themselves. It would seem to take an army to accomplish. In the next scene Louis accuses Avner. He says that he knows that Avner and his crew were not in Lebanon but the Israeli army assassinated Abu Youssef and his colleagues. Avner can neither admit that he was in Lebanon nor pretend that it was the Army which accomplished the mission. Louis says that his father who is the real head of his family spy business wants to meet Avner to find out more about him. Avner has no choice but to agree if he wants their cooperation in finding the rest of the terrorists. Again putting himself in danger, he accedes to wearing a blindfold when going out to meet the boss.

Their driver puts Louis and Avner in the middle of a French country estate. A very long table covered with a white cloth and accompanied by beautifully carved chairs is set out under the trees for a paradisaical lunch. Beautiful children crowd around, welcoming the man they expect to join them for a feast. They are politely curious and very charming. Avner smiles. Louis introduces him to his father who invites Avner to help him cook. The old man instructs him to put some meat into the sink. Avner starts to turn the tap, but the old man explains that you cannot wash the meat without spoiling the taste. Avner asks why put it in the sink. The old man says that keeps the juices from dirtying the kitchen. He shows Avner how to peel the white fat away from the red offal. He looks at Avner's hands, comparing them with his own and concluding that they both have "butcher's hands," not small enough to be real cooks. Using this metaphor he explains that he had been part of the French resistance, had seen his brothers killed and his own father and sister hanged for being in the resistance and had seen the Vichy "scum" replaced by the Gaullist "scum," the Nazis defeated, but Stalin ruling instead of Hitler and had become disenchanted with all governments. Picking unripe fruit he says that it is bitter, but if tortured by being boiled in sugar water it will become sweet. Menace is replaced by kindness; he forgives Avner for having told the Israeli army where to find the three terrorists because "You have to feed your family," but says it must not happen again.

Asked to say grace, Avner gestures as if to cross himself, but the old man tells him he does not need to do that. He asks Louis to do it instead and Louis thanks God for sending him good customers The old man says that his son and daughter are a "minotaur "and a "centaur." They are abashed. What can this mean? They are half human, half animal. Later he says that Avner could be his son but is not. He implies that he could be Jew but is not. If he were, his son and daughter would be half and half. This playfulness about identity seems intolerable to his son Louis, but the old man plays with the notion that Avner may become like him, a renegade who plays the espionage world for money for his family. Avner can lose his humanity and become half animal if he continues in the path that the Frenchman has taken. The attachment to family is like the attachment to country, it cannot be everything or the person becomes inhuman. The human condition requires balancing loyalties, evaluating options, accepting less than paradise. After bringing him back to Paris, Louis offers another name, not on his list, but working as a liaison between the Palestinians and the Russians. Avner hesitates but accepts. He is continuing the mission, just one step further. Now he goes to Athens.

In Athens the team goes to a safe house provided by Louis. As they sleep in the decrepit ruin, a footstep on the stairs alerts them. Palestinian gunmen come in. They assert at gunpoint that this is the safe house Louis provided for them. By standing down, they all feel safe. The scene foreshadows the ending of the movie and, I believe, expresses the moviemakers' conviction that standing down is the only solution to the Israeli-Palestinian conflict. The Palestinians identify themselves; the Israelis claim to be German red faction terrorists. They sleep in the same room. Avner talks with Ali, one of the Palestinians about why the Palestinians are doing this. Avner says they are Arabs and there are many places that Arabs can live. Ali says that this people will wait for their homeland as the Jews did, for 2,000 years if necessary. Avner counters that the land is just rocks and olive trees. Ali says that is what he wants for his family. He is clearly sincere and human. Talking does not solve the problem. The Israeli team goes ahead with their plan. They have leftover World War II grenades that they wire into the TV set in the hotel room of their target. But the bomb does not go off as planned. The Russian and Palestinian bodyguards wait for the man who is their liaison and the Israeli's target. He goes to his room, but nothing happens. One of the Israeli team grabs a grenade, races up to the room, throws it at the Palestinian liaison, slams the door and runs when the bomb goes off. The guards outside shoot at him as he rushes out the door of the hotel. One of them is the gentle Palestinian Ali with whom Avner had talked about homeland and what it means. Avner shoots Ali in self defense. The team gets away, leaving the concierge who had helped them behind. They throw money at him. He throws it in the street in despair. The Russians and Palestinians will kill him.

Ironically the next scene shows Avner talking with Louis as if Louis had not betrayed him by sending the Palestinians to the same "safe house" where they could have killed each other. Louis offers Avner the prize name he had sought as if to make up for having betrayed him. Avner demurs, but Louis tells him that the man is in the pay of the CIA which pays him not to hit American targets and does not inquire into which targets he hits with their money. Hearing this, Avner signs on to kill him. In London the team sights their target, but two apparently drunken Americans bump into them and prevent their getting a clear shot at him. Afterward Avner meets a beautiful woman in a bar but refuses her offer to sleep with him. He runs into the senior member of their team as he is going to his room; the older man suggests that the "drunken" Americans could be CIA or Mossad or that Mossad may be giving the CIA tips or vice-versa. Avner tells him that he is letting the mice run around in his head, accepts the older man's criticism that he is too active and warns him of the "local honey trap" in the bar. Avner goes to his room, calls his wife, hears his daughter's voice and cries. When he has a nightmare about the Munich kidnapping he goes to his friend's room, smells the beautiful young woman's perfume on his friend's doorknob, pushing open the door, he finds the naked dead body of his older team member. He howls and sobs. Saved from death himself, he cannot protect his friend and protector.

Back in Paris Louis' father warns Avner that he is also being hunted. His name and his picture are for sale. He asks him to stop, but gives him the name and picture of the young woman. The old man Avner and his team head for a train to the woman's home in Amsterdam. They lose the bomber—he cannot continue. To be a Jew is to be righteous, he says, and he is afraid that he is losing that. He is losing his soul. Avner tells him to rest—the three remaining team members will take care of avenging the oldest. They kill the woman with blow guns that had been affixed to bicycles as if they were tire pumps. They leave her naked body just as she had left their comrade naked: death for death and dishonor for dishonor. The team is exhausted. That night Avner and Steve look for Hans and find him knifed to death on the waterfront. His wallet and identification are intact.

The killing was not a robbery. They go back to find the young bomber dead, an apparent suicide, but Avner thinks that perhaps he too was killed in retaliation for their killings. He becomes paranoid, looking for bombs and traps everywhere.

Avner waits in front of a kitchen furnishings store. Louis approaches, this time with a German Shepard on a leash. He tells Avner that such things happen to bombers. They accidentally blow themselves up with their devices. Avner does not want to go on, clearly he longs for the kitchen he sees through the glass storefront, but Louis tells him that if he can kill Abu Hassan his handlers will let him go back home. The thought of that is enough to get Avner to agree. He and Steve go in blackface to a meeting where Abu and scores of other Arab men are milling about. They hesitate, a guard sees them, they kill him and run. Avner's black face somehow remains even when he gets to Israel's military airport. The young Mossad soldiers who pick him up want to shake his hand, but he looks as if he has forgotten how. He refuses to tell his handler the name of his contact. He will not give up Louis or the old man. His mother tells him that she is proud of what he did to keep the land for the Jews. She had lost her entire family in the Holocaust, prayed for a son and got him—the son she is most proud of, the son who helped restore the land. But she does not want to know what he did. He is alone with his nightmares.

Back in Brooklyn he finds his wife sitting on the steps of a brownstone with her neighbors. She runs to embrace him. He sees their daughter. They are together at last. But he cannot sleep, holds his gun at the ready, thinks he sees potential assassins when a car pulls out as he walks by holding his daughter. He calls the old man in France who calls him "Avner" rather than the cover name they had used. The old man tells him that he knows who he is but that no harm will ever come to him through the old man. Avner decides the men who are following him must be Mossad. He storms into the Israeli Consulate and screams that they have to leave him and his family alone or he will go to the newspapers with his whole story. His wife tries to calm him by making love to him, but he plays out the end of the Munich Massacre in his mind as they have intercourse. It is at this point in the film that we see the final act of the Munich Massacre. We see the Palestinians shooting the bound and unarmed athletes in cold blood. We see the horror that Avner has avenged. Love and death mingle in his mind. Avner meets his former handler Ephraim on the Brooklyn waterfront. Ephraim begs him to come back to his native land. He refuses saying that he does not believe that his mission solved anything, that there are new terrorists created every day and that war is not the answer. Ephraim plays on his feelings for his aging parents, his wish for his daughter to grow up in her own country. Avner refuses and asks Ephraim to come to dinner at his new home. Ephraim refuses. He walks away. The end titles tell us that nine of the eleven involved in Black September have been killed, including Ali Hassan Salameh. Behind the titles is a view of the twin towers.

Balancing loyalty to family as against loyalty to nation and loyalty to a piece of land, the film shows different kinds of families, nations and places. There is Avner's birth family: his father who was jailed for fighting the British and his mother who is fiercely proud that her son continues the fight for his people. There is the family he creates with his wife: a loving respite from fear and hatred. There is the Palestinian family living in luxury in Paris bemoaning the poverty of their people and the cruelty of the Israelis who have deprived them of their land. There is the French family of Louis, devoted to each other, but hating their family business of selling secrets to assassins. There is the family of Ali, the Palestinian who longs for his forefathers' olive groves. There is the family that is created to avenge the Munich Massacre: Avner and his four team members. By contrasting these families, the movie shows what Avner's choices in response to terrorism can be and what Israel and the world can choose as values against terrorism.

Avner's birth family has fallen, like the Israeli body politic, prey to internal conflict. His parents are divorced and do not speak to each other. The family of Louis has gone from fighting as partisans against the Nazis to being spies for hire, amoral and bought by the highest bidder. Ali has traded blood for olive groves, killing and being killed with no compromise acceptable. Avner's only hope and, the movie proposes—the world's best hope—is for people to build communities around their families. This may be a naive message. Families are vulnerable to terrorist attacks even when they do not retaliate. Passive resistance is a strategy that can be used against a government in which moral principles include protecting the weak and helpless. Gandhi could succeed because he was dealing with the British who believed themselves protectors of the weak, and were exhausted and decimated by two horrendous world wars, Martin Luther King could succeed because he faced a country that had fought against racism at horrendous cost in the War Between the States, and more recently the Second World War. Moreover, both the British and the American whites had fought side by side with the people they were now oppressing. There were reasons that passive resistance worked for the Indians against the British and for the blacks against the whites in the United States. The movie *Munich* makes clear that those reasons fail to hold between the Israelis and the Palestinians. The conversation between Avner and his Palestinian counterpart when they face each other for a brief truce makes this clear. In the end, the Palestinian sees the Jews as the thieves who have stolen his land and the Jew sees the Palestinians as the murderers who want to kill his people. Neither side sees itself as the power in the situation. Both see themselves as the wronged underdogs, both want justice as they see it, both want to protect what they see as rightfully theirs. The conflict in this movie is entirely political. There is no conflict between husbands and wives, none between parents and children, none between rivals for the same lover. When I wondered why such an important and beautifully photographed movie was not more widely admired, I thought of two opposing ideas: propaganda and tragedy. Taking the movie as propaganda, it seeks an end to the revenge killings of Arabs and Jews in Israel and Palestine. Maybe it fails as propaganda because it has no single message. Maybe it fails as propaganda because action fails in the movie and there is nothing and no one to cheer. In the psychoanalytic view that may reflect the idea that if splitting occurs and the other is seen as the embodiment of all that is bad, then one may see himself as all good. To have a god, one needs a devil, to have a self, one needs an other, to have a defense team, one needs an opposition. Perhaps the movie folds in on itself because it does not propose an enemy, but presents both sides as both bad and good.

If splitting does not work, the movie can be a tragedy. And perhaps it fails as art because love and hate are so totally separate; Eros and aggression are so far from each other that the story fails. The people Avner loves are good, the people he is assigned to kill are bad. He never makes the tragic mistake of loving or making love with one of the bad people. Unlike Euripides who demonstrated the tragedy of revenge and the possibility of redemption through lawfulness in the Orestiad, the makers of *Munich* do not believe in a world order of a proportion that could provide hope for the future; all they offer is the bleak New York waterfront, the scene of the World Trade Center disaster. The movie offers pity and fear, but no catharsis. In this, it fails as a tragedy. Neither dumb enough to be successful propaganda, nor brilliant enough to be great tragedy, the movie fails. One can only hope that the subject of the movie, the hope for peace between the Israelis and the Palestinians has only failed so far and still may ultimately succeed.

****
****

Original publication of preceding chapter:

RICHARDS, A.K. (2009). Review of the Movie *Munich*. Internationalpsycho-
analysis.net, Sept. 6.

http://internationalpsychoanalysis.net/2009/09/06/review-of-the-movie-
munich-by-arlene-kramer-richards

Girl Into Woman: Growing Strong
A View of *Pan's Labyrinth*

On one level the film *Pan's Labyrinth* is a political statement. Set in the 1940s, it deals with the bitter end of Spanish civil war, Basque separatism, and Franco fascism. On another level it is a fairy tale about a princess who has to accomplish three tasks to get back to the father who loves her even though he has lost her. At a third level it is a nature story about how plants and animals interact with each other and with people. But the fourth level that is about female development is the one that I would like to focus on for this evening. It is interwoven with the other levels, yet it functions as the thread that pulls them all together.

The three major female characters in the film are three ages of woman. The youngest is Ofelia, the child heroine. Next in age is Mercedes the young woman heroine; next is Ofelia's mother, survivor and bearer of new life. The fourth age is represented by the women who work in the kitchen. Each of these stages of life has its own form of heroism and each has its own weaknesses. The tension throughout is whether each of the women will survive the perils of her age and whether she will keep her own vision of who she wants to be intact. Will she live up to her ideals? Will she give up her ideals and cave in to those who threaten her life? But most of all the film is about Ofelia who appears before the titles; the visual title of the film is her image.

The film begins with sounds: wind, breathing, singing. The first image of the film is the head of a young girl; blood flows from her nose and mouth; she is dying. The film can only be a tragedy. Miraculously the blood flows backward to symbolize going backward in time. Behind this image the narrator tells the story of a fairy tale princess who decided to see the real world. The second image is a journey, a metaphor for life. In it we see Ofelia, the young girl of the first image, but now traveling with her mother in an official looking car. Ofelia reads fairy tales. Her mother suffers through the journey burdened with her pregnancy, nauseated and vomiting. She blames her symptoms on the baby being too active. Only in the fairy tales can people live without vomiting, suffering the pain of having a real living body. At this point Ofelia's living body is still intact. She chooses to live in the fairy tale world.

The fairy tale world appears in the form of rune stone, a message from the world of the past when fairy tales were true. The stone is not pretty even though it is beautiful. It is scary and yet familiar, it is uncanny. Like the stone, the faun she encounters is part of the natural world. But he does not look like a faun in nature; he looks more like Pan, the mythical, goat who stands for joy, sexuality and mischief. At first sight he scares Ofelia and the audience. Sexy is scary. That we are meant to see the faun as Pan is clear from the title of the movie, yet he is always referred to as the faun. The contradiction unsettles and frightens; Pan is uncanny. Like Pan, menstruation enters the world of a girl as both natural and unfamiliar. Throughout, the movie identifies fairy tales with nature, visually depicted as dragonflies as fairies and a mandrake root as a fetus. Ofelia enters the world of the labyrinth to find that she is now a child of the moon. The menstrual imagery continues— the fullness of the moon will bring the crucial event. The entire movie is thus set in the premenstrual part of her first menstrual cycle. The first menses is the crucial moment.

Once arrived at the end of their initial journey, mother and Ofelia are greeted by the Captain, a strict man who orders the mother into a wheelchair and scolds Ofelia for greeting him with her left hand. Patriarchy incarnate, the Captain will not allow any female initiative. He enforces passivity on the mother; he sets the rule of relating for the daughter. But the Captain also introduces her to Mercedes, a young servant woman who runs the household. When Mercedes warns Ofelia not to go into the labyrinth, she seems to be enforcing the passivity that the Captain and patriarchy demand of women. Ofelia does not heed the warning; she enters the labyrinth, thus listening to the call of her body rather than accepting social constraints that would have her deny her new sexuality. She chooses Pan over the subservient woman.

Ofelia settles in as her mother's companion and protector when she sees her mother's fetus and tells him a story to make him less active. She calms him down with a sad tale of a rose living alone on a cold hostile mountain top where no one can reach her: the story of female latency. Here again the image of the ideal woman is one who desired by others, has no sexual desire herself.

Everyone is sure that the fetus is a boy. When the doctor questions this, the Captain goes into a rage. A boy has value, initiative, desire; a girl is nothing. By a brutal scene in which the Captain kills a son and then his father, the story establishes the importance of the father-son relationship and the Captain's unfitness to have a son.

Ofelia disobeys the injunction not to go into the labyrinth; reentering it she meets Pan. By contrast with the patriarchal rules for passivity in women, the Pan requires Ofelia to undertake three tasks in order to get her heart's desire. The three tasks are parallel to the classic tasks required of the hero in many fairy tales where the hero will win the love of the princess and the kingdom by completing the tasks. The faun gives her a book in which the tasks will appear. This empowers her, taking her out of the role of the passive princess who must be won by the active male and putting her into the role of the active princess who is the only one who can save the fairy tale world by her deeds.

In Ofelia's first test she is given a party dress, an external appearance of beauty. She refuses to keep herself looking pristine, takes off the dress and follows the book's instruction that she destroy a greedy toad and get a golden key. She completes the task only to find that she and her dress are now muddy and unfit to appear at the Captain's table. Sad at disappointing her mother, she smiles when her mother tells her that the Captain is even more disappointed with her.

Ofelia's mother dies in a bloody childbirth after the Captain has killed the doctor and assigned a medical orderly to deliver the baby. Mercedes tells Ofelia that she also believed in fairies as a child, but no longer does. She soothes Ofelia with a wordless lullaby—the same song as in the opening of the movie. Mercedes tells Ofelia that having a baby is complicated. Ofelia decides that she will never have one. This refusal of motherhood contradicts what the patriarchy demands of women. It is like giving the left hand in a handshake.

At this, the faun gives her a second task. Her second task is to use the key to get a special dagger. But she must not eat anything when she is in the underworld doing her task. Fear escalates as she takes the trip into the underworld. She walks past a huge banquet displaying the tempting foods that are associated with sexual pleasure. At the head of the table sits a monster who cannot see. His eye sockets are empty: his eyes are on the plate in front of him. This uncanny image seems like the authority to whom all this pleasure belongs. It is his table. Disobeying the faun's prohibition, Ofelia eats a grape and the monster puts one eye into his empty socket.

Ofelia eats another and he puts in his second eye. Now that he can see, he comes after her. She is saved only because two of the fairies guiding her deflect the monster who eats them. The faun is furious. He tells Ofelia that she has lost her chance at immortality. The episode follows the myth of Persephone who lost her right to live with her mother by eating a persimmon when she was down in Hades. It also recalls the myths of Oedipus who put out his eyes to punish himself for killing his father and sleeping with his mother. And it recalls Odysseus feat of putting out the eye of the cyclops who ate men. By eating the forbidden grapes Ofelia is now guilty like Oedipus, separated from her mother like Persephone and barely escaped from being eaten by a monster herself.

The faun gives her a last chance. She must bring the baby to the labyrinth that night because this is the evening of the full moon. The faun takes the dagger she stole from the monster and tells her he needs a drop or two of the baby's blood. She refuses; her own blood flows when the Captain kills her. Mercedes sings her the lullaby as she dies. The bloody opening scene repeats. But in the coda the baby goes to Mercedes who can nurture him. The Captain asks her to tell his son about him and Mercedes defies the law of the patriarchy: the baby will never know who his father was. And the faun tells Ofelia that by disobeying his order to give her the blood of an innocent she has gained the right to eternal life with her mother and father.

The blood imagery goes from the blood of life oozing from the young girl at the first shot to the menstrual blood shown in the faun's book to the mother's blood in childbirth to the infant's blood Ofelia will not allow to be shed and back to her own life blood. When the faun tells her that the blood of an innocent must be shed, Ofelia's mother's blood cannot suffice. The mother has given up her innocence by marrying the Captain (who may have killed Ofelia's father.) Her blood does not qualify as the blood of an innocent.

Ofelia's refusal to hand over her brother makes hers the innocent blood. In the end Ofelia has gained true power by being true to her own moral judgement. So what is the relationship between blood, the moon and moral judgement? According to the logic of the movie, I think that it involves the advent of sexual maturity in a girl that transforms her into a menstruating woman who has the potential to bear children. It is that trans-formation that makes nature's moral imperative to continue the species an immediate issue. The movie deals with blood, the blood of new life in the childbirth scene and the blood of death many times over. For any young girl the first menses is the death of childhood innocence and the birth of womanhood. All of this takes place in the girl-woman's body regardless of the social circumstances and history of object relations in her life.

But it is the particulars of time and place in which the menses begins, the history of the particular girl and her particular family that determine whether the advent of menses is deflating as it is with the girls interviewed by Orenstein or empowering as it is in tribes where puberty rites allow girls to assume the responsibilities and pleasures of adulthood. Just as some societies empower the woman who experiences menses, some families celebrate their daughters' coming of age: just as some societies devalue women, so some families treat young girls more like the equals of their boys, but treat menstruating females as pariahs.

In the Spanish society of the 1940s as reflected in *Pan's Labyrinth,* women are valued mainly as producers of children, nurturers and cleaners. Ofelia's mother is not even given a name, she is valued as the mother by her living daughter and as the potential mother of his potential son by the Captain. Ofelia values her mother's beauty, but it is not clear that anyone else sees her as valuable in herself apart from her reproductive role. In the dinner party scene, Ofelia's mother tells her guests that the Captain had been a client of her husband's and that after her husband died, the Captain had come to her to start a relationship. The older women to whom she tells this story titter as if they inferred that the Captain had gotten rid of her husband in order to start the relationship with her. The Captain himself becomes very angry when he hears this and explains to the other women that his wife is foolish: they are not to believe what his wife's story implies. It is not to be thought that he would value her beauty so much that he would kill for her. Later the Captain tells the doctor that in the birth he is to save the baby, not the mother.

Even less valuable are the women past menopause: the women working in the kitchen. They are so valueless that no one speaks to them except through that younger woman, Mercedes. This reverses a logical order in which an older more experienced women would be likely to be the supervisor, and the younger woman would follow her instructions. But the reason the older women are less valued is clear at the end of the film when Mercedes carries the Captain's baby into the future. The young woman is still beautiful, still capable of producing babies, and nurturing them. She is a carrier of life as the Captain is the instigator of death. She is confident that she can deal with the Captain.

Being a woman entails having within one's body a secret labyrinth of power and mystery. The opening of the vagina has two sources of power: babies come out through it and pleasure comes from both ingress and egress. The film shows how the productive power is valued in a patriarchal society, while the power of pleasure is feared.

All those societies that practice female circumcision recognize the enormous power of the female genital in motivating behavior. By physically removing a girl's power to access this pleasure, they try to ensure that the women will be subservient will be motivated to do their husband's pleasure rather than their own. Similarly, Western societies strive to impose on girls a psychic alienation from their own genitals by forbidding exploration, naming and enjoyment of them. This enforcement particularly comes into conflict with the renewed interest in her genitals awakened by first menstruation. The blood is to be hidden, cleaned away as comes out of the vaginal cavity, or, preferably, absorbed away as soon as it comes down through the cervix, thus eliminating the smell as well as the sight of it. More shameful even than urine or feces, it is to be kept from social reality and even from the perceptions of the menstruating woman herself as much as possible. Young women are taught to hide their menstruation, to be ashamed of it, to be "dainty," not "bloody." I believe that this shame about their bodily function contributes in a major way to the disastrous loss of self confidence and self esteem regularly seen in young girls at the age of first menstruation. The film uses the metaphor of the labyrinth to visually display the prohibition on the vulva and vagina.

How does the patriarchal refusal to allow the young girl pride in her body come about? Greek myths deal with the power of the labyrinth. Ariadne shows Jason how to find his way out of the labyrinth. Thus she saves him from the fate of many other young Greeks. In most version of the myth, he has promised to marry her if she saves him, but after she does he reneges on his promise and in one version he marries her sister Phaedra instead. The message to the young girl is clear.

Do not give a guy instruction on how to manage your labyrinth. He will take the knowledge and use it with your sister instead of you. Sexual knowledge and open sexual desire in a woman are scorned, not rewarded. In one version, Ariadne's pride in her female knowledge is punished by a goddess who turns her into a spider. Better not to know, but if you know, better to hide it than teach it and better to hide it than to take pride in it. The movie *Pan's Labyrinth* underscores the sexual meaning of the labyrinth by connecting it with Pan, the god of sexuality. It thus brings two myths together to create new insight into the dangers of sexual life. Myths explicate the dilemmas humans face. While Freud held up the myth of Oedipus as the universal conflict, others have questioned how widely it applies. Jung was the first analyst to seriously question its universality and to propose a diverse and gender differentiated mythology as the key to human dilemmas. Kulish and Holtzman (2008) propose as the female universal myth the story of Demeter and Persephone. For them, Persephone faces the conflict between love for her mother and love for the man who takes her away from her mother and introduces her to the pleasures of the underworld: sex. They argue that Persephone resolves her conflict by eating the seeds of a pomegranate. Since she eats six seeds, she will spend six months of the year with her lover. Since she ate only six, she will spend six months with her mother. This compromise formation allows her to experience sexual love without losing her mother entirely.

I think that the Persephone myth sheds light on both the movie and the dilemma that young girls face at menarche. In the movie, Ofelia must die. She died in the opening scene. The movie only traces how she comes to die. Unlike Persephone, she cannot choose both. She chooses to save the baby and therefore loses her life to live eternally with her mother and father in heaven; she chooses to remain a daughter. That choice rings true in a Catholic Spain where remaining in a convent is a viable choice, but also rings true for some feminists, some lesbians, and some career-oriented women who choose their passion for their work over having a family. Ofelia has chosen and pays the price for her choice. This myth is another open to girls and young women. I think we need to go in a different direction than Freud in that we need to see the possibilities of more than one myth to support more than one choice.

Tolman (2006) has shown that young women in the United States still overwhelmingly believe that they are good when they do not engage in sex and bad when they do. Further, they believe that only bad girls experience desire and that to be good is to "just say no." I believe that the revulsion at menstrual blood and the demonization of female sexual desire are related. Both keep the girl away from her "labyrinth." If guilt over sexual desire and shame over the blood of fertility contribute to female depression (Jack 1991), this has clinical implications. To know that she has the power to give herself pleasure is to wean a girl from patriarchy. To know that her menstrual blood is the badge of her ability to give life is to give pride in her power. Both pleasure and power counteract depression.

So what do the identifications Ofelia makes in *Pan's Labyrinth* tell us? She can identify with several women: her mother, Mercedes, and the women of the kitchen. From the beginning she is shown refusing identification with her beloved mother when she refuses to call the Captain "father" or to show any real or pretended good feelings for him. She refuses to obey Mercedes when she warns Ofelia not to enter the labyrinth. She identifies with Pan, trusting him and accepting his help and advice. She refuses identification with both her beautiful mother and the female chorus of older women, both the kitchen workers and the society ladies invited to the dinner when she soils her beautiful dress and shoes. She refuses to identify with the abstinent self sacrificing Mercedes when she enjoys the fruit she takes from the monster's banquet table. She identifies with the lovely fairy who leads her into the labyrinth and partly identifies with the three who lead her into the monster's dinner party.

The film contrasts harsh reality with the parallel world of the fairy tale. For our patients and for women in our lives, the role of identification with fictional heroines both in fairy tales and in other art forms is crucial. Choosing to identify and partially identify with traits and values associated with real people is part of the story; choosing to identify with citizens of the fantasy world is another and, to my mind, most helpful part in constructing a self of one's own choosing, a self that feels authentic, a self that can integrate new experience without losing touch with the earlier versions of oneself.

REFERENCES

JACK, D. (1991). *Silencing the Self: Women and Depression.* Cambridge, MA: Harvard

KULISH, N. & HOLTZMAN, D. (2008). *A Story of Her Own: The Female Oedipus Complex Reexamined and Renamed.* New York: Jason Aronson.

ORENSTEIN, P. (1994). *Schoolgirls: Young Women, Self Esteem and the Confidence Gap.* New York: Doubleday.

TOLMAN, D. (2006). *Dilemmas of Desire: Teenage Girls Talk About Sexuality.* Cambridge, MA: Harvard.

****
****

Original publication of preceding chapter:

RICHARDS, A.K. (2008). Review of *Pan's Labyrinth*: "Girl Into Woman: Growing Strong" Online at:
http://internationalpsychoanalysis.net/2008/08/22/arlene-kramer-richardss-review-of-pans-labyrinth.

Matchstick Men: **Psychological Thriller and Therapeutic Paradox**

A little-noticed movie about the psychotherapy of obsessive-compulsive disorder and tics slipped by in 2003 despite a dramatic plot and a great performance in the lead role. The ironic title describes the layered plot and its various characters. Matchstick men are con artists, specialists in creating illusions and getting others to believe in them for the purpose of fleecing them of their money. The irony comes in the plot from the beginning. We see a tense man enter his immaculate house with an immaculate swimming pool outside and clean the windows. He checks his dog: a standard size bulldog which sits next to the couch in his immaculate living room. It is made of hard clean ceramic. He opens and closes doors to a count of three. His house is a con. It looks like a plush setting for a leisured life, but it is actually a hard, cold setting for a life bound by so many rigid rules that it might as well be a concrete cell. If this is a prison, what is his crime?

Called by his slick younger assistant who sounds and looks like a harried ambitious business person, our hero Roy rushes over to close the deal. In a sly pun, Roy's name echoes the french word for king. Aristotle has it that a tragedy requires that the hero start from a high place in order to have room to fall. Roy's Hollywood style house with its white furniture and window wall looking out onto a large pool fits that bill and his name confirms it. Roy leaves his elegant home and drives over to the scam. He enters an ordinary suburban house and sits at the ordinary dining room table with the middle aged husband and wife. Only his briefly flashed badge and his claim to be an FBI investigator differentiate the scene from any sales talk. Roy convinces the husband that what his wife bought was worthless. He offers the services of the FBI in catching the con men who sold her something worth far less than what she paid for it. Roy plays on the husband's eagerness to believe that he is smarter than his wife. In order to prove this, he willingly gives Roy his bank account number, his signature on a paper that allows any transactions the supposed FBI man chooses and thus gives him the means to defraud him of his entire fortune.

One important premise of the con is the idea that a woman is a gullible victim. Another is that the man is in charge of decision making. In order to feel like the smart one, the husband willingly accepts the idea that Roy plants: the wife has been conned. He is so willing to accept the idea that he does not bother to get any proof. Roy has conned him by playing on his masculine narcissism. Just as the con is completed, the woman opens a door to let in their dog. Roy becomes completely panicked. He twitches, shakes, and breathes hard. His assistant has to get him out of the house and back to his own place. Another premiss: the young take care of the old. And dogs represent animal nature, something the hero is terrified to confront. The stage is set.

In a supermarket Roy buys a carton of cigarettes and several cans of tuna fish. He notes that it is "the usual". He barely checks out the check-out lady even though she clearly indicates her interest in him. He reenters his house with all his rituals including carefully leaving his immaculate shoes at the door, checking his immaculate ceramic dog to see that his gun and money are in place inside it, and prepares an immaculate dinner: a well washed can of tuna fish, neatly opened and slid onto an immaculate plate. He uses his sink and garbage disposal to clean away all evidence of his austere dinner. He places the emptied can in a plastic bag and slides that into another plastic bag.

Interestingly, the con man hero takes medication for his mental disorder. He is shown to be completely dependent on it: when he accidentally upsets his bottle of pills into his garbage disposal, panic ensues. A desperate call to the "doctor" from whom he gets them yields worse news. Not only is he out of pills, his "doctor" has skipped town with no forwarding address. What can he do? He hides out. He tries to deal with his anxiety by cleaning the house with a toothbrush. He smokes by holding his cigarette with rubber gloves. He cleans and cleans, but nothing helps. He cannot live without these pills. His assistant rescues him by supplying the name of a psychiatrist who can prescribe for him. There is only one hitch. The psychiatrist, Dr. Harris Klein (a pun on harried and small), insists that he talk if he is to get medication. This doctor seems substantial, real, legitimate. By insisting that Roy talk about his troubles, he is following the best psychiatric practice. But our hero does not want to talk. Yet he has no choice—he needs his medication, so he agrees. He tells the psychiatrist that he developed the symptoms ten years ago. He does not like being outdoors, cannot stand dirt and has had no personal relationships for ten years. The symptoms began when he left his then pregnant wife after beating her because he thought she was two-timing him. The idea that she was conning him was unbearable. Yet Roy falsifies one part of his story. He tells Dr. Klein that he is an antiques dealer. Once again we are back to the theme of the woman as the faithful and real person, the natural person. Like the middle aged wife in the couple he conned, his wife was part of nature, pregnant she was procreating, natural, real. Losing faith in his woman caused his disaster. The con man was created when his earlier self was destroyed by the suspicion that he was being conned.

Dr. Klein tells him that he must contact his ex-wife and find out whether the pregnancy was successful. He must know whether he has a child. Meanwhile the doctor gives him pills that are even better than his old prescription. These pills are so new that the only way to get them is directly from the doctor. Calmed by the pills, Roy tries to comply with the behavioral injunction. He calls, but cannot leave a message when he reaches a recording that indicates that she is not answering her telephone. The contrast between the smooth talking con man who talked another man out of his life savings and the pathetic ex-husband unable to speak to his ex-wife even on the answering machine is a dramatic reprise. Faced with talking to the woman, he is as helpless as he was when the dog came in to the scene in which he was conning the couple to whom he represented himself as the FBI man. Since our hero is unable to make contact with his ex-wife, the doctor agrees to call for him.

In their next session, Dr. Klein tells him that he has a teenage daughter who wants to meet him even though his wife does not want anything to do with him. The idea of meeting his daughter clearly frightens him. He goes to the meeting place, but sits in his car with the windows rolled up watching high school students out on a campus. A cute, roller skating, child-woman identifies herself as his daughter, Angela. Angela appears to be his guardian angel. She inspires him to want to conceal his scamming. Much of the movie shows him gradually softening as he allows his daughter to sleep on his living room couch, order in pizza for dinner and eventually even identify with him by taking part in one of his scams.

As the film progresses, we see the hero learning to trust his daughter, gradually letting her see the money hidden in his china dog, letting her learn where he has a safe deposit box and how to use it. He is now behaving just like the husband in the first scam scene. When our hero shows his daughter where he keeps his cache of money, ironically, the money is in a china dog he keeps in his living room. The cold imitation of a dog is a container for his most cherished possession. Real live dogs frighten him. Does a china dog represent another form of the same animal, or is the china dog a denatured dog as he is a denatured man? Does the man also serve as a container stuffed with money?

His daughter prevails on him to let her run a scam-which she does in a do-it-yourself laundromat. The vision of money and cleaning or "cleaning someone out" of money recurs like a musical theme. By tempting a woman in a laundromat to share in a supposed winning lottery ticket, she plays on the gullibility of a poor person and on the large amount of money that she could supposedly get with no work. She succeeds in getting money from her even though the woman is reluctant to do anything that might be dishonest, like cashing in on someone else's lottery ticket. In a clever reversal of tactics, the daughter convinces the woman that she will be doing the daughter a favor by taking the ticket, only she can put up a little cash up front to get the ticket. Again and again the victim of the scam is someone who wants more for his money or more money than he is entitled to have.

Meanwhile, Roy's apprentice convinces him to participate in a money-laundering scam similar to the one his daughter pulls. When Roy goes out on this serious scam, the meeting is in a strip joint. The sleazy sex for money makes the perfect background for the scamming set-up. The dupe is a man who is willing to exchange British and United States money at far better than the exchange rate. Supposedly the scammers get the currency from a bank.

When he runs out of pills again, the doctor is out of town. He brings a wrapper to a pharmacy and tries to talk the pharmacist into giving him a few pills to tide him over until his doctor returns. Much to his chagrin, the pharmacist tells him that he has been taking vitamins for menopause. Yet the pills had helped him. Was this a con? He is enraged, but confronts his doctor who explains that psychotropic medications like the one he was originally taking are only marginally more effective than placebos. This statement, by the way, has not been challenged by any drug companies or their representatives since the movie came out. That scam is still being perpetrated in the real world. Yet we have seen changes in Roy. How is this possible? He has been talking to the doctor. He has been getting cured. He is participating in a talking cure. He has not been running scams. The real changes he has been making in his life are responsible for the moderation of his symptom. The doctor knows that he is not really an antiques dealer because he did not recognize the valuable antique stool in his office. Even though Roy has not told the doctor the truth as he knows it, the therapy works anyway. Can it be that it is not what is said, but the quality of the relationship that effects the cure?

In a complex scheme Roy's daughter, his doctor and his assistant scam him out of his life savings, he finds out that the "doctor" was not a real doctor and he has lost everything. The picture fast forwards to one year later. He now lives in a small apartment, is married to the clerk at the super-market who is now pregnant. He works in a carpet store where his erstwhile daughter comes in to buy a carpet that will be suitable for a family with a dog. She is clearly not afraid of the natural. She tells him that she was in on the scam but was also scammed out of her share of his savings. She is older than she appeared to be and is now living with a poor musician, but she is happy with her life.

Roy's love for his therapist, his love for his supposed daughter, and eventually his love for his wife and baby-to-be are the signs and the guarantors of his recovery. The raw aggression of beating his first wife has been overcome by the loving induced by his therapist and Angela.

Because he can love, he no longer needs to court punishment; he is able to make a real living rather than living off scams. What is notable and similar to the analytic situation is the therapeutic love that enables real love.

This movie shows a version of a therapeutic relationship cure in which the guilt and fear of his own aggression motivate a man to commit crimes which mirror the initial traumatic fear of being humiliated. Roy's initial crime was beating his pregnant wife. He beat her because he believed that she had been unfaithful to him. His rage was fueled by his imagined loss of masculine pride in inseminating a woman. Losing control of himself and enacting the rage against the unborn baby led to shame and guilt that were excruciatingly acted out in the compulsive cleaning and the phobias that kept him isolated from nature and anything natural.

For most of the movie Roy is unable to tolerate nature, yet he is able to interact successfully in the world of people. Able to inspire trust in the people he meets for the first time, he is unable to sustain deeper relationships even when he appears to be doing that with his apprentice. His apprentice ultimately betrays him as does the putative daughter he feels for and the therapist in whom he confides his shameful and guilty secret. Why does intimacy breed contempt? It appears that when he confides in others they see his self-contempt and treat him accordingly. It is the opposite of the situation in which the successful narcissist is able to inspire love in others because she loves herself. Roy inspires contempt because he holds himself in contempt. This prevents intimacy as effectively as does the narcissist's self-absorption. The paradox that opposite character traits have the same outcome is best understood, I believe, in terms of Bach's theory of fixity of point of view versus flexibility. For Bach, human interaction depends on being able to simultaneously keep in mind one's own point of view and that of the other with whom one interacts. Inter-action, in fact, is the rapid alternation of these points of view so that both participants are taken care of by the interaction. Another way of saying this is in the commentary of Rabbi Hillel, "If I am not for myself, who will be for me? But if I am only for myself, what am I? And if not now, when?"

For Bach, the therapeutic action of psychoanalytic treatment for such people depends on the capacity of the analyst to avoid interfering with the patient's insistence on his own point of view for as long as it takes for the patient to feel sufficiently satisfied that he is being heard so that he is interested in hearing the other's point of view. Is this what happens to Roy? In some ways, it is. The therapist avoids confronting Roy with his lie about being an antiques dealer until the treatment has taken effect sufficiently for Roy to have begun to want to give up scamming. If we see the scamming as a part of a complex enactment of crime and punishment with the tics and phobias as the punishment, we can take the failure to confront as a disruption of the enactment scenario. Roy commits his crime; he lies and he does not get punished. This disruption itself is thought by some analysts to be enough to change the patient's expectations and world view and allow him to give up the pathologic pattern that has routinized and destroyed the spontaneity of his world.

Whatever has happened to cause the cure, Roy has experienced it. He no longer needs the big money, big house and trophy pool that shored up his fragile sense of self worth before the therapy. What is most interesting to me about this movie is the depiction of a complicated syndrome with a narcissistic core, a set of related symptoms and a frank exposition of a theory of cure that involves being fooled. Roy's cure comes about because he was scammed.

Martin Bergmann has posited psychoanalysis as a cure by love. He asserted that the analyst presents a situation in which the patient feels loved because he is understood rather than shamed or condemned for what he believes to be shameful or bad acts. Bergmann posits love as the belief that the other is necessary and sufficient for the lover's happiness. The lover believes that being loved by the beloved is all you really need. The love recalls that of the ideal mother who loves the baby unconditionally. The analyst does not really love the patient in the sense that Bergmann understands love. The analyst does not believe that the patient is necessary for the analyst's well being. But the patient loves the analyst in that way and both sustain the illusion that the feelings are mutual. It is this illusion that is destroyed bit by bit in the course of the analytic work; the patient understands that the analyst is neither omnipotent nor omniscient. She gradually comes to believe that she can live without the relationship she has learned to trust and depend on and then learned to live without. She thus loses the illusion that the analyst is necessary to her well being. She also loses the illusion that she is necessary to the analyst—an illusion that the analyst has never encouraged. She finds her own love outside the analytic relationship when she realizes that the analyst is really not going to leave his wife for her.

The reason that analysts are so shocked and outraged when one of us fails to keep the boundaries we accept as necessary between analyst and patient is that the analyst who falls in love with the patient binds her to him in a way that negates the whole analytic process of gradual de-idealization and gradual acceptance of the inevitable loss of contact with the analyst and need to turn to others in the world for the comforts and ecstasy of loving and being loved.

Could this way of understanding the analytic process contribute to a combined classical drive-relational model of analytic work? Perhaps it reflects a logical outcome of the classical analytic model as transposed to modern American reality.

****
****

Original publication of preceding chapter:
RICHARDS, A.K. (2004). *Matchstick Men*: Psychological Thriller and Therapeutic Paradox. *The PANY Bulletin* 42(2):64–71.
(Also at:
http://internationalpsychoanalysis.net/2007/08/20/matchstick-menpsychological-thriller-and-therapeutic-paradox-by-arlene-kramer-richards)

Woman as Medusa in *Basic Instinct*

The Gorgon Medusa is a goddess of ancient origin and long duration. According to Gimbutas (1989):

*The Gorgon Medusa . . . can turn men to stone. She is capable of tak-
ing the breath away . . . a potent Goddess dealing with life and death,
not the later Indo-European monster to be slain by heroes such as
Perseus. she is linked with Artemis. Artemis and Hecate are one, a
lunar Goddess of the life cycle with two aspects: one, standing at the
beginning of the cycle, the other at the end: one young, pure and beautiful, connected with young life, and the other gruesome, connected
with death. . . . Hekate is described as traveling above graveyards
with her hounds, collecting poison and then mixing deadly potions.
She is a remorseless killer appeased only by bloody sacrifices. Her
eerie howl conveys the presence of death.*

*The Gorgon lived throughout ancient Greece. Her hideous fea-
tures—lolling tongue, projecting teeth, and writhing snakes for hair—
were believed to be protection against the Evil Eye. As a prophylactic
mask, the Gorgon was depicted . . . with snakes emerging horizontally out of her head: she is girdled by two snakes with hissing opposed
heads exuding powerful energy* [pp. 207–209].

Basic Instinct is a movie that promulgates a hateful message with such
artful means that it provoked me to hate myself for loving it. It reminds
me of seeing *Triumph of the Will* or *Intolerance* or *Day of the Locust* in
that regard. It is clearly a part of the battle against women that Susan
Faludi describes in *Backlash*. The story of the movie is a relentless attack
on women. Educated women, this movie tells us, are dangerous, blood-
thirsty lesbians. Even the ones who seem to love men are at least unethical and possibly murderous. The most attractive and openly sexual ones
like Catherine, are the most alluring and the most deadly. Powerful women
and women who achieve things, like writing books or getting a degree in
psychology, are the worst. Women who are older than 30 or overweight
are not worth thinking about. Women are the enemy, and men who are
attracted to them are doomed. Even the friends of men who are attracted
to them are doomed.

Basic Instinct signals its intent with its opening titles. The words are shown over flesh; muscles ripple under skin. The flesh could be male, female, or both. The flesh, seen behind print, teasingly maintains a current of excitement under the rational listing of the movie's title, writer, stars, and director. This device alerts the audience to the importance of words and names in the rest of the movie. The title sequence portends an old-fashioned morality tale; it promises a rational examination of the weaknesses of the flesh. Later, the hero will fall asleep in front of an image of the Medusa. *Basic Instinct* is about woman as Gorgon.

The camera zooms from the opening shot of a door to a mirror reflecting a couple having intercourse. The contrast between the titles and the flesh behind them is repeated in the contrast between the square furniture and the softly curved flesh of the sexual partners. The camera comes on a primal scene as the sexual partners grapple with each other. The woman on top ties the man's hands and plunges an ice pick into him again and again. Her blonde head is shown only from the rear, although portions of her body are seen from the front. Faceless, generic, the woman on top is dangerous, whoever she is. *Basic Instinct* evokes primal fear of the vulva, the Medusa that turns man into stone.

The second scene shows two investigators riding to the scene of the crime, talking with unquestioning loyalty and compradeship like the hero and sidekick of countless westerns. Their camaraderie contrasts dramatically with the murder scene with its depiction of the danger for a man of intimacy with a woman. The ethos of the picture is established by the nicknames the buddies have for each other. The hero, Nick, is called "Hoss" by his sidekick, who calls him "Cowboy." Partners immortalized in countless westerns reverse roles here. While Gene Autry and Roy Rogers loved their horses, they were clearly on top of them. The hero of this movie is a "Hoss" who needs a rider. The rider can be the cowboy, his friend, or the rider can be the woman on top, the lethal woman of the opening scene. The battle between the forces of good and evil is set in motion. The good guys have nothing to do with women or at least don't value the women.

The buddies arrive at the scene of the crime, a bedroom now full of policemen. Despite the situation, tension is lowered. The buddies stop to admire the victim's Picasso, a sign of wealth, culture, and power. The hero points out the commanding officer as loyal to the mayor, a woman. The guy from the mayor's office threatens the hero, warning the audience about men who are loyal to women.

The guys discuss the murder. Blood all over the sheets is assumed to be that of the victim. None of the detectives even thinks that the blood could be menstrual fluid, even though that is the most common cause of bloody sheets. The blood the woman leaves on the sheets is denied. By contrast, the eerily illuminated semen shown all over the sheets is admired by all as the emission of a powerful man. At no time do the detectives consider that the crime could have been committed by a man. No one thinks it could have been a homosexual partner or a jealous husband or lover. Instead, the detectives tell each other what kind of woman could have done this.

Someone suggests that the housekeeper may be the culprit. Another refutes this with the information that the housekeeper is 52 years old and weighs over 200 pounds. This immediately disqualifies her from having had a sexual encounter with the dead man. After all, the guy remarks, the corpse had no bruises. The implication is that, if the man had sex with such a fat woman, he would be bruised. Since no fat woman could have sex, only a thin, attractive woman could possibly have done it. A later scene shows a plump, middle-aged Hispanic woman working as a maid. She, like the housekeeper, is not a suspect. Later, a plump policewoman helps the buddies. The good woman is a sexually unattractive one. Cowboy and Hoss visit the woman who was the girlfriend of the murder victim and the last person he was seen with in public, a Miss Catherine Trammell. Her name has several resonances. Her last name means ensnare. Her initials are C.T., a euphemism for cunt and for "cock teaser." Her first name, Catherine, is that of the shrew in Shakespeare's *Taming of the Shrew.* Unlike Shakespeare's heroine, who is called Kate by the man who tames her, this Catherine is called by her full name throughout the movie. She gets respect. Her name also associates her with Catherine the Great, Empress of Russia and dangerously domineering. By contrast, the hero is called only by nicknames, and his name, as if to underscore the point, is Nick. At a later stage in the movie, Catherine's power over him will be signaled by calling him Nicky, an even more intimate and childish version of his "Nick" name.

The buddies admire Catherine's Picasso, a woman with two faces like the murder victim's, but larger. Catherine has more economic power than a man. The buddies next see a provocatively dressed blond they assume is Catherine looking down on them from a staircase; her position establishes her as intimidating. The two presumably tough cops tell her everything she asks of them. She tells them that she is Roxy, Catherine's friend.

The movie searches for bad women, finding them everywhere. Sexual women in this film are all under suspicion. They lie, cheat, change names, dye their hair, and wear wigs. You can't tell them apart without a score-card. Men are in constant danger from their inconstancy.

The next scene, Catherine's second residence, is even more impressive than her first home because it has a beautiful and treacherous cliff overlooking the ocean. Her two Lotus Climax cars add to the image of her power. The exchange between the buddies and this powerful woman is humiliating to the men. Giving in to her power, they answer her questions. When they ask polite questions, she refuses their softening circumlocutions and talks bluntly. Asked whether she was dating the murder victim, she replies, "No, I was fucking him." It is clear that a woman this brutal could have committed a murder. As the buddies leave the house, Cowboy speaks for the audience. "Nice girl," he sneers.

The partners have had to interrupt their investigation to allow Nick to reluctantly keep the appointment the chief had reminded him of at the crime scene. His appointment is with a female police psychologist. Their interview establishes that they were formerly lovers and that the treatment consists of a series of questions. She asks, he answers. He has given up all his addictions, booze, cocaine, cigarettes, even sex with women. The young, slim, provocatively dressed Dr. Beth Gardner ends the interview by saying, "I still miss you, Nick." Dr. Gardner is a female clinician who cannot sustain a boundary between love and work, like those discussed by the Gabbards (1987) who detailed the role of the seduced female therapist as a movie convention. As in all the cowboy movies, the hero keeps his power by refusing to engage in any of that mushy love stuff that the ladies try to push on him.

Following scenes establish that Miss Trammell has over 100 million dollars, has written several books, and is powerfully intelligent. A male psychologist argues that the killer is a frightening person likely to kill again. This sets the audience up for what I believe to be the most crucial scene in the movie: Catherine's interview at the police station.

The buddy cops return to the beach house to bring Catherine to the police station in order to get more information from her. Again, she turns the tables, getting information about Nick first. As they wait for her to change from her shorts outfit into "something more appropriate," Nick sees a newspaper with a story about his accidental killing of two tourists several months earlier. The scene is shot looking into the room where Catherine is changing. She makes no effort to close the door, displaying herself nude to the buddies as she dresses without underwear. On the way to the police station she challenges Nick to remain a nonsmoker and smokes in his face.

At the police station the guys confront Catherine to determine whether she has committed the murder. Catherine sits on a chair facing the guys. Her dress is seen only above her waist; the camera angle makes her look all naked legs and provocative gesture. She smokes. Informed that there is no smoking in the station, she challenges her putative investigators. "What are you going to do, book me for smoking?" she asks, daring them to take her on. They back down. After a brief exchange, she turns to the hero. "Ever fucked on cocaine, Nick?" As she says this, she uncrosses and recrosses her legs in such a way as to display her vulva, while acting as if she does not notice what she is doing. It seems to me that this is the key moment in the movie.

The woman as evil temptress who leads a man to doom is personified in the conjunction of the question in which the suspect is questioning the cop, the woman is questioning the man, the sexual adept is questioning the ascetic, and the suspect is turning the inquisition into an opportunity to lead the inquisitor into sin. The sight of the female genital stuns the whole roomful of men. She flashes her genitals at them with the same aggressive intent and effect as a male flasher has toward his female victims. Once she has done this, her power seems magical: she outwits the police, she can pass the lie-detector test, and she alienates the hero from his buddies. When he responds to her request for a ride back after she has passed the lie-detector test, they suspect that he is colluding with her. He is on the road to his destruction. The many plot twists after this moment are as inevitable as the downward spiral Othello takes after the moment when Desdemona drops the handkerchief.

In the next scene he has joined the guys at a bar. He drinks for the first time in 3 months. Beth Gardner cheerfully takes him home with her, only to have him rough her up and rape her anally. Afterward, her mood is dreamy, but when he asks for a cigarette, she tells him to get it on his way out. The nice woman enjoys being hurt but rejects him when he becomes self-destructive. Nick leaves her for the police station, where he learns that a professor at Berkeley was stabbed to death with an ice pick while Catherine Trammell was a student there. He rushes off to the Trammell house just in time to see her black Lotus drive off. He follows in his red Plymouth, getting left behind by her superior driving and her more powerful car. He finds the car parked in front of the house belonging to

Hazel Dobkins, another woman who will turn out to be a murderer. This woman has the initials of H. D., a bisexual woman poet of great power. Catherine's pen name is Woolf after Virginia Woolf, a bisexual woman novelist.

Nick visits Catherine at her beach house once again to investigate her connection with this woman and with the professor's murder. She uses an ice pick expertly to hack apart a block of ice. She is using him as the model for the victim of her next book. She accuses him of killing four people and provoking his wife's death. They clinch. Catherine's friend Roxy comes in; Catherine embraces her passionately, dismissing Nick.

A later scene in Nick's apartment shows Beth, the good girl, coming to apologize to him for having given out confidential information. Even the "good" woman betrays the man, this time by a typically feminine failing: she cannot keep a secret. He slaps her around. She apologizes and leaves. He sleeps while a monster movie runs on the television. The face of the monster is a Medusa with a wide gaping mouth full of little pointed teeth and hair all around. The reference leads immediately to a scene in which a cop with whom Nick had a public altercation earlier in the day is found killed with a gun of the type Nick carries.

A hearing shows Nick identifying with Catherine by smoking while being interrogated and, when confronted, repeats her quip about being charged with smoking. Nick is becoming one of Catherine's slave-lovers. The bad woman takes over his past, his memory, and forces her identity on him. Thus, another bad thing about women is that they remake a man in their own image.

Catherine visits Nick again, teasingly telling him about her first book, an account of a murder very similar to the accident in which her parents died. The murderer, she tells him, was the couple's son and sole heir, as she was her parent's sole heir. The difference between the sexes doesn't matter. Money and power do matter. After ignoring a warning from his faithful buddy Gus, Nick goes to a nightclub where he finds Catherine inhaling cocaine with Roxy while seated on a stall in the men's toilet. The two women dance erotically. Catherine is shown as a person who enjoys breaking any rules she can find and as a person untroubled by disgust.

Catherine leaves Roxy for Nick, and they have sex under a ceiling mirror. She binds him with a white scarf. Roxy tells him that she has been watching and that Catherine likes her to watch. In this complex scene, the rapid shifts underline the shiftiness of the woman. In the morning light Nick finds Catherine standing close to a fire on the beach. She has warned him about getting too close to the fire, but he passionately insists that he enjoyed the dangerous sex they had, calling it "the fuck of the century." She replies that it wasn't bad for a beginning. Thus she constantly humiliates him by getting him to overvalue her while she undervalues him.

Sex with Catherine is costly. As Nick leaves a diner, a black Lotus comes after Nick. He manages to force the Lotus off a cliff. The driver was Roxy. Later, Catherine muses, "She never was jealous before."

In a psychological evaluation at the station house, Beth rescues Nick with her sympathetic cover-up of his by now reckless rage. In the next scene flamelike shadows flicker on the wall at the beach house. Catherine sits crying in a rocking chair. She complains that everyone she cares for dies. She mourns them only as lost possessions. Nick comforts her, is again seduced by her, and is mobilized by her confession that she slept with a girl at Berkeley who became obsessed with and copied her. Nick eagerly investigates the possibility that she murders people to pin the murders on Catherine. He does not want to believe that Catherine is the murderer.

Finding that the girl eventually changed her name to Beth Gardner leads Nick to suspect and confront Beth. Her last name, she says, is her husband's and her first name is what he liked to call her. This fits with the good girl image because she has allowed herself to be defined by her man. Her name has more resonance, however. Oberman is an Anglicized version of Ubermensch, the hero who is entitled to kill to express his needs. The resonance of names is like the musical resonance of the sound track.

Catherine shows up at Nick's apartment and has sex with him, and when he suggests that she put a happy ending on her book, she says such a book would not sell. "Somebody has to die," she says. "Somebody always does." Nick resumes the chase and finds out that Beth's husband was killed and that the unsolved murder was rumored to have something to do with the wife's girlfriend. Beth is no longer to be trusted. He goes back to Catherine's house and finds her new novel printing out. She tells him that the novel is finished and the hero is dead. Her older female lover appears and bids her an erotic goodbye on her way out. Enraged, Nick joins Gus on the way to a rendevous with Catherine's former roommate. Since Nick no longer has a gun and is not officially on the investigation, Gus goes in alone. Nick realizes that this may be a trap and rushes in to find Gus dead. The audience has already seen Gus shot by a thin woman in a shiny black raincoat and blond wig. Beth appears, claims to have come to a rendevous set up by a telephone call, and seems to be holding something that could be a gun in her pocket. Nick shoots and kills her, only to find that she was holding her keys to his apartment in her pocket. The police arrive, find a police raincoat, a police gun, and a blond wig on the staircase. Nick has now lost both his buddy and the woman who seemed to really care about him. He is responsible for both of their deaths, yet he does not tell the police that Beth was not the murderer.

Catherine shows up in Nick's apartment, crying. They have sex, she ties him up, she leans back, he suggests that they stay together, "fuck like minks and raise rug-rats." She says she hates rug-rats, he says omit the rug-rats; she leans back, reaches toward the floor in the identical gesture with which the woman in the opening scene reached for the ice pick, reaches over him, and embraces him. The movie ends with a shot of an ice pick on the floor beneath their bed.

Throughout the movie Catherine warns Nick of his fate. Like a spider, she draws him into her web. Playing on his guilt, his curiosity, and his loneliness, she lures him to his doom. Teasing him with the possibility that she may be innocent, she tells him that she will kill him as she has so many others. Her healthy looking face and body contrast with her drug use, open enjoyment of casual sex, bisexuality, and propensity for murder. She looks womanly yet uses an ice pick better than a man. She is the quintessential murderess.

The crucial image in this movie is the image of the Medusa seen on the television screen in Nick's room. By putting this image on the screen, the movie links up to the tradition of Medusa stories (Hamilton 1940) and visual representations that warn men of the danger of the woman, the danger of the Medusa. Analysts (Freud 1923, 1940; Ferenczi 1923; Flugel 1924; Reik 1951; Balter 1969) have noted the importance of the Medusa myth for understanding men's fear of women. I would like to trace the image of the Medusa in the context of the message this movie is promulgating about women.

The Medusa is an image of the vulva, hairy all around; a face, but not a face; a mouth, but not a mouth; and life-giving when young, but horrific to see and death-dealing to the young heroes who encounter her. The symbol of the Medusa is replete with the images of bee and snake. The bee sting, like the ice pick wielded by the dangerous woman, can kill. The lithe body of the snake, like the body in the murder scene of the movie, can mesmerize and kill. When Catherine displays her vulva, she evokes the mesmerizing power, energy, and death-dealing menace of the Medusa. According to Hamilton (1940), the Medusa is one of the three Gorgons, sisters who lived on an island in the sea. Perseus was the hero who sought her head as a present for the man who was marrying his mother Danae. The myth describes the boy as having grown up fatherless and therefore not confronted with his mother's sexuality. He used the Gorgon's head to turn his mother's suitor to stone, thus saving her from marriage by displaying the terrifying image of a vulva.

Arlow (1971) traced the propensity to exhibitionism and fetishism in men to the traumatic effect of the sight of the female genitalia, especially as displayed by an aggressive mother. The castration anxiety men experience leads to fear of their own self-punitive impulses and finally to a perversion or perverse character trait that the man experiences as powerful enough to ward off the dreaded experience of the female genital. The denial of the female genital is coupled with the conviction that it could be fatal. It is too horrible to exist; therefore, it cannot exist. Catherine's character is perfectly expressed in her display of her genitals. By forcing the men to look at it, she immobilizes, fascinates, and destroys them.

The misogynist message is one Faludi (1991) describes in popular culture, politics, and most importantly, in popular psychology in the 1970s. It has resurfaced, as Faludi and others (Rossi 1972) have shown, after each historical period in which women made gains toward equality with men. Its pervasiveness, ubiquity, and historical recurrences (Pantel 1992) lead to questions about why it always comes back. Is there something in the female psyche that allows women to be excited by this movie and that is related to why women allow patriarchy to happen?

This question, I think, brings us back to the question of the title of this movie. What is the basic instinct? Is it a raw sexual desire as exemplified by Catherine's comment that, even if you have no affectionate feelings for the partner "You still get the pleasure?" (Freud 1905). Is it the aggressive wish released in the multiple violent stabbings with an icepick (Klein 1932)? Is it the masochistic wish to be punished that seems to motivate Nick's attraction to Catherine but is a reversal of the usual male-female roles in that the female is the masochist who forces the male to oppress her (Freud 1923)? Is it a question of a need for attachment to others (Bowlby 1969), which gives society the power to coerce women into self-loathing or denigration (Horney 1926)? All of these are possible. The instinct in question is a puzzle to analytic thinkers.

Karen Horney (1926) was the first analyst to point out that: "Like all sciences and all valuations, the psychology of women has hitherto been considered only from the point of view of men" (p. 326). Unfortunately, hardly anybody listened to her call for understanding female psychology from the point of view of women. Male analysts 63 years later still seemed convinced that penis envy is the primary experience of the female genitalia and of femaleness in women. As object-relations and other primary femaleness theorists have posited, femaleness is primary in girls, and the vulva is experienced as valuable by the little girl and by the woman. But do men get it? Or do they believe in envy as the primary female experience? To the extent that they believe penis envy to be the bedrock of female psychology, they must fear retaliation from the envious female. *Basic Instinct* is a statement from the popular culture that tells us that the sexes have different kinds of power. It appeals to both men and women.

When Catherine displays her vulva, she shows her power. The movie gains power by reassuring the audience that sexual women are not mothers. When the housekeeper is eliminated as a suspect because she is old and fat, when Beth who changed her name to her husband's is eliminated as a suspect, and when Catherine tells Nick that she will not have children, the story provides comfort by telling the audience that mothers do not do it. They do not have sex and they do not murder. Balter (1969) showed the Perseus-Medusa myth to be a patriarchal rebellion against matriarchal power. *Basic Instinct* is supportive of power and virility of the male cohort ranged against the mother. It assures men that, by avoiding beautiful powerful women, they can avoid death. It assures women that, by being beautiful and powerful, they can entice men even to their death.

REFERENCES

ARLOW, J. (1971). Character perversion. In: *Currents in Psychoanalysis*, I. Marcus, ed. New York: International Universities Press.

BALTER, L. (1969).The Mother as Source of Power. *Psychoanalytic Quarterly* 38:217–274.

BOWLBY, J. (1969). *Attachment.* New York: Basic Books.

FALUDI, S. (1991). *Backlash.* New York: Crown.

FERENCZI, S. (1923). On the Symbolism of the Head of the Medusa. In: *Further Contributions to the Theory and Technique of Psychoanalysis.* London: Hogarth Press, 1950.

FLUGEL, J. (1924). Polyphallic Symbolism and the Castration Complex. *Internatinoal Journal of Psycho-Analysis* 5:155–196.

FREUD, S. (1905).Three Essays on the Theory of Sexuality. *Standard Edition* 7:249–254.

——— (1921). Medusa's head. *Standard Edition* 18:273–274.

——— (1923).The ego and the id. Standard Edition, 19: 12-66.

GABBARD, K. & GABBARD, G. (1987). *Psychiatry and the Cinema.* Chicago: University of Chicago Press.

GIMBUTAS, M. (1989). *The Language of the Goddess.* New York: Harper & Row.

HAMILTON, E. (1940). *Mythology.* Boston: Little, Brown.

HORNEY, K. (1926). The Flight from Womanhood. *Internatinoal Journal of Psycho-Analysis* 7:324–339.

KLEIN, M. (1932). *The Psychoanalysis of Children.* London: Hogarth Press, 1975.

PANTEL, P. (1992). *A History of Women.* Cambridge, MA: Harvard University Press.

REIK, T. (1951). Modern medusa. *American Imago* 8:323–328.

ROSSI, A. (1973). *The Feminist Papers.* New York: Columbia.

****
****

The preceeding chapter originally article appeared as:

RICHARDS, A.K. (1998). Woman as Medusa in *Basic Instinct. Psychoanalytic Inquiry* 18:269–280.

Gambling and Death

Those—dying then
Knew where they went—
They went to God's Right Hand—
That Hand is amputated now
And God cannot be found—

The abdication of Belief—
Makes the Behavior small—
Better an ignis fatuus
Than no illume at all

—EMILY DICKINSON, 1882

Emily Dickinson trembles at the idea of a world with no supreme being because there is no alternative to death in such a world. There is no guarantee of justice. Chaos is unbearable. She asks for a false god rather than no first principle at all. This paper is about the false god of gambling—a God that some find irresistible when confronted with the death of those they love. There are no odds to death. Everyone dies.

The comforting thing about gambling games is that there are rules, the gambler knows the odds ahead of time—and there are odds. Like death, losing at a casino is inevitable, but on the way to that loss, everything is fair.

In an earlier paper (Richards & Richards 1997) written with Arnold Richards [see chapter 20, current volume], we showed how Las Vegas, the mecca of the gambling world in mid twentieth century, was a vast temple dedicated to denying death. Three movies about Las Vegas showed how the gambler denies his own death. *Bugsy* (1991) showed how Bugsy Siegel created Las Vegas and died for breaking the rules; the movie *Casino* (1995) showed how a character named "Ace Rosenthal" industrialized Las Vegas and died for breaking the rules; and a movie called *Leaving Las Vegas* (1995) showed a loser who accepts the lack of odds and comes to Las Vegas in order to die. Like those who come to Las Vegas to gamble now, the characters in these movies accept their inevitable deaths, but at the same time live as if they know the rules and by keeping to them, they can prevent their own deaths. In this paper I want to extend that theme to show how gambling enables denial of the death of those the gambler loves.

THE MOVIES

In the movie *21* (2008), a group of MIT students is recruited to count cards at Las Vegas for the game of 21. A touching moment of connection shows the young hero with the girl of his dreams who is already a member of the group to which he is being recruited. She tells him about how her father taught her the game, and when he asks about her father, she tells him that he is long gone. His father has been dead for many years as well. Not only does this make it clear that they are going to be lovers, it also makes it clear that the students were fascinated by gambling for a reason. Death ties them to each other and death makes gambling fascinating. What makes the hero love his experience in Vegas is not explained in any other way—this is enough.

It is interesting to compare this with the book on which the movie is based. Called *Bringing Down the House* (Mezrich 2001), the book is a non-fiction "as-told-to" tale of gambling and yet not gambling, only seeming to gamble. And a striking difference between the movie and the book is that the hero of the book has a living father. His father is a successful scientist, as he wants his son to be. But the book describes the son as lonely in his lab, cut off from the living world. Invited to join a glamorous group of fellow students by a charismatic professor, he gladly gives up his scientific career for the gambling life. By counting the cards that have already been played in the deck they can figure out when high cards are likely to come up and then bet accordingly. The point is that they use statistics—a science that was actually invented for gambling—to ensure that they will have the advantage over the house; they will win eventually. The purpose of devoting their considerable talents to this, rather than to science or mathematics is the thrill of being in the moment, not in preparing for a long distant future, not in thinking of the past experience with family, friends, teachers, classmates, but being in the moment with a group of people also there only for the moment.

Yet the book and the movie both center around scenes of the pseudogamblers actually gambling with their lives as they defy the house rules against counting cards in the casino. They know that the casino owners can be dangerous. They have heard stories of card counters being mugged and of others disappearing into the desert. An older gambler warns them:

"Don't let some guy named Vinnie take you on any long drives out into the desert" (p. 73).

They are not gambling at the 21 game, they are gambling with their lives. The knowledge that they are not gamblers in the card game is offset by the thrill of being on the edge, facing what may be the last moment of their lives.

In one interview in both book and movie a woman gambler says: "I found the thrill of the game almost as addictive as the field of consulting. The idea of going up against a huge corporation, finding ways to beat them in their own arena—it was a real high." (p. 124). The interviewer says: "I nodded. I had heard this from everyone on the team. They all saw themselves as little Davids going up against a giant, neon Goliath. Except in their version, David got rich off the battle" (p. 125).

For the woman interviewed, as for the other gamblers, the money was only a token. And the games are played with tokens, reinforcing the difference between the money in gambling and the money used to pay for tangible goods. For real gamblers the token is exchanged for money. For these counters the token stands for life. The interviewer does not see that in the bible story David not only gets rich, he also gets to keep his life and he gets to be king. In other words, what makes the thrill is the heroic stand against the more powerful force. David risked his life. Gambling is a thrill when life is the stake. Another thrill was dressing up for the casino experience. The MIT students went to Las Vegas dressing up as ordinary gamblers, impersonating people from whom the casino could expect to make money. The game of being different from themselves added to the fun. They were like children dressing up for Halloween with the fun and death-defying bravado of pretending. The movie makes it clear that the actual gamblers the MIT team was impersonating also chose special outfits, make-up, hairstyles to create personas for the purpose of impressing the other people at the casino. These impersonations are more glamourous than real life and reinforce the pretence of the casino, the idea that one has not suffered and will not suffer loss. Jeff Ma is the central character in the book. At the end of the second edition of the book the author interviews him about his family and friends' reactions to the story. Jeff says:

But now, well, the reaction has all been pretty positive. I think people understand that the ethics of what we were doing—well, it wasn't like we were going to Vegas to gamble. We were using math to beat the system (p. 260).

He is now out of danger and again in denial of he real risk he took. His loss of the woman he loved is never mentioned—though he clearly understands that his gambling destroyed their intimacy. In the after interview he mentions what the gambling got him: a townhouse and a share in a bar. He does not mention having a new relationship. For him, as for other gamblers, the group around the table is the level of intimacy they want. Winning or losing is almost beside the point, being in the situation is what they prize above intimacy. Once the person that the gambler loved is lost, gambling replaces her and replaces any regrets he might have had about losing her.

A BOOK

But the idea of a system to beat the odds is a very common one among gamblers. It is the point of a gambling addiction. The gambler must believe that he or she can beat the system. In Dostoyevsky's *The Gambler* (1866), two very different gamblers use two very different systems. Both lose. A third person at the gambling tables is "the old lady." But the old lady gambles by betting with the house. She accepts her inability to escape death by gambling. Early in the novel death is introduced when the narrator, the gambler, asks the woman he loves what has happened since he last saw her:

"Nothing, but the arrival of two pieces of news from St. Petersburg, first, that Granny was very ill, and then, two days later, that she seemed to be dying" (p. 11).

This statement outlines the plot of the entire novel. A group of gamblers, their dependents and those to whom they are in debt, are waiting for the death and for the money that they will inherit, swindle or be repaid. Tragic and comedic at the same time, the novel focusses on the addiction to gambling as a way of denying time, death, and the loss for which the odds are inescapable. The gambler who is the hero and narrator of the novel, makes a first attempt at explaining it sociologically:

The Russian is not only incapable of amassing capital, but dissipates it in a reckless and unseemly way. Nevertheless we Russians need money, too, . . . and consequently we are very glad to make use of such means as roulette, for instance, in which one can grow rich all at once, in two hours, without work That's very fascinating to us; and since we play badly, recklessly, without taking trouble, we usually lose (p. 32).

Life with its tiny increments of time—and work with its tiny increments of achievement, earning, and saving with very slow gains—are of no interest to a gambler. What he values is the moment in which time seems suspended, the moment between placing the bet and finding the outcome. Death is what comes in a moment; life is a tedious step-by-step journey. In the novel the Granny, rather than dying and leaving her money to the gamblers, becomes a gambler herself and loses her money. The gamblers had counted on her death as a way to get money with which to continue gambling. The death of a supportive and protective family member is shown as a necessary condition for gambling.

The gambler in the title of the book goes down the gambling road to the end. Dostoyevsky's *The Gambler* describes the experience of the moment from the inside. While writing this novel, Dostoyevsky was also writing *Crime and Punishment* (1866). He was deeply in debt, had been to debtor's prison already and was facing it again. He had contracted to deliver two novels by a certain date. If he did not deliver on time, the publisher would own all of Dostoyevsky's future writings. He would never be able to make his living by writing again. Gambling that he could finish the novel by the given date, he was rushing to finish it in what was in effect a life-or-death struggle. In the novel, the old lady of the gambling table chooses to return to ordinary life in which she will, as Dostoyevsky himself finally did, seek immortality through religion rather than at the card table. As he describes it in *Crime and Punishment,* the choice of religion is a choice of connection with others, a salvation through love. It is the opposite of the choice Jeff Ma makes in *21.*

Gambling in a casino is a spectator sport. The players watch each other, on any one play they are surrounded by watchers. Dressing in particularly eye catching costumes, make-up, hairdos and jewelry is part of the play. Dostoyevsky shows it this way:

"I watched you ma'am," Marfa cackled, and said to Potapitch, "What does our lady want to do?" And the money on the table— saints alive! the money! I haven't seen so much money in the whole of my life, and all around were gentlefolk—nothing but gentlefolk sitting. "And wherever do all these gentlefolk come from

Potapitch?" said I. "May Our Lady herself help her," I thought. "I was praying for you ma'am," and my heart was simply sinking, simply sinking, I was all of atremble. "Lord help her," I thought, "and here the Lord has sent you luck, I've been trembling ever since, ma'am, I'm all of a tremble now" (p. 101).

Like the spectators in Las Vegas, those in Dostoyevsky's Roulette-ville admire the elegance of the players, feel trembling and hope as if they were lovers anticipating orgasm, and trembling afterward as if they had been moved to orgasm and were now coming down to everyday reality from it. If orgasm is the "little death," gambling is the public orgasm, the public little death.

The gambler himself experiences losing all his money as if it were a death: "What am I now? Zero. What may I be tomorrow? Tomorrow I may rise from the dead and begin to live again!" (p. 170). The zero is particularly apt as it is the number in roulette in which everyone's money goes to the bank. All players lose except those who have bet on zero. Plainly only the bank can win. In the end, the bank always wins. Death is inevitable. But the moment before death is worth dying for. The moment when it is still possible that the gambler and not the bank will win this time. And that moment is to the gambler better than the moment of orgasm, the moment that also just precedes death.

Once having experienced the death and rebirth at the gambling table, the gambler no longer wants sexual fulfillment as much as he wants the gambling high moment. In the novel, a Mr. Astley comes to the gambler a year after that first moment and offers him the love of the woman for whom he was gambling in the first place. Astley is the symbol of British prudence. He confronts the gambler:

You have not only given up life, all your interests, private and public, the duties of a man and a citizen, your friends (and you really had friends)—you have not only given up your objects, such as they were, all but gambling—you have even given up all your memories.

The gambler answers:

"Enough, Mr. Astley, please, don't remind me," I cried with vexation, almost with anger, "let me tell you, I've forgotten absolutely nothing; but I've only for a time put everything out of my mind, even my memories, until I can make a radical improvement in my

circumstances, then . . . .then you will see, I shall rise again from the dead" (p. 174).

What he will do when he rises from the dead is to go back to his beloved. He will return to human intimacy. To be resurrected, to be returned from the dead is the promise of religion, in these accounts, the false religion of gambling promises the gambler a new life in which he wins the love of the beautiful woman rather than the death of losing everything to the House.

A MEMOIR

Double Down is a memoir (Barthelme & Barthelme 1999) linking gambling and death. Its authors are brothers, both successful academics and writers. In their book they describe how they managed to lose a quarter of a million dollars, all the money they had inherited from their ambivalently loved father. They observe: "Our fellow gamblers were serious, not like academics but in the furious way that children are serious, concentrating on play, oblivious, intense, yet at ease Essentially, they came to the casino to be children" (p. 74).

The authors, like their fellow gamblers, were acting like they were still children, living in the time before their father died. As they describe it their fantasy was: "Things would suddenly and inexplicably turn in our favor. A hurricane of money and love" (p. 85). Gambling enabled them to escape the reality of their father's death:

Gambling is of course, a very expensive way to beat reason. You can get pretty much the same thing by staying awake for a night and a day, or however long it takes you to get a little psychologically unhinged, destabilized, detached from whatever you believed the day before, and then staring at the cat, the dog, the stapler, the back of your hand, water. Most anything will do once you've shed your silly confidence (p. 97).

Knowing that gambling at a casino was rigged so that over time they had to lose, they tried to understand what they were doing:

. . . we were more serious, more ardent in our courtship of loss. We practiced, we tried harder, we dumped the cash our father had tried so hard to put together for us. Was the message clear? Was it, "We don't want your money"? Or was it, "Consider yourself repudiated"? Or was it more like, "Thanks for this chance to feel

like a loser on a large scale"? Or was it, "This money is a poor substitute for you"? (pp. 116–117).

I think that the answer is one that multiple choice tests provide: All of the above. But the gamble is not only about losing. Winning provides much of the same feeling:

The losing part is not fun exactly, in fact, fun doesn't come into it. but the heat, the dizzying adrenal rush, is much the same whether the chips come back to you, or go into the dealer's rack. . . . play the game, any game, for significant stakes and you'll know. It's not whether you win or lose, its that you play. (pp. 118–119).

The brothers come to understand that: "We lost the money because we played, because we wouldn't give up, because giving up was unheard of, because our parents were dead and there was no order to our lives" (p. 136).

They talk as if gambling would put order in their lives, as if the rules of the game are the important thing, the "ignus fatuus" of Dickinson's poem, the false god that comforts even when the believer knows that the god is false. The brothers only stop gambling when they are kicked out of the casino. Like the players in *21,* the rules of harsh reality supersede those of the magical gambling world, the veil is torn away, the wizard turns out to be a poor reminder that death does exist, human life is finite and the odds do not apply. There is no escape. Everybody loses the people they love.

A psychoanalytic understanding of death has been late in coming. The idea of a death instinct as posited first by Spielrein (1912) and elaborated by Freud (1920), has been rejected by the ego psychologists. The idea of death as one of the feared calamities of childhood was controversial when posited as annihilation anxiety by Hurvich (1989). The idea that a person defends against the threat of death by manic defense fits with the psychology of gambling as I have outlined it here. In the end, gambling provides moments of immediacy of sensation that shut out fears of all kinds, fears of being abandoned, of being excluded, of losing one's powers, and of being deprived of the exclusive love of one's parents. But each of these fears is made concrete in the thought of parental death. These depictions of gambling in fiction, non-fiction and semi-fictional film show the ways gambling fends off the thoughts, feelings and images evoked by the possibility of death.

Freud described a gambling game in "The Theme of Three Caskets." Here the caskets are used as if they were shells in a shell game. He who chooses the golden casket loses, He who chooses the silver casket also loses, and the one who chooses the lead casket wins. Freud understands the gold to represent the woman who gives birth to the man, the silver casket to represent the wife who loves him and the lead casket as representing the Lady Death. Of these varieties of love, the ultimate winner is Death.

If death is the ultimate lover is the death of a loved one a betrayal? Does the survivor wonder: "Did the one I love love death more than he or she loved me?" In the first hand account of the death of her husband and the year she spent mourning him, Didion (2005) attempts to:

> . . . *make sense of the period that followed [the death], weeks and then months that cut loose any fixed idea I ever had about death, about illness, about probability and luck, about good fortune and bad, about marriage and children and memory, about grief, about the ways people do and do not deal with the fact that life ends, about the shallowness of sanity, about life itself* (p. 7).

A remarkable feature of the book is her constant reference to the dates of events, important events like weddings and adoption, public events like assassination of a president, all attached to numbers, all ordered mathematically. The whole book is like a statistical manual, a gambler's memoir, a record of luck, both good and bad. It makes clear how the obsessional defense fits into the gambling activity and the card counting "not gambling" activity of the professional MIT players as a strategy to defeat the death of a loved person.

REFERENCES

BARTHELME, F. & BARTHELME, S. (1999). *Double Down.* New York: Harcourt.

CAROTENUTO, A. (1982;1983). *A Secret Symmetry: Sabina Spielrein between Jung and Freud.* New York: Pantheon Books.

DIDION, J. (2005). *The Year of Magical Thinking.* New York: Knopf.

DOSTOYEVSKY, F. (1866). *The Gambler.* Transl. C. Garnett, ed G.S. Morson. New York: Modern Library, 2003.

――― (1866). *Crime and Punishment.* Transl. D. McDuff, New York: Penguin, 2002.

FREUD, S. (1912). The Theme of The Three Caskets. *Standard Edition* 12:289–301.

——— (1920). Beyond the pleasure principle. *Standard Edition* 18:7–43.

HAYMAN, R. (2001). *A Life of Jung.* New York: W W Norton & Company.

HURVICH, M. (1989). Traumatic Moment, Basic Dangers, and Annihilation Anxiety. *Psychoanalytic Psychology* 6:309–323.

MEZRICH, B. (2002) *21: Bringing Down the House: The Inside Story of Six MIT Students Who Took Vegas for Millions.* New York: Free Press.

RICHARDS, A.K., & RICHARDS, A.D. (1997). Gambling, Death and Violence: Hollywood Looks at Las Vegas. *Psychoanalytic Review* 84:769–788.

SPIELREIN, S. (1912). Die Destruktion Als Ursache Des Werdens. *Jahrbuch der Psychoanalyse* 4; English Transl. Destruction as a Cause of Becoming. by S.K. Witt (1995) in *Psychoanalysis and Contemporary Thought* 18:85–118.

****
****

Original publication of preceding chapter:

RICHARDS, A.K. (2009). Gambling and Death. In *Greed: Sex, Money, Power and Politics* E. Ronis & L. Shaw, eds.

The Terrifying Woman: Latin and Anglo View of Female Sexuality in *Basic Instinct* and *That Obscure Object of Desire*

This paper will compare the views men have toward women in regard to sex and violence in each of two films: *Basic Instinct* and *That Obscure Object of Desire*. Comparison will be made between how men see women in Anglo and Spanish cultures. The men and women characters in each film are also to be discussed as fantasies of the male directors and writers who see women through the concepts developed in their separate cultures.

Particular interest in the vicissitudes of instinctual life in women will focus on: how women express aggression; toward whom that aggression is expressed; when the aggression is shown; and the subjects about which it is expressed. While they cannot be completely teased out from this view of aggression, the following libidinal themes in these movies will be traced: how women express sexual desire; toward whom they express this desire; when it is expressed; and what characteristics of the object are shown to elicit sexual desire in women. Particularly important is how the aggression interweaves with desire, and how it energizes, interferes with, and sometimes overcomes the tender and idealizing aspects of women's desire.

The Gorgon Medusa is a goddess of ancient origin and long duration. According to Gimbutas (1989):

> *The Gorgon Medusa . . . can turn men to stone. She is capable of taking the breath away . . . a potent Goddess dealing with life and death, not the later Indo-European monster to be . slain by heroes such as Perseus, she is linked with Artemis. Artemis and Hecate are one, a lunar Goddess of the life cycle with two aspects: one, standing at the beginning of the cycle, the other at the end: one young, pure and beautiful, connected with young life, and the other gruesome, connected with death. . . . Hecate is described as traveling above graveyards with her hounds, collecting poison and then mixing deadly potions. She is a remorseless killer appeased*

only by bloody sacrifices. Her eerie howl conveys the presence of death.

The Gorgon lived throughout ancient Greece, Her hideous features—lolling tongue, projecting teeth, and writhing snakes for hair—were believed to be protection against the Evil Eye. As a pro-phylactic mask, the Gorgon was depicted ... with snakes emerging horizontally out of her head: she is girdled by two snakes with hiss-ing opposed heads exuding powerful energy (p. 207–209).

Basic Instinct is an Anglo movie. Like *Triumph of the Will, Intolerance* and *Day of the Locust,* it promulgates a hateful message by artful means. It is part of the battle against women that Susan Faludi describes in *Backlash.* Educated women, this movie tells us, are danger-ous, blood-thirsty lesbians. Even the ones who seem to love men are at least unethical and possibly murderous. The most attractive and openly sexual ones like Catherine, are the most deadly. Powerful women who achieve things like writing books or getting a degree in psychology are the worst. Beautiful women are the enemy; men attracted to them are doomed; even friends of men attracted to them are doomed.

That Obscure Object of Desire is a Spanish movie in which the beautiful woman who is desired and sought after through the movie is always on the scene when terrorist explosions are around. Why? Is she linked to the terrorists? The movie teases the audience with hints and suggestions as the beautiful woman teases the protagonist of the film. As she lures him into desire, the audience is lured into the mystery. Who is she? What power does she have over the protagonist? Why does he desire her more than other women? A sense of menace and doom lurks in every scene.

Basic Instinct signals its intent with its opening titles. Seen behind print, naked flesh teasingly maintains a current of excitement, alerting the audience to the importance of words and names in the rest of the movie. The title sequence promises a rational examination of the weaknesses of the flesh. Later, the hero will fall asleep in front of an image of the Medusa. *Basic Instinct* is about woman as Gorgon. The title sequence of *Obscure Object of Desire* is similarly important. Strong Spanish guitar music accompanies shots of swaying palms against a pale blue sky. Nature is lovely, warm and sensuous. But the titles are flame red, bringing a violent contrast and heat. Man is violent, disturbing and clashing. Where there is human imprint, there is danger. The opening scene of traffic shows the machine as polluter and enemy. We are in a tropical city, ready for explosion. *That Obscure Object of Desire* is about woman as destroyer, woman as Medusa.

In *Basic Instinct* the camera zooms from the opening shot of a door to a mirror reflecting a couple having intercourse. The contrast between the titles and the flesh behind them is repeated in the contrast between the square furniture and the softly curved flesh of the sexual partners. The camera comes upon sexual partners grappling. A blonde ties the man's hands and plunges an ice pick into him again and again. Faceless, generic, the woman on top is dangerous, whoever she is. *Basic Instinct* evokes primal fear of the vulva, the Medusa that turns man into stone.

In the first scene of *That Obscure Object of Desire* the hero buys his tickets and in the next scene has gone home where he is greeted by his butler who says: "She has left." We see a gardener carrying a heavy sack, an image that will be repeated. The two men go inside to find a pillow stained with blood and a pair of high-heeled shoes as well as a pair of wet panties. The hero remarks that the blood on the pillow is from a nosebleed, dismissing the notion that it could be menstrual blood or blood from a hymen. The butler tells him that the panties are wet, suggesting the vaginal secretion of sexual arousal. "Burn them all" the hero orders. The butler tells him that a German philosopher said: "If you go with women carry a big stick." The hero goes into his car and says: "To the bank." An explosion and fire startle both men as they sit in the car. The equation between female sexuality, money and explosive rage is in place.

Both films involve a pair of men and a single woman. Both invoke danger with bloody linen. The men pursue the woman, but she is dangerous, a natural beast, endangering the civilized men. Ironically, the pursued is the object of fear.

The second scene of *Basic Instinct* shows two investigators riding to the scene of the crime like the hero and sidekick of countless westerns. Their camaraderie contrasts with the danger, for a man, of intimacy with a woman. The ethos of the picture is established by the nicknames the buddies have for each other. The hero, Nick, is called "Hoss" by his sidekick, who calls him "Cowboy." Partners immortalized in countless westerns reverse roles. This hero is a "Hoss" who needs a rider. The rider can be his friend the cowboy or the lethal woman of the opening scene. The battle between the forces of good and evil is set in motion: guys good, women bad.

The buddies arrive at the crime scene, a bedroom now full of policemen. Despite the situation, tension is lowered. They stop to admire the victim's Picasso, a sign of wealth, culture, and power. The hero points out the commanding officer as loyal to the mayor, a woman. The mayor's man threatens the hero, warning the audience about men who are loyal to women.

The guys discuss the murder. Blood all over the sheets is assumed to be that of the victim. None of the detectives even thinks that the blood could be menstrual fluid, even though that is the most common cause of bloody sheets. The blood the woman leaves on the sheets is denied. By contrast, the eerily-illuminated semen is admired as the emission of a macho man. No one thinks the killer could have been a homosexual partner or jealous husband or lover. Instead, the detectives wonder what kind of woman could have done this. A detective eliminates the housekeeper because "she is fifty-two years old and weighs over two hundred pounds." After all, the guy remarks, the corpse had no bruises. The implication is that if the man had sex with such a fat woman, he would be bruised. Only a thin woman could possibly have done it. A later scene shows a plump, middle-aged Hispanic woman working as a maid. She, like the housekeeper, is not a suspect. Later, a plump policewoman helps the policewoman helps the buddies. The bad woman is the thin sexy one.

Cowboy and Hoss visit the girlfriend of the murder victim, the last person he was seen with in public, Miss Catherine Trammell. Her name has several resonances. Trammell means ensnare. Her initials are C.T., a euphemism for cunt and for "cock teaser." Her first name, Catherine, is that of the shrew in Shakespeare's Taming of the Shrew. Unlike Shakespeare's heroine, who is called Kate by the man who tames her, this Catherine is called by her full name throughout the movie. She gets respect. By contrast, the hero is called only by nicknames and his name, as if to underscore the point, is Nick. At a later stage in the movie, Catherine's power over him will be signaled by calling him Nicky, an even more childish version of his "Nick" name.

The buddies admire Catherine's "Picasso," a woman with two faces like the murder victim's, but larger. Catherine has economic power. When they see a provocatively-dressed blonde looking down on them from a staircase, they assume she is Catherine. Her position intimidates them. The two cops tell her everything she asks of them. She then tells them that she is Roxy, Catherine's friend. The women associated with Catherine are also intimidating. The movie searches for bad women, finding them everywhere. Sexual women in: this film are all under suspicion. They lie, cheat, change names, dye their hair, and wear wigs. You can't tell them apart without a scorecard. Men are in constant danger from their inconstancy.

Catherine's second residence has a beautiful and treacherous cliff overlooking the ocean. Her two Lotus Climax cars add to the image of her power. The exchange between the buddies and this powerful woman is humiliating to the men. Giving in to her power, they answer her questions. They ask polite questions; she talks bluntly. Asked whether she was dating the murder victim, she replies, "No, I was fucking him." It is clear that this woman is brutal. As the buddies leave the house, Cowboy speaks for the audience. "Nice girl," he sneers.

The partners have had to interrupt their investigation to allow Nick reluctantly to keep the appointment the chief had reminded him of at the crime scene. His appointment is with a female police psychologist. Their interview establishes that they were formerly lovers and that the treatment consists of a series of questions. She asks, he answers. He has given up all his addictions, booze, cocaine, cigarettes, even sex with women. The young, slim, provocatively-dressed Dr. Beth Gardner ends the interview by saying "I still miss you, Nick." Dr. Gardner is a female clinician who cannot sustain a boundary between love and work, like those discussed by the Gabbards (1987) who detailed the role of the seduced female therapist as a movie convention. As in all the cowboy movies, the hero keeps his power by refusing to engage in any of that mushy love stuff that the ladies try to push on him.

In *That Obscure Object of Desire* the hero orders his butler to turn the car away from the explosion which he asserts was set by terrorists "here too." They go to the train. The butler goes to second class, the hero to first. The class difference is underlined. In his compartment the hero meets a young mother and her daughter who are his neighbors in Paris. A second man joins them and sits facing forward so as not to get dizzy. The conversation includes a comment that air travel nowadays is hazardous: "two nice young men take you to the desert," A midget enters, settles himself in his seat and reads the paper. The people in the compartment are middle class, not hijackers.

A plainly-dressed young woman hurries alongside the train looking for someone through the windows. The hero spots her, gives a porter some money and meets her as she attempts to board the train. He empties a basin of water on her head, apparently using what he paid the porter to fetch for him. Wet but undeterred, she enters another car.

The main body of the movie is shown as a narrative with flashbacks as the hero tells his traveling companions what led him to throw water on the young woman. On the day of a terrorist trial he met his jurist cousin for lunch in Paris. They ate at his home, truffle omelet and beef with lobster sauce, luxurious dishes in an elegant setting. The hero who is still nameless sees a new maid, a beautiful young woman who tells him that her name is "Conchita." That evening he asks his butler to order her to serve him a chartreuse. He is in his dressing gown. Sitting her beside him, he finds out that she has not been a servant, but hates to work in an office and loves to dance. He kisses her, she makes his bed and leaves the next morning he finds that she has left his house with no forwarding address.

Three months later in Geneva, he is watching swans on a lake in the park. He is mugged on his way back to his hotel by three young men who refuse his wallet, but ask for just 800 francs. Back at his hotel, Conchita appears and returns his money explaining that they are dancers who needed the money to return to Paris. He pushes the money at her, she gives him her address and leaves a scented handkerchief which he holds tenderly.

In the next scene he is in Paris, being dropped off at the slum apartment she shares with her mother. The mother serves him coffee, tells of their poverty and promises to repay him. She gratefully accepts a wad of money from him and leaves him alone with her daughter. When he makes a pass, she says that she is not that kind of girl, but teases him by putting a candy in his mouth seductively. He tells his companions on the train that he went back to that apartment daily for the next month.

One day he comes in to find her rehearsing with her guitarist. She takes off her clothes, washing herself in her underwear. She teases him with a Spanish song, gesturing as if she were shaving him while she sings: "Is anyone listening? No! Want me to tell you? Yes. Do you have a lover? No. Will you be my lover? Yes." "Is it true?" he asks her. She says it is not her words, only a song. The shaving reminds us of Samson being shaved by Delilah. She allows him a kiss, a caress and stops him. He gives her an envelope full of money. The mother comes back. He asks her why she will not have him for her lover and she whispers that she is a virgin. The butler brings the mother to the hero's luxurious apartment where he offers her more money. Suddenly he calls the butler who removes a mouse caught in a spring trap. He will not be running around any more. The mother agrees to bring her daughter back to his place the next night. But the next night the guitarist delivers a note: "I wanted to give myself to you. You tried to buy me. I will never see you again. In their game of cat and mouse, he is the mouse, she the cat. He rushes to the apartment, but it is empty.

Two months later she turns up as the hatcheck girl in a restaurant where he is having lunch. He renews his suit. She calls him by his name "Mathieu" and promises to allow him to have her in his country house. As he drives there, he passes a scene of terrorist sabotage. A man is carrying a heavy cloth sack. At the house she refuses to sleep with him, calls him her love asks him to love her forever, promises to love no one else, but goes into his bed dressed in a tightly-laced girdle he cannot get off her. He cries. She says she doesn't like what she is doing either, but she will live with him and gradually allow him more. He says he is so happy to have her near him he does not need consummation.

She tells him that she doesn't understand why he wants to make love. Now he is carrying a heavy cloth sack as they walk through a park. They go to bed, but she will not have sex. He gently suggests that there are other ways to make a man happy. She becomes indignant. They hear an assassination, she leaves his bed, goes to her room. He finds her hiding the guitar player. He orders her out; she berates him and vows never to see him again.

As the train crosses another bridge, Mathieu tells his cousin that he is afraid he cannot stop himself from going back to her and asks his cousin to rid him of her. The police expel her and her mother in a scene where it is revealed that the daughter's real name is "Conception." This revelation is another turning point. We see that we have never really known this woman whom we thought we knew.

Back in Seville, where he knew he would find her, he gives money to a mother-and-daughter team of beggars with a baby. The daughter unwraps the baby which turns out to be a pig wrapped in a blanket. Mathieu smiles. He asks his butler, Martin, what he thinks of women. Martin replies that he has a friend who loves women very much and thinks that they are "bags of excrement." The canvas bags carried by gardeners, and by Mathieu when he was in the Park with Conchita, are revealed to be the emblem of women. He leaves his sack to be picked up later.

Mathieu sees Conchita working as a dancer in what anyone else would recognize as a brothel, but he accepts as a night-club. She dances. He is enchanted. She excuses herself for a rest. Her friend tells him where he can find her "resting." He sees her dancing nude for a group of men. Enraged, he renounces her. But when she pleads with him he agrees to buy her a little house of her own so that she will be his lover.

He gives her the deed to the house. She promises to receive him at midnight. But, she teases, midnight tomorrow. The next night she gives him her foot to kiss through the locked gate. She dances for happiness at being able to be free of him at last. She tells him he has always disgusted her and that she stayed with him only to ruin him. She displays herself making love to the young handsome guitarist and taunts him with: "The guitar is mine. I play it for whom I want." Returning to his hotel Mathieu is held up by young terrorists who steal the car.

Conchita appears the next morning saying she is disappointed that he did not love her enough to commit suicide. She tells him that he doesn't understand women, that she only wanted to prove that he did not own her. She taunts him into slapping her. Blood pours from her nose as she offers him the key to the house and assures him that the scene of the night before was only a pretense, she has saved herself "intact" for him. Her ultimate seduction is always the hymen. Martin and the maid hear screams. Martin tells her that they are quarreling, but the sounds could be those of a violent primal scene. Back in the room, we see her pleading, but Mathieu is enraged. He throws the keys in her face.

Back in the train Mathieu is telling his companions that this happened the morning before. We realize that the blood on the pillow at the beginning of the movie was from a nosebleed, the shoes were Conchita's and the water he poured on her was the final blow in their battle. But was it? Conchita appears, douses him with a bucket of water and we next see them arm-in-arm as they leave the train in Paris together. We hear a news report of a strange alliance of revolutionary groups as the lovers are shopping in a gallery. They stop to watch a seamstress repairing a rip in a finely-embroidered nightgown. Mathieu fondles Conchita's hand. The music of Wagner's Gotterdammerung from *Die Valkirie* plays so loudly that we cannot hear his words. Conchita pulls away, he walks after her, imploring. A gigantic explosion ends in flames that envelop the screen.

The crucial image in this movie is the image of the bag of excrement. It appears again and again as Mathieu becomes more obsessed with Conchita. It contrasts with the image of purity represented by her insistence on her intact hymen. The narrative contrasts the alluring young virgin with the hideous bag of excrement. The image of the hymen is explored in detail by Holtzman and Kulish (1997). These authors contend that the hymen is a dread image because it can never be replaced or regenerated. Loss of the hymen is a step on the road toward death. Thus, the death at the end of *That Obscure Object of Desire* is an image of the end of the hymen, the moment Conchita has feared will be the moment Mathieu will stop loving her.

Turning back to *Basic Instinct,* we see a similar plot line develop. Following scenes establish that Catherine Trammell has over one hundred million dollars, has written several books and is powerfully intelligent. A male psychologist argues that the killer is a frightening person likely to kill again. This sets the audience up for what I believe to be the most crucial scene in the movie: Catherine's interview at the police station.

The buddies return to the beach house to bring Catherine to the police station in order to get more information from her. Again, she turns the tables, getting information about Nick first. As they wait for her to change her outfit, Nick sees a newspaper with a story about his accidental killing of two tourists several months earlier. He looks into the room where Catherine is changing. She displays herself nude. On the way to the police station she challenges Nick to remain a nonsmoker and smokes in his face.

At the station the guys confront Catherine about the murder. Catherine sits on a chair facing them. The camera angle makes her look all naked-legs-and-provocative-gesture. She smokes. Informed that there is no smoking in the station, she challenges her putative investigators. "What are you going to do, book me for smoking?" she asks, daring them to take her on. They back down. She turns to the hero. "Ever fucked on cocaine, Nick?" As she says this, she uncrosses and recrosses her legs in such a way as to display her vulva while acting as if she does not notice what she is doing. This is the key moment in the movie.

The woman as evil temptress who leads a man to doom is personified in the conjunction of the question in which the suspect is questioning the cop, the woman is questioning the man, the sexual adept is questioning the ascetic and the suspect is turning the inquisition into an opportunity to lead the inquisitor to sin. The sight of the female genital stuns the whole roomful of men. She flashes her genital at them with the same aggressive intent and effect as a male flasher has toward his female victims. Once she has done this, her power seems magical: She outwits the police, she passes the lie detector test and she alienates the hero from his buddies. When he responds to her request for a ride home, they suspect that he is colluding with her. He is on the road to his destruction. The many plot twists after this moment are as inevitable as Othello's downward spiral after Desdemona drops the handkerchief.

In the next scene he has joined the guys at a bar. He drinks for the first time in three months. Beth Gardner cheerfully takes him home with her, only to have him rape her anally. Afterward, her mood is dreamy, but when he asks for a cigarette, she tells him to get it on his way out. She enjoys being hurt but rejects him when he becomes self-destructive. Nick leaves her for the police station where he learns that a professor at Berkeley was stabbed to death with an ice pick while Catherine Trammell was a student there. He rushes to her house just in time to see her black Lotus drive off. He gets left behind by her superior driving and more powerful car. He finds the car parked in front of the house belonging to Hazel Dobkins, another woman who will turn out to be a murderer. This woman has the initials of H.D., a bisexual woman poet of great power. Catherine's pen-name is Woolf after Virginia Woolf, a bisexual woman novelist.

Nick visits Catherine at her beach house once again to investigate her connection with this woman and with the professor's murder. She uses an ice pick expertly in the course of making drinks. She tells him that she is using him as the model for the victim of her next book; accuses him killing four people and provoking his wife's death. They clinch. Catherine's friend Roxy comes in; Catherine embraces her passionately, dismissing Nick.

A later scene in Nick's apartment shows Beth, the good: girl coming to apologize to him for having given out confidential information. Even the "good" woman betrays the man, this time by a typically feminine failing: she cannot keep a secret. He slaps her around. She apologizes and. leaves. He sleeps while a monster movie runs on the television. The face of the monster is a Medusa with a wide gaping mouth full of little pointed teeth and hair all around. The reference leads us immediately to scene in which a cop with whom Nick had a public altercation earlier in the day is found killed with a gun of the type Nick carries.

A hearing shows Nick identifying with Catherine by smoking while being interrogated, and, when confronted he repeats her quip about being charged with smoking. Nick is becoming Catherine's love slave. She takes over his memory, and forces her identity on him. Women can remake men in their own image.

Catherine visits Nick again, teasingly telling him about her first book, an account of a murder very similar to the accident in which her parents died. The murderer, she tells him, was the couple's son and sole heir, as she was her parents' sole heir. She intimates that she killed them. The difference between the sexes doesn't matter; money and power matter. Ignoring a warning from his buddy, Nick goes to a nightclub where he finds Catherine inhaling cocaine with Roxy while seated on a stall in the men's toilet. The two women dance erotically. Catherine is shown as a person who enjoys breaking rules and is untroubled by disgust.

Catherine leaves Roxy for Nick, and they have sex under a ceiling mirror. She binds him with a white scarf. Roxy tells him that she has been watching and that Catherine likes her to watch. In this complex scene, the rapid shifts underline the shiftiness of the woman. In the morning light Nick finds Catherine standing close to a fire on the beach. She has warned him about getting too close to the fire, but he passionately insists that he enjoyed the dangerous sex they had, calling it "The fuck of the century." She replies that it wasn't bad for a beginning. Thus she constantly humiliates him by getting him to overvalue her while she undervalues him.

Sex with Catherine is costly. As Nick leaves a diner, a black Lotus comes after him. He manages to force the Lotus off a cliff. The driver was Roxy. Later, Catherine muses, "She never was jealous before."

In a psychological evaluation at the station house, Beth rescues Nick with her sympathetic cover-up of his by-now reckless rage. In the next scene flame-like shadows flicker on the wall at the beach house. Catherine sits crying in a rocking chair. She complains that everyone she cares for dies. She mourns them as lost possessions. Nick comforts her, is again seduced by her and is mobilized by her confession that she slept with a girl at Berkeley who became obsessed with and copied her. Nick eagerly investigates the possibility that this girl pins the murders on Catherine because he wants to believe Catherine innocent.

Finding that the girl eventually changed her name to Beth Gardner leads Nick to suspect and confront Beth. Her last name, she says, is her husband's and her first name is what he liked to call her. This fits with the good girl image because she has allowed herself to be defined by her man. Her name has more resonance, however. Oberman is an Anglicized version of *Ubermensch,* the hero who is entitled to kill to express his needs. The resonance of names is like the musical resonance of the sound track.

Catherine shows up at Nick's apartment and has sex with him, and when he suggests that she put a happy ending on her book, she says such a book would not sell. "Somebody has to die," she says. "Somebody always does." Nick resumes the chase and finds out that Beth's husband was killed and that the unsolved murder was rumored to have something to do with the wife's girlfriend. Beth is no longer to be trusted. He goes back to Catherine's house, finds her new novel printing out. She tells him that the novel is finished and the hero is dead. Her older female lover appears and bids her an erotic goodbye on her way out. Enraged, Nick joins Gus on the way to a rendezvous with Catherine's former roommate. Since Nick no longer has a gun and is not officially on the investigation, Gus goes in alone. Nick realizes that this may be a trap and rushes in to find Gus dead. The audience has already seen Gus shot by a thin woman in a shiny black raincoat and blond wig. Beth appears, claims to have come to a rendezvous set up by a telephone call, and seems to be holding something that could be a gun in her pocket. Nick shoots and kills her, only to find that she was holding her keys to his apartment in her pocket. Nick has now lost both his buddy and the woman who seemed to really care about him. He is responsible for both of their deaths.

Catherine shows up in Nick's apartment, crying. They have sex, she ties him up, she leans back, he suggests that they stay together, "fuck like minks and raise rug-rats." She says she hates rug-rats, he says omit the rug-rats, she leans back, reaches toward the floor in the identical gesture with which the woman in the opening scene reached for the ice pick, reaches over him, and embraces him. The movie ends with a shot of an ice pick on the floor beneath their bed.

Throughout the movie Catherine warns Nick of his fate. Playing on his guilt, his curiosity, and his loneliness, she lures him to his doom. Teasing him with the possibility that she may be innocent, she tells him that she will kill him as she has so many others. Her healthy-looking face and body contrast with her drug use, open enjoyment of casual sex, bisexuality, and propensity for murder. She looks womanly yet uses an ice pick better than a man.

The crucial image in this movie is the image of the Medusa seen on the television screen in Nick's room. By putting this image on the screen, the movie links up to the tradition of Medusa stories (Hamilton 1940) and visual representations that warn men of the danger of the woman, the danger of the Medusa. Analysts (Freud 1922, Ferenczi 1923; Flugel 1924; Reik 1951; Balter 1969) have noted the importance of the Medusa myth for understanding men's fear of women. I would like to trace the image of Medusa in the context of the message this movie is promulgating about women.

The Medusa is an image of the vulva, hairy all around; a face, but not a face; a mouth, but not a mouth; and life-giving when young, but horrific to see and death-dealing to the young heroes who encounter her. When Catherine displays her vulva, she evokes the mesmerizing power, energy, and death-dealing menace of the Medusa.

According to Hamilton (1940), the Medusa is one of the three Gorgons, sisters who lived on an island in the sea. Perseus was the hero who sought her head as a present for the man who was marrying his mother Danae. The myth describes the boy as having grown up father-less and therefore not confronted with his mother's sexuality. He used the Gorgon's head to turn his mother's suitor to stone, thus saving her from marriage by displaying the terrifying image of a vulva.

Arlow (1971) traced the propensity to exhibitionism and fetishism in men to the traumatic effect of the sight of the female genital, especially as displayed by an aggressive mother. The castration anxiety men experi-ence leads to fear of their own self-punitive impulses and finally to a perversion or perverse character trait that the man experiences as power-ful enough to ward off the dreaded experience of the female genital. The denial of the female genital is coupled with the conviction that it could be fatal. It is too horrible to exist; therefore it cannot exist. Catherine's character is perfectly expressed in her display of her genital. By forcing the men to look at it, she immobilizes, fascinates and destroys them. Similarly, Conchita fascinates and destroys every time she mentions her hymen. Her virginity paralyzes Mathieu.

The misogynist message is one Faludi (1991) describes in popular culture, politics, and most importantly, in popular psychology in the 1970s. It has resurfaced, as Faludi and others (Rossi 1972) have shown, after each historical period in which women made gains toward equality with men. Its pervasiveness, ubiquity, and historical recurrences (Pantel 1992) lead to questions about why it always comes back. Is there something in the female psyche that allows women to be excited by this movie and is related to why women allow patriarchy to persist?

This question, I think, brings us back to the question of the title of this movie. What is the basic instinct? Is it a raw sexual desire as exemplified by Catherine's comment that, even if you have no affec-tionate feelings for the partners, "you still get the pleasure" (Freud 1905)? Is it the aggressive wish released in the multiple violent stab-bings with an icepick (Klein 1932). Is it the masochistic-wish to be punished that seems to motivate Nick's attraction to Catherine, as well as Mathieu's fascination with the completely unscrupulous Conchita, but is a reversal of the conventional female role of masochist who forces the male to oppress her (Freud 1923)? Is it a question of a need for attachment to others (Bowlby 1969), which gives society the power to coerce women into self-loathing or denigration (Horney 1926)?

All of these are possible. The instinct in question is a puzzle to analytic thinkers.

Karen Horney (1926) was the first analyst to point out that: "Like all sciences and all valuations, the psychology of women has hitherto been considered only from the point of view of men" (p. 326). Unfortunately, hardly anybody listened to her call for understanding female psychology from the point of view of women. Male analysts over 50 years later still seemed convinced that penis envy is the primary experience of the developing female and characterizes femaleness in women. As object-relations and other primary femaleness theorists have posited, femaleness is primary in girls, and the vulva is experienced as valuable in the little girl and by the woman. To the extent that they believe penis envy to be the bedrock of female psychology, they must fear retaliation from the envious female. *Basic Instinct* and *That Obscure Object of Desire* are statements from the popular culture that tell us that the sexes have different kinds of power. They appeal to both men and women.

When Catherine displays her vulva, she shows her power; when Conchita mentions her hymen, she shows hers. Both movies gain power by reassuring the audience that sexual women are not mothers. When the housekeeper is eliminated as a suspect because she is old and fat, when Beth who changed her name to her husband's is eliminated as a suspect, when Catherine tells Nick that she will not have children, and when Conchita's mother is the one who is willing to take Mathieu's money only for sex with her daughter the stories provide comfort by telling the audience that mothers do not have sex and they do not murder.

Balter (1969) showed the Perseus-Medusa myth to be a patriarchal rebellion against matriarchal power. *Basic Instinct* is supportive of the power and virility of the male cohort ranged against the mother. It assures men that, by avoiding beautiful powerful women, they can avoid death. It assures women that, by being beautiful and powerful, they can entice men even to their death. *That Obscure Object of Desire* reassures men that only the males can be trusted. The butler is a better friend than any woman can be. He reassures Mathieu that men are trustworthy even though women are not. It also implies that by avoiding beautiful young virgins, they can avert death. It reassures women that their power is in their protestation of virginity and that they can get away with any kind of behavior as long as they maintain the illusion men so much want to believe.

These films are alike in their depiction of women as powerful and evil. Both juxtapose sex and death, sex and money, violence and money.

In the Anglo movie, women who are sexually active are powerful; in the Spanish movie, virgins are the ones who have the power. In other words, the power of women seems to be a common fantasy, while the degree of sexual activity of women seems to be a more culturally-specific icon of their power. Benjamin has asserted that men see women as powerful because they were once little boys at the mercy of their powerful mothers. From these movies, we might be inclined to assert that the power of the woman may or may not reside in her status as mother, but will surely be fueled by her sexuality.

Octavio Paz (1997), fascinated by the erotic works of the Marquis de Sade remarks that: "(R)eigning over these princes of evil is not a man, but a woman. Evil to be beautiful, must be absolute and feminine." This view permeates the Spanish film and the Spanish culture with the constant visual images of virgins who are mothers. The two films have in common the hatred of female power. They differ only in *Basic Instinct* shows the power of the childless sexual woman while *That Obscure Object of Desire* shows the power of the sexually abstinent but reproductively capable woman. Both are fantasies; both have their roots in de Sade and the projection of male fears into female images. Ullman (1998) traces images of Hollywood movies from the turn of the 20th century to show the profound disapproval of the rise of female power at that time. As we approach the turn of the 21st century, we can see that fears of female power continue to fuel our dreams and our art.

REFERENCES

ARLOW, J. (1971). Character Perversion. In *Currents in Psychoanalysis,* L. Marcus, ed. New York: International Universities Press.

BALTER (1969). The Mother as Source of Power. *Psychoanalytic Quarterly* 38:217–274.

FALUDI, S. (1991). *Backlash: The Undeclared War Against American Women.* New York: Crown.

FERENCZI, S. (1923). On the Symbolism of the Head of the Medusa. In *Further Contributions to the Theory and Technique of Psychoanalysis.* London: Hogarth, 1950.

FLUGEL, J. (1924). Polyphallic Symbolism and the Castration Complex. *International Journal of Psycho-Analysis* 5:155–196.

FREUD, S. (1905). Three Essays on the Theory of Sexuality (1905). *Standard Edition.*

——— (1922). Medusa's Head. *Standard Edition* 18:273–274.

——— (1923). The Ego and the Id. *Standard Edition* 19:12–66.

GABBARD, G. & GABBARD, K. (1987). *Psychiatry and the Cinema*. Chicago: University of Chicago Press.

GIMBUTAS, M. (1989). *The Language of the Goddess*. New York: Harper & Row.

HAMILTON, E. (1940). *Mythology: Timeless Tales of Gods and Heroes*. New York: Mentor.

HOLTZMAN, D. & KULISH, N. (1996). The Hymen and the Loss of Viginity. *Journal of the American Psychoanalytic Association* 44:303–332.

HORNEY, K. (1926). The Flight from Womanhood. *International Journal of Psychoanalysis* 7:324–339.

KLEIN, M. (1932). *The Psychoanalysis of Children*. London: Hogarth Press 1975.

PANTEL, P. (1992). *A History of Women*. Cambridge, MA: Harvard University Press.

PAZ, O. (1998). *An Erotic Beyond Sade*. New York: Houghton Mifflin Harcourt.

REIK, T. (1951). Modern Medusa. *American Imago* 8:323–328.

ROSSI, A. (1973). *The Feminist Papers*. New York: Columbia.

ULLMAN, S.R. (1998). *Sex Seen: The Emergence of Modern Sexuality in America*. Berkeley, CA: University of California Press.

****
****

Original publication of preceding chapter:

RICHARDS, A.K. (1999). The Terrifying Woman: Latin and Anglo View of Female Sexuality in *Basic Instinct* and *That Obscure Object of Desire*. *Projections* 12(2):35–52.

INDEX

A

abandonment, in case studies, 289, 297, 308–312

Abelin, G., 106

Abend, S., 296

abortion, effects of, 178–179

abuse

    allowing, 113–115, 371, 411–412, 438

    by mother, 303–304

    in perversions, 164

    women's response to, 112–115

Aciman, A., 284

"After Reading *Mickey and the Night Kitchen* for the Third Time Before Bed" (Dove), 91

agency, promoting, 26–27

aggression, 115, 261, 337

    fear of, 301–302, 312, 314, 326–327

    mothers', 166–167, 415, 441

    in perversions, 36, 153, 163, 165–166, 202–203, 210–211, 213, 222–223, 244

    repression of, 120, 194

    sexuality in service of, 208, 210, 213–214

    in training analysis, 336–337

    in transference, 96–97

    women and, 85, 94, 242

aggressor, 26

    identification with, 6, 255, 265

Almansi, R.J., 235

American Psychoanalytic Association (APsaA)

    debate on training analysis, 339–341

    on frequency of sessions, 319–329

    on loneliness, 15, 317

    on telephone analysis, 331–334

    training of nonmedical analysts and, 6–7

"Anal and Sexual" (Andreas-Salomé), 75, 77

anal pleasure, 119–120, 147

Andreas-Salomé, L., 73–78, 81

anger, analyst allowing patient's, 305, 307–308

Anthony, Susan B., 66

anxiety, 29, 273, 400. *See also* castration anxiety

phallic, 247
on primal scene, 116

masturbation
  female, 119, 243–244
  mothers' response to, 123
  perversions and, 149, 226–227
  sphincter clenching as, 116, 125
Matchstick Men, 399–405
Mayer, E., 103–104, 112, 121
McDougall, J., 121, 233, 235
McKillop, Anne, 13
Medusa, 104
  Basic Instinct using image of, 408, 414, 430–431, 440
  myth of, 407, 416, 429–430
  vulva as image of, 414–415, 440
Meir, Golda, 379
Melting the Darkness (Poland), 317
memory
  emotions and sensory experiences in, 272–273
  involuntary *vs.* voluntary, 272, 275
menstruation, 392, 394, 396–397
mental health, 329, 336
  appropriate grooming as sign of, 171, 173
mental illness, 140
  perversions classified as, 223–224
  religion's influence on conceptions of, 33–34
Messager, A., 189
messiness, in case study of Ms. A, 289, 292
Mezrich, B., 427
Michels, R., 244
Miller, J.B., 85, 258, 270
Millet, K., 68
misogyny
  Freud accused of, 65
  resurfacing after gains in equality, 415, 441
Mitchell, 85
money, 365, 371, 373, 431
  death's relation to, 369, 424
  equated to life, 359, 361–362
  guilt and anxiety over, 178–179
  between love and death, 361, 364
morality, 34, 394, 410, 431–433